Moving Toward Positive Systems of Child and Family Welfare

Moving Toward Positive Systems of Child and Family Welfare

Current Issues and Future Directions

Gary Cameron
Nick Coady
Gerald R. Adams
editors

Wilfrid Laurier University Press

WLU

This book has been published with the help of a grant from the Canadian Federation for the Humanities and Social Sciences, through the Aid to Scholarly Publications Programme, using funds provided by the Social Sciences and Humanities Research Council of Canada. We acknowledge the financial support of the Government of Canada through the Book Publishing Industry Development Program for our publishing activities.

Library and Archives Canada Cataloguing in Publication

Moving toward positive systems of child and family welfare : current issues and future directions / Gary Cameron, Nick Coady, Gerald R. Adams, editors.

Includes bibliographical references and index.
ISBN 978-0-88920-518-5

1. Child welfare—Canada. 2. Family services—Canada. 3. Social work with children—Canada. 4. Family social work—Canada. I. Cameron, Gary II. Coady, Nick, 1951– III. Adams, Gerald R., 1946– IV. Title.

HV745.A6M69 2007   362.70971   C2007-901529-8

Cover design by Sandra Friesen. Text design by Catharine Bonas-Taylor.

Contents

Introduction

Finding a Fit
Family Realities and Service Responses

Gary Cameron
Nick Coady
Gerald R. Adams

Listening to Other Voices

As researchers and as service providers, it is easy to behave as if we have an accurate, and perhaps superior, understanding of the people who use child and family welfare services.[1] In official conversations, where we make important decisions that affect people's lives, our voices are privileged, as are our determinations about what aspects of others' lives are important to consider and what behaviours are appropriate. Our professional environments and our professional and personal self interests combine to make us publicly confident in our judgments and unquestioning about our right to decide. We take our benevolence for granted.

Professional and academic portraits of families using child protection services, with recommendations for improving the families' lives, provide important illustrations of this privileged discourse. It is particularly concerning that the prevalent images of these families are negative and colour our expectations and interventions. In her analysis of the literature, Nancy Freymond (2003a) concludes that mothers involved with child welfare are portrayed "as having difficulties of such magnitude that the likelihood of any substantial change is remote" (pp. 19–20). In addition, she makes an argument that is fundamental to the logic of this volume:

> The child welfare system is conditioned by the biased understanding of the lives of biological mothers. The ways that mothers ... understand their world, and their behaviour in it, do not fit neatly into the contexts of child welfare. Mothers do not merely absorb and comply with the

advice of professionals. They attempt to interpret and to incorporate that advice into their daily living contexts. When child welfare expectations contradict what is "common sense" in the world of biological mothers, the expectations are met with frustrations and resistance. (p. 1)

Few groups evoke less sympathy than who the general public imagines these parents to be. This "hard" perspective leads to an expectation that the public child-protection authorities be "hard" with these "bad parents." One of the motivations for this book is to question the usefulness of this dominant discourse about parents and families involved with child welfare. If we accept these dominant profiles, ambitions to create productive partnerships with such parents seem naive.

The papers in this volume were prepared as part of the program of research of the Partnerships for Children and Families Project.[2] The Partnerships for Children and Families Project is a Community University Research Alliance funded by the Social Sciences and Humanities and Research Council of Canada (2000–2005). A major focus of its program of research was how family members involved with Children's Aid Societies and children's mental health services portray their own lives and their involvements with these authorities. In addition, this program of research examined the nature of front-line child protection and children's mental health work and the perceptions of service providers regarding their jobs and the families that they serve. Finally, the Partnerships for Children and Families Project explored other countries' systems of child and family welfare and "alternative" program models in Canada and elsewhere.

Some of the papers in this volume provided the conceptual frameworks to guide different aspects of the Partnerships for Children and Families program of research. Other discussions incorporate selected findings from this research. In addition, several authors use international comparisons of systems of child and family to enrich their considerations of positive future directions. Collectively, these chapters provide a description and critique of existing child and family welfare systems in Canada and make suggestions for policy, administration, and service delivery reforms.

More specifically, the objectives of this book are:

- to provide a general description and critique of Canadian child and family welfare;
- to examine Canadian child and family welfare holistically, drawing on a variety of perspectives and methods of investigation;
- to ground these considerations of Canadian child and family welfare in information about family living realities and service involvement experiences and in data about front-line service provider employment conditions;

- to use international comparisons of child and family welfare systems to clarify a range of system design choices for Canadian child and family welfare; and
- to present a selection of specific possibilities for innovation in Canadian child and family welfare, extrapolating from literature and research reviews and original research.

While these objectives provide the overall framework for the book, readers will be interested in using specific chapters for different purposes. Therefore, we have taken care to make sure each chapter includes enough contextual information to be useful as a separate resource, as well as a complement to the other chapters.

A basic premise of our focus on developing positive systems of child and family welfare in Canada is the need to improve the congruence between the assistance families receive and the demands that they face in their everyday lives. From our perspective, there are two primary dimensions to this challenge: (a) providing a broader range and higher levels of useful assistance to family members than is currently the norm; and (b) delivering help in ways that are welcome to families and lead to more co-operative helping relationships between family members and service providers.

Family Realities

The Partnerships for Children and Families research highlighted patterns of family living that need to be accommodated by child and family welfare. This chapter presents an overview of central patterns in the data identified in the life stories collected as part of a broader program of research. These patterns provide an initial "grounding" from which to consider the discussions of child and family welfare in the remainder of the book.

Lives of Lesser Privilege

From its earliest days, "Anglo-American child protection systems" have focused their attention on the most impoverished segments of the population, as well as on immigrant and other "marginalized" groupings (see the discussion by Cameron, Freymond, Cornfield, & Palmer in chapter 1). Over the years, the rationales for the disproportionate involvement of these disadvantaged groups have included maintaining economic productivity, public safety, and proper moral standards and rescuing children from "dangerous and unwholesome" environments (Freymond, 2003b).

Privilege in this discussion refers to access to valued education and employment and to the sufficiency of financial resources to provide adequate access to daily living resources. *Lesser* is in comparison to the educational, employment and financial circumstances of the author of this chapter and to many child protection personnel in contact with these families. Both concepts refer to living conditions during childhood as well as in adult life. It is impossible to read these stories of family life from the Partnerships for Children and Families research without confronting dramatic evidence of the ongoing pressures of living with lesser privilege and the extraordinary efforts required to survive and to overcome such obstacles. For example:

Elizabeth: Elizabeth currently lives with her daughter and a female friend in the back section of a house in a noisy neighbourhood with a lot of drug dealing and prostitution. Elizabeth survives on funds from Workers Compensation and from the orphan's benefits that she receives due to the death of Steven, the father of her oldest child. These sources of income provide her with $900 a month. Elizabeth should also receive child support from Ben, her ex-partner; however, she says that he recently quit his job to avoid the monthly payments.

Throughout her life, Elizabeth has survived by taking advantage of any means available to her. She describes:

> I'm really resourceful. I have a lot, and, when I move into a community, I find out a lot about the community, the things that the community has to offer um, so I go that way resourceful. I've survived a lot. Not as much as others but to me it's a lot. Um, you have to because, if you're sitting there with no money and no food, you have to find a means for it, you know. There's different ways, umpteen ways you can get food, and you just gotta figure out a way to do it.

Three broad interpretive themes related to lives of lesser privilege emerged from the analyses of mothers' life stories in the Partnerships for Children and Families research.

First, child welfare involves communities and generations of individuals and families with ways of living that reflect their ideals, norms, and exigencies of childhood, parenting and family. Such patterns of living cannot be understood solely in terms of individual characteristics and responsibilities. In addition, this program of research identified gaps between the daily realities of mothers and fathers and those of service providers—emotional, intellectual, social, and practical—that are difficult to bridge when helping families and communities.

Rebecca: A typical day for Rebecca is long and busy. She is responsible for the majority of the work required to maintain a home. Rebecca describes what a typical day looks like for her when she comes home after an overnight shift at her job:

I'd come home, and ... they'd be up already. And the fighting would already be starting.... some of them would get up at six o'clock. They just can't sleep longer.... if they still didn't have their lunches made, sometimes I would help them, other times, I would just sit here, and kind of ... supervise. And encourage them to get ready faster. And be out the door so I could go to bed.

She then tries to get some sleep. Her children begin to return home around 3 p.m. so she has to be up. Rebecca goes back to bed after supper, sleeps until 11:00 p.m., and then heads to work for 11:30 p.m. Rebecca estimates that for the past several years she has been getting an average of four hours of sleep each day. Her sleep is often disturbed by events at work or home. Sometimes, Rebecca has worked Sundays at her mother's restaurant.

Paul: Paul and his family have lived in the same housing co-operative for 17 years. He likes where he lives but also talks about the challenges drugs and delinquency in the neighbourhood pose for his children. He has worked for the same employer in the textile industry for 28 years. His wife is on a long-term disability pension. Coping with limited finances with five children is an ongoing challenge. At the time of the first interview, Paul could not afford to have his car repaired and was commuting by bus:

I've been in that department 'til, to this day. (So, you like your job?) Oh no. [laughter] Yeah, yeah. Yeah, you need a job. Potatoes and stuff on the table and get groceries ... I've been there a long time ... I get five weeks for my vacation time. And basically it's not too bad if you've been there for quite a few years ... thank God for my drug plan ... my kids are on this medications, over a hundred and fifty dollars a shot ... One of my wife's pills are over four hundred and something dollars. (So is that stressful, like are finances stressful?) Oh yeah. Yeah, that can be more stress, I think that worries me out, worries me more ... I got food on the table, and stuff like that, you know, it could be a lot worse, you know. A lot of people are a lot worse than us.

Second, lives of lesser privilege are often characterized by high levels of adversity, daily stress, and periodic crises, from childhood into adult life. The challenges confronted by these families are well known to service professionals: conflict and violence, addictions, unstable homes, job and income insecurity, emotional challenges, and poor physical health.

Amber: During Amber's childhood, her father went to jail for several years for drug trafficking. After her parents' separation, Amber, a First Nations woman, "bounced around a lot" between family members and foster homes. When Amber was 14, she lived on the street, slept on park benches, and she would sneak into bars to drink and use drugs. Amber recalls that she was close to the sex trade, but she couldn't bring herself to become a prostitute. By age 16, Amber had returned home to live with her mother, but she left again because of the sexual advances of her mother's partner. She moved to Alberta to live with her stepfather.

Zack: Zack came from a childhood home that had many of the same characteristics of his recent marriage:

> ... I grew up, uh, skinny as I am now—only a lot skinnier actually. And, uh, no self-confidence, no confidence in myself at all. I had a dad and a mom ... they were together for many, many, many, many years until she died at 48 I guess.... dad did not make a lotta money, same as me. Uh, my dad had 5 children, same as me.... My, uh, my dad drank. And, uh, and I really believe that he passed off some genes to me. Uh, unfavourable genes ... my idea,... was to, you know, die by the time I'm 30 of alcoholism.... Dad and mom didn't get along really that well. I mean, because of his drinking ... he'd scream and yell, you know, if you didn't do something ... that's where ... the fear came in ... was that he'd scream and yell at ya. Uh, so, it was, it was unpleasant growing up. I mean I wanted to be out on my own ... my mother was not a good housekeeper.... It was a total disaster from Sunday to Sunday and when I grew old enough I, uh, I started to clean it. I was probably 12 or 13 when I first started.

Zack has struggled with a serious alcohol addiction for all his adult life. The children's aid society apprehended his five children when his second wife left them with him to move out with her boyfriend. His children were returned to him only after he had completed a residential addictions program and remained alcohol free.

Most of the mothers and many of the fathers in the Partnerships for Children and Families life story research have at some point been single parents. For the women, this typically coincided with a substantial drop in their income. Most of the mothers have been on social assistance at least once. About an equal number of parents did not complete high school. Long hours of work, shift work, low pay, and limited benefits were common. Living space typically was rented and modest, sometimes in neighbourhoods considered harmful by the mothers. Almost all of these women and many of the men described financial and living circumstances that left them very vulnerable to disruptions.

Particularly striking was the level of daily living stress described by some parents, because they invested so much of themselves into working to pay the bills, caring for their children, keeping their families together, and maintaining a home. For example, **Karen**, who left her adoptive home at 14 and then moved through several foster homes, lived on her own at a young age. She and her partner worked overlapping shifts six days a week, trading off care of the children. Between getting her two boys off to school in the morning and doing housework late at night after work, Karen did not get many hours of sleep. She described their efforts as "running really hard just to live on the margins." **Sandy** also talked about working very long hours at a variety of low paying jobs, while she cares for her "hyperactive and aggressive" young daughter and babysits two neighbour children during the week. Her husband often works six days a week and then helps out with some of Sandy's jobs outside the home. **Caleb** met his current partner, Christine, when they both worked alternate shifts at a gas station. Caleb talked about the busy schedule required by his wife's shifts in a factory and his delivery work. Not surprisingly, parents frequently talked about being emotionally and physically exhausted. They did not have surplus time or money to invest in self care.

Third, less recognized by service professionals are the efforts by parents—mothers in particular—to manage this adversity over many years and their personal victories along the way. Readers of these parents' stories frequently comment on the endurance and persistence of these parents and marvel at how many of them manage to keep hope alive in their lives.

Annette: Growing up, Annette was the target of her father's abuse. Annette performed very well in school, but the stress from her home life eventually caught up with her. In grade eight, her grades plummeted, but, despite difficulties at home, Annette worked hard to finish high school; she planned to leave home when she received her diploma. Annette recalls her graduation from high school:

> ... that was one of the happiest days of life, to get that diploma in my hands. I carried that everywhere. I didn't care how wrinkly it got, but that was my ticket to freedom. And I graduated in June and I hitchhiked up here in October. And that was an experience in itself. The best thing I ever done. Because my mom says, you get on that highway, and you don't look back. You look back, you're going to come back. And I didn't look back once, only to see if there was more traffic coming, but that's about it. And I've been a survivor since.

After graduating from high school, Annette hitchhiked from her home province to Ontario. Along the way, a friendly truck driver gave her fifty dollars. Once she reached her destination, Annette used this fifty dollars to stay in a hotel and immediately went job hunting.

George: George (41) grew up in a northern Métis community. He spoke of his early adulthood when he lived a "gangster life" and how having a child turned him away from drugs and a violent lifestyle. George recounted how his ex-wife's drug addiction and prostitution led to their family's involvement with the children's aid society. He spoke of the hardships he faced holding his family together and attributed his current success in life to his faith, determination, and business skills:

> So I really at this point, was just dumbfounded, not knowing what to do … I grabbed my daughter and I prayed … I asked God … "Just give me some direction where you want me to go." … I was very sad and I cried a bit, and Faith was playing with the tears as they fell down my face and, and I [said] … "I'm glad you're so small. You don't realize how I feel right now, what I'm going through and how hard I fought I to get you and how I wish I had more to give you." And, and I just said … "God, tell me where you want me to go." And we went to bed, it was very humbling time … [I] woke up the next day and there was a knock at the door and it was the St. Vincent de Paul. … I put an ad out, and, and the, I think the very next day, a Christian couple, or a lady came with her son … rented that basement off me for five-fifty a month.

Currently, George lives with his three daughters, Faith (8), Grace (5), and Gabriella (4), and his girlfriend, Madison, with her two daughters, Mia (15) and Chloe (21).

Continuity of Family

The child welfare literature focuses a great deal on the struggles within families: inadequate or harmful parenting, hurtful childhoods of parents, conflict and violence between partners, and unstable relationships and homes for children (Freymond, 2003a). The Partnerships for Children and Families research certainly illustrated the dramatic nature of these struggles for many families. However, there is another story fundamental to understanding these families. It is a tale about the continuity and central importance of family in the lives of these parents and their children, and the persistent desire and effort of many parents to have a family and a home. These contrasting stories coexist and researchers and practitioners need to understand them in relationship to each other as we hear about ways of living that may be very different from our own.

When women in this program of research discussed their partnerships, most told of a series of relationships with different men over time. At some time most had been involved in a physically and emotionally abusive relationship with a live-in male partner, some with several. Many of their children were not living with their biological fathers, and many had minimal if any contact with their "dads." Siblings had different biological fathers in quite a few families. Most of the fathers also talked about difficulties in their partnerships and many were no longer with the mother of their children. Some had taken on the responsibilities of a single parent.

There is another side to this image of partnerships, however. These stories tell of a strong motivation to partner, to try again, particularly among the women, coupled with a strong desire for a "normal" family and home. In addition, in most of their current partnerships, the women feel that they are doing better than with past partners and, in many, if not all, tales, there are descriptions suggesting that these perceptions are accurate.

The portraits of some families describe continuing "chaotic and unstable" living arrangements. Some parents talked of their very difficult trials in parenting an "explosive child." Many children in these stories have endured the loss of a father or mother, a number of "step-parents" coming and going, violence and conflict in the home, parents with alcohol or drug abuse problems, and unstable living arrangements. The stories describe many parents struggling to manage the stress of their work/school, parenting, and home-management responsibilities. The childhood stories of perhaps half of these parents suggest that they might not have much to draw on in terms of a "map" to guide their own parenting. Some are clearly repeating behaviours from their own difficult childhood homes.

Nonetheless, in the Partnerships for Children and Families research, these families remained central to parents and children "being well" and "feeling that they belong and that someone cares." Many mothers, including many with quite "horrendous" childhood experiences, continued or re-established contact with their own mothers and other extended family members as adults. Family is the most common source of emotional and practical support for many parents. Many of these mothers and fathers and children did much of their socializing within their extended families. A critical point is that, in almost all of these stories, mothers, and less frequently fathers, provided the only continuity of parenting and family for their children over time. In many of these stories, becoming and being a "mom" or "dad" was central. Many mothers and fathers, but not all, talked fondly about "who their children are" and strove to maintain a family and a home for themselves and their children, sometimes under very difficult circumstances.

Anyone who grew up experiencing the turmoil and disruptions of many of these families can understand the fear, anger, and confusion of children in such homes. They know about the price children pay over a lifetime—a price many of the parents in this research continue to pay in their own lives because of their childhoods. Nonetheless, it is critical to emphasize that these are the families in which almost all of the children in this research continued to live and, for most parents and children, these families represent connections that will be desired for all of their lives.

Lives as Children

Mothers and mothering receive much of the attention in child welfare interventions. The Partnerships for Children and Families research showed that, even when there is a long-time male partner in the home, he typically only becomes a focus of the child protection investigation if he is a perpetrator of child or partner abuse (Frensch & Cameron, 2003). Even with a partner at home, the mother often felt that she was held accountable for controlling or removing the "danger" that he might pose for her children. Some fathers talked about feeling excluded or characterized as a "negative stereotype" by child welfare service providers.

Mothers were most often the primary caregivers of the children in this research. They provided much of the continuity in children's lives, because biological fathers were frequently absent or sometimes excluded from their children's lives. Nonetheless, some fathers made active long-term investments into parenting their children, and others wished for a chance to be able to do more. As mentioned previously, a pivotal recognition is that, even for the children in this research who have been in care, the overwhelming majority continued to live in a parent's home and to depend upon her or him for their sense of belonging. The well-being of these parents were central to these families' well being, yet many of them told truly horrendous stories of what they had to overcome in their own childhoods and the impact this has had on their adult lives.

Sandy's mom and dad were both alcoholics, and her dad was abusive to her mom. Sandy described in detail a particular instance when her mother was seriously hurt. Her parents were divorced by the time she was four years old. They were poor and Sandy suspects her mother worked as a prostitute, until she married Sandy's stepfather. Sandy was sexually abused by her oldest brother, who was responsible for caring for the family, because her mom and step-dad were out most of the time. Sandy's mom and step-dad also drank together, and both would become quite violent.

Amy was in foster care as an infant and returned to a mother with substance abuse problems. Her mother was very abusive toward her, and was eventually diagnosed with a bipolar disorder. Her mom brought lots of men home, and when she was in a relationship, she and Amy's step-dad fought constantly. **Amber** came from "a very dysfunctional family" and was in a foster home at eleven. She was pregnant at fourteen and living on her own on the streets, "close to prostitution." **Karen** was adopted at two years old and, after being sexually molested by an adopted brother, moved through three foster homes until she lived on her own at seventeen. **Annette**'s dad was an alcoholic and dangerously abusive, and she left home at sixteen and hitchhiked on her own to Ontario.

Paul was adopted as a young child through the children's aid society. His non-biological brother was also adopted. His parents were older when they adopted the two boys. Paul talks positively about his parents but sees them as having been strict disciplinarians. His mother became very ill, and Paul describes taking care of her and assuming extra responsibilities around the home. She died when he was fourteen. **Caleb** describes being separated from his biological mother when he was three years old. He has no memory of this time but has been told that it was because his mother was physically abusive and struggled with a variety of personal challenges. **Dean** said that:

> I grew up with an alcoholic father. I've got a couple of brothers who are in and out of jail all the time ... one's really bad. Like he's spent 85% of his adult life behind bars. Yeah. And yeah my dad used to just yell and scream. I used to hide in a little, a round, forty-five gallon drum in the closet, put clothes over my head. And we'd jump out the windows, and run when dad come home drunk. And that gave me a lot of anger. And built up over the years.

The life stories of the First Nations participants in the Partnerships for Children and Families research have unique themes requiring attention. Besides being about very difficult personal journeys, these are also tales of collapsed communities. The parents of these mothers and fathers were often themselves "products" of foster care and detention homes. These stories illustrate the pervasive challenges facing many First Nations communities (for example, see the discussion by Mandell, Clouston Carlson, Fine, & Blackstock in chapter 3) that have prompted a call for community healing as an essential core for Aboriginal child and family welfare models.

None of us could live the challenges many of these mothers and fathers have faced and emerge unscathed. Many child welfare service providers recognize this reality; however, in their emphasis on dealing with their personal issues (Cameron & Hoy, 2003), they often don't acknowledge the time and resource constraints in the lives of these parents and the great amount of time and effort such personal healing efforts require. Equally important in understanding these parents is the great persistence and courage many of them have shown in facing and sometimes overcoming such obstacles. There is desire and strength in many of these stories usually not recognized in "official" dialogue about these mothers and fathers nor encouraged in our helping models.

A commonality in many of these stories, particularly surprising in circumstances of very abusive childhoods, is the central role held by relations with parents and other family members. For example, **Jen** talked to her mom everyday, lives near her dad, was close with her brothers, and lived with her grandparents. **Caleb** gets together with his dad weekly and had re-established communication with his mom and her other children recently. **Amy**'s bipolar mom was particularly nurturing to her in the last five years before she died. Amy stated that she could not have made it with four kids without the support of her parents. **Eric**, his wife, and their children spent much of their free time socializing with his parents, siblings, and extended family. **Sandy** got together with her mom, step-dad and brother regularly. **Amber** was trying to rebuild her relationship with her mom. **Dean** lived with his dad while he tried to establish a home where his daughter could visit. **Elizabeth** talked most days with her mom and believes that her mom really loves her. She wants to move with her kids to live closer to her mom and her step-dad. **Carlos** and his infant daughter returned to live with his parents while he was on probation.

There is an endurance and continuity of family in these stories that is central to understanding the lives of many of these mothers, fathers, and their children. There are strengths in these family networks that are often unrecognized in our focus on past and ongoing troubles. However, these families will be around for many of these parents and their children long after child welfare services have gone away.

Children as a Challenge

Children's mental health centres where we live reserve about 50% of their residential beds for children placed through children's aid societies. In the Partnerships for Children and Families research about 40% of families with a child placed in care by child welfare were struggling with the challenging behaviour of a child. In addition, most of the families with a child placed in residential mental heath care had prior involvement with child welfare organizations. Our research showed that children's aid societies had difficulty recognizing and responding adequately to these families.

Three themes from our program of research with these families are germane to providing a context for the discussions in the rest of this book. First, families with such a "difficult" child live "under state of siege," experiencing an intensity of ongoing pressure and disruption unlike any other families in the Partnerships for Children and Families research (Cameron, de Boer, Frensch, & Adams, 2003):

> He'd break the furniture, put holes in the walls, hurting my animals ... he used to try and hurt the young one ... he once took her head and banged it against the table and she lost all her teeth ... he was going to kill me because he had threatened me many times. (O127, p.66)

> ... week after week after week ... when they're uh ... in an elevated state ... they're not sleeping, and neither ... you're not getting any sleep. And it's just constant chaos. And, it just ... it drains you. (O86, p.72)

Second, mothers, in particular, in these families make extraordinary sacrifices often with substantial costs to their physical and emotional health as well as to their relationships with partners and to their social and work involvements:

> I would wake up in the morning, huge anxiety attacks, most of the time I would physically vomit before even actually ... getting on with the day ... so I guess I sunk into a pretty deep depression and had a lot of anxiety ... in anticipation of what's going to happen next. (Y134, p.128)

> It was the police that gave me a call ... between the crying and the near throwing up ... I quit my job, I couldn't function ... it completely destroyed me ... I left my job for my kids ... I've got to find the money to live somehow but they need me. (Y88, p.129)

Finally, parents' efforts to find someone to believe what is happening in their homes and to find help for their "challenging child" typically go on for years:

> We were desperately searching for something for [focal child] to participate in ... We probably had looked into a number of things from [child welfare agency], from the hospital, starting to explore things, them giving me information so I can do my own research and try to find out what's available. (O104, p.104)

> Three weeks of summer school and they're kicking him out. I had to beg the principal to please keep him. One more strike and he's out though. And I've been doing that for years with teachers. And pleading and phoning ... (O99, p. 133)

> I almost felt sometimes like I was banging my head against a wall. And I wasn't getting anywhere because I was trying to tell these doctors that I knew something was wrong and they were trying to tell me that I didn't know what I was talking about ... it was awful. (Y90, p. 134)

Most of the mothers coping with "challenging children" had contact with child welfare organizations at some point in time and, when help was forthcoming, particularly in the form of parenting relief and child placement, it was appreciated. However, most of these women also talked about the great difficulty of getting a response from child welfare authorities, feeling judged as bad parents when they did, and, in many instances, not receiving much useful assistance.

Service Responses

While some argue that Anglo-American child protection systems do what the public expects of them reasonably well (Parton, Thorpe, & Wattam, 1997), others have raised increasingly insistent concerns about these child protection systems in the English-speaking countries in which they predominate. Among the most persistent critiques are the low level of assistance provided to most families and the rapidly escalating costs of these systems, with little tangible evidence of enduring benefits to parents or children. Many note that a substantial proportion of parents fear and resist involvement with child protection agencies, and that a lack of congruence exists between the help offered and the realities of the lives of many families. In each of these English-speaking countries, researchers actively search for solutions to the increasing pressures on their child protection system. (For example, see the discussions in chapters 1 and 2 of this book).

The Partnerships for Children and Families program of research reported important positive elements in many families' experiences with child protection services. For example, many mothers talked about making a welcome connection with a child protection worker. Families most often appreciated having someone who would listen to them and who believed that they were doing their best. Service providers were also appreciated for offering practical advice and finding useful resources. Some women credited the children's aid society with helping them get out of an abusive relationship, though they did not necessarily appreciate how this was done. Women also talked about helpful programs and services that they either voluntarily used or were ordered to use by child welfare.

These positive experiences, however, were not the dominant themes in this child welfare research. For a family, having several child protection workers while a case was open was the norm. Many mothers commented about having infrequent contact with child welfare workers and how hard it was to get a response to their calls. Some child welfare workers were clearly perceived as insensitive and judgmental, and mothers felt that some workers assumed they were guilty until they proved themselves innocent.

Fear was a prevalent theme in most of these stories—fear when a child welfare employee first showed up and fear that they might come back. Even "voluntary clients" talked about feeling that they had no choice except to agree with what the agency wanted. Also of note is that most of the families' lives in this research seemed to continue after child welfare involvement much as they had before. Crises have abated and families may have learned a few new behaviours, but there is little evidence of substantial and enduring benefits for children, parents, or families. Child welfare service providers prescribed a fairly standard and limited range of interventions for families: individual and group counselling of various types, anger management and parenting courses, and alcohol and drug testing and treatment were most common. Parents were monitored to make sure that they followed through with agency prescriptions and that they behaved "appropriately" with their children.

A particular issue raised in this research was the use of short-term foster care placements (from five days to four months) as a precaution and as leverage to secure changes in family functioning. These placements were horrible ordeals for mothers. Most of the mothers of young children, who were apprehended and then returned home, talked of the insecurities and confusion of their child afterwards. Our contention is that, rather than taking a child out of his or her home for a short period of time for such purposes, it is both practical and humane to create alternative, more "family-friendly" choices (for example, see the discussion by Freymond in chapter 4).

How these mothers and other family members talked about their lives has clear implications for improving Canadian child and family welfare. The most salient concern is the limited level of assistance forthcoming to most families involved with child protection services and the modest benefits for children, parents, and families from these efforts. The price of child protection's single-minded focus on specific conceptions of harm to children is that too many families resent and fear an unwanted and unhelpful intrusion into their lives.

Building a more balanced and flexible child and family welfare system requires establishing greater congruency with the elements of the lives of parents and families identified in the Partnerships for Children and Families research. Lack of access to adequate resources and opportunities for enhancing child, parent, and family well-being, high vulnerability to disruption in existing supports, and high levels of daily-living stress were common themes in this research. Many mothers and fathers confronted tremendous personal challenges in their childhood and adult lives and endured painful disruptions in their relationships with partners and their family functioning.

Nonetheless, these parents—mothers in particular—and these families remained very important in their children's lives, often providing the only source of continuity and belonging. Many of these mothers' and fathers' stories illustrated persistence and the overcoming of obstacles, as well as a continued commitment to their children and a desire for a stable home and a family. Despite some horrendous beginnings, families in this research exhibited continuity and strength. New partnerships formed, and families of origin often provided assistance and social connections.

The core challenge for child and family welfare remains connecting with the shared daily living realities of communities and of children and their parents in ways that family members find acceptable and sensible. Several authors in this volume argue that it is essential to increase the level and diversity of helping options available, allowing for greater flexibility and collaboration in service delivery. This implies moving away from the stand-alone model of child protection that predominates in Canada toward sharing the child and family welfare mandate across various service and community organizations. It suggests the value of greater partnerships among formal services and informal family and neighbourhood networks in promoting child and family safety and well-being.

A corollary implication is an acceptance of the principle of shared parenting. Holding stressed and distressed mothers and/or fathers responsible for remedying troublesome family circumstances is an insufficient response. The principle of shared parenting requires involving broader groupings of service providers and family and community members as long-term partners in caring for children. It also involves the development of "empowerment spaces," creating opportunities for mutual aid, social connections and friendships, and communal co-operation. It complements professional helping with mutual reliance among families, neighbours, and others confronting similar life challenges. Finally, shared parenting accepts the importance of compassion and creativity in facilitating healing and personal growth for the adults in this research area.

Overall, and in various ways, the chapters in this book elaborate the argument that there is no contradiction between protecting children and promoting their welfare within families and communities. It is within our grasp to envision a more balanced and inclusive child and family welfare system in Canada.

Organization of the Book

In chapter 1, Gary Cameron, Nancy Freymond, Denise Cornfield, and Sally Palmer examine the characteristics of Anglo-American child protection systems. They contrast these systems with various family service systems in continental Europe and with community healing/caring models of child and family welfare developed by Aboriginal populations in Canada and elsewhere. These three general systems are compared on dimensions common to all systems of child and family welfare. The authors highlight the differences in the responses of various systems to common challenges and the implications of these variations. They contend that there is nothing inevitable about the current organization of child and family welfare in Canada and illustrate the value of international comparisons for thinking about positive innovations.

Freymond and Cameron, in chapter 2, use findings from the Partnerships for Children and Families research to illustrate the daily living realities and child welfare involvements of mothers whose children at some point have been placed in out-of-home care. They contrast these portraits with the most common images of such women and their families in the child welfare literature. They argue that child welfare interventions are often incongruent with the lives of these mothers and their families and discuss the nature of more positive alternatives.

In chapter 3, Deena Mandell, Joyce Clouston Carlson, Marshall Fine, and Cindy Blackstock provide a comprehensive analysis of First Nations' past and ongoing experiences with Canadian child welfare. They examine different models of funding and service delivery for Aboriginal child and family welfare, and they elaborate First Nations' visions for respectful community-caring models of child and family welfare and the challenges faced in implementing these approaches.

Freymond, in chapter 4, uses examples from Canada and Europe to examine how to develop "intermediary spaces" in child and family welfare—where children, parents, communities, and service professionals can come together to negotiate and to create strategies for helping. She focuses on reducing adversarial relationships between families and child welfare professionals and lessening the system's reliance on coercive legal authority.

In chapter 5, Fine, Palmer, and Nick Coady summarize the findings from various forms of qualitative and quantitative evidence, exploring service participants' perceptions of their involvements with child welfare, children's mental health, and psychotherapy services. Their focus is on identifying the characteristics of service involvements that service participants identified as enhancing helping relationships.

In chapter 6, Freymond presents the results of her qualitative investigation into the cognitive, social, and emotional processes affecting child protection workers as they make decisions to apply for crown wardship for children, permanently severing the legal bonds between parents and their children. She describes sequential stages of identification, chance-giving, negotiation, and legal decision-making in this process. She also elaborates concepts of identity formation and de-individuation to explain how service providers manage such difficult decisions.

Cheryl Harvey and Carol A. Stalker, in chapter 7, review the research that explains the nature and causes of professional burnout in social service organizations. They supplement this with data from their study of employment realities in selected Ontario children's aid societies. They conclude with a discussion of the implications of their findings for improving child and family welfare.

In chapter 8, Karen M. Frensch, Cameron, and Gerald Adams provide an overview of the research literature on the placement of children and adolescents in residential mental health centres. This is supplemented with data from their study of families involved with residential treatment in selected Ontario children's mental health centres. They highlight the substantial overlap of these families with families involved with child protection authorities and the very different responses families receive from these two systems. They conclude with a discussion of the implications for service delivery.

Chapter 9 extrapolates major themes from the proceeding chapters and highlights their implications for social policy, systems design, service delivery, and future research in Canadian child and family welfare.

Notes

1 The more inclusive term child and family welfare is used instead of more common terminology such as child welfare or child protection to accommodate the discussions of alternative approaches in this volume. Child welfare or child protection is used intentionally in this chapter only in reference to the narrower focus of existing Canadian procedures.
2 More information about this past and ongoing program of research as well as access to review papers and research reports is available at www.wlu.ca/pcfproject

References

Cameron, G., de Boer, C., Frensch, K. M., & Adams, G. (2003). *Siege and response: Families' everyday lives and experiences with children's residential mental health services.* Waterloo, ON: Wilfrid Laurier University, Partnerships for Children and Families Project.

Cameron, G., & Hoy, S. (2003). *Stories of mothers and child welfare.* Waterloo, ON: Wilfrid Laurier University, Partnerships for Children and Families Project.

Frensch, K. M., & Cameron, G. (2003). *Bridging or maintaining distance: A matched comparison of parent and service provider realities in child welfare.* Waterloo, ON: Wilfrid Laurier University, Partnerships for Children and Families Project.

Freymond, N. (2003a). *Child placement and mothering ideologies: Images of mothers in child welfare.* Waterloo, ON: Wilfrid Laurier University, Partnerships for Children and Families Project.

Freymond, N. (2003b). Mothers' Experience of Child Placement: A Reflexive Methodology. Unpublished doctoral dissertation proposal. Wilfrid Laurier University, Waterloo, ON.

Parton, N., Thorpe, D., & Wattam, C. (1997). *Child Protection: Risk and the moral order.* London: Macmillan.

|1|

Positive Possibilities for Child and Family Welfare
Expanding the Anglo-American Child Protection Paradigm

Gary Cameron
Nancy Freymond
Denise Cornfield
Sally Palmer

Introduction and Overview

Policy and practice intended to protect children living in "unsafe" environments and to facilitate their proper development have a limited common foundation across settings. No necessary line of reasoning leads from the circumstances confronting children and their families to a country's particular configuration of community, service, and legal responses. The creation of the "problem of child maltreatment" and how we deal with it are best understood as discourses that grow out of specific histories and social configurations:

> As Gelles (1979) pointed out 20 years ago, child abuse and neglect amounts to a social construction ... Child abuse has been created as a social problem. It is not just there, it is a discourse ... This means that objective statements are impossible because they are inherent to the social context in which the problems arise. (Marneffe & Broos, 1997, p. 178)

This chapter challenges the idea that the Anglo-American child protection paradigm, as seen in Ontario, is an inevitable or superior option. This paradigm is best understood as a particular configuration rooted in our vision for children, families, community and society. Other settings have constructed different responses that reflect their own priorities and desired outcomes. We argue here that "realiz[ing] that elsewhere things are done differently expands one's confidence in the belief that 'different' things can be done" (Hetherington, Cooper, Smith, & Wilford, 1997, p. 124).

Another aspect of our argument is that every child and family welfare system[1] creates its particular configuration out of the necessity to balance a common set of requirements. All systems must come to terms with similar challenges and choices. It is the nature of the choices made, and the balance struck among competing priorities, that gives each approach its unique strengths and weaknesses. For example, every delivery system reflects deliberate or unconscious choices about:

- the extent to which interventions give precedence to the interests of children, families, communities, or society;
- how broad the intervention mandate should be;
- the balance required between local discretion and bureaucratic control over decision making;
- how separate the child welfare/protection system should be from the broader social welfare network;
- the types and extent of authority to be used when working with children and families;
- what linkages are optimal with the judicial and police systems; and,
- the emphasis placed on individual change, on shared provision of social resources, and on collective empowerment and action.

Different priorities and choices are reflected in child and family welfare systems. We see these as choices with consequences, with each configuration having its particular strengths and limitations. The reported consequences of these choices for children and families, as well as for service providers working in these systems, differ greatly from place to place. For example:

> Child abuse reports reveal a large degree of variance ... ranging from a low of 2/1000 in Finland to 70/1000 in California ... In general, it appears that the Anglo-American countries with reporting systems oriented towards child protection register much higher rates of reporting than the family-service oriented systems such as the Netherlands, Finland, and Belgium, for the data that are available. (Gilbert, 1997b, p. 235)

Child and family welfare practices mirror the cultural (both current and historical) and institutional contexts in which they have evolved. These local cultures impose strong constraints on the shapes any child and family welfare project will be allowed to take in a certain setting (O'Hara, 1998). For example, the focus on individual rights and the separation of family and state in Anglo-American contexts will make it difficult for practices to evolve toward more activist and collectivist orientations, which are common in parts of continental Europe. Nonetheless, the fairness and the consequences of the Anglo-American child protection paradigm are being increasingly questioned, and understanding other service realities can stimulate our search for improvements. Both to generate hope and to stimulate creativity, it is worthwhile examining our child protection system in the context of a continuum of existing and suggested alternatives.

Child welfare has been described as an "ideological battleground" (Wolff, 1997), an arena where fundamental differences in values about children, family, and society are contested. In considering possibilities, we are not engaged in a neutral exercise. Support for existing arrangements or for new departures draws on deep wellsprings of emotion and strongly held convictions. How we view children and families and how we treat those who get into trouble divide us as people and as citizens. Although this chapter cannot offer proof of better options, it can begin to define the spectrum of possibilities. The readers' consideration of these alternatives will be coloured by their values and priorities.

The purpose of this chapter is twofold: (a) to illustrate and to comment on a range of child welfare/protection design options as manifested in Europe and North America; and, (b) to examine the place of the Anglo-American child protection paradigm in this continuum. Although we make no claim to comprehensiveness, we are confident that the scope of material included is representative of the broad service patterns and issues raised in our discussion. To accomplish the purposes of this chapter, we investigated a variety of related topics:

- History and characteristics of the Ontario child protection paradigm: This brief historical overview describes the roots and main development patterns for the child protection system in Ontario. Its purpose is to provide a context for later considerations of alternative approaches.
- Common traits of Anglo-American child protection systems: Child protection systems in England, United States, and Canada/Ontario have evolved similar operating patterns. In addition, comparable concerns are found in the literature about the child protection paradigm in all three countries. This section highlights these commonalities as a precursor to examining other design options.
- Ideologies and contexts: The organization of child welfare/protection takes place in settings with different conceptions of preferred relationships among children, families, communities, and the state. These differences influence ideas about how families should be supported and children protected. Understanding this variance provides a lens through which to consider the underpinnings of Ontario's child protection orientation and the possibilities and constraints these represent for change.
- Explanatory models: All child welfare/protection systems are organized around explicit or unconscious assumptions about the reasons families experience difficulties and children need protection. The differences in

core explanations that guide policy and intervention in Continental European, Anglo-American, and First Nations approaches have important implications for the involvements of children and parents with child welfare/protection systems. This section provides an overview of these differences and their implications for our helping efforts.

- Choices in child and family welfare system design: This analysis identifies several system-design and service-delivery dimensions along which various child welfare/protection orientations are compared. The purpose is to begin to highlight the nature and range of choices available to inform future discussions about improvements.
- Concluding comments—Lessons and future directions: This section summarizes the major patterns and issues from the above topic investigations and examines their implications for future reflections about changes to the child protection paradigm in Ontario.

History of the Anglo-American Child Protection Paradigm

Ontario Child-Saving History

In the 1990s, the Ontario child protection system faced a barrage of criticism about its inability to protect children from death as a result of abuse. One of the official responses has been the introduction of a risk-assessment model, a protocol that child protection investigators apply to evaluate various aspects of the care a child is receiving. The risk-assessment protocol purportedly adds a "scientific" or more "objective" dimension to the difficult and often uncertain work of detecting children most at risk of harm. Another official response has been the introduction of legislation that works in tandem with the new investigative procedures to ensure that the process of permanently removing children deemed at "high risk" from their abusive parents is accelerated.

In principle, this seems very distant from the 1984 child welfare legislation that insisted on the "least intrusive" interventions in order to preserve families. In 2006, in response to a massive escalation of child protection costs under the new system, following earlier shifts in the United States and in Alberta, the Ontario government is proposing moving toward a two-track differential response model (see the discussion later in this chapter).

How is it that in less than two decades the preferred response to "at risk" children in Ontario seems so varied? This discussion looks at the historical underpinnings of our current child welfare system and the evolution of child welfare practices in Ontario. It also explores how our responses to "at risk" children continue to be constructed through a child-saving lens that both frames our understanding of this work and simultaneously restricts and obscures options for intervention. This brief overview is intended to provide a reference point for subsequent discussions about a range of possibilities and choices in the design of child welfare/protection systems.

Industrialization is the historical event most associated with the beginnings of public assistance to children. Any period of history marked by rapid societal change finds itself caught between new understandings of human need and society's traditional responses. In the pre-industrialized world in England, the family and the church bore the responsibility of meeting needs associated with ill health, poverty, or other unexpected misfortune. As rural farming communities gave way to the urban centres of the mid-19th-century industrial revolution, the increased visibility of the effects of poverty and fears about the rampant spread of disease added new urgency to the dilemmas of responding to human need. Traditional helping mechanisms became inadequate to the task, in terms of both skill and available resources.

In England, religious conviction compelled middle-class reformers to attempt to save children who fell prey to the villains of the darker sides of social developments (Dahl, 1985). These philanthropists blamed the state for the social upheaval of the time and considered the state to be incapable of compassion. Even though, through the poor laws, the state maintained the final authority for children in need, these philanthropists regarded the state as a dreadful last resort. A child saver would become focused on saving children from falling into the state's clutches by offering to assume responsibility for the care of the child victims of industrialism. This view gave rise to the concept of *in loco parentis*, a legal doctrine whereby parental responsibility could be assumed by others, although not by the state (Dahl, 1985).

The world of 19th-century England was viewed through Christian beliefs, the foundation of which was the struggle between God and Satan for human souls. Hence, much of their world was seen as either good or evil—a world of saviours and villains. This dichotomy of good and evil informed the foundations of the child-saving movement. Child savers saw the state, society's moral decline, and the hazards of urban life as evils from which children required saving.

Child savers were not concerned about the feelings of the child, in fact, public awareness of the emotional world of the child came at a later period in history (Sutherland, 1976). Nor was it about rescue from any particular suffering or hardship that the child might be enduring. To save was to train, discipline, and render obedient the wayward waifs, who, once a resource in a rural economy, were now discarded on city streets. The goal was to transform them into future resources and contributors to society (Chen, 2001). To save was a high calling: it was a demonstration of Christian faith and the antidote to society's moral downturn.

The period of the infamous English institutions followed the inception of the child-saving movement. Delinquent children were sent to the reformatory and neglected children to industrial schools to learn factory work. The last half of the 1800s saw a substantial rise in the number of children interned in industrial schools. The demand for placements far exceeded available charitable resources. State grants became available and beleaguered charitable institutions, despite their former low opinion of the state, were happy to accept the financial relief. The philanthropic approach to child saving was further eroded by the emergence of the professions, which tended to direct demands toward the state rather than private benefactors (Dahl, 1985).

By the late 19th century, the charitable donations and efforts of well-intentioned philanthropists had mostly been replaced by government funding and emerging professionals in social welfare, whose expertise rested on new advances in the scientific community. The state gradually became the chief supporter of the child-saving movement. Children were now understood as having distinct needs, separate from those of adults; they were, in essence, blank slates, susceptible to external influences that shaped their character. Thus, when children were found in poverty, roaming the streets, or were found guilty of delinquent acts, the problem was attributed to poor influences. Parental conduct toward children was understood as the primary influence and the chief source of difficulty when problems arose (Chen, 2001).

In 19th-century England, the upper class considered poverty to be caused by immorality. In their Christian framework, prosperity was understood as clear evidence of God's blessing. It was the immoral who were unable to secure blessing and were therefore destined to poverty. In addition, the emerging view of children as unfinished beings reinforced the child savers' belief that the implantation of immoral ideas would lead to immoral instincts, on which these children would act later in life (Dahl, 1985). Therefore, the greatest cause for concern was the transmission of parents' bad morals, as evidenced by their poverty, to their children (Piper, 1999). To save individual children, and to save society from continued moral decline, it was necessary to separate the child from an immoral parent. The substitution of the moral parent for the immoral one is an original and fundamental underpinning of foster care.

England was the home of industrial capitalism and, in this capacity, it demonstrated to the rest of the world the impact of industrialization on society (Dahl, 1985). Decades later, when similar social problems developed in the industrializing colonies, they turned to England for answers. Their strong political, social, and cultural similarities with England ensured that the remedies from the motherland were readily transported. The adoption of English solutions is clearly evident in Ontario's child welfare history. Ontario's current child welfare system is firmly rooted in the 19th-century English child-saving philosophy that saw children initially as the innocent victims of an industrializing nation and later as products of deficient parenting.

By 1870, Ontario was facing the social consequences of industrialization. Toronto was becoming a large and important commercial centre, and concerns about the growing visibility of poverty were unfolding, just as they had in London a half-century earlier. Rather than instituting a Poor Law to ensure a minimum standard of care, Canadian attitudes decreed that, in this land of plenty, those who could not fend for themselves were lazy and/or immoral (Jones & Rutman, 1981). As in England, middle-class philanthropists led the child-saving movement. They were concerned both that the souls of children be saved from a death without Christianity and that children be kept from harmful, immoral influences to ensure a stable, crime-free future for the nation (Jones & Rutman, 1981; Sutherland, 1976).

J. J. Kelso is credited with establishing the first children's aid society in Toronto. He directed its establishment and played a role in the development of similar societies across Ontario and in other English-speaking provinces. He was widely acknowledged at that time as the leader of the child-saving movement (Jones & Rutman, 1981; Macintyre, 1993) and as a key moral entrepreneur in the movement (Hagan & Leon, 1977). Like his British predecessors, he became a child saver because of the visible plight of street children in an industrializing Toronto.

Kelso believed that the removal of children should be permanent and that they needed an upbringing in loving Christian families (Jones & Rutman, 1981). But he was also concerned about parental rights, and, in response to criticism, he said that he advocated for the improvement of the home life by timely intervention, so that removal of children from the home might not be necessary (Jones & Rutman, 1981). It was this home life, however, that was viewed as the source of the problem and the reason that children needed help. Locating the problem in the home persists today, and the tension between advocacy for permanent removal and for supporting improvements in the child's home is still felt at the beginning of the 21st century.

In 1893, new legislation allowed for the establishment of children's aid societies in Ontario. Their work focused on individual families and separating children from the immorality found in their homes and communities. The legislation described young children as dependent and neglected, but older children, who had already suffered from prolonged exposure to bad conditions, were referred to as immoral and depraved (Bala, 1999). Without knowledge of the emotional world of a child, this saving by separation seemed to make sense to Ontario authorities just as it had in England, and the broad discretionary powers granted to the children's aid societies ensured that the practice became well established.

In the 1920s, Freudian principles of psychotherapy reconstituted immorality as psychopathology. These new ideas broadened and made more "scientific" the understanding of why children needed help. This fresh approach, while identifying a different parental deficiency as the reason children required saving, did not alter or challenge the original principles on which child welfare is predicated.

During the first half of the 20th century, North American families struggled to cope with the effects of a crippling depression and two world wars. Families were devastated first by their disillusionment that hard work in the land of plenty did not necessarily secure prosperity and then by the loss of lives in the wars. As families, and the nation, pulled together in the face of these difficulties, the public face of the child savers was very low key (Costin, Karger, & Stoesz, 1996). Rarely were parents who expressed an interest in caring for their children prevented from doing so (Bala, 1999).

In the 1960s, an American pediatrician, C. Henry Kempe, pioneered the identification of what became known as battered child syndrome, urging doctors to report to the authorities any evidence of broken bones in infants and children. This raised new concerns about the extent to which parental psychopathology could place children at risk. Child savers became conscious of the need to challenge parental explanations of injuries and became more focused on the investigative aspects of their work.

Issues of Aboriginal child welfare, as well as provincial responsibilities for services on federal First Nations reserves, also found resolution in the 1960s. Just as the institutional "big houses" had failed the child savers a century earlier, residential schools, designed to assimilate First Nations children through discipline, education, and separation from Aboriginal ways of life, were publicly acknowledged to have failed (McGillivray, 1995). The 1867 British North America Act had placed First Nations under federal jurisdiction, although child welfare was a provincial jurisdiction. In 1947, the Canadian Welfare Council and the Canadian Association of Social Workers, in a brief to a subcommittee on the Indian Act, drew attention to the conditions for children on First Nations reserves. In response, amendments were made that secured the constitutional authority for the provision of provincial services on federal reserves. After considerable federal/provincial wrangling, the federal government signed cost-sharing agreements with the provinces for the provision of child welfare services on reserves (McGillivray, 1995). Saving First Nations children through practices of apprehension and adoption became standard and widespread.

The late 1970s and the 1980s ushered in concerns about the effects of the renewed child saving efforts of the 1960s. Concerns emerged about the broad discretionary powers of social workers and the violation of the rights of parents and children, concerns that were firmly lodged in concepts of family autonomy and the individual rights movements. It became incumbent on social workers to more clearly articulate and defend decisions to apprehend children. Second, there were increasing reports of the overuse of apprehension and adoption policies, particularly in First Nations populations (Hepworth, 1985). There was continued First Nations resistance both to the cultural destruction caused by provincial child welfare policy and to the erosion of individual Aboriginal identities through foster care and adoptions outside the community.

In addition, concerns were raised about the number of foster children adrift in the child protection system, without adequate attachment to a primary caregiver. Goldstein, Freud, and Solnit (1973; 1979) argued for the importance of children having continuity of care, an argument that underpins the current emphasis on permanency planning for children. It has been used both in support of family preservation and as a rationale for early removal and adoption of children.

The result was an emphasis on parental rights and on family preservation in the 1984 Child and Family Services Act, which insisted that agency intervention give priority to "least disruptive" alternatives. This legislation also added a new dimension to the "best interests of the child" by recognizing the need for stable attachment, fostered through continuity of care, and stable family relationships. Thus, from 1980–1989, the number of foster children in Ontario dropped by an estimated 22% (Trocmé, 1991). However, this family preservation orientation was handicapped by the fact that there were no fundamental changes to the way child welfare services were organized. Furthermore, throughout the 1980s, social service expenditures in Ontario stayed relatively constant, despite dramatic increases in the numbers of families receiving in-home support services (Trocmé, 1991). The family preservation orientation was further constrained by the child-saving mentality of child welfare professionals; many workers lamented that their efforts on behalf of children were frustrated by the number of opportunities given to parents to make changes.

In the 1980s, the child-saving movement focused on child sexual abuse. The Badgley Report in 1984 described the widespread occurrence and the massive under-reporting of child sexual abuse. Adult disclosures of childhood sexual abuse contributed to increased public awareness, which, in turn, caused a sharp increase in the number of reported cases and the increased availability of treatment. In the 1990s, attention shifted to addictions that interfere with parenting and the controversies around mothers who expose babies to illicit drugs while pregnant. Moreover, public concerns about the number of children who die as a result of abuse and ensuing legislative changes have effectively dismantled the earlier emphasis on family preservation.

A shift in the social climate emerged in the 1990s. Neo-conservative political policies stressed individual responsibility, fiscal restraint, and increased negative judgments regarding those seen as inadequate parents. These factors strengthened the emphasis on reporting child abuse and on social workers' quasi-scientific assessments of risk. New definitions in the 2000 amendments to the CFSA also widened the scope for involuntary state intervention into families. Accelerated legal processing and the use of sophisticated psychological testing to assess children's attachment to their families pointed to a future where the reliance on apprehension and out-of-home placement rivalled that of the 1960s. The more recent interest in a differential response child welfare system for Ontario—maintaining the new procedure-driven emphases in "core" child protection services but encouraging a service response to less "dangerous" family situations—indicates a recognition that this future has arrived. This shift follows earlier differential response reforms in Alberta and the United States (Alberta Children's Services, n.d.). The balance sought between these two patterns of responses, how they will be realized, and their impacts on families and service providers remain to be determined (Differential Response Sub-Committee, 2005; Ontario Ministry of Children and Youth, 2005; Ontario Ministry of Children's Services, 2003).

For the past 100 years, child-saving principles have been the foundation of Ontario's child protection system. Regardless of how appropriate they are, these principles restrict the range of our responses to concerns about children's welfare. Child welfare has been characterized as engaging in solutions that have been tried before, which suggests a reform process that fails to benefit from the wisdom of hindsight (Van Krieken, 1986). As long as child welfare is understood as primarily child saving, our ability to respond innovatively to the complexities facing children and families will be limited by the principles on which our system is based.

Child saving principles continue to influence our child welfare system. Saving implies a rescue from danger, and it implies that someone or something places children in danger. At the root remains the belief that child maltreatment is the result of parental psychological difficulties and/or immorality, and that it is from the influence of these damaged or unworthy parents that children must be saved. Concerns about immorality continue to seep into and blend with psychological explanations (Swift, 1995). Separation from the "psychologically deficient" person and placement with a family that is "psychologically healthy" remains central to the child welfare system.

The focus on saving obscures other explanations for child maltreatment. It ignores exposure to social conditions such as poverty, crime, and environmental depredation, which compromise the well-being of children. It does not give enough weight to communities' inability to offer children social, educational, and health opportunities, economic conditions that disenfranchise, and government policies that increase the burden on families. Understanding and responding to struggling families and risks of harm to children are complex challenges that defy simple solutions (see the discussions later in this chapter). Conversely, Ontario's child welfare system has always demonstrated a narrow perspective and range of response to these complexities.

Common Traits of Anglo-American Child Protection Systems

To understand the current child protection system in Ontario, it is necessary to understand some of its core characteristics, as well as those from child protection systems in England and the United States, which function in a similar manner. In this paper, these Anglo-American child protection systems will often be referred to as threshold systems, making reference to the shared trait that families must meet minimum levels of "dysfunction" to qualify for formal entry into these systems.

Although there are strong advocates for the appropriateness of threshold child protection systems, our analysis suggests that these arguments are being heard less often than they were in the past. Discussions in the recent literature often involve concerns about the ways children and families are treated by Anglo-American child protection agencies. It is striking that these concerns are similar across countries that have created threshold systems. Before discussing a range of possibilities for child and family welfare system design, this section describes the common characteristics of these Anglo-American threshold systems. In addition, this discussion summarizes both the rationale for current threshold systems and the emerging critiques of these systems.

Traits of threshold systems. The child protection systems in Canada, the United States, and England have evolved similar ways of working. All share roots in Anglo-American liberal democratic traditions. These are threshold systems in which English thinking initially dominated, although since the Second World War they have been heavily influenced by American ideas. Not surprisingly, very similar observations about these three systems have appeared in the literature.

Threshold systems function within societies that place great emphasis on individual responsibilities and rights. This valuing of personal discretion can be seen in concepts of family that deem to parents sole privilege and responsibility for the care of their children. Swift (1997) comments that, in

Canada, there is a "belief that parents bear the primary responsibility for the welfare of their children and a concomitant right to raise their children in accordance with their own wishes" (p. 38). Intrusion by the state into the private lives of families is only permitted when parents violate minimum standards of care and treatment of their children. Even then, agents of the state are required to prove allegations of parental maltreatment in court before the parents' right to privacy can be overridden (Larner, Stevenson, & Behrman, 1998).

Because of this legal requirement to demonstrate parental incapacity or misconduct before the state can intervene, workers spend much time gathering evidence suitable for use in formal legal proceedings (Larner, et al., 1998; Swift, 1997; Pires, 1993). The primary mandate is to protect children from harm in their immediate living environments, most often from their parents. Trocmé and his colleagues (2001) note that, in 1998, 61% of child investigations in Canada involved allegations against biological mothers. Cases are closed on families whose circumstances under investigation are judged not to be serious enough. They are sometimes referred elsewhere for services; however, many investigated families do not receive any assistance from the child protection agencies. Furthermore, these agencies have only minimal working linkages with other social welfare institutions that provide assistance to families: child care, recreational programs, scholastic assistance programs, and so on (Hetherington, et al., 1997; Lawrence-Karski, 1997; Waldfogel, 1998). In addition, rather than voluntarily seeking help or accepting offers of service, the majority of parents and children who become involved with threshold systems do so because of an agency-initiated investigation of their lives.

Both the United States and Canada have legislation around mandatory child abuse reporting. Service professionals and others must report any suspicions of child maltreatment. Over the past three decades, the number of reports received by these threshold systems has increased greatly (Parton, 1997; Waldfogel, 1996). For example, one children's aid society reports a 60% increase in community reports about child abuse over four years (Family and Children's Services of Guelph and Wellington County, 2000).

The threshold system's required first response to each abuse report received is a formal investigation to determine the validity and seriousness of the alleged maltreatment. Only families that fall below the prescribed minimum child care standards enter into the formal child protection system. If, based on this initial assessment, parents do not fall below this minimum level of care, their investigation is closed, and they usually do not receive any services or assistance from the agency (Chen, 2001; Ontario Ministry of Community and Social Services, 2000b). In addition, the proportion of families who have no involvement beyond an initial investigation is increasing.

For example, according to Lawrence-Karski (1997), in 1976, 70% of reports investigated in California received services beyond the initial screening; whereas, in 1992, only 6% of reports received services. Likewise, in Canada, 36% of cases received services after the initial investigation in 1998 (Trocmé et al., 2001).

After an investigation has been completed and a child protection case opened at the agency, responses include referrals to other programs to assist the family with their difficulties, supervision contracts/orders (voluntary and involuntary) to ensure parents are complying with agency expectations of parenting standards, and out-of-home placement of children (usually involuntary). In addition, there is extensive and increasing use of an adversarial legal system to ensure that parents comply with the expectations of child protection professionals. For example, in 2000, between 50% and 70% of the cases open at the two children's aid societies participating in the Partnership for Children and Families program of research (2000–2005) involved a formal application to the court (personal communication). Because of the importance placed on individual rights and due process in court applications, legal representation typically is required for all parties to the dispute—the agency, the parent, and older children—as soon as the court becomes involved in a family's case.

Protection of children (usually from physical or sexual harm by caregivers) is the primary mandate for these threshold systems (Ontario Ministry of Community and Social Services, 2000b; Panel of Experts on Child Protection, 1998). Therefore, although child neglect still constitutes the largest proportion of cases that are opened in threshold systems, physical and sexual abuse have become more prominent issues since the 1960s. In fact, child abuse has become the organizing framework for much of the child protection legislation, within which neglect is a subcategory (Swift, 1997; 1998).

Furthermore, although it was stated in the Ontario Child Welfare Act (1965) that "every Children's Aid Society shall be operated for the purpose of providing guidance, counselling, and other services to families for the prevention of circumstances requiring the protection of children" (McEachern & Morris, 1992, p. 157), the focus of Ontario Children's Aid Societies centres almost exclusively on child protection. Despite new interest in differential response systems, legislation and funding criteria at present are concentrated on the protection of children from physical, sexual, and emotional maltreatment. Initiatives for preventing abuse and optimizing children's well-being invariably receive lower priority in threshold systems. (Costin et al., 1996; Larner et al., 1998; Luckock, Vogler, & Keating, 1996; McEachern & Morris, 1992).

Another defining trend in threshold systems is the decreasing amount of discretion given to child protection workers in working with families.

This move toward standardized procedures stems both from a lack of willingness to trust workers' judgements about what to do, partly as a result of public inquiries into system "failures," and from an increasing belief in the power of "science" and the "rational" organization of procedures to predict when children are at risk of being harmed and to protect them from harm (Lawrence-Karski, 1997; Ontario Ministry of Community and Social Services, 2000b; Parton, 1997; Swift, 1997). A by-product of these standardized procedures and legal recording requirements is that workers invest more time in assuring compliance with these expectations, leaving less time to spend with families (Chen, 2001; Swift, 1995). Regehr, Leslie, Howe, and Chau (2000) noted in their recent study of the Children's Aid Society of Toronto that "at times workers were seeing people to write something about them instead of helping them ... they felt their work at the agency was focused on meeting the needs and requirements of legislation, rather than providing service to clients" (p. 7).

Rationale for the Ontario child protection system. A clear argument for this child protection system is found in the rationale for the amendments in 2000 to the Child and Family Services Act. Those who advocated for the amendments describe the benefits of moving to a standardized child protection system that is more focused on the rights of the child. In response to the deaths of Ontario children who were receiving child welfare services, a panel of experts was brought together in 1998 to make recommendations for legislative changes to help prevent further tragedies. They recommended more emphasis on standard risk assessments, definite timelines for investigation, recording, and intervention, and a broader definition of what constitutes a child in need of protection (Panel of Experts on Child Protection, 1998). These recommendations resulted in changes in the legislation that moved the Ontario child protection system in the same direction as the systems in the United States and England.

The paramount principle in the current Ontario child protection legislation is that "each child is entitled to safety, protection and well-being ... and that all other purposes are secondary" (Panel of Experts on Child Protection, 1998, p. 13). The Panel of Experts on Child Protection (1998) stated that the legislation must be clear that all other objectives are of lesser importance because in the past:

> These other objectives have been interpreted in such a way as to overemphasize the rights and interests of parents rather than the needs of the child ... In the event of conflict between the rights of the parents and the needs of the child, the lack of clarity as to which principle has priority has compromised the safety, protection, and well-being of some children. (p. 13)

In addition, it was argued that the definition of a child "in need of protection" needed to be broadened to include the "risk that the child is likely" to be in danger of maltreatment. This amendment broadened the previous definition, which required that the child be at "substantial risk" of harm; the change was intended to more adequately protect children, by allowing child welfare workers to intervene earlier. Proponents of this threshold system want child protection workers to be able to investigate families at the first signs of potential harm to the child in order to prevent or to minimize harm to children:

> The ability of protection workers to intervene early and assess the family's ability to meet the child's physical, developmental and emotional needs is crucial. The focus on non-intrusion into the family by the state has contributed to barriers in obtaining crucial information about a child ... It is hoped that earlier intervention will prevent or at least minimize the damage to vulnerable children and increase the opportunities for effective and earlier services to children and parents. (Panel of Experts on Child Protection, 1998, pp. 8–9)

Advocates of the Ontario child protection system argue that having to prove that a child is in serious danger of being harmed restricts workers' ability to protect the child: "the use of the test of substantial risk has left children in dangerous situations" (Panel of Experts on Child Protection, 1998, p. 17). Child protection workers should be able to investigate families as soon as it is determined there is "risk that the child is likely to be harmed" (p. 17).

Furthermore, these proponents wanted a more consistent approach to service delivery across the province and advocated for a standard means of assessing whether a child is in need of protection. As a result of children's death involving children's aid societies, there has been much public criticism about the quality of workers' judgements about children and families. Standardized tools were seen as potentially useful in helping workers make more informed and consistent child protection decisions (Ontario Ministry of Community and Social Services, 2000a).

A few authors have argued that the investigative focus of threshold systems is justified from a public safety perspective on child abuse. Those who support this argument, which is especially prevalent in the United States, contend it is important to be able to gather evidence and prosecute offenders and that the abuse of children should be understood in the same light as other forms of assault. As Costin and colleagues (1996) note, "in order to provide children with safety, it is necessary to criminalize child abuse and neglect" (p. 181). From this perspective, there is no logical difference between criminal violence against women and the violence done to children. Some proponents of this idea support the division of the child protection system into one that would perform "policing" functions and another that would provide support for families who need assistance but do not pose a serious threat to their children (Costin et al., 1996).

Common critiques of threshold systems. The child protection literature from England, United States, and Canada shows that common criticisms of these systems are emerging across these settings. American authors voice the strongest concerns about the manner in which their child protection system is evolving; however, similar criticisms are surfacing about the 1989 child protection reforms in England. Although the reforms to the Ontario child protection system are more recent, they have produced effects similar to those in England and the United States. This section presents an overview of the most common critiques found in the literature of Anglo-American threshold systems.

Within these threshold systems, the number of child abuse reports has increased dramatically over recent decades (Family and Children's Services of Guelph and Wellington County, 2000; Waldfogel, 1996). Partly because they are required to formally investigate every report, the rise in reports has inundated child protection agencies (Larner et al., 1998; Pires, 1993; Regehr et al., 2000; Waldfogel, 1996). Not only are there insufficient resources, it appears that the new procedures draw more families into the investigative system. These systems are overwhelmed by reports that must be investigated, leaving inadequate time to provide useful assistance to families in need. Furthermore, the systems' inability to deal with the increase in reports leads to increased job pressures for workers and higher levels of worker frustration, resulting in higher turnover (Regehr et al., 2000; Waldfogel, 1996; 1998). (See the discussion in chapter 7.) In fact, according to a study of the Children's Aid Society of Metropolitan Toronto, intake workers stayed with the agency for a median of only one year, and family services workers stayed with the agency for a median of only three years. The same study also reported a two-year front-line turnover rate between 46% and 90% for child welfare practitioners (Regehr et al., 2000).

Threshold systems have been criticized for formally investigating too many families whose problems stem from shortages of resources and difficulties with child-care responsibilities. Consequently, less emphasis has been placed on providing appropriate assistance and guidance to these families. In the United States, this has led to 70% of cases either not being investigated at all or being closed after investigation (Waldfogel, 1998). In addition, because so much time is spent investigating families who could benefit from less coercive services and supports, there is concern that fewer resources are available to intervene effectively with families where children are truly at risk of harm.

Within threshold systems, there has been consistent debate over child protection agencies' dual mandates (to provide assistance for and to exercise legal authority over families). Some critics argue that this dual focus results in neither function being carried out effectively and that these functions should be separated into a formal "policing" operation and a separate system providing positive supports (Besharov, Robinson Lowry, Pelton, & Weber, 1998; Callahan, 1993; Costin et al., 1996; Hetherington et al., 1997). In contrast, in settings that do not use the threshold system, there is greater capacity to provide non-coercive assistance to families, and managing the dual mandates of caring and controlling creates less overt tension (Hetherington et al., 1997). Because of the heavy emphasis on control in threshold systems, it may be that dissatisfaction with the dual focus stems from a perceived imbalance in the functions of care and control, rather than the dual mandate itself, which exists in all systems reviewed.

The challenges facing families that come into contact with the child protection systems are multiple and complex (Cameron & Rothery, 1985; Peirson, Laurendeau, & Chamberland, 2002; Schorr, 1989; 1997). However, the responses offered by threshold systems are limited and not very adaptable to the needs of particular families (Besharov et al., 1998; Waldfogel, 1996; 1998). As Lindsey (1994) comments, the problem in child welfare is that "instead of freely choosing from among a spectrum of services, clients have only one choice, for which they must qualify" (p. 47).

The first step for every family that comes in contact with the threshold systems is an investigation, the results of which disqualify the great majority of families from service (Lawrence-Karski, 1997; Parton, 1997; Waldfogel, 1998). For families deemed in need of help, instead of practical and welcome supports, "assistance" often comes in the form of expectations with which parents must comply, or in some cases, the removal of children from the home. The most common system response to clients of the Ontario child protection system is an intervention in which the system prescribes certain requirements that the family must meet to ensure that the children are not at risk of harm. This intervention can take the form of a supervision order or an agreement with the family (although clients often feel they had little option but to agree). Although evidence is accumulating about the value of positive supports that could help many of these families, critics of the threshold approach complain that the response from these systems continues to be singular and unchanging (Besharov et al., 1998; Lindsey, 1994; Waldfogel, 1996; 1998).

Additionally, threshold systems have been criticized for their excessive focus on the protection of children from abuse by their caregivers. Children are often left in impoverished homes, with little thought to their long-term health and well-being, provided there are no immediate "safety" risks. In threshold approaches, human miseries other than child safety are often not considered in decisions to intervene, except as they are considered to place a child in jeopardy (Besharov et al., 1998; Chen, 2001; Swift, 1995; 1998). Furthermore, when the state does intervene, the decision to remove children from their homes is often problematic. Although out-of-home placement is clearly an improvement for some children living in dangerous or severely dysfunctional homes, the ability of threshold systems to provide loving and nourishing long-term environments for children is questionable (Hepworth, 1985; Kufeldt, Vachon, Simard, Baker, & Andrews, 2000; Lindsey, 1994; Swift, 1998; Wharf, 1992). Kingsley and Mark (2000) note that in England, "mental health workers, foster parents, and DSS [Department of Social Services] workers all indicated that the current system takes children and youth with attachment disorders and puts them in situations that intensify that disorder" (p. 38).

The societies in which threshold systems operate tend to have individualistic ideologies about family and parental responsibilities. Some critics argue that threshold systems evaluate families' situations out of the context of their daily living realities, thereby overlooking important factors that impact both on families' functioning and on the opportunities available to them (Callahan, 1993; Cameron, Vanderwoerd, & Peirson, 1997; Swift, 1998; Wharf, 1995). Additionally, although the official rationale for intervention is the protection of children, a more covert dynamic is the allocation of blame and appropriate punishment to wrongdoers. Social and economic conditions that hinder parents from adequately caring for their children are largely irrelevant to this accounting and are seldom a focus for helping strategies (Chen, 2001; Hughes, 1995).

Proponents of threshold systems have challenged that all child and family welfare alternatives that do not place a clear priority on the protection of children sacrifice the safety of children to the interests of the parents. However, in our review, there was no evidence to support the conclusion that children in contact with non-threshold systems were being hurt with greater frequency or severity than those dealing with threshold systems. Across the different child and family welfare systems reviewed, children are removed from situations perceived to be dangerous with similar frequency (Gilbert, 1997a). However, in non-threshold systems, the removal of children is more often done with parental agreement, whereas parents in threshold systems typically resist this decision (Hetherington et al., 1997). In light of this information, threshold systems' overarching justification for their often coercive interventions—that they are better at protecting children from harm—loses much of its power. Holding families responsible and punishing transgressions seem less persuasive justifications for a protection orientation as the core rationale for threshold systems.

The threshold systems in England, the United States, and Canada have recently experienced serious problems with recruiting and retaining staff. Child protection work can be emotionally demanding, and frequently requires workers to interfere in dramatic and coercive ways in the lives of struggling families. Furthermore, child protection work has recently changed in these settings, giving professionals much less discretion in their jobs. This results in more adversarial relations with families and the need to invest a great deal more time complying with new documentation requirements (Costin et al., 1996; Pires, 1993; Swift, 1995). Between 1997 and 1999, the Ontario Ministry of Community and Social Services "twice invested additional funding for hiring nearly 1000 new front-line workers" (Chen, 2001, p. 10). However, despite this increase in available funding and intense recruitment efforts, agencies have had difficulty finding and retaining well-trained professionals to work in the field (personal communication with the executive director of a children's aid society, September 2000; Regehr et al., 2000). These employment issues were not typically highlighted as problems in our review of the literature about non-threshold child and family welfare systems (Hetherington et al., 1997).

A less common but persistent criticism of threshold systems is that they are systems of oppression of the most disadvantaged parents and children in our society. The threshold systems' roots are in the child-saving movement, in which one class of established people "rescued" children from a lower class of "bad" parents and the "immoral" influences of poor communities (Swift, 1995). This tendency continues today; almost all the families that come to the attention of the threshold system are working class and poor (Cameron & Rothery, 1985; Cameron, Hayward, & Mamatis, 1992; Callahan, 1993; Costin et al., 1996; Courtney, 1998; Swift, 1995). Conversely, middle- and upper-class families are rarely drawn into these systems; when they are, they have shown a greater capacity for organized resistance (Martin, 1985). Also, the evidence is overwhelming that, in North America at least, it is the poorest of minority families—First Nations, Black, and Hispanic—whose children are removed in disproportionate numbers (Pires, 1993; Saskatchewan Children's Advocate Office, 2000; Swift, 1995; 1997). Critics also point out that many of the mothers who come within the mandate of threshold systems have been victims of personal violence and addictions in their childhood and adult homes. They often live in unsafe and deteriorating neighbourhoods, where it is hard to hold on to hope (Belsky, 1993; Hughes, 1995).

Although these factors are well known to many of the architects and employees of threshold systems, they are not officially a primary concern and are viewed as illegitimate focuses of helping. Indeed, one of the paradoxes of the new formalized risk assessment procedures used in threshold systems is that concerns such as poverty have been emptied of their emotional and political content. They have become technical demerit points for parents in the assessment of child safety rather than reasons for compassion and assistance (Callahan, 1993; Chen, 2001; Swift, 1998).

Many concerns have been expressed in the literature about the manner in which the threshold systems operate and about the consequences of their interventions for families and children. The recent move to more standardization, bureaucracy, and evidence-gathering has drawn a lot of criticism. However, despite these concerns about threshold systems, there is less clarity about what remedies would be preferable.

In Canada, many service professionals and members of the public assume that the threshold or Anglo-American child protection paradigm is the only available option. Our hope is that, by examining arrangements in other countries and in First Nation communities, we can open our thinking to other possibilities. The remainder of this chapter highlights some of these alternatives for ensuring the well-being of children and families. Our challenge is to step off well-worn pathways and to be open to considering other ways of relating to children, families, and communities.

Ideologies and Contexts

Relationships among the State, Communities, Families, and Children

Concepts of children and families vary greatly across cultures. Shaped by historical, political, and cultural contexts, they directly influence our views on protecting children and supporting families. This section examines the ideologies that colour perspectives on the relationships among children, families, communities, and the state in selected societies. Specifically discussed are the ideologies framing these relationships in Anglo-American, selected continental European, and First Nations settings. We examine the implications of these relationships for child and family welfare systems.

Our intent is to provide a brief overview of various viewpoints. This discussion does not do justice to the complexities of relationships in each setting; nonetheless, these cross-cultural comparisons help to clarify the rationale behind policy choices, stimulate awareness of alternative views, and place the emphases of various child and family welfare orientations in context.

Stasis in ideologies. Values and ideologies are developed over long periods of time and are firmly entrenched in the history and culture of a society. These ideologies set the boundaries for what is acceptable in the development of public policies. In addition, these differences help us to understand the variations in public policy from one country to another

(O'Hara, 1998). It is evident that a society's perspectives on children, families, communities, and the state are reflected in their child and family welfare policies and practices.

Because these ideologies are so entrenched in the culture and history of particular places, child and family welfare policy and practice tend not to change radically, nor cause significant shifts in established relationships between the state, communities, families, and children. As Majone (1989) notes, "major policy breakthroughs are possible only after public opinion has been conditioned to accept new ideas and new concepts of the public interest" (as cited in O'Hara, 1998, p. 47).

Thus, despite tremendous growth in our knowledge of children and families, and their changing needs over the past century, the mandates and structures of Ontario's children's aid societies have varied only within relatively narrow parameters. Child welfare service delivery ideas and programs that fall outside the established ideological boundaries have remained on the fringes of mainstream thinking and methods. However, we do not see such arrangements as completely immutable. For example, Sweden had extremely high level of coercive removals of children from their families in the first half of the 1900s but has more recently placed a very strong emphasis on social provisions and supporting families (Olsson Hort, 1997). A beginning point in any reconsideration is an understanding of the reasons for current arrangements, along with an examination of alternative possibilities.

Anglo-American Rugged Individualism

The ideology of rugged individualism, which values individual initiative, ambition, self-sufficiency, and the principle of competition, has become North America's moral, social, political, and economic ideal. Societies that embrace this ideology believe that people must be free to pursue their interests (Djao, 1983; Sapiro, 1990). Individualism is rooted in a laissez-faire approach to economics, based on the 18th-century writings of Adam Smith (1723–1790), who contended that government interference in business is harmful. In addition, he argued that individuals who pursue their own interests will ultimately produce the highest level of good for the most people. This ideal is also rooted in the writings of Thomas Hobbes (1588–1679). A century earlier, Hobbes had asserted that the state should become involved only to prevent wrongdoing arising from unchecked individual self-assertion. He believed that the state's role in relation to the rest of society was one of provider and regulator of a social and moral framework (Hetherington et al., 1997).

Concepts of family. The ideals of rugged individualism, and of laissez-faire economics have set the family apart from the state in Anglo-American societies. The effects of late 19th-century industrialization and urbaniza-tion fragmented extended families, which were crucial for survival in farm-ing communities, and ushered in the nuclear family as the preferred model (Macintyre, 1993). Extended family networks, once the chief caregivers of children, were replaced by biological parents whose dominant virtue, through the lens of individualism, became self-reliance (Swift, 1995). The nuclear family ideal became the standard to which all Anglo-American societies aspired, as well as the standard by which all families were to be evaluated:

> So effective were the nineteenth- and twentieth-century promoters of
> the Victorian family model that today's society has great difficulty accept-
> ing the fact that other models have developed in other parts of the world
> and that alternative family models exist in growing numbers within our
> own society. (Pence, 1985, p. 237)

In individualistic societies, families are expected to survive in a free mar-ket based on their own talents and efforts. These societies believe that inter-nal family matters should be protected from the state. As Baker and Phipps (1997) have noted, in Canada (and other Anglo-American societies), laws and policies "have incorporated the values of self-reliance, individualism, and family privacy" (p. 105). Thus, in social welfare programming, a residual approach dominates, whereby state aid is available primarily in situations where parents have failed to adequately provide for the needs of family members. According to individualists, social welfare is for emergencies only, and should be withdrawn once the proper balances between the individual and marketplace have been restored, lest it erode the ideal of family respon-sibility (Baistow, Hetherington, Spriggs, & Yelloly, 1996; Djao, 1983).

Child protection, as part of the range of social welfare programming, is also intended for emergency or crisis situations. Ideally, temporary provi-sions for the care of children are provided by the state until such time as the family regains its own means of providing for its children (Swift, 1997). Critics of the system contend that disenfranchised single mothers are most often the focus of child protection interventions in Anglo-American soci-eties because they are ideologically distant from the ideal of self reliance (Pires, 1993; Swift, 1998; Thorpe, 1994). Interventions are concentrated on parents who fail both to meet minimum standards of child care and to demonstrate economic self-reliance. These critics argue that the child pro-tection systems are not equipped to respond to issues of child care in mid-dle- and upper-income families; when economically self-reliant parents fail to meet the prescribed minimum child care standards, they are much less likely to come under the purview of child protection authorities (Costin et al., 1996; Martin, 1985).

Concepts of children. In Anglo-American societies, the state's relationship to children varies considerably from its relationship to families. The state is in the conflicted position of wanting to both protect family privacy and enforce parental obligation, while at the same time ensuring the protection of children from harm (Nelken, 1998; Ronen, 1998). Changing constructs of childhood have shaped this dilemma. For example, in both England and Ontario, school attendance rose sharply during the late 1800s.This gave rise to studying children as a distinct group from adults, laying foundations for ongoing studies in child development (King, 1998).

School attendance was also a major contributing factor to making visible the plight of the children who had become the casualties of the Industrial Revolution (Hendrick, 1990; Sutherland, 1976). Coupled with emerging ideas about the social, educational, and psychological needs of children were constructions that framed childhood as a period of vulnerability requiring protection.

Because Anglo-American societies were so steeped in individualism, the valued response to such a public demonstration of need was to both protect the vulnerable children and to equip them for survival in a society that valued competitive capitalism. In turn, it was felt that society would be protected from becoming overburdened with future costs associated with the deviancy that might result from past cruelty and neglect of children (Armstrong, 1995; Bala, 1999). Foster placement—and particularly placement in middle-class, nuclear families—seemed to be the best solution. Today foster care remains a foremost intervention in child protection systems.

One of the chief complaints that critics have of the Anglo-American child protection paradigm concerns its disregard of the importance of family relationships. The state's relationship to the child and the state's relationship to the family are seen differently. Parents are often cast in the role of villain and children in the role of victim (Besharov et al., 1998; Chen, 2001). Although there may be specific cases where this perspective is accurate, there are many situations where the child's best interests are served by strengthening the relationship between parent and child. However, the Anglo-American system is not designed to actively support parent–child relationships and often sees the interests of parents and children as pitted against each other (Besharov et al., 1998; Chen, 2001; Swift, 1995).

Concepts of community. The role of the broader community in ensuring the well-being and protection of children is not central in the Anglo-American child protection paradigm. For example, Ontario's 54 provincially-funded children's aid societies are administered by local boards of directors who, in theory, have the responsibility of identifying community needs and allocating service resources appropriately. Ideally, the community is accounted for in such an arrangement; however, in practice, the provincial ministry seldom makes funding available that surpasses the minimum requirement for required day-to-day operations (McEachern & Morris, 1992). Alternative approaches such as family preservation, mutual aid programs, family group conferencing, and community development initiatives have shown considerable promise, but remain outside the mainstream service delivery (Cameron et al., 1997).

Some child protection critics see a possibility for community involvement in Anglo-American child protection systems as an intermediary structure between the state and the family. They contend that organized community involvement can help children, parents, and communities to find a voice and to engage the state in meaningful dialogue (Wharf, 1992; 1993).

Implications for child and family welfare. The Anglo-American emphasis on individualism means that parents are assumed to have the sole rights and responsibilities for raising their children (Swift, 1998). There is a belief that most families will raise their children with little difficulty and that the state should refrain from interfering into their private affairs. If a family experiences difficulties, the parents are often held responsible for ensuring the well-being of their children; any societal factors contributing to the family's problems are generally overlooked (Swift, 1998). As a result, to a great extent, child protection work is carried out with families on a case-by-case basis:

> Investigations take place in the private domain, with particular families as their focus ... The case-by-case approach instructs us to see the problem as individualized; our attention is directed to the unique circumstances and behaviours occurring in this particular family and to the specific effects on particular children ... This way of organizing child welfare moves the social and economic issues affecting these families to the background. (Swift, 1998, p. 169)

First Nations Notions of Interdependence

First Nations ideas about children, family, and community are rooted in beliefs about the interdependence among the environment, people, and the Creator; many First Nations emphasize the necessity of living a balanced life in relation to all creation. When change occurs in an individual, it necessarily impacts the family, community, and surrounding environment; therefore, to speak of the individual as self-reliant is contrary to a First Nations world view (Maidman & Connors, 2002; Morrissette, McKenzie, & Morrissette, 1993).

These Aboriginal principles embrace not only interdependence but also total inclusion. Ideally, this perspective ensures that all members of the community, each of whom is seen as uniquely gifted, contributes to the survival of the community as a whole (Maidman & Connors, 2002). Hence, there are no conceptual separations or boundaries between the community, family, or children. The elders lead through the sharing of wisdom, but actual decision-making is accomplished through consensus of all community members (Morrissette et al., 1993).

Concepts of family. Aboriginal desires for families differ in fundamental ways from Anglo-American nuclear family ideals. Extended families play an active role in the care of children. In many First Nations communities, children are raised by their grandparents or others in the family (Morrissette et al., 1993). Maidman and Connors (2002) argue that "these kinship patterns and traditions result in a person identifying numerous people as kinship equivalents of fathers, mothers, and siblings" (p. 396). According to tradition, in First Nation communities, all members of a family have some responsibility for the upbringing of children.

> within the tribal family: (a) older siblings provide protection, love, and teaching, (b) parents provide love, teaching, food and shelter, (c) elders/ grandparents provide love, care and teaching, (d) aunts and uncles often act as additional parental figures, and (e) clan members and community members monitor and provide expectations for socially appropriate behaviour. (Maidman & Connors, 2002, p. 385)

In Aboriginal communities, great emphasis is placed on keeping children within their family and the community. It is believed that all other forms of care are secondary and, above all, community members should support the efforts of parents in trying to raise their children in a safe, healthy environment (McKenzie, 1995; Wharf, 1992).

Concepts of children. In Aboriginal thought, the child is not a separate entity; her or his identity is understood in relation to others in his/her family or community. As members of the community, ideally, children have certain responsibilities to fulfill, and they learn that neglecting these expectations can cause hardship to themselves and others in the community (Maidman & Connors, 2002; Morrissette et al., 1993). Ideally, First Nations children attain a sense of individuality and belonging through tribal traditions that allow them to develop their potential, while still acting in harmony with the needs of the family and community (Maidman & Connors, 2002).

The late-19th-century concept of childhood in Anglo-American societies made a significant contribution to the state's rationale for practices of assimilation centred on the separation of Aboriginal children from their tribal communities (Morrissette et al., 1993). It has been argued that it is inappropriate to separate the well-being of Aboriginal children from that of their families and communities and that the practice of large-scale removals of First Nations children from their homes and communities has culminated in a legacy of cultural destruction (Kingsley & Mark 2000; Morrissette et al., 1993; Royal Commission on Aboriginal Peoples, 1996; Saskatchewan Children's Advocate Office, 2000).

Concepts of communities. Aboriginal perspectives are steeped in principles of interdependence, seeing the well-being of children in relation to strengthening family and community. Large extended family networks and others in the local community ensure the provision of adequate care for children (McKenzie, 1995). Ideally, continued community membership and communal responsibility for caring for each other ensure children's survival in an Aboriginal community.

Implications for child and family welfare. The ideals of rugged individualism have always been at odds with Aboriginal ideology. These differences ultimately led to the mass destruction of First Nations communities and Aboriginal ways of life. The colonists sought not only to conquer territory but to secure their claims through acculturation, so that all children would receive Anglo-Canadian citizenship in a Christian culture (Kingsley & Mark, 2000; Maidman & Connors, 2002; Morrissette et al., 1993; Royal Commission on Aboriginal Peoples, 1996; Saskatchewan Children's Advocate Office, 2000). The dominance of individualism, its ethnocentricity, and its impact on child welfare philosophy have marginalized Aboriginal ideology and have alienated most First Nations communities from ways of life that sustained them for thousands of years:

> [Intrusion into First Nations communities has been] ... paternalistic in nature, condescending and demeaning in fact, and insensitive and brutal ... children have been taken from families and communities first by residential schools and then by child welfare authorities. Both ... have left Aboriginal people and societies severely damaged. (Manitoba Public Inquiry into the Administration of Justice and Aboriginal People, 1991, p. 509)

It is only through Aboriginal resistance to the destruction of their communities (caused in part by child welfare policies of apprehension and adoption into non-native homes), and the persistence of First Nations communities in obtaining self-government, that Aboriginal ideology is now beginning to be heard in child welfare (Maidman & Connors, 2002; McKenzie, 1989; Morrissette et al., 1993).

First Nations concepts of children, families, and community have strong implications for the design of child welfare/protection systems. Ideals for

First Nations child welfare include the use of traditional teachers and healers in its practice, addressing the need for healing both within families and within communities (Morrissette et al., 1993; Saskatchewan Children's Advocate Office, 2000). Aboriginal helping efforts do not place an emphasis on the individual rights of children; they focus on working with parents to support them in their roles, and remove children from their families and communities only as a last resort (McKenzie, 1989; 1995; 1997; Wharf, 1992). In addition, because of the emphasis on collective responsibility and interdependence, First Nations child welfare ideals involve consultation with parents, extended family, and the local community to make decisions about the well-being of a child (Morrissette et al., 1993; Wharf, 1992).

Continental European Notions of Collective Responsibility

Similar ideas of collective responsibility for the well-being of children and families are shared among some western European nations. Although these countries are influenced more by ideals of individual achievement and responsibility than are First Nations, there are competing ideologies that influence their ideals about relationships between state, community, family, and children. Political theorist Jean Jacques Rousseau (1712–1778) believed that the basis of any state was a collective consciousness and that the people must remain sovereign, both in the development of their society and in the exercise of their own rule making (Bronowski & Mazlish, 1960). The role of the state is to express the will of the people, and the role of the law is to operate on the consent of the whole population. The state gives political expression to social character (Hetherington et al., 1997).

In contrast to Anglo-American laissez-faire and individualist ideals, Europe's dominant ideologies have been protectionist and collectivist (Heidenheimer, Heclo, & Teich Adams, 1975). It is difficult to characterize one model that typifies Europe, however; there are important differences among European countries that will not be captured in this general overview. Overall, principles of social solidarity and subsidiarity are key notions in European social ideology. These principles are emphasized in varying degrees throughout continental Europe (Hetherington et al., 1997).

Subsidiarity and social solidarity. The subsidiarity principle forms the basis for understanding relationships among the state, the community, and the family. Subsidiarity is predicated on Catholic social philosophy, which is embodied in the 1931 encyclical of Pope Pius XI, *Quadragesimo Anno*. This thinking dates back to 1871, when the Catholic Church explored alternatives to socialism and liberalism. It states:

> (Sections 79–80) ... it is an injustice, a grave evil and a disturbance of right
> order, for a larger and higher association to arrogate to itself functions

which can be performed efficiently by smaller and lower societies.... The State therefore should leave to smaller groups the settlement of business of minor importance, which otherwise would greatly distract it ... Let those in power, therefore, be convinced that the more faithfully this principle of subsidiary function be followed, the greater will be both social authority and social efficiency, and the happier and more prosperous the condition of the commonwealth. (as cited in Lorenz, 1994, p. 25)

Social solidarity encompasses ideals of mutuality, reciprocity of obligations, and social cohesion. Solidarity lies primarily within the family, secondly in the community, and thirdly in the state, an order reinforced by subsidiarity (Hetherington et al., 1997). It postulates a strong relationship between the family and the state, an emphasis on social inclusion, and an emphasis on maintaining family integrity. In countries such as Sweden, Norway, Finland, and Denmark, solidarity is so strongly embedded in the culture that distinctions between state and society are blurred. Scandinavian vernacular refers to the welfare state as *folkhem*, literally "the people's home" (Leira, 1994).

Social solidarity and subsidiarity combine to define an ideal of "a state whose legal, economic and social system is founded on the principle of social security (avoidance of material distress for the citizen), social justice and social equality (of opportunity)" (Dyson, 1980, as cited in Lorenz, 1994, p. 26). Hetherington et al. (1997) describe the social context these principles provide for child welfare as follows:

Where services for children are enshrined by the principles of social solidarity, subsidiarity and citizenship, one consequence is that the institutions which organise, deliver, and shape local responses to child protection are structured into, and derive their authority from a total conception of society. (p. 34)

A collective conception of society ensures that child welfare is understood in broad ways. Countries like Denmark, for instance, make little distinction between policies aimed at well-being and those aimed at risk. In Germany, the general thinking is that, in one way or another, all families could be understood as at risk. It is expected that those who need help can and will seek it (Pringle, 1998; Wolff, 1997). Another example exists in Sweden, where it is part of the normal course of life that families receive public welfare services (Olsson Hort, 1997). However, some critics have expressed concern that such an inclusive approach to child and family welfare opens the possibility that child abuse will not be recognized and/or will not be taken seriously enough, leaving children in potentially dangerous situations (Pringle, 1998).

Concepts of family and children. In many European societies, the family is identified as a fundamental social institution, and the state's role is one of broadly protecting the health of families; a right to family support is assumed. The family is understood as having basic rights, and "conflicts of rights between family members are likely to be subordinated to questions of family welfare" (Hetherington et al., 1997, p. 94). Thus, from this perspective, it is inconsistent to sever child and family connections when trying to protect children, unless other options have been explored first. Living with the biological family is valued as the most desirable environment for children. Therefore, family maintenance and support is often the dominant to approach to child and family welfare (Madge & Attridge, 1996; Olsson Hort, 1997; Poso, 1997; Tuomisto & Vuori-Karvia, 1997).

The idea that the child is an inseparable part of the biological family is deeply embedded in most European societies, and the social welfare emphasis is on family services, therapeutic help, and prevention (Cooper, Hetherington, Baistow, Pitts, & Spriggs, 1995). When necessary, the placement of a child is often accomplished in a co-operative arrangement between state and family, with permanent severing of the parent–child connection less common than in Anglo-American jurisdictions (Baistow et al., 1996; Hetherington et al., 1997). However, concern has been expressed about the degree to which the child's perspective may be obscured. These orientations have also been criticized for not dealing with the realities of oppression and power imbalances in families where child abuse does occur (Pringle, 1998).

Conceptions of community and child welfare. In many European countries, fostering proper child development and care is not seen as the sole responsibility of their parents. For example: "children are not just the private responsibility of parents, but rather are a collective resource that add to France's demographic and economic strength, and therefore have a place in state policy" (White, 1998, p. 13). Many European societies have acknowledged this responsibility in material ways, supporting relatively high levels of taxation to ensure higher levels of care and provisions for all families and children. Likewise, European communal ideologies often value prevention and community development initiatives:

> the principles of subsidiarity and solidarity give social work a broader, preventive, and community development mandate: not to separate individuals from society, but to promote healthy relations between and within groups, and to see that as a process of encouraging participation of the marginalised from below, aided by resources from above. (Cannan, Berry, & Lyons, 1992, p. 46)

Concluding Remarks

It is essential that we understand that child and family welfare systems manifest preferences about the complex representations of the relationships among state, community, family, and children. Child and family welfare mirrors these relationships, which are rooted in the historical, economic, and cultural underpinnings of the society. These roots present barriers to transporting "good" ideas from one culture to another. Nonetheless, these barriers are not impermeable; as argued in the introduction to this chapter, knowing about the existence of other ways tells us that strategies other than those most familiar to us are indeed possible.

The intent of this discussion is not to weigh the relative merits or disadvantages of the different ways of understanding relationships among children, families, communities and the state. Rather, the purpose is to acknowledge that there are many ways of understanding these relationships. These differences are often neglected in discussions of possibilities in child and family welfare, because we are limited by conventional understandings of the context in which we live.

Explanatory Models: Why Do Families Experience Difficulties?

At the root of every child and family welfare system are central ideas about the nature of child maltreatment and the reasons why families have difficulty providing adequate care for their children. Child welfare/protection systems are constructed around these values and explanations, which are deeply rooted in the societies in which they have evolved. Therefore, it is helpful to understand the ways in which family difficulties are viewed; these explanatory models influence the interventions favoured by various systems. There is no single set of explanations of child maltreatment common to all child and family welfare systems. By examining the range of ways in which family difficulties are conceptualized, we encounter a spectrum of possibilities outside the realm of current preoccupations.

There is near unanimity in the literature that child maltreatment is a very complex problem with many contributing elements (Ammerman & Hersen, 1990; Cameron et al., 1997; National Research Council, 1993; Peirson et al., 2002). Every child and family welfare system acknowledges the contributions of the following to family breakdown: parental history, parental functioning, emotional and physical illness, substance abuse, lack of knowledge, social isolation, lack of developmental opportunities, violence, economic distress, and community disintegration. Nonetheless, few, if any, child and family welfare systems are organized so that this full range of contributing factors carries equal weight in their understanding of distressed families. Likewise, no system is solely influenced by only one explanatory model. Each child and family welfare system places greater emphases on some of these rationales, and the particular combination of perspectives empha- sized influence the ways help is given to distressed children and families within that system.

Table 1 summarizes various models or explanations that have emerged from our review about why children are maltreated. Some of these perspectives exert great influence on existing child and family welfare systems, while others have achieved recognition only within smaller pilot projects. This section discusses each of the explanatory models in Table 1.

Parental deficiency. One approach taken is to hold parents solely responsible for providing adequate care for their families. This is the de facto emphasis in threshold systems that have evolved in child-saving societies. Historically, their emphasis was on "rescuing" children from incompetent or immoral parents and removing them from the dangerous and deviant influences in their living environments. As Swift (1995) notes, in Canada, "both the system and our conceptions of child neglect have remained remarkedly [sic] consistent to the original [child-saving] model" (p. 4). In threshold systems, parents are both entitled, and expected, to provide proper care for their children. If minimal norms for child care are violated, it is because the parents will not or cannot take proper care of their children (Marneffe & Broos, 1997; Martin, 1985; Schene, 1998; Swift, 1995; Tunstill, 1997).

Within this perspective, parents are often described as having personality characteristics that prevent them from adequately providing and caring for their children. As a result, interventions often focus on producing change in individual parents (usually the mother) rather than in the environments they live in (Martin, 1985; Tunstill, 1997). Hughes (1995) argues that, in Canada, government services "tend to attribute poverty to personal defect and emphasize remedial casework strategies presumed to help break the 'cycle of poverty'" (p. 783).

There is also an implicit assumption that families do not normally need assistance with their child care, and it is presumed that families in trouble will not realize that they need help or will not seek help voluntarily (Armitage, 1993). Consequently, the majority of families are brought into contact with the system through third-party reports and agency investigations. Furthermore, because parents are often considered to represent a danger to their children, there is an insistence that they carry out their child care responsibilities or face losing their children to another home where they can be adequately protected (Schene, 1998).

Table 1: Why Do Families Experience Difficulties?

	Explanations	Implications of this model
Parental Deficiency	• Parents who maltreat their children often have problematic personality characteristics that are the root of the problem. • Parents are solely responsible for the care and well-being of their children.	• State, community, and extended family members are not expected to contribute to child well-being. • Parents will not come forward voluntarily for assistance. • Parents are generally assumed to be the major source of risk to children. Thus, children should be removed from parents, if it is thought to be in the child's best interest. • If families have problems, parents are responsible.
Family Breakdown	• Child maltreatment occurs when the family is not functioning as a healthy unit. • Poverty, environmental stress, and lack of appropriate supports contribute to family dysfunction and child care problems.	• Emphasis is placed on supporting families and maintaining child–family connections. • Children will only be removed from the family's home without the parents' permission in extreme cases. • Parents are expected to voluntarily seek help if they need assistance. • Emphasis is placed on higher levels of support and social provisions for families.
Societal Breakdown	• Child maltreatment results from inadequate support and resources. • Child care and development are shared responsibilities of society. • Family breakdown is as much a failure of society as individuals.	• Emphasis is placed on high levels of support and social provisions for families. • There is greater involvement of the community in the functioning of families. • Parents are expected to voluntarily seek help if they need assistance. • Children are removed from home as a last resort, usually only temporarily.

Continuum of Normal Behaviour	• Child maltreatment is an exaggeration of normal behaviour in society. • At some point in their lives, most families will receive some sort of assistance.	• Emphasis is placed on high levels of support and social provisions for families. • Children will only be removed from the family's home without the parents' permission in extreme cases. • Parents are expected to voluntarily seek help, if they need assistance.
Risk and Protective Factors	• There are risk and protective factors that contribute to the likelihood that families will experience difficulties. • Families with several risk factors are likely to experience more problems than others.	• To be effective, treatment and prevention programs should address many of these risk and protective factors. • Programs may need to cross service jurisdictional boundaries, and may need to be intensive and long-term.
Economic Distress and Community Disintegration	• Family difficulties result from economic distress and community disintegration. • Most consistent predictor of child welfare involvement is living in extreme poverty and deteriorating neighbourhoods.	• Focus is on placing child and family healing within the context of the healing process for the whole community. • Emphasis is placed on high levels of support and social provisions for families. • Focus is on maintaining children within their communities and/or extended families.
Systems of Oppression	• Child maltreatment issues are rooted in economic, class, gender, and racial oppression. • Child welfare/protection agencies are seen as reinforcing these oppressive relationships and destructive of the ways of living of the people they "target."	• Agencies need to reform relations with oppressed groups. • Emphasis is placed on high levels of support and social provisions for families. • Focus is on collective, participatory responses to empower communities. • Calls for child welfare/protection workers to advocate for social change based on their knowledge of their clients' lives.

Family breakdown. In some continental European systems, child mal-treatment is seen as a symptom of family dysfunction or breakdown. Within this frame of reference, the concern is with the health of the families as basic units of socialization and child development and with the help families need to function properly. Family and parenting problems are exacerbated by external circumstances such as poverty and environmental stress; viewing family problems as resulting only from parental inadequacies is considered "blaming the victim" (Fox Harding, 1991). This view of family difficulties leads to an emphasis on supporting families and maintaining child–family connections. This perspective has been influential in Belgium where:

> Both the abuser and the child are perceived as victims influenced by broad sociological and psychological factors beyond their control ... Protection of the child is a priority, but the child is more often maintained in the child's family together with the provision of services to support the parents and help them cope. (Marneffe & Broos, 1997, p. 181)

Only in exceptional cases, where children are in severe danger, will a child be removed from the family home without the family's permission. Within this approach, it is assumed that families will voluntarily seek help with their children (Marneffe & Broos, 1997; Olsson Hort, 1997; Roelofs & Baart-man, 1997).

Societal breakdown. A different perspective is taken by First Nations and some more collective European societies, who view child development as a shared responsibility of the society. Family breakdown and child mal-treatment are as much a failure of society as of individual families. This approach leads to an emphasis on social provisions to support families and children. Denmark exemplifies this perspective, as their "social infrastruc-ture reflects a cohesive national concept of what constitutes quality of life for the individual and a belief that society has a collective responsibility to ensure that individuals have equal access to attaining quality of life" (Pires, 1993, p. 47). In addition, this way of viewing family difficulties leads to cul-tural support for greater involvement of the community in the functioning of families and in the care for children. Evidence of this frame of reference can be seen with Aboriginal societies, as exemplified by the Champagne/Aishi-hik Band, where the "planned involvement of family members and friends transforms the private matter of child welfare to a community concern" (Wharf, 1992, pp. 116–117). (See the discussion in chapter 3.)

Continuum of normal behaviour. Another influential perspective on child maltreatment was developed in the Berlin child protection centres. This perspective views child maltreatment as a continuation or exaggeration of patterns found in most families and in society as a whole. In fact, child abuse does not differ significantly from patterns of oppression and violence that are both obvious and even praised elsewhere in society (Marneffe & Broos, 1997). For example, physical and sexual aggressiveness are evident in many sports and popular entertainment. From this perspective, there should be no stigma attached to families who seek help and no implication that they are somehow abnormal. Under the proper conditions, any of us is capable of inappropriate care giving.

In systems influenced by this perspective, child abuse is not identified as a specific problem and is not a necessary or even typical precursor for families' involvement with authorities. Finland exemplifies this viewpoint with a child welfare system "in which child abuse as such is seldom reported or diagnosed as a specific problem for treatment ... From this perspective, it is difficult to identify child abuse as a separate problem requiring special treatment" (Poso, 1997, p. 160). Within the continuum of normal behaviour, it is assumed that, at some point in their lives, most families will receive social welfare assistance (Marneffe & Broos, 1997; Olsson Hort, 1997; Poso, 1997). This perspective leads to the design of child and family welfare systems in which a heavy emphasis is placed on making resources and supports available to all families. In addition, the emphasis is on maintaining the parent–child bond, whenever possible (Wolff, 1997).

Risk and protective factors. Another perspective has evolved from research on risk and protective factors for various social problems, including child maltreatment. This research concludes that these complex difficulties are influenced by multiple factors. Families involved with child and family welfare agencies usually have difficulties in many areas of living, such as family functioning, addictions, physical and mental health, economic distress, and socially disintegrating communities. Also, research shows that these difficulties cluster together into common profiles for many distressed parents and children. Furthermore, various disadvantaged populations, such as young offenders, psychiatric populations, and child protection clientele, have similar difficulty clusters (Cameron, O'Reilly, Laurendeau, & Chamberland, 2002; Nelson, Laurendeau, Chamberland, & Peirson, 2002; Peirson et al., 2002).

Within this framework, there is no clear theoretical or empirical way to isolate one or more problems as the key points for intervention. To be effective, a range of risk and protective factors for both parents and children needs to be addressed simultaneously and sequentially. Proponents of this perspective believe that prevention of neglect and abuse should include programs targeted to assist children with many aspects of their lives. Ideally, many promising program models cross jurisdictional boundaries and provide access to help that is both intensive and frequently long-term (Cameron et al., 1997; Cameron, O'Reilly et al., 2002; Nelson, et al., 2002; Schorr, 1989; 1997). In North America, a number of demonstration projects with multiply disadvantaged populations have produced superior results building upon these principles. Unfortunately, despite these encouraging results, such promising initiatives have remained at the margins of threshold systems (Cameron, Karabanow, Laurendeau, & Chamberland, 2002). Perhaps because of greater access to a range of social provisions for children and families, some continental European child and family welfare systems have made this a more central reality (Poso, 1997).

Economic distress and community disintegration. Another perspective is to view family breakdown and child maltreatment as consequence of economic distress and community disintegration. Proponents of this explanatory model point out that the most consistent and strongest statistical predictors of having an open child protection case are living in extreme conditions of poverty and neighbourhood dissolution; this relationship is even stronger for families with children in out-of-home care (Costin et al., 1996; Courtney, 1998; English, 1998; Lawrence-Karski, 1997; Peirson et al., 2002).

During economic hard times, the number of families that experience difficulty caring for their children increases, as does involvement with the child and family welfare system (Hughes, 1995). In addition, economic hardships for families are more prevalent in countries with lower levels of social provision (Phipps, 1999). For example, Canada's poverty rate is almost double that of many European countries (Hughes, 1995).

Some First Nations have focused on placing helping child and family clearly within the context of a healing process for the whole community (Maidman & Connors, 2002; McKenzie, 1989; 1995; 1997; Morrissette et al., 1993). From this perspective, it is futile to blame individuals or families for their difficulties: "Innu and Inuit concepts of justice are very different from white concepts of justice ... the words 'guilty' and 'innocent' don't even exist in Inuktitut ... the emphasis in Inuit culture is on solving the problem, not punishing the offender (Toughill, 2001, February 3, p. K3). Attempts at community healing in threshold systems are relatively new and ill-understood efforts, and we have a great deal to learn. However, a few examples exist in the United States, where a community-healing rationale has been the basis of intensive and multi-faceted neighbourhood development projects, with an emphasis on child well-being and protection. The results from some of these projects are encouraging for children, families, and communities (see examples in Cameron, O'Reilly, et al., 2002).

Systems of oppression. Some authors see family breakdown and child maltreatment as rooted in economic, class, gender, and racial oppression. Threshold systems are seen as reinforcing these oppressive relations and

Choices in Child and Family Welfare System Design   37

being destructive toward people and traditional ways of living (Armstrong, 1995; Callahan, 1993; Swift, 1998; Thorpe, 1994). For example:

> because the foundation of patriarchal public policies is based on the traditional beliefs about women and their place in society, these policies become self-fulfilling ... stingy services are provided by ill-paid women to women and their children, selected because of their inability to provide for themselves. The status quo is maintained. (Callahan, 1993, p. 196)

This perspective prescribes a radical shift in thinking and in existing relations. Proponents favour more generous social provisions and, in particular, they propose collective and participatory responses that respect and empower families and communities (Maidman & Connors, 2002; McKenzie, 1989; 1997; Morrissette et al., 1993; Swift, 1995; Wharf, 1992).

This perspective on systems of oppression has been influential in First Nations conceptions of child welfare and in a small number of North American neighbourhood demonstration projects (Cameron, O'Reilly et al., 2002; Maidman & Connors, 2002). In addition, some feminist social services have been heavily impacted by this point of view. For instance, in her 1993 review of feminist service organizations, Callahan (1993) argued that their most important attributes are their commitment to social change and their attempts to meet the often overwhelming needs of those who come to them for assistance.

To improve outcomes for children and families, it is essential that we first realize that there are various ways of conceptualizing the reasons families experience difficulties. Perspectives on the cause of family difficulties and child maltreatment dramatically influence the approaches taken to assist children and families. Because culture and values play such an important role in how our world is understood, it is easy to forget that there are alternatives to our way of understanding these difficulties. Again, our contention is that knowing this range of possibilities has the potential to expand the boundaries of our existing notions about how to help families and children.

Choices in Child and Family Welfare System Design

Gilbert (1997c) proposes that child and family welfare systems can be classified into the following categories: (a) child protection systems (for example, the United States, Canada, and England); (b) family service systems with mandatory reporting (for example, Denmark, Sweden, and Finland); and, (c) family service systems without mandatory reporting (for example, Belgium, Netherlands, and Germany). These three orientations focus their interventions on the circumstances of particular children and families. Our review suggests a fourth orientation: (d) community caring systems (for example, some First Nations communities). This orientation places help-ing children and families in the context of a healing process for the whole community. Although this orientation is much less common and not well established, it represents a more communal understanding of the problems facing children and families and of how responses are best organized (Maid-man & Connors, 2002; McKenzie, 1989; 1997; Morrissette et al., 1993). Child protection systems can also be differentiated into those with manda-tory reporting (for example, Canada, and the United States) and settings without mandatory reporting legislation (for example, England). In our examination of choices in child and family welfare system design, reference will be made to each of these orientations.

Our review of child and family welfare systems identifies dimensions along which these systems may be compared. These are summarized in Table 2. These comparisons identify a spectrum of possibilities in system design and demonstrate that there is nothing inevitable about how child protection is organized. Ontario's child protection system, which represents choices from a substantially broader set of alternatives, is grounded in the values, priorities, and institutional contexts of the province. As mentioned at the beginning of this chapter, we believe that child and family welfare systems are not neutral responses to problems; they represent some of our most powerful statements about our values concerning children, family, community, and state.

Managing Dual Mandates

Each of the child and family welfare orientations compared operates within a dual mandate, incorporating requirements to provide care (offering pre-ventive, supportive, and remedial assistance to children, parents, and fam-ilies to enhance their well-being and functioning) and to exert control (using professional and communal authority as well as legal/police mandates to enforce community standards of child care). Notwithstanding their generic nature, there are important differences in how various child welfare/protec-tion orientations manage these mandates.

First response and view of legal authority. Threshold orientations increasingly focus on monitoring and controlling the behaviours of parents in "high-risk" families and, as a consequence, provide minimal supports to families. The initial response of threshold systems is a mandatory, legal investigation of allegations of child maltreatment, with any "care" responses coming later in the process if at all: "In England, the response ... was to extend control to more and more families via a framework of investigation, regulation, procedure, and through child protection conferences which moved 'therapeutic' intervention to one side" (Hetherington et al., 1997, p. 27).

Table 2: Choices in Child Welfare/Protection System Design

Topic	Questions	Choices
Managing Dual Mandates	What is the system's first response to families in difficulty?	• Investigation of the family to assess risk of harm to the child. • Offer of services to support the family.
	How is the use of legal authority viewed?	• Use of the formal, adversarial legal system to force parental compliance. • Use of informal, inquisitorial legal processes to negotiate a plan of action that is agreed to by the family. • Avoidance of the legal system whenever possible. Family, friends, and others in the community are brought together to develop a plan of action for the family.
	Who provides services for families?	• Family services are often contracted out to other agencies and not viewed as an integral part of the child welfare/protection system • Family services are integrated into the overall child welfare/protection system.
Relationship with the Legal System	What is the role of the police and formal legal authority?	• Child welfare workers work in tandem with police to investigate parents and gather evidence in case it is needed later in formal court proceedings. • Child welfare workers attempt to avoid the involvement of police and court-mandated interventions whenever possible, for example, through the use of voluntary services, informal negotiations through the Judge for Children's Office and lay mediation committees, and community involvement through First Nations band councils.
	How is authority conferred to child welfare/protection workers?	• Child welfare/protection workers' authority is enforced through the power of the legal system. • The well-being of children is understood as a collective responsibility of the community. Parents feel entitled to support and often interventions are negotiated with families, lessening the need for coercive enforcement.

Table 2 (*continued*)

Topic	Questions	Choices
Relationship with the Legal System (continued)	Who is most involved in decision-making in the child welfare/ protection system?	• Child welfare/ protection is the realm of specialized professionals; non-professional voices are rarely heard in the development of intervention plans for families. • The Child welfare/protection system makes some use of non-professionals in decision-making (e.g., boards of lay people). • Non-professionals are highly involved in decision-making and services are often governed by the community.
	Is reporting of suspected cases of child maltreatment mandated by law?	• Reporting to the child welfare/ protection system is mandatory. • Reporting to the child welfare/ protection system is voluntary.
	Is mediation provided as an intermediary between voluntary involvement and legal coercion?	• Access to the legal system is the primary dispute resolution mechanism. • Intermediary mediation bodies are part of the normal intervention options.
Separate or Embedded Child Welfare Organization	How is responsibility for child welfare/ protection services allocated?	• Responsibility is allocated solely to a specialized unit (e.g., children's aid societies) • Responsibility is shared across several social welfare units, such as health, education, recreation, financial assistance services, etc. • Care is separated from control, so that some units are responsible for the investigation of families and others are responsible for any services provided. • All or most child welfare/protection functions are the responsibility of the same unit.
	How do families enter the system?	• Services are given only to families with confirmed danger of child maltreatment. • Services are only offered to families deemed to be at risk. • Services are accessible to all families.

- Services are provided at the insistence of the child welfare/protection agency through legal mandate.
- Services are given on the basis of a family's request for/acceptance of support.
- There must be evidence of child maltreatment for services to be provided.
- Families must demonstrate need of assistance before assistance is given.
- Services are given to families who request them.

How is ending the parent–child relationship viewed?

- Permanent state guardianship and adoption are common interventions, often without the permission of the parents.
- Permanent state guardianship and adoption are rare and often with the permission of the parents.

How much effort is expended before severing the parent-child connection is considered?

- If parents cannot comply with agency demands to ensure the child's safety, the child will be removed. Few services are offered directly by the agency, although the family is often referred to other services available within the community.
- Permanent removal of the child is a last resort. Many services and supports are provided to the families before severing the parent–child connection is considered.

How do conceptions of children and families affect intervention priorities?

- Societies that emphasize individual rights typically make the well-being and safety of the child their paramount concern. The child's best interests takes precedence over the well-being of the family. These societies are more likely to permanently remove children from their parents.
- Societies that place great importance on the well-being of families typically do not place greater emphasis on the well-being of the child's rights than on the rights of the family. Families of origin are seen as fundamental to children's well-being. Family maintenance is a priority. These societies tend to avoid the permanent severing of parent–child relationships.

Maintaining Families and Supporting Children

Table 2 (*continued*)

Topic	Questions	Choices
Maintaining Families and Supporting Children (continued)	What is the organizing framework for the child welfare/protection system?	• Child abuse is the organizing framework. The system focuses on finding children who are at risk of harm and protecting them. Parents are often considered to be the source of risk to the children and are seen as being responsible for the problems. • The well-being of the child and the family within the community is the organizing framework. All families are eligible for services and support. Factors such as health, financial difficulties, and family dysfunction are viewed as common sources of difficulty.
Discretion and Control	How much discretion is available to child welfare/protection workers?	• Workers rely on standardized tools to assess risk to children. Standard timelines and guidelines must be met to ensure workers are following procedures and protocol. • Workers are trusted to use their discretion and experience in assessing risk to children and developing intervention plans.

On the other hand, the initial response of family service systems typically emphasizes the provision of service to maintain the family and the parent–child bond, the priority being finding ways to support family functioning, except in extreme situations. For example, in Finland, where preventive, non-stigmatizing, and supportive measures and services are emphasized, the focus has been on interventions that encourage and support the maintenance of children in their own homes:

> Maternity and child health clinics have expanded and diversified family training, and intensified co-operation with families. In day care, various forms of co-operation supporting parental participation were developed. Also home help services have been developed to support child rearing by parents. (Tuomisto & Vuori-Karvia, 1997, p. 92)

In these family service systems, the option to use formal and legal authority is still available, if necessary. However, coercive and legally mandated interventions are regarded as last resorts and are generally avoided, if possible. Conversely, legally contested, formal court proceedings are much more common in threshold systems. In fact, one European commentator noted that:

> [it is] interesting that all of the countries except Canada and the United States were moving to clarify in policy the concept of the state as an agent for empowering parents to carry out their responsibilities to their children. ... [in European countries] ... state efforts to assist parents are construed as strengthening, not diminishing, parental rights, roles, and responsibilities. Participants also pointed out that this attitude toward state role coincides with policy efforts to achieve greater involvement of parents in decision making and a greater preponderance of voluntary placements of children who require care. (Pires, 1993, p. 68)

Some family service systems (for example, France and Belgium) make frequent use of the authority of family judges (often specially trained for this purpose) in a less formal fashion when negotiating intervention plans with families and service providers. Other countries, such as Finland, Germany, and Denmark, have also legislated informal negotiations with families to resolve child care concerns. This legislation is based on the principle that assistance to families should be framed as an offer of help, rather than as a command from a legal authority; the intent is to offer parents some freedom of choice about their families and to foster a feeling of self-help, rather than control (Bering Pruzan, 1997; Wolff, 1997).

Ideals for First Nations community caring systems also stress providing support to families and maintaining children in their own community. They place the highest emphasis on the involvement of relatives and others in the local community in the process: "Aboriginal social work practice will include the use of traditional teachers and healers, a community based approach to the planning and implementation of service, and the incorporation of traditional methods of healing" (Morrissette et al., 1993, p. 103). The approach taken by the Champagne/Aishihik Band, in Yukon, reflects these principles of healing and involvement of the local community. Parents, extended family, and community members work together to develop a plan of action and identify resources for the family within the community. Parents' hardships are acknowledged, and although they are not blamed, there is an insistence that parents take ownership of the difficulties and take an active role in problem-solving. Community involvement can facilitate parents in connecting with helping resources and can provide support for the family (Wharf, 1992).

Despite important differences, it is important to realize that these broad child and family welfare orientations do not operate in complete isolation from each other. Increasingly, influences from North American child protection systems have fostered changes in European child and family service systems. England's *Looking After Children* model of state care for children has influenced policy and practice elsewhere in Europe and in Canada (Kufeldt et al., 2000), and England has recently introduced new policies reflective of some continental European countries' emphasis on social provisions for children and parents (see the discussions in Freymond & Cameron, 2006). First Nations community caring systems have been substantially influenced by the child protection orientations of the state jurisdictions in which they are nested (see the discussion in chapter 3).

Who provides services for families. Child and family welfare systems also differ in the extent to which they house the care and control dimensions of their mandates within one agency. Threshold systems usually invest the child protection mandate in a single public or parapublic agency. These systems operate under specific legal guidelines and have close connections to the courts and, increasingly, to the police. The involvement of other social service and community organizations in the protection mandate (unless under contract to supply specific types of child protection services such as foster care or in-home supports) is minimal and unclear.

Conversely, many family service systems involve their broader social service networks, as well as particular support agencies. For instance, until 1998, Confidential Doctor Offices (CDO) in the Netherlands acted as a first line for providing child and family welfare services, including working with families where child maltreatment was a concern. Families were approached on a voluntary basis by the service, even though the CDO were officially connected to the Child Care and Protection Board. Depending on the nature of the family's problems, the CDO referred the case to a specialized agency.

Treatments included having school personnel or family doctors speak to the family and offer advice on child rearing, regular visits from social workers to provide support for the family, and/or individual or family therapy. More intensive treatments included out-of-home placements, either on a voluntary basis, or on the basis of a child protection order (Hetherington et al., 1997; Roelofs & Baartman, 1997).

In addition, family service systems typically have separate jurisdictions for child abuse specialists and the management of formal legal actions and child placements. Some family-focused systems have created intermediate strata between voluntary service and legal coercion, which allow for less formal, but authoritative, negotiations among family members, service professionals, and judges. Belgium exemplifies this approach by having two separate functional areas for its care and control operations. This separation allows for "an intermediate zone in which difficult cases [can] be assessed and managed" (Hetherington et al., 1997, p. 27).

Based on these examples, some critics of the threshold systems have argued that one way to improve them would be to create more intermediate alternatives between voluntary involvement and legal coercion (Hetherington et al., 1997). Also, some systems in the United States have experimented with dividing their child welfare/protection system into two tracks:

> One strategy for improving [the general threshold model] ... would create an alternative less adversarial system for handling reports that appear not to present a serious threat to the child's safety ... Missouri has used this two-track system since 1994, and approximately 80% of reports of suspected maltreatment are handled in the voluntary "assessment" track. [There are similar reform initiatives in Florida and Iowa]. (Larner et al., 1998, p. 11)

Investigating every "maltreatment" report is an expensive, unappreciated, and unnecessary response to many families. A differential response model limits investigative responses to urgent or high risk situations, while assessment and support responses are offered to families whose circumstances are considered less "threatening" to children. The effectiveness of the differential model depends on methods that appropriately sort referrals into high and low risk response categories. In this model, low to moderate risk situations are most appropriately served by community agencies that provide voluntary help (where families agree to involvement) to stabilize families and protect children (Schene, 2002). Differential response models require extensive community partnerships in which child protection agencies play the lead role but share the responsibility of protecting children with community service providers (Waldfogel, 2001).

In the 1990s, several American states implemented demonstration differential response models. Although this model has the potential for multiple tracks of service delivery, most of these states developed dual-track response systems (Trocmé, Knoke, & Roy, 2003). From our perspective, the rift in the Anglo-American child welfare paradigm between protecting children and supporting families predisposes proponents toward a bifurcated system of first responses. The separation of care and control functions into distinct delivery systems led to a debate in these systems over the classification of referrals into those who merited assessment and community intervention and those who required investigation and standard protection interventions.

Another design option is to develop a flexible first-response system that maintains a constructive flow of involvements between support units and protection units. Many families involved with child and family welfare systems could benefit from a mixture of compassionate and authoritative assistance. In addition, in a child protection culture, where protection trumps all other concerns, there is a danger that the supportive function will be under valued and poorly supported.

A differential response system depends on strengthening the involvement of community service organizations in the child welfare mandate. Because the United States has invested its child protection mandates in stand-alone agencies, in which the role of external community agencies is marginal, an emphasis on creating service partnerships has become central to creating differential response models.

For example, in Jacksonville, Florida, the development of community partnerships has focused on five public-housing developments. In conjunction with formal and informal leadership in the communities, the public child protection agency has developed neighborhood networks that include a range of partners, including service agencies, government departments, grassroots associations, churches and civic groups (Schene, 2002). Additionally, there is a focus on strengthening informal sources of support. Friends and neighbors are identified by child welfare workers and families as sources of potential support and "a community safety agreement is then developed, detailing what the community resource person will do to support the family and under what circumstances the person will re-contact CPS [Child Protection Services]" (Waldfogel, 1998, p. 155).

The co-location of services in neighbourhood settings has proved to be important in expanding the role of community agencies in differential response models of child welfare. This co-location of services is also convenient for families. Schene (2002) also argues that co-location facilitates the coordination of interventions, supports relationship building between professionals and indigenous community leaders, and allows professionals to develop an understanding of the community in which they work (Schene,

2002). Clearly, for a differential response approach to be of real value to families, there has to be a richness of formal and informal helping and community involvement resources available.

Many neighbourhoods in Canada have made extensive progress in the building of active partnerships among service organizations, including, in some cases, the local child protection agency. In addition, many Canadian communities have made extensive gains in empowering local residents and in developing an increased community capacity to respond to its own challenges. For example, most of the demonstration neighbourhoods in the Better Beginnings, Better Futures Primary Prevention Project in Cornwall, Toronto (Regent Park), Kingston, Ottawa, Etobicoke, Sudbury, and Guelph (Onward Willow community) have made exemplary gains, to varying degrees, in creating partnerships among service providers and between local residents and professional helpers, and in empowering local neighbourhood leadership (Cameron & Cadell, 1999; Cameron, Hayward, McKenzie, Hancock, & Jeffery, 1999; Pancer & Cameron, 1994). There are other neighbourhoods in Ontario with many of the prescribed requisites for a successful flexible response model in child welfare. These are communities in which experiments could begin to elaborate an enriched and flexible response model for child welfare.

For example, Family and Children's Services of Wellington, a mandated child protection agency, was the initiator and the original sponsoring organization for the Onward Willow Better Beginnings, Better Futures Primary Prevention Project and the Shelldale Centre: a Village of Support. The Shelldale Centre includes 16 program partners co-located in a refurbished school, including primary prevention programs, child, youth, and family recreation, early childhood development programs, adult education and employment training, clinical and family counselling, community policing and victim services, violence-against-women support programs, family health services, and child welfare services. The Onward Willow Better Beginnings, Better Futures project moved into the Shelldale Centre and has space for its child and parent programming, access to kitchen facilities, a gym, and meeting rooms for recreational and community-development initiatives. Alcoholics Anonymous and other community groups also use the space for meetings. Having a child welfare agency successfully initiate the Shelldale Centre illustrates that space can be created for partnerships and community empowerment, even within Ontario's current child protection mandates.

Relationship with the Legal System

Role of police and formal legal authority. One of the central choices in constructing child and family welfare is defining the role of the legal system (judges, courts, police). Formal legal authority plays an important part in every child and family welfare system; however, the point at which formal legal authority is used and the role of the legal system vary widely across settings.

In threshold child protection systems, families have a right to privacy and the state, as represented by the child protection agency, only becomes involved if there is suspicion that minimum legal standards of child care have been violated. From the beginning, in investigations of reports of child maltreatment, the worker must be conscious of gathering evidence to ascertain (and, if necessary, to prove in court) that a transgression has taken place, in order to justify the agency's continued intervention with the family. In England, social workers and police often work together in child protection investigations. England has an adversarial legal system, similar to the United States and Canada, in which the child's best interest is the chief consideration for the courts (Hetherington et al., 1997). In Canada, policies requiring social workers to refer many cases to the police have existed since about 1984. For many families, Karen Swift (1997) contends that "a report to child welfare is a report to the police ... an eventuality that exposes the family to highly intrusive investigation" (p. 52).

During the investigation, social workers must complete standardized recording forms. This recording is purposeful and is based on the legal requirements of gathering evidence that can be used in court. Threshold systems work with adversarial legal systems, in which the role of the judge is to decide between formal arguments presented by lawyers representing each party to the dispute (often the parent, the child, and the child protection agency). Due process considerations are paramount in this system and have led to "new training programs, new legislation and procedures designed to increase specificity and 'objectivity' to the evidence gathering procedure" (Swift, 1997, p. 52). Similar patterns have been described in the English child protection system: "Local authority social workers work closely with the police in child protection investigations ... The legal system is adversarial ... the welfare of the child is the paramount concern of the court ... The court hearings are formal and conducted by lawyers" (Hetherington et al., 1997, pp. 76–77).

The intention in family service systems is that the first responses to reports of child maltreatment be an assessment of the family's situation and an offer of help to the family. How this help is given is more often guided by professional judgment and local interactions than by prescribed procedures or the evidence gathered for possible legal proceedings. First contact is often with systems involved with a variety of families—not only families suspected of child maltreatment. Usually, there is a stated intention to maintain the family and the parent–child bond and avoid involvement with the formal legal system.

Some family service systems have created intermediate structures (for example, lay child protection boards in Belgium, the family judge's office in France) between front-line voluntary service and formally contested court applications. This intermediate space is where negotiations between the family members, the service workers, and the judge can take place (see the discussion in chapter 4). Family service systems are typically found in societies with inquisitorial legal systems. This tradition allows judges to take a more active role in asking questions and gathering information than is allowed in adversarial legal systems. In inquisitorial systems, fewer cases go to contested court hearings, and most service decisions—even those involving the placement of a child—occur with the agreement of parents.

From a liberal rights perspective, these family service arrangements might allow excessive state and community involvement in families' lives. Luckock and his colleagues (1996; 1997) argue that these arrangements disguise the fact that professional and communal authority is used to coerce parents' compliance with professional recommendations. They favour the restraints on professional authority and the balancing of various parties' rights that are provided by due process in the English legal system.

On the other hand, family service systems do allow for greater discretion and more voluntary, or at least less adversarial, involvements in helping. Most importantly, they shift the emphasis to offering a broader range of helping options, in cultures where this type of communal assistance is more normalized, before the full force of legal authority is brought to bear on the family. The following examples provide a brief description of these relationships in selected European family service systems and First Nations community caring approaches.

The Belgian approach to child welfare is based on the principle of subsidiarity and makes supportive services available to families separate from coercive interventions ordered by the legal system. This separation reportedly "allows social workers, doctors, and other professionals concerned about children to consult with the VAC [Confidential Doctors Office] teams without reporting to the judicial system ... The VAC ... provide an intensive therapeutic service to [self] referred families" (Luckock, Vogler, & Keating, 1997, p. 109). The Belgian system also attempts to avoid unnecessary court involvement with families through a lay mediation procedure. Only when all of these voluntary involvements cannot be made to work is the coercive power of the formal legal system typically invoked (Luckock et al., 1997). Reportedly, self-referrals by "abusive" parents rose from 2% to 38% under these arrangements, the risk of a child being reinjured was reduced, and, between 1986 and 1994, 81% of children in care were returned to their families (Marneffe & Broos, 1997).

In France, intermediary procedures are introduced, usually before more coercive, legal action is taken. Families can and do make use of the Judge for Children's Office to receive assistance and referrals. Hetherington and her colleagues (1997) note that:

> the process of the hearing is informal and the family is in direct discussion with the judge ... By law, the judge has to attempt to get the agreement of the parents to any order he makes and failure to do this can be the grounds for appeal. (p. 65)

Judges in threshold systems would not see many of the cases that come before French judges—either because the families would not have met the criteria for services, or there would not have been sufficient evidence to take the families to court. In contrast, "French participants estimate that only about 10 percent of the cases that come before Children's Judges involve maltreatment" (Pires, 1993, p. 46). The Judge for Children receives many referrals, not only from social workers, but from parents as well. Parents are also motivated to seek help from a Judge for Children because it qualifies them for access to increased social service support. It is also important to note that in France adoption is not generally an option without the parents' permission (Hetherington et al., 1997).

Similarly, the inquisitorial courts in Germany provide an intermediary structure for families in the child welfare system. The German courts operate on the principle of voluntary jurisdiction or *freiwillige Gerichtsbarkeit*:

> Parties can be represented and witnesses can be heard but the judge holds sole responsibility for the investigation ... Judges have a mediating as well as an investigative function and will frequently conduct "round table" discussions which take into consideration all the provisions available under the KJHG *Kinder und Jugendhilfegesetz* (Children and Youth Services Act)] to help a child and its family. (Wilford, Hetherington, & Piquardt, 1997, pp. 18–19)

German families are normally involved in all decisions concerning their welfare, especially when developing a plan of action in cases of crisis or need (Wilford et al., 1997). However, in cases of extreme severity, or when agreements cannot be reached, interventions for families can be legally mandated (Wolff, 1997).

The formal legal system does not play a large role in the First Nations' conception of an approach to child and family welfare congruent with their traditions and living realities. The adversarial and authoritarian nature of contested court procedures run counter to the importance First Nations place on self-determination and community empowerment. For example, in 1980, the Spallumcheen Band in British Columbia passed a by-law in which they assumed full control of child welfare services. The by-law allowed all authority for child welfare to be transferred to within the community. Under this by-law, "apprehending authority and final decision-making reside with the ... Chief and members of the Band Council, placement and review decisions are made by means of a vote at Band Council meetings following lengthy informal discussion by all who wish to speak" (McKenzie, 1989, p. 9). However, First Nations in North America and elsewhere (for example, Maori in New Zealand and Aboriginals in Australia) have rarely been able to proceed beyond delegated authority to apply state procedures within their communities (Bennet & Blackstock, 2002; Love, 2002; see discussion in chapter 3). Their desired relationships between community processes and formal legal proceedings have yet to be completely articulated and consistently applied.

A Canadian variant of intermediary mediation structures has been tried in British Columbia, where the Child, Family and Community Services Act and Rules guide judicial processes designed to avoid contested applications to the courts. A judicial case conference is mandatory in new apprehensions and acts as "the gateway for future process toward the ultimate decisions for the benefit of the child by the parents, social workers, aboriginal bands or the judge" (Schmidt, 2001, p. 3). Legal counsel, the parents, social workers, and representatives of an Aboriginal band frequently attend case conferences. Judges engage parents and social workers in discussion for the purposes of resolving disputes. A case conference does not address whether a child is in need of protection, but may order temporary or continuing care in an effort to keep the focus on the needs of the child, rather than the fault of the caregiver (Schmidt, 2001). Issues such as parental access, the duration of existing orders, and the expectations of social workers are suitable for mediation in this context. Judges may make an order to refer particular issues to community mediators, or make recommendations or orders that move the case to a formal hearing. In the urban centres of Surrey, Vancouver, and Victoria, approximately 26% of cases that have case conferences proceed to trial (Schmidt, 2001).

The nature of authority. Some parents will always resist intrusions into their homes, regardless of how they are approached. Eventually each orientation must be able to use formal authority to compel family compliance or to remove children from the home. However, systems differ in the extent to which they use authority other than the coercive power of the law to encourage family involvement. In threshold systems, operating in social settings that stress individual rights and family privacy, the legal power of the state is the prime mode of ensuring access to families. In more communal societies, such as some continental European countries and some First Nations communities, the well-being of children and families is understood as a more collective responsibility. Ideally, this approach causes community norms to be accepted more readily by families as reasons for their engagements with professional or community helpers. The flip side of this social contract is that families also expect assistance with the responsibilities of child care.

A core component to consider in the design of child and family welfare systems concerns the bases of authority or legitimacy used in engaging families, and the timing of agency interventions. Another basic choice is the extent to which service principles are to be based in concepts of individual rights and responsibility and/or concepts of social solidarity and co-operation in the care of children. For example, in England, "the last 15 years have witnessed a consolidation of ideologies of individual rights ... and a general decline in ideas of collective responsibility" (Hetherington et al., 1997, p. 93). However, in many family service systems, a greater emphasis has been placed on the notions of solidarity, subsidiarity, and collective responsibility:

> The idea of "solidarity" is important in understanding the socio-political context in which many European child welfare systems are embedded ... thus the [Flemish child protection] committee is understood by those involved more as a social organism than an administrative body, and as such its continued evolution, improvement, and integration within the wider social fabric is accepted. (Hetherington et al., 1997, p. 32)

> German social policy is informed by the principle of subsidiarity ... The principle needs to be understood in the context of solidarity: the social contract between citizens and state places an obligation on the state and the Federation of States to strengthen the smallest social unit at base so that it can fulfill its responsibility in relation to the community and the state ... [these philosophies] view family support and child-care services as a social responsibility as well as a buttress to the family as the basic social institution. (Wilford et al., 1997, pp. 12–13)

Likewise, First Nations community caring systems place a great value on community support and notions of collective responsibility. Within these systems, it is believed that strong communities are built by strong families and, ideally, there is a powerful sense of commitment to supporting others within the community (Maidman & Connors, 2002). Morrissette and his colleagues (1993) note that "the development of Aboriginal culture involved the exercise of responsibility on the part of all members for the benefit of the group" (p. 93).

Who is involved in decision making? A related consideration is the extent of the role of lay people and civic groupings in child and family welfare systems. In threshold systems, for all practical purposes, child protection is the purview of service and legal professionals. In contrast, non-professional involvement is most dramatic in some First Nations communities, where child protection services are directed and delivered through self-governing institutions and community networks. Consulting with non-professionals is heavily emphasized in some Innu and Innuit communities. For example, in these locations, when a decision must be made about the removal of a child from his/her family, ideally, the judge will ask "everyone involved in the child's life, from distant aunts to family friends, to come talk at the hearing ... He understands that here people are not individuals, that [they] are a part of a very extended family" (Toughill, 2001, February 3, p. K3). Likewise, in the approach developed by the Champagne/Aishihik First Nation in Canada:

> First the primacy of family care means that any form of substitute care is by definition secondary and temporary. Where family care breaks down the first response is to provide support in the form of counselling or temporary respite care by relatives or friends. If these responses are inadequate, a placement in a Native child-care home may be required ... this pattern contains the distinct benefit of ensuring that children remain in their community, can attend the same school, and can keep their friends ... Second, the assistance of family and relatives is sought when parents experience problems. Family meetings are initiated and chaired by the child welfare co-ordinator to plan for the care of the children and to resolve the difficulties facing parents. In turn, this planned involvement of family members and friends transforms the private matter of child welfare to a community concern ... Since they live in the small communities in which they work, child welfare staff have a comprehensive and detailed knowledge of families and child-care ... Third, this approach to practice requires community-based resources. In Haines Junction and Whitehorse, Indian child-care homes have been established. (Wharf, 1992, pp. 116–117)

To a lesser extent, involvement of lay helpers and civil society in child and family welfare is evident in some European systems, reflecting their concepts of social solidarity. For example, in Sweden, professional roles and authority are not as institutionalized as in threshold system countries and, as a result, local social welfare committees are responsible for overseeing child protection interventions when it is felt that a child is at risk (Olsson Hort, 1997). In Denmark, the power to authorize involuntary, out-of-home placements is vested in local, elected Children's Boards (Bering Pruzan, 1997). Belgium also exemplifies this involvement of lay helpers in its child and family welfare system: "each Committee [Special Youth Assistance] consists of a council of 12 volunteers active in child welfare and each carries responsibility for an administrative district" (Luckock et al., 1997, p. 104).

Mandatory reporting. Systems differ in whether they require by law (with the threat of penalties) community professionals and the general public to report to child and family welfare authorities any suspicions they have about maltreated children. Both threshold and family service systems are found in societies with mandatory reporting requirements (for example, Ontario and Finland). Likewise, both types of systems are found in societies without mandatory reporting laws (for example, England and Germany).

The argument for mandatory reporting is the belief that more vulnerable children will receive protection from harm. The danger is that parental fear of the intrusions of the child protection authorities, in threshold systems at least, will attach itself to other service organizations. As a result, parents needing help may be less willing to come forward. An additional concern for the threshold child protection systems that require mandatory reporting has been the overwhelming number of reports child protection agencies receive: "[In the United States] the system is so overburdened with cases of insubstantial or unproven risk to children that it does not respond forcefully to situations where children are in real danger" (Besharov, 1985, pp. 539–540).

Mandatory reporting may have a different meaning for families where the system's first response is an offer of assistance, rather than a formal investigation. In addition, in our review, we found no evidence clarifying whether finding and providing assistance to children at risk of maltreatment is more effective in systems with mandatory reporting:

> in the United States the rate of child fatalities has continued to rise, despite mandatory reporting of child abuse and neglect and a huge rise in such reports. In Canada also over the past twenty years resources have increasingly shifted into child protection, but there has been no measurable decline in child homicide ... the weight of the evidence points to the conclusion that child death rates in this and other Western countries from homicide or possible homicide have remained much the same over a long period, and that the introduction of child protection procedures has had no effect on them. (Gibbons, 1997, p. 80)

Consistent with their respect for self-determination, First Nations feel that it is important to refrain from intrusive interference in families whenever possible. However, that does not mean that inappropriate child rearing practices are accepted by others in the community. Ideally, family, neighbours, and friends share a more collective commitment to children's welfare:

> Tribal families promote mutual respect for the individuality of members ... It is also considered important to not interfere with an individual's actions as this may show disrespect for their rights of self-

determination. Non-interference is enacted within child rearing environments in which children are constantly monitored by the community and encouraged by expectation to emit socially appropriate behaviour. These styles of relating contribute to the development of strong, self-confident and independent persons [sic] who ultimately contribute maximally to the strength of the family and the community. (Maidman & Connors, 2002, p. 385)

Separate or Embedded Child Welfare Organization

Allocation of responsibility. A basic decision made in child and family welfare system design is whether to allocate child protection mandates exclusively to a specialized unit or share them across several social welfare and/or justice units. As discussed earlier, in the United States and Canada, some critics of the dual mandate of existing threshold systems call for a complete separation of the care and control functions into distinct systems. They argue that this reform would allow the police, courts, and social workers to each do what they do best. We have argued that this prescription ignores some deep requirements of creating more effective child and family welfare, not to mention the danger of the care function being poorly supported.

It is not possible or humane to classify families neatly into those who merit support and those who should be investigated or prosecuted. In addition, well-designed systems maintain a constructive flow of involvements between units with more supportive/therapeutic mandates and those charged with investigation and enforcement. Even with families with verifiable instances of child maltreatment, except in the most extreme cases, continued connections are important to children's development and for providing continuity and belonging in children's lives. The endurance of family connection is demonstrated by the observation that many children raised in the care of the state re-establish various forms of contact with family members once they are on their own (Palmer, 1995).

Creating gradations along the care/control continuum (such as opportunities for authoritative mediation or for alternative living circumstances for parents and children) is more productive than an artificial separation. We have argued that impermeable boundaries between care and control system components in child and family welfare are neither functional nor desirable:

the difficulty of sorting cases by level of risk is a challenge for all narrowing proposals ... begs the question of how the [American] system should respond to the range of families within each group, who are not all alike ... means considering ways to move beyond the standardized, one-size-fits-all response to families that CPS currently provides. (Waldfogel, 1998, p. 110)

Threshold systems in England, United States, and Canada have invested their child protection mandate in "stand-alone" public or parapublic organizations. The rest of the social welfare delivery system has no clear role in carrying out the protection mandate, although other agencies are often involved with the same families. Increasingly, these threshold systems emphasize the investigative and enforcement components of their mandates, and the legal requirements of control tend to dominate their work environments. Concerns about this trend are arising in the literature.

[In England]: ... how can any social consensus ... be protected and given a chance to develop, flourish and contribute to renewed social cohesion rather than just the narrow project of "protecting the child" in isolation from its social surroundings. (Hetherington et al., 1997, p. 34)

[In US]: While the child welfare system may indeed be "broken and in need of fixing," it cannot be fixed by attending to child welfare alone. (McCroskey & Meezan, 1998, p. 68)

In family service systems, the child and family welfare mandate is shared across multiple partners in the social welfare and youth justice systems. It is common for local general service organizations to provide assistance to distressed families and to be the first contact with many families suspected of maltreatment. Some social service organizations, like the Confidential Doctors Office in the Netherlands, until 1998, had a formal mandate within the child protection system. Other elements of the social welfare systems in these countries, such as day care and community nursing, are frequently used to enrich the protection efforts. These systems also have specialized units, usually within the youth justice system, that focus on investigation and enforcement. For example:

This non-punitive response to child abuse and neglect was developed simultaneously in several western European countries in the early 1970s. The Confidential Doctors Bureaus were the first to be created in the Netherlands ... Kind in Nood (Child in Need) in Belgium ... and the Fifth Province in Ireland ... followed, reflected the same background philosophy as introduced by Reinhart Wolff in the Berlin Child Protection Centre in 1975. (Marneffe & Broos, 1997, p. 177)

[In Finland:] The child welfare legislation reforms of 1990 emphasise preventive, non-stigmatising, and supportive measures and services. One of the central objectives of the reform was to shift the emphasis of child welfare from extra familial care to measures that encourage and support the maintenance of children in their own home. As a result, work methods of all welfare services, were adapted toward strengthening child rearing by carers. Maternity and child health clinics have expanded and diversified family training, and intensified co-operation with families. In day care, various forms of co-operation supporting parental participation were developed. Also home help services have been developed to support child rearing by parents. (Tuomisto & Vuori-Karvia, 1997, p. 92)

[In Germany:] Youth Offices, which oversee all child and youth services from recreation to child welfare, are mandated to work with families to prevent serious difficulties from arising. Only in the event of danger to a child's well-being and lack of parental consent for recommended services does the Guardianship Court step in. (Pires, 1993, p. 47)

The boundaries between the care and control components of these family service systems have been described as somewhat fluid, with information flowing informally both ways. For Luckock and his colleagues (1996; 1997), this informality raises some questions about confidentiality of information about families.

Entering the system. A related choice in child and family welfare is how families enter the system. Entry options include:

1. through social services accessible to all families, or those focusing on families in difficulty, or agencies specializing in investigations of allegations of child maltreatment;
2. on the basis of a family request/acceptance of service, or the insistence of a child protection agency enforcing a legal mandate; and,
3. on the basis of a request for service, demonstrated need of assistance, or evidence of child maltreatment meeting minimal criteria mandating state intervention into family life.

Threshold systems have single access points, as well as the narrowest and most coercive criteria for entering the child protection system. Most involvements come on the basis of third party reports of suspected abuse, which are then substantiated or dismissed in the process of a formal investigation by the child protection agencies. In Ontario, as the range of supports offered by children's aid societies has narrowed, and as the criteria for system entry have become more specific, the number of families calling children's aid societies on their own for assistance has fallen. To enter the formal child protection system, families must be "proven" to be abusive or neglectful of their children or likely to become so in the near future; increasingly fewer of these engagements are on the basis of mutual consent. A trend toward filtering families out of the system was also evident in a study in England:

At first, 25 percent were filtered out by social work staff at the duty stage without any direct contact with the child or family. At the second [stage], the investigation itself, another 50 percent were filtered out and never reached the initial case conference. Of the remainder, just 15 percent were placed on the Child Protection Register. Thus six out of every seven children who entered the child protection system at referral were filtered out without being placed on the Register ... (for 44 percent of those investigated) there was no intervention to protect the child nor were there any services provided. In only 4 percent of all cases referred were children removed from home under a statutory order at any time during the study (Parton, 1997, p. 7). Many Continental European family service systems have several access points, including social welfare agencies serving the general population or serving a broad range of families in difficulty. Most families become involved either by a parent or child requesting assistance, or on the basis of an offer of service from the agency following up on a report of suspected maltreatment. Almost all these involvements, including placement of children, are on the basis of mutual (negotiated) agreement. There are no specific criteria indicating maltreatment necessary in order to receive assistance. For example:

[In Sweden] Child abuse or neglect is not a necessary or even typical precondition for beginning child welfare services. It is part of the normal course of life that children receive child health and welfare services. (Olsson Hort, 1997, p. 107)

[In France:] There are no specific grounds such as being "in need" that defines whether or not a child is eligible for help. (Hetherington et al., 1997, p. 65)

Maintaining Families and Protecting Children

All child and family welfare systems must balance the goals of maintaining the family as a viable social unit for child development and protecting the child's right not to be harmed physically, sexually, or emotionally in his or her home. All systems have the capacity to temporarily or permanently remove children from their parents' home; likewise, all have the capacity to assist families with their child-rearing responsibilities. However, the differences in relative emphasis upon supporting families across systems are striking.

Severing the parent–child connection and supportive services to families. Some family service systems rarely sever the connection between children and their parents completely (that is, adoption is seldom used). In addition, all the family service systems reviewed place great importance upon parental agreement with intervention plans (sexual abuse is an exception in some of these countries and leads to quick involvement with the justice system). As well, all family service systems go to greater lengths to provide supportive services to families than threshold systems are able or disposed to do. For example:

> An interesting and long-established response to child behaviour prob-
> lems in the Netherlands has, since early this century, been to place chil-
> dren in special centres after school. There are now around a hundred of
> these centres across the country, with children attending at least three
> days a week over a period of around two years ... The strategy is to offer
> group therapy to the children while at the same time working with the
> families. Children are screened every six months to monitor their progress
> and usually leave the centre when both the child and the family seem
> able to cope on their own. There is apparently little stigma attached to
> attending these centres. (Madge & Attridge, 1996, p. 144)

Gilbert's (1997a) data suggests that children may be placed outside the home in European family service systems as often as in North American threshold systems; however, prior to this decision, and with other families where child removal is not called for, family service systems place a much greater emphasis on providing resources to support the family (Gilbert, 1997b). This family support is exemplified by Germany's Child and Youth Service Act (1990) which emphasizes providing extensive "preventive and supportive measures to help with the care and education of children in their families" (Hetherington et al., 1997, p. 68). This approach is also evident in Denmark's child and family welfare system, which recognizes that family difficulties should be resolved in a holistic manner. Thus, Danish policy is designed to "facilitate a voluntary, family-oriented approach to the problem of child abuse" (Bering Pruzan, 1997, p. 126).

Conceptions of children and families and intervention priorities. In the family service systems, healthy families are viewed as fundamental for social cohesion and the proper education of children. As a result, the Swedish approach to child and family welfare places an emphasis "on the right of birth parents to provide continuing care and, at least, to have ongoing contact with their children if out-of-home care [is] required" (Olsson Hort, 1997, p. 109). In these more communal cultures, the well-being of families is not secondary to protecting individual rights and freedoms. Direct assistance is offered to keep families together whenever possible, and many of these systems place an emphasis on prevention and the development of strong families. For example, in Belgium, 17 centres for the prevention and treatment of child abuse and neglect have been established since the mid-1980s. Marneffe and Broos (1997) list these centres' three main functions:

1. To offer direct assistance to the families whenever possible to keep the family together: "Even if a safe place has to be found outside the family, the parents are involved in the decision making" (p. 167).

2. To offer supervision, support, and counselling for social workers who have to deal with child abuse in their professions.
3. To help in prevention: "The focus is more on changing public opinion than trying to change the family because child abuse and neglect cannot be reduced to a problem of bad or pathological parents" (p. 167).

Similarly, permanently severing the bonds between children and their parents is discouraged in First Nations conceptions of child and family welfare. There is great emphasis placed on keeping children in their families, and all other forms of care arrangements are viewed as being secondary and temporary by nature:

> Placement priorities, in order of preference, are the extended family, families within First Nations communities in the tribal council area, other First Nations families, and non-First Nations caregivers.... extended family placements outside the community and family foster homes within the community were given relatively equal weight. This indicates the importance attached to community as well as family connections. (McKenzie, 1995, p. 644)

Love (2002) talks about the concept of an ensembled self for the Maori in New Zealand. These concepts of self are inextricably bound to an individual's place of origin (land), genealogy, extended family, and tribe/community. Whereas in threshold systems the decision to separate children from parents draws on clearly bounded Western ideals of individual selves, from the perspective of ensembled selves, this decision is not seen as rational.

In Ontario, the child's right to be protected from harm takes precedence by law over any consideration of the family's need for assistance to care for the child. Threshold systems intervene to protect the child from harm in his/her home and to hold the parents accountable for ensuring the child receives good care. If parents cannot or will not comply, they risk losing legal guardianship of their child. Increasingly, English and North American threshold systems offer very limited supportive services to families themselves and operate within a broader social environment that has also reduced support to disadvantaged families. For instance, American child protection agencies are only mandated to carry out investigations of families, to coordinate and manage foster care services, and to licence child day-care facilities (Schene, 1998). All other supportive services for families fall outside their jurisdiction.

Organizing framework. A related choice in the design of systems is whether to use the concept of child abuse as the organizing framework or to operate within a broader framework of child, family, and community welfare. Beginning with the "discovery" of child abuse in the 1960s in America, the focus of threshold systems has narrowed from an already limited conception of child welfare and neglect to a complete concentration on child abuse. From this perspective, child neglect is viewed as a specific category of harm to children rather than a symptom of family living circumstances (Swift, 1995). Conversely, family service systems are incorporated into a broader philosophy of societal, family, and child welfare, in which the concern is not solely protecting children from maltreatment. Child protection, defined as intrafamilial protection from harm, is not the central organizing principle in most western European child welfare systems (Hetherington et al., 1997). In these family service systems, a more collective ideology is reflected in their higher levels of social provisions and less blame is placed on families who are experiencing difficulties. For example:

> [In Finland]: From the multi-problem perspective, physical violence or child abuse in the family is seen as too narrow a category that emphasizes the symptoms of the problem more than the basic causes and stigmatizes or blames the perpetrators too easily. (Poso, 1997, p. 153)

Discretion and Control

A fundamental choice in the design of child and family welfare systems is whether to allow local service providers to use their judgment and training to make decisions or to rely on the standard prescriptions and controls characteristic of formal bureaucratic organization. This choice has deep implications for the child and family welfare experience of parents and children, as well as the work environments of service providers (Regehr et al., 2000).

Continental European and First Nations systems typically endorse more discretion, rather than relying on detailed rules and regulations to guide assessments and interventions like the threshold systems in England, America, and Canada do. These non-threshold systems have not placed a priority on using a formal standard risk assessment procedure with families, as is common in the Anglo-American systems. On the other hand, a few family service systems, such as the Netherlands, are introducing more formality into their processes; there has recently been a move toward increasing requirements in the Dutch system for social workers to provide judges with evidence of child abuse (Hetherington et al., 1997). Notwithstanding these modifications, family service systems generally put more faith in the discretion and judgments of professional social workers. These systems typically endorse welfare and social work principles as their preferences in working with families and rely on local deliberations and professional decision-making about how to proceed (Hetherington et al., 1997; Olsson Hort, 1997; Poso, 1997). As Hetherington and her colleagues (1997) note, a Belgian social worker has no standardized procedures to rely on to "reassure her that she is 'doing the right thing,' but she does have a team who she turns to for consultation and support" (p. 20).

While information is limited, in one study, social workers in First Nations community healing systems were described as having more discretion, as well as more input into child welfare policies:

> in a ministry often characterized by low morale and frequent staff turnover, staffs of the Native unit are enthusiastic about and committed to their work. ... They went on to talk about the mission—to work with and provide services to a group of people who have rarely received satisfactory services from the ministry. Thus there is identification with a cause, a sense of being different and distinctive. The distinctiveness is revealed in part by the way clients are treated—as friends, rather than people with problems. Second, staff see themselves as innovators and creators. Rather than simply and only implementing established policy, the Native unit is helping the ministry develop policy for Native child welfare. (Wharf, 1992, pp. 108–109)

On the other hand, threshold systems, perhaps influenced by their child-saving heritages, the pressure felt due to media-fuelled "crises" about abused children, and the increasing requirements of their legal systems, have become increasingly reluctant to trust local professional and community decision-making about "maltreating" families.

In Ontario, over the past decade, reliance on standardized information recording and formal "people-processing" procedures has increased substantially. These bureaucratic procedures have been combined with a standard child abuse risk-assessment instrument intended to increase the accuracy and objectivity of making decisions about families. As a result, worker discretion has been substantially reduced in deciding how to interact with families, and their time spent fulfilling formal recording requirements has greatly increased. In England (and other threshold systems), there is concern that "child protection work has become an administrative routine" (Hetherington et al., 1997, pp. 17–18). However, compliance with standard procedures has become a way for workers to avoid blame, should they make a decision that allows children to be further mistreated in a family. Furthermore, these risk-assessment procedures are considered a means to screen the increasing number of reports the agencies receive (Lawrence-Karski, 1997).

It is no coincidence that threshold systems are experiencing a crisis of confidence, both from families and their own service providers. For example, a recent study of working conditions at the Children's Aid Society of Metropolitan Toronto reported in *The Globe and Mail* newspaper "paints a portrait of front-line workers in child protection swamped by an almost impossible workload that includes more paperwork than actual visits to children at risk of abuse and neglect" (Philp, 2001, February 20). She adds: "a growing number of social work graduates are turning their backs on child-protection work, which is legendary for being stressful and has been excoriated in the media over the past several years." No equivalent sense of crisis is found in the literature about European family service systems, although they too are not without their scandals and critics (see Grevot, 2002; Veldkamp, 2002).

Less Explored Choices

Options not generally found in most comparisons of child and welfare systems remain nonetheless useful in the consideration of possibilities for improvement. A complete discussion of these options is beyond the scope of this review, but a brief explanation of the nature of several of these considerations follows.

Most discussions of child and family welfare assume that professional casework is the dominant service modality, and differences centre on how this casework can best be organized and supported. However, this predominant emphasis on individual cases might exclude other valuable helping strategies for disadvantaged and distressed parents and children (Cameron et al., 1997). Studies of program models that produce the most encouraging results for people confronting challenges in many areas of their lives emphasize that the ways in which these programs are staffed and involve participants differ in basic ways from mainline services (for illustrations, see the reviews in Cameron, O'Reilly, et al., 2002; Cameron et al., 1997; Nelson et al., 2002; Schorr, 1989; 1997).

Equally important, similar operating patterns have been identified across many promising programs for a range of distressed populations. Common patterns include: addressing multiple protective and risk factors; allowing for high levels of involvement and continuity of involvement over longer periods of time; enabling flexible responses; tailoring patterns of involvement to particular circumstances; incorporating informal helping; responding quickly in times of crisis; and actively reducing concrete, psychological, and social obstacles to participation. It is clear that, if we are to take advantage of these lessons from promising programs, we should investigate new and more varied service content and organizational forms for the daily work of child and family welfare.

Many forms of assistance for troubled children and parents require neither an assessment nor an investigation by a service provider for families to access them, for example, family resource centres, Alateen and Al-Anon, daycare, and parent support groups. Both parents and children benefit from having greater opportunities to control how they will become involved. There are also many useful, collective programs involving parents and children that are under-represented in our thinking about child and family welfare, such as collective kitchens, parent mutual-aid organizations, recreation programs, and faith groups. In addition to providing professional assistance, we need to help people to find each other and facilitate community empowerment. Finally, there is almost a complete absence of any organized voice for parents and children in existing child and family welfare systems. When considering possibilities for the future, it is important to respect the right of parents and children to influence what happens to them. To ensure that the voices of professionals are not the only voices in the debate, families involved in the systems must be heard.

Concluding Comments: Lessons and Future Directions

In addition to exploring the institutional context for child protection services in Ontario, the Partnerships for Children and Families program of research considered the everyday realities of service providers and service participants, and developed the following set of ideal guiding principles for positive systems of child and family welfare: Assistance would be provided in ways that are welcomed by most of the parents and children involved. There would be emphasis on current, promising programming for disadvantaged children, parents, and families. While keeping children safe from harm would be a priority, it would be understood as complementary to the preceding principles. There would be an emphasis on ensuring that service providers find their work worthwhile and feasible. Systems would be able to accommodate variations in the ways of life and service requirements of particular families and communities. Systems would focus on enhancing the motivation, talent, and judgment of family members and service providers alike.

If the analysis in this chapter is accurate, it is apparent that the Anglo-American child protection paradigm fails to satisfy many critics on at least some of these criteria. We concur with authors who argue that the threshold paradigm is in urgent need of reform, but that this cannot be accomplished if we restrict our thinking to protecting children from a narrow range of dangers within their homes (Hetherington et al., 1997; McCroskey & Meezan, 1998).

This chapter does not make specific recommendations about what should be included in a revised child and family welfare system. Our ambitions in this chapter have been twofold: (1) to free us to imagine alternatives—to disturb conventional certainties about the inevitability or the superiority of current procedures in our child protection system; and, (2) to identify possibilities in various areas of system design as signposts for future explorations of positive improvements.

Observations about the persistence of the "child saving" orientation over time in the Ontario child protection system potentially lead to pessimism about the possibility of meaningful reforms in our policies and practice. Indeed the obstacles to new ways of thinking and working are formidable. Nonetheless, our historical review highlights substantial shifts in our child protection orientation over time; for example, changes in the supports made available to families, in the emphasis on apprehending children, in the reliance on bureaucratic controls, and in the nature of involvements with courts and police. As observed earlier, a new sweep of reforms is underway in Ontario's child protection system. It may prove fruitful to begin our search for improvements by focusing on changes potentially compatible with our local cultures and institutional contexts.

At some point, however, evolution confronts the barriers of the basic values and strategies of existing arrangements. There is a limit to what we can hope to accomplish, even within the broad parameters of our existing child protection paradigm. Our belief is that the fundamentals of the Anglo-American child protection paradigm need to be challenged and reformulated in a more positive fashion. Such deep shifts in ideas and practice are rare, but they have taken place elsewhere; we can learn from these experiences.

If we are not to be frozen into believing in the inevitability and immutability of our current arrangements to "protect" children, we require both a vision of what might be more satisfactory and achievable, and some steps with which we can begin the journey. This chapter concludes with a discussion of some possibilities to consider in planning this voyage.

Our child protection system is increasingly preoccupied with "protecting" children from harm within their own homes. Interventions centre on holding parents accountable for the care of their children and removing children from "danger." These guiding principles are too limited and too often lacking in compassion for the lives of children and parents. We need a more inclusive and acceptable vision to guide the enterprise, which includes promoting the ongoing well-being of children and their families.

Our current child protection systems provide very low levels of useful assistance to children and families, because disproportionate shares of time and resources are absorbed by administrative and legal control requirements. An additional concern is that, as the budgets of the child protection agencies expand rapidly, as they have in Ontario over the past five years, driven by increased costs of court and out-of home placements, fewer resources become available for other assistance strategies. Paradoxically, we have no evidence that these new "protection" emphases safeguard children better, even against the narrow criterion of intra-familial harm, than more communal child welfare orientations (Gibbons, 1997).

It is imperative to provide much higher levels of positive assistance to more families—both to parents and directly to children (a seriously under-valued and underutilized protection and welfare strategy). We need to take advantage of what is known about programming that is promising for dis-advantaged and distressed children and families (Cameron et al., 1997; Cameron, O'Reilly, et. al., 2002; Nelson et al., 2002). Our first response to most families must become an offer of assistance; while maintaining the capacity to intervene quickly with legal authority when warranted.

To move in this direction, child welfare should not remain the preserve of a single mandated authority. Practical arrangements to share responsi-bility (including mandated authority in some instances) among child pro-tection services, other service organizations, and members of host communities must be created. Our vision of child welfare must broaden considerably and cross traditional jurisdictional boundaries. For such part-nerships to be viable, more resources have to become available for positive ways of helping. This will require reallocating a portion of the resources cur-rently absorbed by child protection investigations, legal processes, manda-tory supervision of families, and out-of-home placements.

Our contention is that processes central to the Anglo-American child protection paradigm—formal investigations, involvement with the police and courts—have to become subsidiary to the main enterprise of child and family welfare. That is, they need to be more specialized, easily accessible, and well connected to sectors providing assistance for children and families, but no longer at the heart of our conception of the child and family welfare challenge. In addition to exploring how to create flexible front-line responses to families and multiple points of entry into the system, substantially increas-ing the proportion of "voluntary" or negotiated involvements with families should become a priority. More families should receive positive responses to their requests for help and be open to acceptable offers of assistance.

Positive reform requires greatly reducing formal court applications for supervision orders or for short-term precautionary out-of-home placements of children. The creation of intermediary, mandated space for negotiated or mediated service and caring for children agreements among parents, child protection service providers, and others should be explored.

One of the driving forces behind the recent rapid increase in state guardianship of children in Ontario has been the greater use of short- and medium-term out-of-home placements of children as a precaution—until family circumstances are better understood or assistance put in place. Such placements are frequently extremely painful experiences for both the par-ents and the children involved (see discussion in chapter 2), increasing resentment and resistance to child protection authorities. An alternative is to explore adding a range of intermediary options between leaving children in the home in unchanged conditions and their involuntary apprehensions. These include: in-home support and observation, access to contact families/persons where a child can visit or stay a few days a week (as in Sweden; Andersson, 2003); foster homes taking parents and children together (as most foster homes in Sweden are licensed to do; Andersson, 2003); care of children in conjunction with working with their parents, in after school centres (as in The Netherlands; Madge & Attridge, 1996) and in daycare centres for younger children. Creating such a diversity of responses would require some diversion of resources from traditional investigative and place-ment responses.

Research shows an increasing level of stress on most Canadian families (Rick, Charlesworth, Bellefeuille, & Fields, 1999). In addition, traditional conceptions of family have been the focus of persistent criticism and suspi-cion for several decades (Hewlett & West, 1988). Whatever we wish would happen, the evidence is unequivocal; almost all of the children who come to the attention of child protection authorities—including a large majority of children who enter state care—will grow up in the care of their nuclear and/or extended families. Many of these children and their parents will con-tinue to live in "disadvantaged" communities. To improve the safety and well-being of these children, we must invest in the families and the com-munities in which they are going to live, even if the permutations and com-binations of living arrangements differ from what professional helpers (who often have radically different living experiences and access to privileges than most of these families) consider ideal. This investment requires a commu-nally accepted rationale and authority for child and family welfare inter-ventions that is much broader and more amenable to service users than exists in Anglo-American child protection systems.

If we proceed down this road to reform, what will happen the next time a child dies in his or her home while involved with child and family wel-fare or in the care of the state? Child and family welfare authorities are in the unique and unenviable position of being held solely responsible for preventing such deaths and are subject to merciless media and public scrutiny if something goes wrong. Unless child welfare service providers, managers, and policy officials are reasonably buffered from these periodic bouts of public condemnation, they are unlikely to be willing to proceed with investigating the value of these types of reforms. To move ahead, front-line service providers have to be confident that the responsibility for plans of intervention with children and families is shared (for example, with an authorized multi-disciplinary/agency case conference; Hetherington, 2002). Similarly, child protection authorities need to be supported through mandated partnerships with other organizations for services and supervision of children and families (Schene, 2002).

The paths from "here to there" are long and unfamiliar. We are unsure how to make changes in any of these areas and about the consequences reforms. Prudence and concerns about feasibility argue against sweeping changes. Past experience has also taught us that there is no "silver bullet" or one-dimensional solution to these challenges (Cameron, Karabanow et al., 2002; Schorr, 1989; 1997). However, we are not without promising directions to explore.

The time is appropriate in Canada for delivery system experiments that incorporate a few or perhaps many of the above suggestions. Such experiments require adequate guidance, assessment, and resources as well as modifications or suspension of existing legislative expectations and controls (for an expanded discussion see Cameron, Karabanow et. al., 2002). The strengths and limitations of our child and family welfare paradigm are well known; levels of user and provider satisfaction will not increase significantly by refinements to our traditional child-saving paradigm. Our basic challenge is to define a new vision for child and family welfare in Canada. We need opportunities for reflection and discussion and to learn from thoughtful experiments with new approaches. We need to find realistic ways to begin this journey.

Note

1 We use the more inclusive term child and family welfare instead of the more familiar North American labels of child welfare or child protection to accommodate the differences among the different paradigms in this chapter.

References

Alberta Children's Services. (undated). *Alberta response model: transforming outcomes of children and youth.* Calgary, AB: author [www.child.gov.ab.ca].

Ammerman, R. T., & Hersen, M. (Eds.). (1990). *Children at risk: An evaluation of factors contributing to child abuse and neglect.* New York: Plenum Press.

Andersson, G. (2003). *Child and family support in Sweden.* Waterloo, ON: Partnerships for Children and Families Project, Faculty of Social Work, Wilfrid Laurier University.

Armitage, A. (1993). The policy and legislative context. In B. Wharf (Ed.), *Rethinking child welfare in Canada* (pp. 37–63). Toronto, ON: Oxford University Press.

Armstrong, L. (1995). *Of sluts and bastards: A feminist decodes the child welfare debate.* Monroe, ME: Common Courage Press.

Baistow, K., Hetherington, R., Spriggs, A., & Yelloly, M. (1996). *Parents speaking: Anglo-French perceptions of child welfare interventions, a preliminary report*. London: Brunel University.

Baker, M., & Phipps, S. (1997). Family change and family policies: Canada. In S. B. Kamerman & A. Kahn (Eds.), *Family change and family policies in Great Britain, Canada, New Zealand and the United States* (pp. 103–206). Oxford: Clarendon Press.

Bala, N. (1999). Reforming Ontario's child and family services act: Is the pendulum swinging back too far? *Canadian Family Law Quarterly, 17*, 121–173.

Belsky, J. (1993). Etiology of child maltreatment: A developmental-ecological analysis. *Psychological Bulletin, 114*(3), 413–434.

Bennet, M., & Blackstock, C. (2002) *First Nations child and family services and indigenous knowledge as a framework for research, policy and practice*. Waterloo, ON: Wilfrid Laurier University, Partnerships for Children and Families Project.

Bering Pruzan, V. L. (1997). Denmark: Voluntary placements as a family support. In N. Gilbert (Ed.), *Combatting child abuse: International perspectives and trends* (pp. 125–142). New York: Oxford University Press.

Besharov, D. J. (1985). 'Doing something' about child abuse: The need to narrow the grounds for state intervention. *Harvard Journal of Law and Public Policy, 8*, 539–589.

Besharov, D. J., Robinson Lowry, M., Pelton, L. H., & Weber, M. W. (1998). Four commentaries: How can we better protect children from abuse and neglect. *Future of Children, 8*(1), 120–132.

Bronowski, J., & Mazlish, B. (1960). *The western intellectual tradition: From Leonardo to Hegel*. New York: Harper and Row.

Callahan, M. (1993). Feminist approaches: Women recreate child welfare. In B. Wharf (Ed.), *Rethinking child welfare in Canada* (pp. 172–209). Toronto, ON: Oxford University Press.

Cameron, G., & Cadell, S. (1999). Empowering participation in prevention programs for disadvantaged children and families. *Canadian Journal of Community Mental Health, 18*(1), 105–122.

Cameron, G., Hayward, K., & Mamatis, D. (1992). *Mutual aid and child welfare: The parent mutual aid organizations in a child welfare demonstration project*. Waterloo, ON: Wilfrid Laurier University, Centre for Social Welfare Studies.

Cameron, G., Hayward, K., Mckenzie, A., Hancock, K., & Jeffery, H. (September 28, 1999). *Partnerships and programs: Service provider involvement in Better Beginnings, Better Futures*. Kingston, ON: Better Beginnings research Coordination Unit, Queen's University, 89pp.

Cameron, G., Karabanow, J., Laurendeau, M.-C., & Chamberland, C. (2002). Program implementation and diffusion. In I. Prilleltensky, G. Nelson, & L. Peirson (Eds.), *Promoting family wellness and preventing child maltreatment:*

Fundamentals for thinking and action (pp. 339–374). Toronto, ON: University of Toronto Press.

Cameron, G., O'Reilly, J., Laurendeau, M.-C., & Chamberland, C. (2002). Programming for distressed and disadvantaged adolescents. In I. Prilleltensky, G. Nelson, & L. Peirson (Eds.), *Promoting family wellness and preventing child maltreatment: Fundamentals for thinking and action* (pp. 289–338). Toronto, ON: University of Toronto Press.

Cameron, G., & Rothery, M. (1985). *The use of family support in Children's Aid Societies: An exploratory study.* Toronto, ON: Ontario Ministry of Community and Social Services.

Cameron, G., Vanderwoerd, J., & Peirson, L. (1997). *Protecting children and supporting families: Promising programs and organisational realities.* New York: Aldine de Gruyter.

Cannan, C., Berry, L., & Lyons, K. (1992). *Social work and Europe.* Basingstoke: Macmillan.

Chen, X. (2001). *Tending the gardens of citizenship: Child protection in Toronto 1880s–1920s.* Unpublished doctoral dissertation, University of Toronto, Toronto, ON.

Cooper, A., Hetherington, R., Baistow, K., Pitts, J., & Spriggs, A. (1995). *Positive child protection: a view from abroad.* Lyme Regis: Russell House Publishing.

Costin, L. B., Karger, H. J., & Stoesz, D. (1996). *The politics of child abuse in America.* New York: Oxford University Press.

Courtney, M. E. (1998). The costs of child protection in the context of welfare reform. *Future of Children, 8*(1), 88–103.

Dahl, T. S. (1985). *Child welfare and social defence* (G. Nyguist, Trans.). London: Norwegian University Press.

Differential Response Sub-Committee of Ontario Children's Aid Directors of Service. (2005). *A differential service response for child welfare in Ontario.* Toronto, ON: author.

Djao, A. W. (1983). *Inequality and social policy.* Toronto, ON: John Wiley & Sons.

English, D. J. (1998). The extent and consequences of child maltreatment. *Future of Children, 8*(1), 39–53.

Family and Children's Services of Guelph and Wellington County. (2000). *1999–2000 Annual Report.* Guelph, ON: Family and Children's Services of Guelph and Wellington County.

Fox Harding, L. (1991). *Perspectives in child care policy.* London: Longman Group UK.

Freymond, N., & Cameron, G. (2006). *Towards positive systems of child and family welfare: International comparisons of child protection, family service and community caring systems.* Toronto, ON: University of Toronto Press.

Gelles, R. J. (1979). The social construction of child abuse. In D. G. Gill (Ed.), *Child abuse and violence* (pp. 145–157). New York: AMS Press.

Gibbons, J. (1997). Relating outcomes to objectives in child protection policy. In N. Parton (Ed.), *Child protection and family support: Tensions, contradictions and possibilities* (pp. 78–91). London: Routledge.

Gilbert, N. (Ed.). (1997a). *Combatting child abuse: International perspectives and trends*. New York: Oxford University Press.

Gilbert, N. (1997b). Conclusion: A comparative perspective. In N. Gilbert (Ed.), *Combatting child abuse: International perspectives and trends* (pp. 232–240). New York: Oxford University Press.

Gilbert, N. (1997c). Introduction. In N. Gilbert (Ed.), *Combatting child abuse: International perspectives and trends* (pp. 1–6). New York: Oxford University Press.

Goldstein, J., Freud, A., & Solnit, A. J. (1973). *Beyond the best interests of the child*. New York: Free Press.

Goldstein, J., Freud, A., & Solnit, A. J. (1979). *Before the best interests of the child*. New York: Free Press.

Grevot, A. (2002). *The plight of paternalism in French child welfare and protective policies and practices*. Waterloo, ON: Wilfrid Laurier University, Partnerships for Children and Families Project.

Hagan, J., & Leon, J. (1977). Rediscovering delinquency: Social history, political ideology and the sociology of law. *American Sociological Review, 42*, 587–598.

Heidenheimer, A. J., Heclo, H., & Teich Adams, C. (1975). *Comparative public policy: The politics of social choice in Europe and America*. New York: St. Martin's Press.

Hendrick, H. (1990). Constructions and reconstructions of British childhood. In A. James & A. Prout (Eds.), *Constructing and reconstructing childhood: Contemporary issues in the sociological study of childhood* (pp. 35–59). London: Falmer Press.

Hepworth, H. P. (1985). Child neglect and abuse. In K. L. Levitt & B. Wharf (Eds.), *The challenge of child welfare* (pp. 28–52). Vancouver: University of British Columbia Press.

Hetherington, R. (2002). *Learning from difference: Comparing child welfare systems*. Waterloo, ON: Wilfrid Laurier University, Partnerships for Children and Families Project.

Hetherington, R., Cooper, A., Smith, P., & Wilford, G. (1997). *Protecting children: Messages from Europe*. Lyme Regis: Russell House Publishing.

Hewlett, S. A., & West, C. (1988). *The war against parents: What we can do for America's beleaguered moms and dads*. New York: Houghton Mifflin.

Hughes, C. (1995). Child poverty, campaign 2000, and child welfare practice: Working to end child poverty in Canada. *Child Welfare, 74*(3), 779–794.

Jones, A., & Rutman, L. (1981). *In the children's aid: J. J. Kelso and child welfare in Ontario*. Toronto, ON: University of Toronto Press.

King, M. (1998). You have to start somewhere. In G. Douglas & L. Sebba (Eds.), *Children's rights and traditional values* (pp. 1–14). Dartmouth: Ashgate.

Kingsley, C., & Mark, M. (2000). *Sacred lives: Canadian Aboriginal children and youth speak out about sexual exploitation.* Toronto, ON: National Aboriginal Consultation Project, Save the Children Canada.

Kufeldt, K., Vachon, J., Simard, M., Baker, J., & Andrews, T.-L. (2000). *Looking after children in Canada.* Fredericton: University of New Brunswick, Muriel McQueen Fergusson Family Violence Research Centre, and The Social Development Partnerships Division of Human Resources Development Canada.

Larner, M. B., Stevenson, C. S., & Behrman, R. E. (1998). Protecting children from abuse and neglect: Analysis and recommendations. *Future of Children, 8*(1), 4–22.

Lawrence-Karski, R. (1997). United States: California's reporting system. In N. Gilbert (Ed.), *Combatting child abuse: International perspectives and trends* (pp. 9–37). New York: Oxford University Press.

Leira, A. (1994). Combining work and family: Working mothers in Scandinavia and the European Community. In P. Brown & R. Crompton (Eds.), *Economic restructuring and social exclusion* (pp.86–107). London: Routledge.

Lindsey, D. (1994). *The welfare of children.* New York: Oxford University Press.

Lorenz, W. (1994). *Social work in a changing Europe.* London: Routledge.

Love, C. (2002). *Maori perspectives on collaboration and colonisation in contemporary Aotearoa/New Zealand child and family welfare policies and practices.* Waterloo, ON: Wilfrid Laurier University, Partnerships for Children and Families Project.

Luckock, B., Vogler, R., & Keating, H. (1996). Child protection in France and England—authority, legalism, and social work practice. *Child and Family Law Quarterly, 8*(4), 297–311.

Luckock, B., Vogler, R., & Keating, H. (1997). The Belgian Flemish child protection system—confidentiality, voluntarism, and coercion. *Child and Family Law Quarterly, 9*(2), 101–113.

Macintyre, E. (1993). The historical context of child welfare in Canada. In B. Wharf (Ed.), *Rethinking child welfare in Canada* (pp. 13–36). Toronto: Oxford University Press.

Madge, N., & Attridge, K. (1996). Children and families. In B. Munday & P. Ely (Eds.), *Social care in Europe* (pp. 126–161). London: Prentice Hall.

Maidman, F., & Connors, E. (2002). A circle of healing: Family wellness in Aboriginal communities. In I. Prilleltensky, G. Nelson, & L. Peirson (Eds.), *Promoting family wellness and preventing child maltreatment: Fundamentals for thinking and action* (pp. 375–466). Toronto, ON: University of Toronto Press.

Manitoba Public Inquiry into the Administration of Justice and Aboriginal People. (1991). *Report of the Aboriginal Justice Inquiry of Manitoba*. Winnipeg, MB: Public Inquiry into the Administration of Justice and Aboriginal People.

Marneffe, C., & Broos, P. (1997). Belgium: An alternative approach to child abuse reporting and treatment. In N. Gilbert (Ed.), *Combatting child abuse: International perspectives and trends* (pp. 167–191). New York: Oxford University Press.

Martin, M. (1985). Poverty and child welfare. In K. L. Levitt & B. Wharf (Eds.), *The challenge of child welfare* (pp. 53–65). Vancouver: University of British Columbia Press.

McCroskey, J., & Meezan, W. (1998). Family-centered services: Approaches and effectiveness. *Future of Children, 8*(1), 54–71.

McEachern, C., & Morris, P. (1992). *Children first: A historical review of the Children's Aid Society of London and Middlesex 1893–1992*. London, ON: Children's Aid Society of London and Middlesex.

McGillivray, A. (1995). Therapies of freedom: The colonization of Aboriginal childhood. *U.B.C. Legal History Papers*. Retrieved March 1, 2001, from web2.uvcs.uvic.ca/courses/lawdemo/webread/mcgill.htm

McKenzie, B. (1989). Child welfare: New models of service delivery in Canada's Native communities. *Human Services in the Rural Environment, 12*(3), 6–11.

McKenzie, B. (1995). Child and family service standards in First Nations: An action research project. *Child Welfare, 74*(3), 633–653.

McKenzie, B. (1997). Developing First Nations child welfare standards: Using evaluation research within a participatory framework. *The Canadian Journal of Program Evaluation, 12*(1), 133–148.

Morrissette, V., McKenzie, B., & Morrissette, L. (1993). Towards an Aboriginal model of social work practice: Cultural knowledge and traditional practices. *Canadian Social Work Review, 10*(1), 91–108.

National Research Council. (1993). *Losing generations: Adolescents in high-risk settings*. Washington, DC: National Academy Press.

Nelken, D. (1998). Choosing rights for children. In G. Douglas & L. Sebba (Eds.), *Children's rights and traditional values* (pp. 315–335). Burlington, VT: Ashgate.

Nelson, G., Laurendeau, M.-C., Chamberland, C., & Peirson, L. (2002). A review and analysis of programs to promote family wellness and prevent the maltreatment of pre-school and elementary school-aged children. In I. Prilleltensky, G. Nelson, & L. Peirson (Eds.), *Promoting family wellness and preventing child maltreatment: Fundamentals for thinking and action* (pp. 221–288). Toronto, ON: University of Toronto Press.

O'Hara, K. (1998). *Comparative family policy: Eight countries' stories* (CPRN Study No. F/04). Ottawa, ON: Canadian Policy Research Networks.

Olsson Hort, S. E. (1997). Sweden: Toward a deresidualization of Swedish child welfare policy and practice? In N. Gilbert (Ed.), *Combatting child abuse: International perspectives and trends* (pp. 105–124). New York: Oxford University Press.

Ontario Ministry of Community and Social Services. (2000a,). Harris Government Announces ... More Support for Vulnerable Children. Retrieved March 27, 2001, from www.oacas.org/resources/OACASJournals/2001March/MinistersAnnouncement.pdf

Ontario Ministry of Community and Social Services. (2000b). *Risk assessment model for child protection in Ontario.* Toronto, ON: Queen's Printer for Ontario.

Ontario Ministry of Children's Services. (2003). *Child welfare program evaluation report.* Toronto, ON: Author.

Ontario Ministry of Children and Youth. (2005). *Child welfare transformation 2005: A strategic plan for a flexible structural and outcome oriented service delivery model.* Toronto, ON: Author.

Palmer, S. (1995). *Maintaining family ties: Inclusive practice in foster care.* Washington, DC: Child Welfare League of America Press.

Pancer, S.M., & Cameron, G. (1994). Resident participation in the Better Beginnings, Better Futures prevention project: The impacts of involvement. *Canadian Journal of Community Mental Health, 13,* 197–211.

Panel of Experts on Child Protection. (1998). *Protecting vulnerable children.* Toronto, ON: Ontario Ministry of Community and Social Services.

Parton, N. (1997). Current debates and future prospects. In N. Parton (Ed.), *Child protection and family support: Tensions, contradictions and possibilities* (pp. 1–24). New York: Routledge.

Peirson, L., Laurendeau, M.-C., & Chamberland, C. (2002). Context, contributing factors, and consequences. In I. Prilleltensky, G. Nelson, & L. Peirson (Eds.), *Promoting family wellness and preventing child maltreatment: Fundamentals for thinking and action* (pp. 39–122). Toronto, ON: University of Toronto Press.

Pence, A. R. (1985). Day care in Canada. In K. L. Levitt & B. Wharf (Eds.), *The challenge of child welfare* (pp. 236–252). Vancouver: University of British Columbia Press.

Philp, M. (2001, February 20). Children's aid staff face burnout. The *Globe and Mail.* Retrieved March 3, 2001, from http://www.globeandmail.com

Phipps, S. (1999). *An international comparison of policies and outcomes for young children* (CPRN Study No. F/05). Ottawa, ON: Canadian Policy Research Networks.

Piper, C. (1999). Moral campaigns for children's welfare in the nineteenth century. In M. King (Ed.), *Moral agendas for children's welfare* (pp. 33–52). London: Routledge.

Pires, S. A. (1993). *International child welfare systems: Report of a workshop.* Washington, DC: National Academy Press.

Poso, T. (1997). Finland: Child abuse as a family problem. In N. Gilbert (Ed.), *Combatting child abuse: International perspectives and trends* (pp. 143–166). New York: Oxford University Press.

Pringle, K. (1998). *Children and social welfare in Europe*. Buckingham, UK: Open University Press.

Regehr, C., Leslie, B., Howe, P., & Chau, S. (2000). *Stressors in child welfare practice*. Retrieved April 5, 2001, from Centre of Excellence for Child Welfare website: http://www.cecw-cepb.ca/Pubs/PubsOther.html

Rick, F., Charlesworth, J., Bellefeuille, G., & Field, A. (1999). *All together now: Creating a social capital mosaic*. Ottawa, ON: Vanier Institute of the Family.

Roelofs, M. A., & Baartman, H. E. (1997). The Netherlands: Responding to abuse—Compassion or control? In N. Gilbert (Ed.), *Combatting child abuse: International perspectives and trends* (pp. 192–211). New York: Oxford University.

Ronen, Y. (1998). Protection from whom and from what? Protection proceedings and the voice of the child at risk. In G. Douglas & L. Sebba (Eds.), *Children's rights and traditional values* (pp. 249–263). Burlingont, VT: Ashgate.

Royal Commission on Aboriginal Peoples. (1996). *Gathering Strength* (Vol. 3). Ottawa, ON: Canadian Communications Group.

Sapiro, V. (1990). The gender basis of American social policy. In L. Gordon (Ed.), *Women, the state and welfare* (pp. 36–54). Madison: University of Wisconsin Press.

Saskatchewan Children's Advocate Office. (2000). *Children and youth in care review: Listen to their voices*. Saskatoon: Saskatchewan Children's Advocate Office.

Schene, P. A. (1998). Past, present, and future roles of child protective services. *Future of Children, 8*(1), 23–38.

Schene, P. A. (2002). *Forming and sustaining partnerships*. Waterloo, ON: Wilfrid Laurier University, Partnerships for Children and Families Project.

Schmidt, D. E. (March 2001). *The child, family and community services act British Columbia: Judicial case conferences*. Materials prepared for the National Judicial Insititute, Vancouver, B.C.

Schorr, L. (1989). *Within our reach: Breaking the cycle of disadvantage*. New York: Doubleday.

Schorr, L. (1997). *Common purpose: Strengthening families and neighbourhoods to rebuild America*. New York: Doubleday.

Sutherland, N. (1976). *Children in English-Canadian society: Framing the twentieth-century consensus*. Toronto, ON: University of Toronto Press.

Swift, K. J. (1995). *Manufacturing 'bad mothers': A critical perspective on child neglect*. Toronto, ON: University of Toronto Press.

Swift, K. J. (1997). Canada: Trends and issues in child welfare. In N. Gilbert (Ed.), *Combatting child abuse: International perspectives and trends* (pp. 38–71). New York: Oxford University Press.

Swift, K. J. (1998). Contradictions in child welfare: Neglect and responsibility. In C. T. Baines, P. M. Evans, & S. Neysmith, M. (Eds.), *Women's caring: Feminist perspectives on social welfare* (pp. 160–190). Toronto, ON: Oxford University Press.

Thorpe, D. (1994). *Evaluating child protection.* Buckingham, UK: Open University Press.

Toughill, K. (2001, February 3). Judge Jim: An Inuk's compassion and understanding transform his people's view of the justice system. *Toronto Star,* pp. K1, K3.

Trocmé, N. (1991). Child Welfare Services. In R. Barnhorst & L. C. Johnson (Eds.), *The State of Children in Ontario* (pp. 63–91). Toronto, ON: Oxford University Press.

Trocmé, N., Knoke, D., & Roy, C. (2003). *Community Collaboration and differential response: Canadian and international research and emerging models of practice.* Ottawa, ON: Centre of Excellence for Child Welfare c/o Child Welfare League of Canada.

Trocmé, N., MacLaurin, B., Fallon, B., Daciuk, J., Billingsley, D., Tourigny, M., et al. (2001). *Canadian Incidence Study of Reported Child Abuse and Neglect: Final Report.* Ottawa, ON: Minister of Public Works and Government Services Canada.

Tunstill, J. (1997). Family support clauses of the 1989 Children Act: Legislative, professional, and organisational obstacles. In N. Parton (Ed.), *Child protection and family support: Tensions, contradictions, and possibilities* (pp. 39–58). London: Routledge.

Tuomisto, R., & Vuori-Karvia, E. (1997). Child protection in Finland. In M. Harder & K. Pringle (Eds.), *Protecting children in Europe: Towards a new millennium* (pp. 77–100). Aalborg, Denmark: Aalborg University Press.

Van Krieken, R. (1986). Beyond social control. *Theory and Society, 15,* 401–429.

Veldkamp, A. W. M. (2002). 'When one door shuts, another opens': Turning *disadvantages into opportunities.* Waterloo, ON: Wilfrid Laurier University, Partnerships for Children and Families Project.

Waldfogel, J. (1996). *Toward a new paradigm for child protective services.* Cambridge, MA: Malcolm Wiener Center for Social Policy, John F. Kennedy School of Government, Harvard University.

Waldfogel, J. (1998). Rethinking the paradigm for child protection. *Future of Children, 8*(1), 104–119.

Waldfogel, J. (2001). *The future of child protection: How to break the cycle of abuse and neglect.* Cambridge: Harvard University Press.

Wharf, B. (1992). *Communities and social policy in Canada.* Toronto, ON: McClelland and Stewart.

Wharf, B. (1993). Rethinking child welfare. In B. Wharf (Ed.), *Rethinking child welfare in Canada* (pp. 210–230). Toronto, ON: Oxford University Press.

Wharf, B. (1995). Toward a new vision for child welfare in Canada. *Child Welfare, 74*(3), 820–839.

White, L. A. (1998). *Welfare state development and child care policies: A comparative analysis of France, Canada, and the United States.* Unpublished doctoral dissertation. Toronto, ON: University of Toronto.

Wilford, G., Hetherington, R., & Piquardt, R. (1997). *Families ask for help: Parental perceptions of child welfare and child protection services—an Anglo-German study.* London: Brunel University.

Wolff, R. (1997). Germany: A nonpunitive model. In N. Gilbert (Ed.), *Combatting child abuse: International perspectives and trends* (pp. 212–231). New York: Oxford University Press.

|2|

Mothers and Child Welfare Child Placements

Nancy Freymond
Gary Cameron

Canadian child protection systems focus on child maltreatment, which is generally attributed to deficient parenting. Systems of child protection have established procedures for evaluating parenting in relation to the risk factors associated with child maltreatment. Although parenting is now considered to involve both mothers and fathers, child welfare remains primarily concerned with the evaluation of biological mothers (Callahan, 1993; Miller, 1991; Swift, 1995, 1998). The risk of child maltreatment is considered to be a function of the number and the severity of problems affecting mothers' capacity to parent. As the risks of maltreatment increase, so does the likelihood that the child will be placed in foster care.

In child welfare literature, the portrayal of mothers with children in foster care is exclusively problem-focused. Mothers' broader, daily living realities that extend beyond the problems associated with child maltreatment are obscured and misunderstood. The consequence is a biased understanding of the lives of these mothers.

The purposes of this chapter are twofold. One is to shed light on the lives of biological mothers who experience the out-of-home placement of a child. A second purpose is to understand how mothers make sense of the out-of-home placement of their children. This analysis reveals profound incongruence between the primary interventions used in child welfare and the lives of these mothers.

Images of Mothers in Child Welfare

Child welfare literature describes characteristics of parents who maltreat their children and appropriate methods of intervention when child maltreatment is suspected. Decisions about placing a child in foster care depend mainly on the attributes of the parents, particularly those of mothers (Shapira & Benbenisty, 1993). Maluccio (1981) describes the biological parents of children in placement as "burdened by a variety of complex reality problems, psychological conflicts, and inter-personal difficulties" (p. 16). Such descriptions of mothers are common. For example, Fernandez (1996) indicates that child welfare workers use labels such as "inadequate, dangerous, unwilling or unable to provide care for their children" (p. 7). In addition, the media contribute to our images of mothers who have their children placed in care. In Ontario, intense media scrutiny prompted public inquires into child deaths, which became the impetus for a variety of child welfare reforms in the latter part of the 1990s (Chen, 2001). Public descriptions of incidents involving child death produce images of unstable mothers and their partners committing heinous harm to their children.

Mothers are understood in terms of their many deficiencies that, when found in combination, are particularly detrimental to their children. These mothers are described as facing inadequate environmental conditions, involvement in abusive relationships, and internal psychological challenges. They have difficulties of such magnitude that the likelihood of any substantial change is considered remote.

Journalist Karen Patterson writes that "a good mother swaddles her child in a sturdy weave of love and care." Before she describes mothers who kill their children, she stresses that "motherhood is considered a sacred duty" (Patterson, 2002, p. B1). Forna (1998) writes:

> The ideal mother is everywhere in art, poetry, fiction, film ... The motherhood myth is the myth of the 'Perfect Mother.' She must be completely devoted not just to her children, but to her role. She must be the mother who understands her children, who is all-loving and, even more important, all-giving. She must be capable of enormous sacrifice. (p. 3)

"Good" mothers are distinguished from "bad" mothers by such idealized notions of motherhood, and there is a huge gulf between mothers who experience problems that lead to the placement of their child in substitute care and these idealized images of good mothers.

The socio-environmental, relational, and psychological factors that predispose a mother to maltreat her child provide the framework through which child welfare workers understand mothers. Child welfare workers are trained to assess and to intervene with "bad" mothers. That these mothers might display strength, resilience or courage in the midst of tremendous adversity is obscured by the context of child welfare service.

In child welfare in Ontario, mothers' strengths are also camouflaged by the use of formal risk-assessment models when child maltreatment is suspected. A standardized risk-assessment model that identifies factors associated with child maltreatment is integral to the work of child welfare service providers (Dawson, 2001). Callahan (2001), whose research examines the experiences of mothers and youth in care, writes:

> Mothers state that risk assessments focus on their deficits and not what they are doing well, blame them for things beyond their control, and force them to answer questions posed by people with different values and unrealistic expectations, whom they may never see again and do not trust. (p. 158)

One of the fundamental issues in challenging the images of bad mothers is that mothers' voices are largely missing from child welfare research and practice. "Without these voices, we run the risk of continuing to see the mothers as deficient and needing repair" (Davies & Krane, 1996, p. 19). The research presented in this chapter illustrates that mothers' understandings of their lives differ fundamentally from the descriptions that dominate child welfare. Attention to the voices of mothers stimulates an enriched understanding of these women and their families and highlights possibilities for more congruent and acceptable ways of helping.

The Research Process

Personal stories function to link subjective experience with the events in the external world; they establish memories, define communities, and identify the concerns of people in a particular time and place in history (Plummer, 2001). Personal stories are moral constructions, where the just and the unjust are identified, and the ethics that guide our lives are made known (Plummer, 2001). People use personal stories to share what is meaningful about their lives.

Attending to the stories people share provides a pathway into the culture. The ethnographic research tradition understands culture as everyday life, emphasizing meanings that are attributed to particular phenomena by members on the basis of their own life experiences. (Van Loon, 2001). Ethnographic research attempts to understand life events by placing them in a meaningful context (Tedlock, 2000).

This chapter begins an analysis of the culture of biological mothers who share the experience of a recent placement of a child in the foster care system. It is based on an analysis of interviews with biological mothers. Mothers were asked to describe the environments in which they live, important relationships that they have, and the day-to-day challenges that they face. They were also asked to describe their involvement with child welfare services and the impact of foster placement on themselves and on their families. Mothers responded by telling stories of their experiences. The analysis of these stories emphasizes meanings that mothers attach to daily living realities and how these meanings function to shape their understanding of the placement event.

Ethnographic research assumes that interaction with people in their daily contexts facilitates a better understanding about their beliefs, motivations, and behaviours (Fetterman, 1998). Almost all of the research interviews were conducted in the mothers' homes. At the conclusion of the interviews, each interviewer recorded analytical notes about their impressions of the mothers and their surroundings. All interviews were audiotaped and transcribed for analysis.

Two interviewing strategies were used in the collection of this data. The first strategy involved a single interview ranging from 1.5 to 2.5 hours in duration. Each participant was asked to talk about positive and negative life events from the past five years. The second part of the interview focused on how the women experienced their involvement with child welfare. The second interviewing strategy developed oral stories based on three conversations between 90 minutes and two hours each, with each mother. The initial interview consisted of a grand tour question (Spradley, 1979), asking the participants to tell the story of their lives. The flow of the conversation had minimal structure and was rarely interrupted. Between interviews, the researcher listened to the tape and prepared some general questions for the next interview. Seven mothers participated in these oral story interviews.

The first step in the process of analysis involved comparing each transcript with the recorded interview for purposes of ensuring accuracy. Listening to the taped interview also facilitated an increased understanding of the complex emotional content of the interviews. Patterns in the mothers' personal lives, current living contexts, and significant life events were noted to develop a beginning list of themes. Emerging themes were compared constantly with previously identified ones and were modified, omitted, or integrated when appropriate. A coding schema emerged with nine major categories. Each of the nine categories was elaborated by specific codes; in total, 62 specific codes were developed. QSR NUD*IST Vivo (Nvivo), a computer program designed to manage qualitative data was used to code and analyze the data.

Caution in generalizing these findings is appropriate, because all of the women in this study received services from the same child welfare agency. Of the 31 mothers who were interviewed, 30 were born in Canada and identified English as their first language. One mother was born in Laos, and identified Laotian as her first language; however, her English was fluent. Two mothers had five children; three mothers had four children; three mothers had three children. The remaining 23 mothers had either one or two children. Mothers ranged in age from 20 to 52 years; the mean age was 33.

The mothers who participated in the research described three general patterns of placement experience. Mothers experienced involuntary placement when children were apprehended[1] against the wishes of the mother. The stories of 18 mothers are consistent with this pattern of placement. Mothers also experienced placement on a voluntary[2] basis, requesting placement for their child. The stories of six mothers are consistent with this pattern of placement. The third pattern of placement involved mothers who consented to voluntary placement, but did so because of the absence of other suitable alternatives for their child. This placement pattern is found in seven of the mothers' stories. Mothers involved in voluntary placements consistently identified the behavioural issues of their child as the precipitating factor in the placement. Usually, only one child from the family was placed, usually an adolescent. In ten of these narratives, mothers specifically mentioned the diagnosis of Attention Deficit Disorder with Hyperactivity (ADHD). The average age of mothers in this group was 40.

Socioeconomic and Relational Contexts

Academics, child welfare professionals, and others have ideas about the lives of non-privileged mothers, but the voices of disadvantaged mothers are rarely found in the literature (Holloway, Fuller, Rambaud, & Eggers-Pierola, 1997). Similarly the voices of mothers involved with child welfare have received almost no attention (McCallum, 1995). The first section of this analysis explores the socioeconomic living environments of mothers who experience the out-of-home placement of a child. It examines employment and neighbourhood realities, friendships, community involvements, and familial support and discusses how child welfare interventions lack congruence with these daily living realities. The second part of this section explores how mothers manage problems. In contrast to the literature, in which these women are portrayed as unable or unwilling to address the problems in their lives, the mothers encountered here are actively involved in overcoming adversities. When child welfare intervenes, their efforts can confound mothers' attempts to manage their problems.

Employment realities. Although some of the mothers interviewed depend on social assistance, many more belong to the ranks of the working poor. Thirty percent of the mothers are married or live in common-law relationships. The income of these partnered mothers is important to the economic survival of the family. One woman said:

> I went back to work before [my son] came home from the hospital, cause I don't collect unemployment. I'm self-employed ... I was supposed to be off my feet for six weeks at least without lifting more than five pounds, but I was working, cause we needed the money ... We're still living cheque to cheque and still paying off debts.

Often the availability of work is not dependable. There are persistent concerns that the work hours will diminish or that jobs will suddenly become unavailable. Another woman, who works as a cashier in a grocery store, spoke of these worries:

> I only get about nine hours a week ... they keep hiring and hiring, so we get no hours. My husband's down to about 35 a week. He's a machinist at a small factory. There's only four workers there ... He used to get about 48 hours a week, now it's down to 35. They just laid off the one guy, so he could get more hours. It's tough right now because the money's not there and we're trying to pay the bills. It's tough.

Mothers who work part-time are often employed in more than one job and schedules are generally hectic. For many, the need to improve financial circumstances results in working long hours and time spent away from families. Working the night shift is one solution to this dilemma; despite the strains of sleep deprivation, it does allow mothers opportunity to care for children during daytime hours.

For non-privileged mothers, there are no simple solutions to these realities. In a privileged world, the recommendation is an appropriate balance between home and work life. However, this requires that families have the option of making choices to bring about favourable outcomes. In non-privileged households, choices are restricted and outcomes less favourable. For instance, mothers choose between having enough money to survive or having enough time available to adequately care for an acting-out child. Non-privileged mothers must "make the best of bad situations," rather than seek an ideal balance.

None of the mothers who experienced an out-of-home placement of a child have a career, the potential to start a career, or the education required to advance a career. Many of them talked about living through chaotic adolescent years. Homelessness, addiction, and strained relationships with family members persist in these narratives. These realities often precluded the completion of secondary school. Some mothers do return to school once their children are old enough to be in school, and high school graduation is seen as a substantial accomplishment.

One of the most fundamental contradictions between the needs of these mothers and child welfare interventions occurs when mothers are denied financial and other forms of tangible assistance. When placement occurs, mothers either lose a portion of their welfare assistance or are expected to contribute from their wages to the costs of their child's care. The result for mothers is increased financial strain. One mother made this point, contrasting a helpful and an unhelpful child protection service provider:

> Like, we would ask her [referring to the worker] if we can get a voucher for extra food, because we have the kids Wednesdays, Saturdays, and Sundays. And, ... she says, well, our agency isn't out for doing that. Like, we can't give it to you all the time. And we're like, why not, you're supposed to be there to help, and we don't get no money or extra stuff for the kids ... That's what I mean about helping out. And then one time, my car broke down, and I couldn't get the kids. And I asked if she could, get a cab, or ... somehow, they can drive him over here. But she was working, so she couldn't do it. The other lady that was involved, she was very helpful. Like, she would understand and talk to us, and understand our feelings, and what was going on and stuff. And she would give us a voucher every month.

Neighbourhood realities. The homes and neighbourhoods of these mothers were frequently described by the interviewers in their analytic notes. The biases in these descriptions are perhaps not unlike those of child welfare workers:

> It is a large single family home in a residential/industrial neighbourhood. Busy street, small lawns poorly kept, no trees. Not a great neighbourhood for children, I think.

> The interviewee lived in what would be conceived as a slum setting ... Her one bedroom apartment was very tiny, and it would almost be possible to touch opposite walls in the living room with outstretched arms. The apartment was extremely messy, with clothing and other items all over the floor, such that I would have to constantly be stepping over things to move around. Furniture and other items were old or in bad repair, with the only exception being a relatively new and large TV set (approx 25–29 inches).

> This was a semi-attached dwelling on a street surrounded by more affluent self-contained homes. Her particular dwelling was rented and the exterior was not well maintained. I was greeted at the door by three large dogs, including two Rottweilers [fortunately friendly]. I was somewhat taken aback by the clutter and some of the interior conditions. They were not as extreme as some other places and there were four kids and two adults living in a fairly small unit. Apparently, the place has been fixed up quite a bit [paint and cleaning] since the CAS involvement. They thought dirt and uncleanliness were one of the major agency concerns initially.

Some mothers talked about wanting more privacy for themselves and their families. One woman says in reference to other families in the same building: "It makes you mad. I don't know, but they, they just know your business. And you got to like, try and keep it to yourself and it's hard. When one person knows it, they blab to everybody else and then everybody knows it."

Concerns about neighbourhood safety are everyday realities for non-privileged mothers. One mother was confused by a child welfare worker's inability to comprehend her daily living realities:

> I had the door open and, you know, it doesn't close all the way because there's a gap in the door. And so, she asked if I could keep it closed and locked. And, I'm like, "well why?" And she's like, "oh well, what happens if somebody's there, and you tell them to come in and, it's some big murderer?" And I'm like, "well, what happens if the door is locked and somebody is knocking on my door, and it's some big murderer, and I open up the door?" I'm like, "it's not going to stop, no matter what." And she's like, "well, he could just walk right in." And I'm like, "well he could just walk right in when I open up the door too."

For women who have experienced life on the streets, the unsafe living conditions of low-income housing complexes pale in comparison. One mother spoke about fears for her safety during a period of homelessness:

> I ended up moving to a shelter, the YWCA, and that's probably the scariest place for a person to live. It's kinda scary in there. Like a lot of older women who have problems and talk to themselves and a lot of people who do drugs, like bad heavy drugs and I was scared living there. I didn't fit in at all. Like I made a couple friends but not really. Like, I was going through a lot and kinda stuck to myself.

Safety is a relative concept. In non-privileged communities, the requirements for safety extend far beyond locked doors. Mothers view their environments from a vantage point that differs from that of child protection workers. There is a normalcy about these living conditions for them, and these women are aware of the limitations of housing options available to them. They are often reluctant to comply with child welfare expectations for change that feel incongruent with what they know.

There is no indication from any of the narratives that mothers received assistance from child welfare to pay for or to locate accommodations that were more suitable. One mother spoke of the extreme challenges she faced finding housing:

> Not a lot of people with five children are looking to rent. So I don't know how people end up moving from a rural situation to a city situation, unless they have money. But we couldn't get ahead because we were stuck in one of the unemployment areas of the country. There was a wait-

ing list that was five years for us for co-op housing/subsidized housing—
five years, so I didn't even bother applying.

The housing that this mother located developed unsafe well-water conditions.
Child welfare's response was to contact the public health unit. While this
mother negotiated to secure another home through Habitat for Humanity,
her children were removed. She described her confusion:

> nothing was ever offered. I'm the one that's applied for Habitat for
> Humanity.... We were right at the head of the priority list. We had a
> house within three months. We lost our kids and at the same time we lost
> the house. Two weeks before the kids were taken, we got a house through
> Habitat for Humanity. We signed papers the day after the kids were
> taken ... all I ask for, is some help to get out of where we weren't doing
> well, with the bad water, which was a concern. They [child welfare] were
> asking me about that. Like well, you know if you wanna call the public
> health unit, call the public health unit. You're not gonna listen to me. If
> they woulda just said, "how about some respite for the summer while
> you guys work on this house for habitat?" we would have been fine ... It
> was bizarre. It's like 'you knew that we were going some place; why are
> you doing this now?

Friendships and community involvements.   Most women who experience the out-of-home placement of a child do not speak of friendships that
are dependable, reliable, or long term. Some women make ongoing connections through social service agencies, particularly women's shelters and
some report enjoyable working relationships with colleagues. However, the
majority of the mothers interviewed have limited social engagements and
minimal community involvements.

These minimal involvements are in sharp contrast to the friendships
and community involvements of Lynn, the only economically "well-off" and
university-educated woman in the study. When faced with relocation to a new
community, Lynn actively sought out friends, who became "just like family."
She defined community connections as resources for support for herself
and for her family. The importance of her community involvement was highlighted when she lamented that her ability to form community connections
was hampered by the need to be at her father's farm on weekends. Lynn's
relationship with friends and community stands in stark contrast to the following mother:

> I know [neighbours's name] will, listen to me, if I have to really talk to
> somebody, but ... I talk to my mom, now and then, over the phone. Like,
> we do talk and visit, maybe once a month, maybe. But that's about it.
> I'm better sometimes, by myself. I'm just, I'm, I feel like I'm a loner ... I

don't mind having friends, I like friends, and other people, but I like spending time by myself.

There is no mention in the other interviews of mothers of joining community organizations or attending social events. Most of these mothers expressed uneasiness with socializing and friendships.

There are a number of plausible reasons that mothers who experience the out-of-home placement of a child do not actively establish community connections. The obvious explanation is that non-privileged mothers lack time, energy, and financial resources for community involvements and socializing. Additionally, many of these mothers have a history of abusive relationships, causing a mistrust of others. The limited social spheres of these mothers might also be a consequence of the acting-out behaviours of a difficult child. Mothers of children who have committed crimes in neighbourhoods or who have negative reputations in the classroom, experience prejudices. Sometimes these mothers and children are ostracized within their neighbourhoods. Mothers are also concerned about the stigma of their involvement with child welfare, particularly of having a child in foster care:

> You know, I hear a bunch of kids playing in the backyard, and it's like oh no, you know, mine used to be out there. But now, I kind of miss that. So I kinda, stay in, or you know, I don't want to get too close to other kids right now ... I don't think their parents would appreciate it. Cause they know I'm involved with [child welfare]. Like, I may be a bad influence on them. So I don't need it.

Familial support. Approximately half of the women receive some form of support from their extended families. Mothers appreciated when family members were supportive during child protection interventions:

> My dad's always known from day one how much of a good parent I am ... So he drove all the way from up north down here. [He] called my aunt to come and take care of me too ... I didn't know what to do. I was so scared.

Mothers of children with behavioural difficulties frequently stressed the importance of a family member who understands their parenting struggles. Generally, because of the extreme nature of the behaviour, most mothers did not seek parenting relief from family members. Perhaps the most intense expressions about familial supports came from mothers whose infants or young children were apprehended. These mothers often talked about their struggles to attempt to establish independence and form intimate adult relationships while adjusting to parenting a young child, managing the realities of non-privilege, and perhaps coping with the traumas of recent abuses. When familial support was available, it was highly valued.

Sometimes the support that women received from their families was unreliable or indifferent:

> My mom's way too busy to call me so she's sort of not around a lot. I guess to cope with that I just, sort of, close the doors on them. If I call them and leave a message two or three times and she doesn't call me then it's not worth it to me. Cause if she doesn't have enough respect to call me, and call me back, then I won't bother with her. She has no time.

Themes of betrayal are found in the stories that some women told about relationships with their parents. One woman believes that her family conspired with child welfare for the removal of her children. Another woman felt betrayed by her mother after she disclosed that her father had sexually abused her. Both of these young mothers expressed hurt and longing for supportive familial relationships. And finally, for some women, relationships with family members are hostile:

> And the only way you're going to communicate with her [in reference to her mother] is with violence and so finally, like, I got violent ... I always told her, "well, one day I'm going to be bigger than you and you're going to have to be looked after and I'm going to treat you the same way you treated me." And she's like, "well, that will never happen."

Eight of the mothers interviewed described supportive familial relationships; six described minimal supports; four described conflicted relationships with family members; two described support from some family members, but conflicted relationships with other family members; ten made no mention of family support. Overall, the familial supports for the mothers in our sample tended to be limited or unavailable.

Implications for interventions. The daily-living contexts of mothers who experience the out-of-home placement of a child are fundamentally different from these of privileged mothers. Despite these differences, privileged and non-privileged mothers share many of the same concerns for themselves and for their children. Non-privileged mothers worry about providing economically for their children and about locating suitable neighbourhoods in which to live. They are cautious about community involvements, but desire positive connections in their lives. They hope for supportive connections with family members and friends for themselves and for their children.

Mothers make decisions about their lives and about their children congruent with their daily-living realities. Despite profound barriers, non-privileged mothers find ways to survive financially in climates where social assistance is minimal and unpopular. Poor job conditions lead to significant demands on the time and the energies of non-privileged mothers. Limited time, energy, and money are major barriers to establishing parenting methods acceptable to social workers.

Sometimes mothers require concrete forms of assistance, whether money, housing, or housecleaning. One mother referred to a former child protection service provider who helped her by supplying food vouchers. Although living with limited resources was pervasive in these stories, this was the only example of concrete assistance offered. Mothers' preoccupation with basic survival was essentially unacknowledged by the child protection system.

Mothers require interventions that are discreet and respectful of their needs for privacy. They worry about what neighbors will believe about their involvements with child welfare. The stigma associated with child welfare involvement may cause mothers to become more isolated within their neighborhoods. Interventions that are mindful of a mother's need for privacy demonstrate a level of respect that enhances positive and cooperative working relationships.

There is an absence of family members and friends on whom to rely for parenting relief for many mothers. This is particularly prevalent when children exhibit behavioural problems and in the stories where mothers have strained relationships with extended family members. These mothers do not have sufficient opportunities for a reprieve from childcare routines. Again, the value of practical support such as childcare services or respite care is evident but often unavailable to these women.

Finally, particularly when support from family and friends is unreliable or unavailable, mothers benefit from empathetic helping relationships, and they appreciate helping relationship where collaboration and support are central processes.

Facing Adversity

Adversity is so commonplace that it is an expected and an accepted part of life for mothers who experience the out-of-home placement of a child. One mother used a metaphor to illustrate her expectation of constant challenges, "it's just a bunch of hurdles ... there's still probably going to be a thousand more hurdles in my life. So I'll still get over them, just like an Olympic athlete or something." Another mother said, reflecting on the birth of her child, "that was like my one good thing [in] the last five years that's happened and anything else has just been horrible for the last five years. It's just been obstacle after obstacle to overcome." Mothers live with no expectation that the hurdles will end:

> I don't try to force anything ... God only knows what next week's going to bring. I could not have told you in January that I was going to go for

surgery ... I wonder what this year is going to be like? Well this year, my daughter was in a mental hospital [on] New Year's Eve because she was threatening suicide. And I'm sitting there at a party going, as long as next year's better than this year, that's all I care about.

Another mother speaks of the pervasiveness of life's hurdles saying, "every time I turn around, I'm getting pushed down."

Despite their pervasive problems, these mothers are not mired in helplessness. Another mother says, "I'm one of those people that you don't expect to go somewhere. And it's nice ... yes, I did survive. I was given a shitty life, but I managed to get out of it." This ability to be triumphant in the face of major adversities is a persistent theme in the stories these mothers told about their lives.

Abusive relationships. Since women tend to understand themselves in the context of relationships (Chodorow, 1978; Miller, 1991), it is not surprising that relationships for mothers who experience the out-of-home placement of a child are critical. Many of the women described their most intimate relationships as non-supportive and abusive and spoke of feeling betrayed when parents, boyfriends, and husbands abused them. The pervasiveness of the abuse toward women who have experienced the out-of-home placement of a child is startling. Eleven of the women interviewed were victims of childhood abuse.[3] Nineteen spoke of violence in their intimate, adult relationships; fourteen of these women identified the fathers of their children as being one of their abusers. Three women suffered abuse in more than one intimate, adult relationship.

There are very painful accounts of childhood abuse in nine of the narratives:

It was traumatic. I ended up moving out at 14 and living off my dad and that was like the most traumatic thing I ever had to go through was 10, 14 years of being beat up. I don't know how far it went for, that's all I can remember. And my life was always being pushed around, or beat up, or name called ... and nothing was ever done right. And my mom used to say I was the black sheep of the family.

Mothers living with domestic violence feel powerlessness about the abuse in their intimate relationships:

I just didn't care anymore ... I got married at 18 to this guy I didn't even know. And that lasted like two weeks and he beat me up pretty good all the time. So I left, and then he found me again and of course I went back and tried it again and he did the same thing again, except we were out in public and the cops got him and took him in ... And his mom used to watch him beat me up, and didn't care.

Often the absence of options and persistent feelings of powerlessness prolong the abuse. Trapped in this cycle, women face incredible challenges coping with the disruptions that violence causes in their lives.

Addictions.   Drug and alcohol addiction figure predominately in the stories of these mothers. Eighteen of the 30 mothers spoke about the impacts of addictions on their lives. Some were born into families where there was chronic substance abuse by one or both parents; others developed their own addictions in adolescence or young adulthood or became involved in intimate relationships with men addicted to drugs, alcohol, or both.

Eight of the mothers shared stories about their childhood experiences with addicted parents. One spoke about growing up in a home where both parents were alcoholics:

> I remember she [referring to her mother] came in my room when I was in grade seven, I think. We were at the cottage and her and my dad were drinking and had a fight. She comes in my room and beats the hell out of me because it's all my fault they got married. You know, it was just bizarre behaviour. Like he pissed in her face. It was just bizarre growing up there ... All my friends and just ones that knew me, they all knew it. Our house was the one where there was yelling, fighting and they give booze to anybody.

Six of the mothers spoke about a personal struggle with drugs or alcohol. Of the six, four spoke of abusing alcohol, one of drug addiction, and one of addiction to both drugs and alcohol. Twelve women became involved in relationships with men with addiction problems. One woman said:

> I was in a common law relationship for ten years ... the relationship was not a good relationship. I have an older daughter that was before that relationship. My youngest daughter is from that bad relationship. I'm normally a strong person. I know I can handle a lot of things. I know I'm a very patient person. I needed to end that relationship with my youngest daughter's father. It was dramatic. It wasn't having a good effect on myself or my children. He was an abusive man. He was a dope smoker. He was into drinking a lot.

Problems with emotional health.   Barriers to secure employment caused these women to experience feelings of stress and depression. This mother spoke of the emotional effects of unemployment:

> My unemployment ran out and I started getting depressed because I wasn't working and I couldn't go out and buy this for [son]. It seemed every job I got, they closed the place down and moved. To this day if I put an application in somewhere, all the places I used to work are not here

no more. So which is not a benefit. But nobody wants to work and have a job as bad as I do.

Abuse in childhood with trauma in adulthood can be the catalyst for depression:

> Well, because July 15th, '94 rolls around, it's hard. That's when he [husband] got murdered. It's just hard when that date rolls around. I feel depressed. So, I try to keep myself busy that day. I try not to think of it. It's hard.

Violence by a partner frequently leads to feelings of depression. One mother vividly described the impact of abuse:

> We weren't quite together for a year and I got pregnant. And when I was six months pregnant I was ready to leave him because he had beat me. And after being away from him for a week he sucked up to me big time and told me that "I will not hit you again" and "I apologize for what I did" ... I dragged it out for another eight and a half years after that ... I was miserable ... I was stressed out. I was looking very old. I was not healthy. I couldn't function. I was sick all the time. I wasn't taking care of myself. I didn't have energy. I just was continually miserable. I was depressed, big time depressed. As soon as I got rid of him though, that changed. I had lots of energy and everything else.

When abusive partners accuse mothers of inadequate parenting, feelings of betrayal deepen, as do feelings of injustice if professionals fail to comprehend their realities.

Mothers who contend daily with a child with behavioural difficulties often experience depression. Exhaustion sets in if the behaviours continue to escalate:

> I guess I sort of had a bit of a mental breakdown ... and just, ended up just totally and emotionally a wreck. And it had been a situation when I had asked (daughter) to watch her brother for me ... I was angry. The kids were fighting. And I was so angry. I thought, oh, I've got the leave the house because if I don't, I'm going to lose it. I don't know why she [daughter] did this, but, she had been trying to scare her brother, and he was younger. And, at one point, she had threatened him with a knife. She said, "I'm going to cut your fingers off." And he locked himself in the bathroom. And, he was screaming ... He was terrified, and he ended up running to the neighbours, and this was ... well, it happened in wintertime, because he had nothing on his feet ... Every time I would turn around, she was getting on my case. She was fighting with me. She was lashing out at me. And, it probably got scary for both of us cause I was at the point where I couldn't take it anymore. I was like, something's got to be done here.

In these stories, mothers parenting children with behavioural problems often talked about being exhausted and feeling powerlessness.

In addition, some of these mothers had organic psychological difficulties. This mother began her story by describing her struggle with postpartum depression and schizophrenia:

> I was diagnosed with postpartum depression in 1993 with my first child. Nobody, my family didn't know about it, like they didn't know about the illness I had so they took me to the hospital ... When they first found out I had it, they were all upset ... I always have to be on medication for life, forever. I was hearing voices, I thought, like my mom gave the medicine to my baby and I thought it was going to kill her. I was so scared. I thought she was going to kill the baby. I was having thoughts that were not true. I heard voices. I thought people were talking to me on the TV. I don't want to go out, I don't want anything to do. I just want to be in the house because I'm afraid. And I look around and I feel strange.

Overcoming Adversity

Child welfare literature portrays mothers as mired in helplessness, with minimal prospects for change (Fernandez, 1996; Maluccio, 1981); however, this research encountered mothers who actively manage hardships. Mothers make choices about managing their problems congruent with their daily living realities. In these stories, mothers relied on four broad coping strategies to overcome adversity.

Wanting a different road. The women in this research found an inner resolve to stand against the influences of addiction, violence, and psychological difficulties in their lives, and this resolve marked the beginning of the process of change. Painful memories inspired mothers to create circumstances different from those of their childhood. This desire for a "different road" is a persistent theme in these stories. A mother who had developed a very serious drug habit spoke to her own inspiration for wanting a different road. She showed the interviewer photographs and said:

> I look at all these pictures. This is my mom. This is my grandmother. These are the two people I've hurt the most, not to mention my children, my son Doug, my daughter, Alisha, my daughter Stacey, and Ashley. It's like a little shrine. And I just look at all these things, you know? And look at me, look how horrid I look. I was on drugs ... And I just deserve so much more. So, this is what's stopped me from getting high. [The names have been changed.]

The most common source of inspiration for changing their lives was becoming a mother. Mothers felt responsible for providing their children with a different life. A woman who was gang-raped described her strong bond with her daughter:

> I lived and breathed for her. I still do ... there's a reason I'm still here. There's a reason those guys didn't kill me in that alley. There's a reason for everything. I looked at her [daughter] and said you know what? We're going somewhere.

Another woman speaks of her determination to make a better life for her children:

> My son asked me about three months ago what my childhood was like and I had to leave the room. I went to the bathroom and started to cry, because I couldn't think of anything good to say to him. And I thought, this is not going to be coming out his mouth. He's not going to stop when someone asks him that. He's going to be proud.

Forming a positive relationship. These women know that wanting a "different road" is only a beginning in the process of change. They require external supports, and finding someone who loves them is highly valued. Meeting someone who offers love is rare and almost unexpected. One mother was asked why the relationship with her new boyfriend was different and was surprised by the question. She responded: "He loves me. He truly, genuinely loves me for me, for who I am. So, he loves my strengths. He admires me. How can I not love him?"

Many mothers believed that friends and family cannot provide necessary support. In these situations they spoke of the extremely important role of counsellors:

> Strangers were more helpful than family ... when I go to my counsellor, we talk, and, I feel good, feel like someone's trying to, give me some advice and stuff. ... [The counsellor is] helpful, like, he tells me to open up and talk to people, and ... then they can understand how you're feeling and stuff ... Cause he said if you don't open up, then nobody knows what you're feeling or thinking, or what you're going through.

With supportive relationships, mothers begin to rebuild trust and develop skills vital for positive relationships.

Changing surroundings. Mothers with addiction problems or those experiencing the ill effects of addictive and violent behaviour of partners, often wanted to change their surroundings. Women with limited financial resources were often forced to move from one situation to another, sometimes without hope for positive change. In their world, changing environments is key to overcoming adversity. A mother, whose addiction to drugs led to a life on the streets, spoke of her new, drug-free lifestyle and her previous life:

"People that have seen me downtown, they do not recognize me. Like, I walk up to certain ones ... you still tend to still keep an eye out looking for them. You know, checking to see if they're okay." Another woman changed her immediate surroundings to manage her psychological depression:

> Every day is a new beginning for me. I don't dwell on something. So at night when I start letting my mind wander and I start wondering why the world is the way it is, why I got brought up the way I did, I pick up a pen and paper, I write down the negatives and positives of everything. And then I'll think of a project, something that's been neglected by someone else, and how am I going to make that beautiful, and that's my memory of how come I don't feel depressed a lot, because I have all these things to put time into to make it look beautiful. And I can look at certain things in my house right now and know how I was feeling before I started it and I usually get up from the table, walk around the apartment, kiss both my children, and sit back down and think how wonderful life is.

When women are involved with violent men, a change of environments often happens in response to a crisis. Women spoke of leaving abruptly, despite having known for some time that they needed to end the relationship. This mother knew that she must leave, but her limited resources presented a major barrier:

> eventually, after the marriage, within weeks, like maybe two weeks, we came back to [this geographical area] and that's when I knew ... [that] I had to get out. I had to get away from this man. And the only source of income I had was baby bonus ... I ran.

The absence of opportunity to escape the ill effects of violence or addiction should not be confused with unwillingness.

Acknowledging triumphs. Mothers' symbols of triumph were congruent with their daily living realities and appear as announcements in their stories. One prefaced her narrative with:

> I'm a recovering drug addict. That's one of the best things ... Drugs aren't the only thing on my mind. It's not the first thing I think about ... You know, I can wake up and go gee, what am I going to do today? Before it was oh, gee, where am I going to get the next hit, you know. That's what's nice. It's nice having money in your pocket when you go out.

These women saw triumphs in their relationships with children, family, and friends. Their understanding of their ability to build more supportive and loving relationships is an important acknowledgment of hurdles already crossed:

> I've got a much better relationship with my children. They're more open with me ... well, my oldest [daughter], she'll be 12 next month, she's very

comfortable in talking to me about anything and I love it. I really do. Like it's not just a mother-daughter thing, it's a friend thing ... It's really nice and it's something I've always wanted ... she realizes that, you know, her mom's not this messed up person anymore

Like, me and [husband] didn't communicate very well. Like, he'd do all the talking, pretty much, and if I gave my opinion, I was being a bitch, you know? It's like, my opinion didn't matter, but, it does. We're learning it, slowly but surely ... I'm going to continue my counselling, hopefully, you know, get over my problems, and my drinking and stuff like that. But um, my overall goal, is for us to be a family again. But a better one than before. And we're not going to quit until we do.

My family totally gave up on me. They kicked me out when I was 12 but now I'm just starting to get back in with my mom. Like I'm starting to get back into like a good relationship with her. Starting, like it's getting better, but I think it's too because she knows that I'm not on drugs anymore, she knows I've cleaned up.

Descriptions of renewed improved relationships were persistently cited by mothers as evidence of their triumph over adversity.

Some mothers marvelled at their own ability to accomplish what had seemed impossible. This mother speaks of her courage to give birth to children and her subsequent ability to parent:

I never thought that I could be a parent. I didn't have a very good upbringing with my mother, so I thought I was kind of hesitant to have children. I thought, well, it's a big responsibility, you know, I didn't think I could handle it. But as the time went on ... it just fell into place.

Parenting symbolizes her triumph over childhood abuse.

More privileged mothers and helping professionals might take some of these triumphs for granted:

I've been off drugs maybe a year and a half. It's been about a year in a half, almost two years since I've been in jail. I've held down jobs, real jobs, real paying jobs ... The clothes on my back, I bought. I did not steal them. You know? Even this cigarette [that] I am smoking, I paid for it. I did not bum it, and I did not go and steal it.

Implications for interventions. Despite many barriers, non-privileged mothers do overcome hurdles, such as violence, addiction, and depression. Their strategies for overcoming are consistent with the opportunities available within their daily living contexts. Child welfare interventions should build upon the resourcefulness and resolve of these mothers and increase their access to relevant resources to mitigate barriers.

The daily living contexts of mothers are discounted when child welfare authorities view mothers as powerless yet responsible for failing to protect their children. Their strengths and resilience in overcoming adversity remain unacknowledged. Dorothy Roberts (1999) writes that:

> Blaming mothers for harm to their children regardless of the social context ... allows the state to focus its attention on regulating mothers rather than transforming the social order. And it cuts off support for alternative visions of mothers' relationships with their children. (p. 47)

Child welfare service providers should consider that when mothers want "a different road," they are striving to change their lives. Their motivation for change is grounded, not in court orders, but in their desire for improved relationships and particularly by their desire for improved lives for their children. A beginning for meaningful help is collaborating with mothers in discovering and following their "different road."

For child welfare service providers to be more helpful, it would be useful if they understood mothers' changing surroundings as evidence of a desire to challenge adversity, rather than as instability. This understanding could create new possibilities for positive engagements with mothers when helping to manage adversities.

The mothers in our research who were facing adversities valued respectful and encouraging helping relationships. They spoke appreciatively of counselling in which they felt heard and understood. However, in their stories, appreciated counsellors tended not to be from child welfare but from other social service settings. Child welfare must cultivate more co-operative relationships with mothers based on an understanding of daily living realities and an appreciation of how they strive to overcome adversities.

In this study, 56% of the mothers whose children were apprehended had already seen them return home, while another 25% anticipated an imminent return. Only 13% were no longer hopeful about the return of their children. Given that a large majority of apprehended children return to their mother's care, it is critical that mothers and their families are assisted to overcome adversities. When child protection does not provide relevant assistance, it becomes another obstacle for mothers to overcome. Interventions that are not congruent with the adversities facing mothers and families increase the stress on already burdened mothers.

Mothers' Experience of Child Placement

Before I had put (my stepdaughter) in foster care, I really believed in our children's social system. I no longer do. I think it's a system that needs to be looked at hard. I think it's a system that needs to set up and be what they say they are—in the best interest of the children.

Mothers who have experienced out-of-home placement have intense feelings about this event. Depending on the crisis that prompted the involvement of child protection, mothers may be either emotionally devastated or relieved. The placement of their children dominated the mothers' narratives about their child welfare involvement. Children entered substitute care because they were apprehended, because mothers wanted help and specifically requested placement, or because mothers wanted help and accepted placement as the only option.

When children are apprehended, mothers do not have a choice about the placement. Apprehensions are preceded by difficulties in the family; however, mothers frequently do not connect these difficulties with the risks of child maltreatment identified by child welfare authorities. They are confused by the apprehension and feel accused of being "bad" mothers. Imposed conditions focus on changing the mother's behaviour and these mothers are typically highly resistant to child welfare involvement. The stories of 18 mothers in this research study are consistent with this pattern of placement experience.

Mothers requesting placement because they have difficulty coping with the behaviour of a child represent a second pattern. These mothers often have older children with challenging behaviours and have exhausted other community social service programs. When child welfare concurs with the need for placement, these mothers feel relieved. They understand themselves as "good" mothers who coped as well as could be expected. The stories of six mothers are consistent with this pattern.

Mothers in the third placement pattern acknowledge that they need help, and they consent to the placement; however, their consent is given reluctantly because of a perceived absence of alternatives. Many have exhausted community social service programs. Mothers who consent reluctantly to placement often resist certain aspects of the placement process, feeling tremendous concern that their child will be "warehoused" by the system. The stories of seven mothers are consistent with this pattern.

Escalating difficulties

Regardless of the pattern of placement experienced, mothers spoke of the escalating difficulties that brought child welfare into their lives. When apprehension was the result, they focused predominantly on difficulties that impacted negatively on mothers' capacities to parent. When voluntary placement was the result, the dominant focus was on the unmanageable behaviour of the child.

Life hurdles intertwine in the following mother's description of the crisis that precipitated the apprehension of her children:

I had a lot of stress on me, like, thinking of my childhood and trying to deal with my future … He [partner] drank a lot, and done a lot of drugs. On the end of it, he started doing crack, and selling the kids' toys for crack … It was frustrating, like, he used to smash beer bottles over my head, and [it was a] hard life … And, I just … was stressed out a lot, and that's probably what made me have a breakdown … Like, I was seeing my kids on TV, and they weren't really there.

Sometimes the precipitating problems clearly relate to the conditions of non-privilege. This mother described unsupportive relationships and investigations prompted by malicious reporting:

I'd have someone living with me that got mad at me, and they'd call—that sort of stuff—you know, revenge. But they [child welfare] would come, and they would talk to me, and then they'd close the case. So it wasn't really anything.

Eventually her children were apprehended because of an anonymous report:

Even now I still don't know why they pulled the kids but, you know … the last phone call, I don't know who it was, but someone called and said that my house was an appalling state due to dogs and dirt. So, that was why they came.

The most frequent frustration of mothers who asked for help was that they were unable to get child welfare to respond to their request. Notice this mother's frustration after soliciting help:

They didn't help me is what I'm trying to say. I was crying out to them. I was saying, "I've got a drug problem, help me" … but they weren't even giving me no research, nothing, to get help for my drug problem. Nothing … I didn't understand. I was like okay, I guess nobody's going to help me here. So, I got myself a live-in babysitter so I could keep my stripping, keep doing my dancing. She was collecting welfare. So, I was getting money from her, I was getting money from dancing, and I was getting my baby bonus money.

Refused help, she reverted to familiar coping strategies. Her addiction spiralled out of control and eventually her children were apprehended. Another woman spoke of her concerns about her child's behaviour and the challenge of getting child welfare to respond:

I was afraid of him, of my own child. I don't think I honestly believed that he would really do something to hurt me, but I couldn't trust him with his baby sister. I didn't … know why he was doing these things. When I got on the phone to the children's aid, I was extremely mad because they said they can't do anything for me. They said unfortunately, he's the one that's abusing and not you, so we can't do anything.

This woman reframed her understanding of an assault on her by her boyfriend as a "blessing," because it captured the attention of child welfare:

And this is exactly what I told the courts, it is a blessing in a sense what happened with [boyfriend, in reference to his assault on her].Because I can guarantee in my life sitting here now that if that didn't go down ... I would be in the same boat I was in.

Investigation

The investigative process is usually frightening. Many mothers know about child welfare's reputation for apprehending children. As soon as the child welfare worker arrived at the hospital, one mother was alarmed and unprepared. She thought, "oh my gawd, they're going to take my kid." Another mother spoke of her first exposure to child welfare:

They're like "can we sit down?" I'm like "fine." And I get in hysterics. I should have stayed calm, but I couldn't. They kinda just sat down and start throwing questions at you. You have no chance to just know what they're saying, cause they sound like chipmunks ... Everything's in fast. So, I was like, what are you talking about? ... Like the first minute they walk in that door, you can't breathe. You don't even know what to do. And then before you know it, your whole life's gone.

Given this intense climate of fear, the differences between the daily living contexts of these mothers and those of the investigating social workers, and the requirement that investigations be completed within prescribed time frames, communication breakdowns are likely:

They came across and said, did you take [son] to the doctor's. And I'm like, "no, I thought they were bruises and you don't usually take a baby to the doctor's for bruises. If he bumped his knee, are you going to tell me I've got to take him to the doctor's because he's got a bruise on one knee." And they misplaced that saying that I did take him to the doctor's, and the doctor told me it was bruises ... I told them straight out, that I never took him to the doctor's because I thought it was bruising myself.

Discrepancies between what mothers mean and how workers interpret their statements can carry over into written legal materials. When a child welfare worker demanded that a physician see this child immediately, the mother prepared a bottle for the baby in the presence of the investigating workers:

I didn't think that we had time for the full sterilization thing and so I just used pure hot water underneath the tap and there was soap in there and cleaned it all out ... They said, "is that how you always do it?" And

I'm like "no, usually I sterilize it." … In the documents, they said that I said that's how I always do it. That's not what I said.

The differences between daily living contexts of the child welfare workers and these mothers is reflected in their language:

I feel I'm not using proper wording when I talk to them. I feel like I'm not being heard … I don't know these big words. And that's the only way they'd understand me. Like if I start swearing and cursing well, then they just think I've got no education. Well, I don't want them to think that, right?

A lack of time is one of the barriers to sorting through communication breakdown and language differences. Decisions about apprehension happen quickly and often result from the first contact with a mother.

As mothers become aware that their explanations are not understood, or are not believed, desperation sets in. One woman related this experience:

You come in here in my home telling me that I'm this and this. And she goes, "are you not on anti-depressants?" And I said, "ya, but I'm not taking them." She goes, "why?" I said, "cause I don't need them." She said, "why?" I said, "cause I didn't say that I was depressed, he [partner who called child welfare] said it." And he looks at me and kinda grinned. I'm like "you asshole." She's like, "well, we have to take [daughter]." I said, "like hell you do" … She said, "do you know of anybody that can come here because we don't know if you're gonna kill yourself." And they wouldn't let me call my dad or nobody so I could have somebody there and have her there … And they still looked at me like, and then they said do you slit your wrists? Well I said, "look at my wrists." I showed them my wrists … And they looked at them and she said, "oh there's nothing there." And he said "well she cuts it through her sweaters." I'm like, "you wanna see all my sweaters in my closet?" She's like, "no, we believe him."

Realizing that she was powerless to convince the worker that she was not suicidal, she resorted to a response congruent with her experience:

So by then I was really mad; I was crying; I couldn't even breathe … started getting mean. I called her every word in the book cause she kept saying, "you slice your arms; you try to kill yourself, don't you?" … I said he's an alcoholic who doesn't know what he's talking about and I'm getting labelled … And I said, "can I have my daughter back please?" She said, "no." I said, "how long?" She goes, "I don't know."

Amidst the fear and desperation that result from an investigation, it is unlikely that mothers will be able to make convincing explanations and negotiate an acceptable plan of care for the child. Many times mothers are unclear about why apprehension decisions are made. This confusion speaks to the disparities between child welfare culture and the daily living realities of mothers. For instance, one mother, whose child had injuries on his hand was not alarmed until she discovered that the injuries were bruises rather than the blisters that were familiar from her childhood experience of discipline. From a privileged perspective, getting drunk, or waiting until the morning to view the bruises, or being less concerned about blisters, appears irresponsible. But this mother does not think in those ways. And when the apprehension occurred, she did not understand:

> And I kept telling them, listen, I didn't do anything wrong, why are you taking the baby away from me, why are you doing this, why do you have to do that? And they're like because we don't know which one abused the baby. I'm like I've got witnesses upon witnesses upon witnesses upon witnesses that could say where I was, when I was, and when that baby got hurt. And they're like oh, well that doesn't matter to us. It was one of you guys and that's all we can say. Until we know what happened, you're not getting your baby back.

Although it was commonplace for mothers to be unclear about which child protection concerns prompted the apprehension, no mother denied the existence of problems. These women understand their problems from within their own daily living contexts. They do not necessarily make connections between their problems and child welfare perceptions that their children are at risk. During investigations, child welfare workers and mothers are typically unable to agree about the nature of the problems. In situations where mothers desire placement, the investigative processes are more positive and there tends to agreement about the nature of the concerns. In situations of apprehension, mothers feel accused and powerless; whereas in situations of voluntary placement, mothers more often feel validated.

Ongoing Involvement

In this study, child welfare service providers developed similar plans of service in each situation of apprehension. Regular and often supervised visits with the child were stipulated. Mothers were required to attend a parenting course and, when applicable, a nutrition course for babies. Counselling and random drug testing were required when addiction issues were identified. When violence was involved, both the mother and her partner were required to attend anger-management counselling. In some stories, mothers were obliged to leave violent relationships and to enter individual counselling in order to improve their self-esteem.

Although the child welfare service plans are oriented toward long-term risk reduction, mothers of apprehended children are focused on the short-term return of their child. When mothers participate solely to secure the return of their child, their commitment to embracing the proposed strategies for long-term change is questionable. For them, the terms of the service plan are often not congruent with their lives. Conversely, in situations of voluntary placement and reluctant placement, the barriers to mothers engaging fully in the service plan are not as pronounced. Because these mothers acknowledge problems and want help, the terms of the service plan are more likely to make sense in terms of their life experiences.

Mothers respond to situations of apprehension with intense and negative feelings, including grief, fear, and shame. One mother spoke of her grief: "it was hard; I cried every night"; while another mother said, "everything we've planned has been taken away from us." Feelings of grief and loss were expressed in all stories, even when mothers agreed with the placement. Such feelings, however, were pervasive in the apprehension stories. The mother whose child was apprehended because of the bruising on his hands said:

> I almost died giving birth to this baby. I'm like, "and then you're going to go and rip him out of my arms?" I didn't get to say bye to him, and I didn't get to see him for like a whole week ... And I felt like why would somebody do this to you? Like why would God let that happen to you after all I've been through. Why would he take my baby away from me too? Why would he do that? He knows I wouldn't do it. Like I just kept blaming, like it had to have been God, he had to have been the one.

Mothers also struggle to understand themselves in relation to having their child placed. They feel shame and fear the label of "bad mothers." One mother said "at first it was really tough ... I felt like the worst mother on the earth." Another comments, "for me, it was hard. It was very emotional ... I felt like ... I wasn't really doing my job as a mother."

Women whose children are apprehended seldom understand or agree with the protection concerns identified by child welfare. Nonetheless, they may comply with agency's terms when they see them as relevant. A mother who initially sought assistance with her drug addiction was co-operative with the addictions counselling component of her plan of service, but resisted participation in counselling she considered non-relevant:

> They made me take like parenting courses and stuff like ... I took grade 12 parenting and yeah, I get to take home like the electronic baby, which has a computer. And like I got an A on the project ... so what do I need to go to baby class for? And they're like "oh, well we need you to, you know, learn a little bit more." So, I took a baby class and took a baby course and other stuff, how to discipline your child properly. And then they wanted us to go into counselling. They told [boyfriend] he needs to go into anger management counselling. So, I'm like, "okay, that's cool." They told me I need to go into relationship counselling ... They just said,

"you know, there's some things that you've got to learn to deal with" ...
And they're like, "you need to go build your self-esteem." And I'm like,
"I already have enough self-esteem. I'm so aware of myself it's unbelievable." Like I tell all my friends I'm the damn best looking thing you ever
seen in your entire life ... I know there's some odds and ends to me that
could be fixed up and stuff, but I'm okay.

Mothers whose children are apprehended have little power in relation
to child welfare professionals. Regardless of their protests and counter-pro-
posals, mothers feel that they are left with little choice but to comply. As
one mother said, "I didn't have no choice in anything ... I had no say in anything ... we're trying to explain to her ... she just won't understand it ... she
just seems to make it worse ... by throwing more accusations in there." Most
often, "participation" amounts to the mother being informed of a list of
court-ordered conditions with which she must comply. Legal processes reinforce this helplessness:

It was like, I had no chance, or no choice, or no say, or nothing which I
don't think is right ... I wished I could have got up in the court and said
what I felt. But, it was like, nobody gave me a chance to do it. Like, the
C.A.S. worker was up there, talking in the courtroom, and he was just
going on and on and on and on and on, and all these lies and stuff. Like
making it out like we're these bad people, you know. I wasn't able to get
up and say what I wanted.

Another barrier to mothers engaging willingly in a service plan is the
strained working relationships between mothers and certain workers. When
children are apprehended, mothers frequently criticize workers for being
"cold," "unfeeling," and "rude." In addition, workers are perceived as demanding and controlling. One mother said, "they're more or less trying to run
your life, telling you how to do stuff."

After an apprehension, mothers separate their emotional reaction to the
apprehension from feelings about the individual service providers. The primary criterion used to evaluate workers is the mothers' perception of the
amount of support received. Even though a very distressing apprehension
was the result of the investigation, this mother appreciated the apprehending worker:

She was very understanding; this was the intake worker. She was more
on our side as well. She couldn't understand what the teacher was saying. Why was the teacher coming up with these things? Why wasn't this
stuff confronted with us [child welfare]. But the only thing she had to be
bound on was the sexual abuse. So that's what they had to go on that
one. Then she kept telling me about her son; she had trouble with her son
and this and that. So she was more or less on both sides. She'd take the

agency's side for the sexual bit and our side for the other bit. She was very understanding.

The sense that service providers are "on your side" is important for mothers. In the midst of adversity, the feeling that someone cares is valued.

Regardless of the obstacles that prevent mothers of apprehended children from engaging fully in service plans, some reported beneficial involvements. One mother said of her experience with an addiction seminar:

I found that pretty interesting. I didn't know a lot of stuff, like, to do with alcohol and stuff, and what it does to your body, and it was helpful ... I enjoyed the group. It was a three-hour group. It was only the one time.

Another mother, who was highly resistant to child welfare involvement, described how the counselling helped her to manage her anger and stop hitting her children:

She said where do you feel your body changes and this and that. At this point, I feel my body shaking. She said well that's your boiling point. That's when you gotta come up, and back down. So it's more or less a learning thing for myself as well ... Hitting our kids, that's automatically stopped. Don't do that anymore.

Although some mothers experienced positive outcomes, the number of mothers who linked child welfare interventions with positive changes in their lives was minimal. This raises questions about the effectiveness of coercive processes of apprehension in reducing long-term risk in families. Investigations lead immediately to coercion when mothers resist. Might these women, if approached with offers of assistance, and if differences of opinion provoked efforts at mediation and negotiation, co-operate more actively with helping efforts? Certainly, when placement is voluntary, the obstacles to collaboration are much less pronounced.

Resolution

In this study, mothers perceived few satisfactory resolutions of the experience of having their children in foster care. In situations of apprehension, mothers were critical of workers who did not visit once children were returned to their care. They were confused and angered by this abrupt withdrawal of services. One mother said, "they disturbed my life. They gave her [daughter] back, and if I was so bad then they just dropped it like that." The mother whose daughter was apprehended because of concerns about her slicing her arms and attempting suicide said this:

So I got a new worker. It was okay, I guess ... they're so worried about you and what you do, and they put a supervision order on you. And for that whole six months they only checked on me once. What if I was suicidal? What if I was gonna kill somebody? They don't even bother you. What's the whole point of that order, if they're not gonna check on you. That's the part I didn't understand.

Some mothers also talked about the negative consequences for their children of being in care:

She goes through, I guess it's anxiety, or feels like I'm gonna leave again. That's why she cries when she goes with her dad. She doesn't think I'm gonna come back anymore ... I'm gonna tell her the truth when she's old enough. I'm gonna tell her what happened.... Even if I go to the store without her, she gets mad and upset.... You can't explain to a two and a half year old, three year old, that you know, what happened ... I'll never like Children's Aid for doing this, the way they did it. They didn't listen and now I have my daughter, I have to deal with every day to get her to understand.

Another woman spoke of the negative impact of foster care on her daughter's development:

Lots of delays, lots of regression. [My daughter] went back to talking baby talk. It seemed like she was gonna walk a year ago, she's not walking yet. She's just starting to get to the point where she starts to take a few steps. A lot of things that she was doing a year ago, she can't do.

Many mothers talked about feeling insecure in their ability to discipline their children after they returned home:

We're more afraid ... I'm afraid because they're going to turn around and say I want to go back to [foster parents]'s kind of thing. Because I don't know if they even discipline them over there. We're disciplining them, but not harshly. It's tough right now.

Another mother described herself as "paranoid" that police cars will arrive to remove her daughter again. There is little ongoing support to mothers or children after care in these stories. They are left to cope as well as they can.

In situations of voluntary placement, some mothers talked about placement having a positive effect on the family. One described building a positive relationship with her daughter who eventually returned to her care. Where child behaviour is a primary concern, mothers felt validated when their parenting challenges were acknowledged. They were relieved to have a break from the stresses associated with daily parenting and to share the burden of these strains with other caregivers. For these mothers, these were positive outcomes.

The Challenge of Congruence

Child welfare priorities and the lives of many of these mothers are not congruent. These women struggle with issues of non-privilege and create strategies for dealing with adversity that make sense in their worlds. Child welfare policy and procedures impede service providers from responding to the pervasiveness of disadvantage in mothers' lives and the strength and persistence shown by many mothers. They prevent workers from responding in ways that are credible in light of the lives of these women and their families.

In the past decade, child protection services have been repeatedly scrutinized in public because of concerns about child deaths. In Ontario, the standardization of child welfare practices has been the political response to public criticism that children have suffered fatal maltreatment because of the negligence of the child welfare system. The concern about negligence reached a climax when a Toronto-area child welfare worker was criminally charged in the 1997 death of an infant. Even though the charges were withdrawn in 1999, the climate in which child welfare is practised has been profoundly altered. Regehr, Bernstein and Kanani (2002) write, "in this social climate, child welfare workers feel under siege and perceive themselves to be at high risk of criminal prosecution and civil liability" (p. 38). In this climate, workers must protect themselves.

A key component of self-protection is service providers' careful adherence to formal procedures and timelines. Service providers report that the experience of having a colleague arrested and charged has made them more suspicious of parents and more skeptical of parents' explanations (Freymond, 2003). With decreased discretion, the likelihood that service providers can adapt effectively to the lives of these mothers and families diminishes.

Persistent communication problems between mothers and workers are the norm in these stories. Mothers often felt that workers did not listen, and they did not understand what was going on in the families' lives. The potential for developing helpful service alliances in this climate of misunderstanding and mistrust is compromised, and there is little opportunity for negotiated, mutually agreeable solutions. Mothers must comply with child welfare stipulations and often do so by "playing the game." Another consequence is that many mothers view the imposed plan of service as largely irrelevant to their lives. Compliance becomes a vehicle for securing the return of their children, rather than an opportunity for meaningful change.

Whittaker and Maluccio (2002), in their reflective essay on child placement, describe child welfare as "preoccupied" with the physical location of the child to the point that it "directs attention away from the twin goals of promoting healthy child development in a safe, nurturing context and enhancing the adequacy of family functioning" (p. 108). Alternative and perhaps more acceptable and effective helping strategies are not recognized.

A regrettable consequence of the lack of congruence between child welfare interventions and mothers' lives is the added burden placed on already overwhelmed mothers. Mothers often talk of child welfare as another hurdle to get over. Some women acknowledged that child welfare involvement motivated them to seek assistance and to change some aspects of their lives. But the questions remain, at what cost are such gains made, and would higher levels of active co-operation result in more impressive benefits for children and families?

Fortunately, in situations of voluntary placement, service providers and mothers were more likely to agree about family circumstances and what should be done. In these stories, mothers often welcomed future child welfare involvements. For example, a mother who talked about very positive relationships with child welfare service providers sought continual reassurance during the research interview that her anonymity would be protected. Her fear was that service providers might not respond as positively in the future if they knew what she was saying. The availability of voluntary placement and service provider support are important resources for this mother.

Even in situations of voluntary placement, however, mothers are aware that the problems of their child intensify long before placement occurs. Child welfare cannot intervene until their eligibility criteria for "risk of harm" to a child are satisfied. Many mothers are unaware that child welfare focuses on their parenting inabilities, rather than on their child's negative behaviours. By the time child welfare responds to repeated requests for help, the child's behaviours often have seriously escalated.

Toward Positive Child and Family Welfare

How mothers talk about their lives has implications for child protection in Ontario. Most salient is the limited level of assistance forthcoming to most families and the modest benefits for children, parents, and families from these efforts. Some argue that the existing child protection paradigm does a reasonable job of what many consider its core function: the detection of and intervention into the dangerous living circumstances of the most vulnerable children (Parton, Thorpe, & Wattam, 1997). Nonetheless, the price of this single-minded focus is that too many parents resent and fear an unwanted and unhelpful intrusion into their lives.

Ontario's child protection system in general, and child placement in particular, continues to involve poorer and less privileged segments of our population. Lack of access to adequate resources and opportunities for enhancing child, parent, and family well-being, high vulnerability to disruption in existing supports, and high levels of daily living stress are commonplace in these families. In addition, many mothers confront tremendous personal challenges in their childhood and adult lives. Many experience painful disruptions in their relationships with partners and in family functioning.

Nonetheless, these mothers, including a large majority of mothers with a child in care, remain very important in their children's lives, often providing their only source of continuity and belonging. These women's stories illustrate persistence and the overcoming of obstacles as well as continued commitment to their children and the desire for stable homes and families. There is a continuity and strength of family in these women's stories. New partnerships form, and families of origin provide assistance and social connections for some women (Cameron & Hoy, 2003). Most relevant, these are the families in which almost all of the children in these stories continue to live. The core challenge for child and family welfare remains connecting with the shared daily living realities of these children and their parents in ways that they find acceptable and congruent with their lives.

Although an extended discussion of promising possibilities for child and family welfare system design is beyond the scope of this chapter,[4] there are some general strategies that emanate directly from these stories. It is essential that we increase the level and diversity of helping options available to families and service providers, allowing for greater collaboration. This implies moving away from a stand-alone model of child protection toward sharing a child protection mandate across service and community organizations. This model benefits from greater partnerships among formal services and informal family and neighbourhood networks in promoting child and family welfare.

A corollary requirement is an acceptance of the principle of shared parenting. Holding stressed and distressed mothers responsible for remedying troublesome family circumstances is an insufficient and inappropriate response. This paradigm includes broader groupings of service providers and family and community members as partners in caring for children. In addition, an easily accessible but substantially unexploited avenue in protecting children from harm and promoting their well-being is the development of children's direct supports.[5]

This paradigm accommodates the substantial strength and resilience evident in these women's and families' stories. It includes the development of "empowerment spaces," creating opportunities for mutual aid, social connections and friendships, and communal co-operation. It complements professional helping with mutual reliance among families, neighbours, and others confronting similar life challenges. In addition, it values compassion and creativity in facilitating healing and personal growth for the mothers in these stories.

Such a paradigm requires the priority expansion of intermediary space between voluntary agreement and coercive legal action (Hetherington, Cooper, Smith, & Wilford, 1997). When agreement is not forthcoming between service providers and parents about family concerns or what needs to be done, the first recourse would be to access formal or informal mediation services to attempt to secure a mutually agreeable service plan. Formal court applications, except in emergencies, would be a last resort. In addition, an expanded range of "family-friendly" placement options such as homes for mothers and children together and respite care would reduce the prevalence of coercive apprehensions and enhance the likelihood of co-operative helping alliances.[6] Greater co-operation between foster parents and mothers would be encouraged, assisting mothers to feel supported and to maintain connections with their children. This would shift attention away from mothers' deficits toward what is best for their children's development.

These suggested changes represent basic shifts in principle and practice from existing arrangements, arrangements that have proved resistant to modifications to core procedures for many years. Nonetheless, niches for innovation in Ontario's child protection system exist, and changes can happen over time. There is no contradiction between protecting children and promoting their welfare within families and communities. It is within our grasp to envision a more balanced and inclusive child and family welfare system, including a more constructive array of child placement options.

Notes

1 The term apprehension is applied to situations where child protection becomes involved with a family and the children are placed in foster care against the wishes of the parent. Apprehensions happen when the investigating worker determines that there is sufficient evidence to demonstrate that the child is "at risk of harm" while in the care of the parents.

2 Note that the term voluntary is sometimes used in a legal sense to suggest that mothers and the child welfare authority have reached an agreement on the terms of the placement. However, there may be considerable state coercion involved in the voluntary placement of a child, and therefore distinctions between voluntary placement and coercive placements can be illusory (Mnookin, 1973). In this study, the term voluntary is not used in the legal sense. Voluntary implies that mothers requested the placement, agreed to the placement when it was proposed, or agreed because they felt there were no other, or better, alternatives.

3 Ten women who provided interviews did not speak about the circumstances of their childhoods.

4 For a discussion of some of these possibilities readers are referred to Cameron, Freymond, Cornfield, & Palmer, 2001 and Cameron & Freymond, 2003.

5 See the discussions in Nelson, Laurendeau, Chamberland, & Peirson, 2001 and Cameron, O'Reilly, Laurendeau, & Chamberland, 2001.

6 See Freymond (2003) for an expanded discussion of these options.

References

Callahan, M. (1993). Feminist approaches: Women recreate child welfare. In B. Wharf (Ed.), *Rethinking child welfare in Canada* (pp. 172–209). Toronto, ON: Oxford University Press.

Callahan, M. (2001). Debate: Risk assessment in child protection services. No: "These tools ... do not reduce risk for children." *Canadian Social Work Review, 18*, 157–162.

Cameron, G., Freymond, N., Cornfield, D., Palmer, S. (2001). *Positive possibilities for child and family welfare: Options for expanding the Anglo-American child protection paradigm.* Waterloo, ON: Wilfrid Laurier University, Partnerships for Children and Families Project.

Cameron, G., & Hoy, S. (2003). *Stories of mothers and child welfare.* Waterloo, ON: Wilfrid Laurier University, Partnerships for Children and Families Project.

Cameron, G., O'Reilly, J., Laurendeau, M. C., & Chamberland, C. (2001). Programming for distressed and disadvantaged adolescents. In I. Prilleltensky, G. Nelson, & L. Peirson (Eds.). *Promoting family wellness and preventing child maltreatment: Fundamentals for thinking and action* (pp. 273–317). Toronto, ON: University of Toronto Press.

Chen, X. (2001). *Tending the gardens of citizenship: Child protection in Toronto 1880s–1920s.* Unpublished doctoral dissertation, University of Toronto, Toronto, ON.

Chodorow, N. (1978). *The reproduction of mothering.* Berkeley: University of California Press.

Davies, L., & Krane, J. (1996). Shaking the legacy of mother blaming: No easy task for child welfare. *Journal of Progressive Human Services, 7*(2), 3–23.

Dawson, R. (2001). Debate: Risk assessment in child protection services. Yes: "an integral part of casework practice." *Canadian Social Work Review, 18*(1), 151–154.

Fernandez, E. (1996). *Significant harm: Unravelling child protection decisions and substitute care careers of children. Perspectives of child welfare workers and biological parents.* Aldershot, UK: Avebury.

Fetterman, D. M. (1998). *Ethnography: Second edition.* Thousand Oaks, CA: Sage.

Forna, A. (1998). *Mother of all myths: How society moulds and constrains mothers.* London: Harper Collins.

Freymond, N. (2003). *Understanding mothers whose children are placed in foster care.* Waterloo, ON: Unpublished doctoral comprehensive paper, Wilfrid Laurier University, Waterloo, Ontario.

Hetherington, R., Cooper, A., Smith, P., & Wilford, G. (1997). *Protecting children: Messages from Europe.* Dorset, UK: Russell House Publishing.

Holloway, S. D., Fuller, B., Rambaud, M. F., & Eggers-Pierola, C. (1997). *Through my own eyes: Single mothers and the cultures of poverty.* Cambridge, MA: Harvard University Press.

Maluccio, A. N. (1981). Casework with parents of children in foster care. In P. A. Sinanoglu & A. N. Maluccio (Eds.), *Parents of children in placement: Perspectives and programs* (pp. 15–32). New York: Child Welfare League of America.

McCallum, S. (1995). *Safe families: A model of child protection intervention based on parental voice and wisdom.* Unpublished doctoral dissertation, Wilfrid Laurier University, Waterloo, ON.

Miller, J. B. (1991). The development of women's sense of self. *Women's growth in connection* (pp. 11–26). New York: Guilford Press.

Mnookin, R. H. (1973). Foster care—in whose best interest? *Harvard Educational Review, 43*(4), 599–638.

Nelson, G., Laurendeau, M.C., Chamberland, C., & Peirson, L. (2001). A review and analysis of programs to promote family wellness and prevent the maltreatment of preschool and elementary-school-aged children. In I. Prilleltensky, G. Nelson, & L. Peirson. *Promoting family wellness and preventing child maltreatment: Fundamentals for thinking and action* (pp. 220–272). Toronto, ON: University of Toronto Press.

Parton, N., Thorpe, D., & Wattam, C. (1997). *Child protection: Risk and the moral order.* London: Macmillan.

Patterson, K. (2002, February 22). What makes mothers kill? *Hamilton Spectator*, pp. B1–B2.

Plummer, K. (2001). The call of life stories in ethnographic research. In P. Atkinson, A. Coffey, S. Delamont, J. Lofland, & L. Lofland (Eds.), *Handbook of ethnography* (pp. 395–406). London: Sage.

Regehr, C., Bernstein, M., M., & Kanani, K. (2002). Liability for child welfare social workers: Weighing the risks. *OACAS Journal, 46*(1), 32–39.

Roberts, D. E. (1999). Mothers who fail to protect their children: Accounting for private and public responsibility. In J. E. Hanigsberg & S. Ruddick (Eds.), *Mother troubles* (pp. 31–49). Boston: Beacon Press.

Shapira, M., & Benbenisty, R. (1993). Modeling judgments and decisions in cases of alleged child abuse and neglect. *Social Work Research and Abstracts, 29*(2), 14–19.

Spradley, J. P. (1979*). The ethnographic interview.* New York: Holt, Rinehart & Winston.

Swift, K. J. (1995). *Manufacturing "bad mothers": A critical perspective on child neglect.* Toronto, ON: University of Toronto Press.

Swift, K. J. (1998). Contradictions in child welfare: Neglect and responsibility. In C. T. Baines, P. M. Evans, & S. Neysmith, M. (Eds.), *Women's caring: Feminist perspectives on social welfare* (pp. 160–190). Toronto: Oxford University Press.

Tedlock, B. (2000). Ethnography and ethnographic representation. In N. K. Denzin & Y. S. Lincoln (Eds.), *Handbook of qualitative research: 2nd ed.* (pp. 455–486). Thousand Oaks, CA: Sage.

Van Loon, J. (2001). Ethnography: A critical turn in cultural studies. In P. Atkinson, A. Coffey, S. Delamont, J. Lofland, & L. Lofland (Eds.), *Handbook of ethnography* (pp. 273–284). London: Sage.

Whittaker, J. K., & Maluccio, A. N. (2002). Rethinking "child placement": A reflective essay. *Social Service Review, 76*(1), 109–134.

|3|

Aboriginal Child Welfare

Deena Mandell
Joyce Clouston Carlson
Marshall Fine
Cindy Blackstock

As the relationships change between Canada's Aboriginal[1] peoples and the state, the issue of Child Welfare is in the foreground, because it is around the well-being, education, and care of Aboriginal children that much of the painful historical relationship between First Nations and the Canadian government has been played out. In this chapter we consider the major issues in Canadian Aboriginal child welfare, drawing on an extensive review and synthesis of current theory and research. Although there is an abundance of material available concerning Aboriginal child welfare, much of it exists outside mainstream academic child welfare literature. Salient work on Aboriginal child welfare is contained in the justice literature, in evaluation reports, operational reviews, submissions to government bodies, and in oral stories and testimony. Our[2] goal has been to cull these sources to present a coherent understanding of Aboriginal child welfare issues that encompasses history, theoretical analysis, politics, visions, realities, education, evaluation, and aspirations.[3]

Given the significant diversity of Aboriginal peoples, no discussion on child welfare can be entirely representative or exhaustive in its scope. This chapter acknowledges that diversity while identifying in a general way what differences in philosophy, culture, language, and experience exist between Aboriginal and non-Aboriginal peoples that can inform best practices in social work. We include a brief overview of the place and meaning of children in Aboriginal societies as a cultural backdrop for the subsequent historical overview of the Aboriginal experience in the Canadian child welfare system. The story of that experience takes on a different meaning when told in the context of Aboriginal values pertaining to children, family, and community. We then discuss the analytic perspectives on the issues we found in the child welfare literature and the justice literature respectively. Finally, we consider the significant changes occurring in the field of Aboriginal child welfare and related services as well as the role that the social work profession and its educators might play in those developments.

Aboriginal Children in the Child Welfare System

> In my first social work job after graduating in the early seventies, I recall going to the apartment of a young Aboriginal woman to investigate a report of "neglect." The woman had two young children—a toddler and a newborn baby. Tears streamed down her face and she said little but was immensely sad. I'll never forget her weeping.[4]

A 1983 publication, *Native Children and the Child Welfare System,* prepared for the Canadian Council on Social Development by Patrick Johnson, provided overwhelming evidence of massive removal of Aboriginal children from families and communities. Using data from the federal Department of Indian and Northern Affairs (INAC)[5] and from provincial and territorial social services, Johnson's figures were cited by the Royal Commission on Aboriginal Peoples (RCAP, 1996c) to demonstrate that Aboriginal children were consistently over-represented in child welfare systems across Canada.[6]

In 1981–82, status First Nations children represented 2.6% of Quebec's children in care, the lowest level for any province. As a proportion of children in care, the percentage was in the low range in the Maritime provinces (from 3.9 to 10.7%) and in Ontario, where the overall rate was 7.7% (but reaching 85% in one northwestern agency), the intermediate range in Manitoba and Alberta (32 and 41% respectively), and the high range in the Yukon, at 61%, and Saskatchewan, at 63%. Only in the Northwest Territories, where the rate was 45% of children in care, were Aboriginal children not disproportionately represented (RCAP, 1996c, p. 25). Provincial statistics often reflect only status Indian children, because child welfare directorates were unable to provide statistics for non-status and Metis children. The proportion of children in care is greatly increased when estimates of Metis and non-status children are included.[7] A 1980 study by Hepworth, for example, (cited in Johnston, 1983) estimated that the inclusion of non-status and Metis children would increase from 32.1% to 60% the proportion of Aboriginal children in care in Manitoba. A 1981 survey by Saskatchewan social services that included Metis and non-status children, estimated that 76.8% of the total number children in foster homes under the supervision of Saskatchewan Social Services were Native (Johnston, 1983). This is particularly concerning, because the statistics also indicate that 91.5% of these children were in the care of non-Native families.

An example of the sharp increase in apprehensions in one community is found in the Spallumcheen Band of British Columbia. A study by MacDonald indicated that the estimated number of status children in care increased from less than 1% in 1955—when British Columbia was just beginning to provide services on reserve and residential schools were still operating there—to 34.2% in 1964, just nine years later (as cited in Johnston, 1983). More than a just problematic proportion of child apprehensions the fact that "as many as one in four status Indian children was spending at least some part of childhood away from the parental home" (Armitage 1993, p. 147)[8] implies stories of childhood disruptions and changed family cultures.

The problem has not been resolved with the passage of time. By the 1990s, the number of Aboriginal children in care had increased in almost every province. For example, in 2001, British Columbia reported that Aboriginal children composed 43.8% of the children in care of the province, the province of Saskatchewan reported Aboriginal child in care populations exceeding 70%, and in Manitoba Aboriginal children constitute about 21% of Manitoba's population under the age of 15 but they account for 78% of children in the care of the child and family services system (Aboriginal Justice Inquiry-Child Welfare Initiative (AJI-CWI), 2001). A submission to the Ontario government by that province's Association of Native Child and Family Service Agencies (2001) regarding recent child welfare reforms states that in some northern Ontario Aboriginal communities, up to 10% of the children are in care. Many of the children taken into care continue to be placed in non-Aboriginal foster homes and residential facilities (McKenzie & Morrissette, 2002). These provincial patterns are reflected in national trends. Timpson (1995) cites federal statistics indicating that in 1991 the proportion of Native children removed from their homes for their protection was ten times that of non-Native children. Data from INAC show a national increase in the number of children in care of 71.5% between 1995 and 2001 (where an eligible child is defined by the funding formula as a status Indian child resident on reserve) (McKenzie, 2002). Three times as many First Nations children are in child welfare today than there were at the height of residential schools operation in the 1940s. The primary reasons that First Nations children come to the attention of the child welfare system are neglect/poverty, substance abuse, and inadequate housing.

What has caused the over-representation of Aboriginal families in the child welfare system? What do the numbers reflect about the system's institutions, policies, and practices? What do they mean in relation to the Aboriginal communities' experiences with that system? We will explore the literature pertaining to the issues of child welfare in relation to Aboriginal communities in Canada. Although the themes of cross-cultural insensitivity and racism are to some degree similar to the relationship of other non-dominant groups with the child welfare system (see, for example, Courtney, Barth, Duerr-Berrick, Brooks, Needell & Park, 1996; Korbin, 1994; and Owen & Farmer, 1996), the significant issues of assimilation and colonization within Canada are unique to Aboriginal peoples, and thus the analysis of the First Nations experience within a strictly multicultural framework is inadequate (Bennett & Blackstock, 2002).

The Child in Traditional Aboriginal Societies and the Disruption of Traditional Relationships

Children hold a special place in Aboriginal cultures. According to tradition, they are gifts from the spirit world and must be treated very gently lest they become disillusioned with this world and return to a more congenial place ... They bring a purity of vision to the world that can teach their elders. They carry within them the gifts that manifest themselves as they become teachers, mothers, hunters, councillors, artisans and visionaries. They renew the strength of the family, clan and village and make the elders young again with their joyful presence. (RCAP, 1996c, p. 23)

Given the cultural diversity among Aboriginal peoples, any general summary of beliefs and values is unlikely to be universally representative, or reflective of the nuanced contexts in which they were expressed. The information summarized here is therefore necessarily oversimplified in an attempt to outline, in very general terms, some of the differences and similarities between Aboriginal and non-Aboriginal ideologies of child and family caring.

In Aboriginal cultures, family has traditionally included grandparents, aunts, and uncles. Caring for a child was shared among immediate family and extended members, and kin networks had important functions in the education of children. Elders, for example, recounted stories and legends that delighted children and gave them insight into the habits of animals and birds and would enable them to learn about the natural world; this was critical for their survival (Carlson, 1994). Legends were also used to instill values, beliefs, and understanding of the whole continuum of life experiences and contexts. Children were considered part of the interdependent web of life connected to all life forms, the environment, and spiritual world. All relationships, including family and community, were emphasized as sites of respect and learning.

Connors and Maidman (2001) offer a summary of the beliefs and values that they understand as guiding traditional Aboriginal parenting practices and the child rearing principles that flow from them. Along with the concept that children are gifts "on loan from the Creator" (p. 357) and bring gifts to the community for their collective benefit, it is believed that the development of these gifts is determined and guided by the Creator. The role of adults is to support this development. Another belief is that anger should be controlled (in the sense of being expressed with respect), that teaching proper ways of behaviour to children is best done by example, and that the Creator is aware of when one has done his or her best. These beliefs lead to some practices that are comparable to contemporary Euro-Canadian culture and some that are different. Traditionally, Aboriginal parents are very respectful of their children and the perspectives they offer. Children are also taught to be humble. Supporting child development incorporates practices that could be viewed as "minimal" interference by mainstream standards, in that the interruption of children's activities and coercion to comply are avoided within certain limits (Connors & Maidman, 2001, p. 357).

The concepts of minimal expectations and non-interference take on different meanings from an Aboriginal perspective than they would in Euro-Western–based cultures. Cree Elder Stanley McKay has noted that within the community of his childhood there was a strong belief that children should be permitted to learn from their own mistakes. In addition, youngsters were more free to eat when hungry and sleep when tired. McKay acknowledges that these values may be interpreted by outsiders as permissiveness or negligence, and he emphasizes that children were also taught to develop responsibility. They learned how to handle a canoe at a very early age, for example, and to hunt skilfully and with care. Although they were given a great deal of responsibility, they were not placed in situations beyond their abilities. From a very early age, children were expected to understand aspects of life that European society would consider more adult-like. For example, even quite young children were not separated from adults at funerals, weddings, or other community gatherings (S. McKay, personal communication, September 2002).

Although all Aboriginal communities share a holistic world view and value interdependence, there are significant differences in how these are expressed. Historical experiences and contemporary contexts of communities also differ widely. The notion of children being valued as gifts with associated benefits, for example, was not historically the sole basis for children's relationships with and value to adults. Adults, including Elders, had a responsibility to nurture, care for, and guide children in a variety of ways, the balance of which was best determined by the nature of both the child and the teaching. In many communities, unlike the laissez faire approach often inferred from the principle of non-interference, the nurturing and teaching of children to maturation was considered extremely important, and considerable emphasis was placed on child development. Non-inter-ference might constitute a legitimate approach only within accepted guide-lines and boundaries. The value of humility was meant to emphasize respect for others rather than a lack of pride in oneself, one's family and community, and the control of anger may be understood as one way of ensuring respect, rather than being a value in itself (Blackstock, 2001).

Consequences of disrupted child care traditions. Because family, composed of an extended kin network, anchored an individual's identity and helped him or her to make sense of the world, disruption of these fam-ily ties placed the child in an alien world without the support to compre-hend it. Unlike dominant societal communities, in which schools operate as supports to families, in First Nations communities, schools have often been experienced as negative. The functions provided by the "mediating institutions" of urban societies (RCAP, 1996c, p. 18), such as associations, clubs, and formal family supports, have parallels in formal community struc-tures like Aboriginal feasts and in informal structures such as relationships with elders.[9] For Aboriginal children, the impacts of ruptured relationships with family and mediating community institutions were further amplified by their separation from their culture and language and from the land.[10] Separated from land and community, children lost more than family; they lost a way of relating to and understanding the world. In addition, because the socialization process involves deep communication of values and expec-tations across generations, Aboriginal children might not be able to fully understand the expectations in the new environment, or how to relate to people or to community resources (McKay & Clouston Carlson, 2003[11]; RCAP, 1996c).

As suggested above, an important traditional Aboriginal value was iden-tity in community. Chandler's work on youth suicide (2002) indicates that the formation of personal identity in Aboriginal youth relies on the nature and extent of an individual's relationships with the people and world around him or her to a far greater extent than with non-Aboriginal children. Main-taining relationships is critical for positive identity formation and suste-nance. Disrupting relationships through forced removal of children to residential schools or to child welfare settings was experienced as devastat-ing. Individuals were "set adrift" outside of their communities. The RCAP (1996c) traces the family dysfunction of many contemporary communities to an inability to show affection and a lack of parenting skills, both conse-quences of disrupted relationships resulting from residential schools and other experiences of colonization. The report suggests "the effects are broader and more diffuse than can be traced in a direct cause and effect relation-ship" (p. 36). A submission to the RCAP by the chair of a family services council described the "pain and humiliation" of families and communities at removal of their children (RCAP, 1996c, p. 28). This experience has been related by many community leaders (Carlson, 1995; McKay & Clouston Carlson, 2003) and is described in MacDonald's recounting (2002) of Aboriginal women's experiences of having children placed, or at risk of being placed, in the child welfare system.

As a part of its assimiliation policy, the government of Canada, with several Christian churches, began operating residential schools during the 1870s. Aboriginal parents were compelled by law to send their children aged 5–15 to these schools, whose often poor conditions resulted in many deaths of children from disease, and whose staff were inexperienced and sometimes abusive and neglectful. The goal of the schools was to displace a child's Aboriginality with Euro-Western Christian ways of knowing and being. Children who were sent to residential schools learned skills that were not always applicable to their home communities, and at the same time were unable to acquire skills such as hunting, fishing, tanning, and so forth, which were essential to enable them to live in traditional ways. Missing, too, during formative years, were the experience and modelling of good parenting, the development of independent judgment, and stable emotional attachments. Skills needed to survive in the residential school setting, such as stealing food, on the other hand, established internal conflict in children who had been taught in their families and communities that this was wrong (Carlson, 1994). Godin-Beers and Williams, in their "Report of the Spallumcheen Child Welfare Program," documented one chief's account of how common cheating, lying, and stealing were in such institutions, and how destructive these actions were when taken back to the home community (as cited in RCAP, 1996c, p. 36). As a result of being taught in the schools that their cultures were something to be ashamed of, some of these returning children also showed a lack of respect for community leaders and values. Community leaders needing to address this had few precedents in their value system. The chief of the Spallumcheen First Nation suggested that the greatest difficulty was "the unemotional upbringing they [the children] had" which led to loss of identity, self worth, and self esteem (as cited in RCAP, 1996c, p. 36). It is important to add that there were Aboriginal children who succeeded in developing skills for independent judgement and the capacity for emotional attachment despite the difficult context of the residential schools, so that the destructive consequences outlined above were not the case for all the children (Canadian Broadcasting Corporation (CBC), 2000).[12]

In addition to the abuse and neglect [13] experienced by many in the residential schools, children who were placed in them were raised in institutional settings, growing to adulthood without models of parenting, although some were able to maintain some relationships with family or to benefit from other role models. Dakota Elder Gladys Cook notes that when these individuals became parents themselves, many succeeded in recovering traditions more positive than the institutional models of their childhoods (Cook & Carlson, 1997). Disruption of parent–child relationships was transmitted across generations, as Maggie Hodgson (2002) explains in the story of her own family. She describes her mother's experience in the schools during an epidemic; multiple student deaths occurred in a context where children were expected to suppress emotions. The unexpressed pain was often later dealt with through use of drugs and alcohol. Hodgson (2002) recounts her mother's decision to send Maggie away to school to protect her from her mother's alcoholism. Hodgson also explains that many who had been in the schools became very punitive parents.

The sacred trust that traditional Aboriginal communities felt with the gift of a child and the care they were able to provide in traditional, economically self-sufficient communities contrasts sharply with the picture of neglect, despair, and suicide often currently represented in mainstream society. What accounts for these contradictory images?

Historical Overview of Child Welfare and Aboriginal Communities

Armitage (1993) divides the evolution of Canadian policy and practice regarding Aboriginal child welfare into three historical phases: the assimilationist period of 1867–1960, the child welfare period, 1960–1980, and the period from 1980 on. The first phase reflected the broader assimilationist aims of Canadian social policy; the second focused on integrating services to status Indians with existing mainstream services, and the third favoured a system for Aboriginal child welfare that entailed "some degree of community and administrative self-government under the terms of tripartite (federal–provincial–band/tribal council) agreements (Cassidy & Bish, 1989)" (as cited in Armitage, 1993, p. 133). Prior to elaborating Armitage's analysis, it must be said that a different position can be found in the literature, which is that neo-colonialism lives on in the current delegated model of child welfare (Bennett & Blackstock, 2002; Brown, Haddock, & Kovach, 2002; Hudson & McKenzie, 1981; MacDonald, 2002). This position will be discussed further in the section below on jurisdictional models. Armitage's conceptualization is presented here to give a chronological context rather than a definitive perspective.

The assimilationist period. During the assimilationist period, the principal child welfare institution was the residential school, based on a statutory requirement under the Indian Act. In Quebec, day schools predominated;

in the western and prairie provinces, residential schools were predominant. Indian education at that time was church run and government funded. It was designed to separate Indian children from both their own and non-Native societies while instilling missionary teachings, values, and beliefs that were in conflict with those of First Nations. Armitage (1993) concludes that students emerged from the schools ill prepared for life either on the reserve or in urban white communities. The primary function of residential schools shifted gradually from educational institution to "alternative parenting institution," as successive generations of former students who were ill prepared for parenthood themselves became parents (Armitage, 1993, p. 144). Previously, if a child were in need of alternate care, members of extended family often provided it; in some cases, the federal Indian agent might have made arrangements for the child to live with another family or sent the child to a residential school (Johnston, 1983; McKay & Clouston Carlson, 2003; Saulteaux, 1997). The involvement of child welfare agencies in Aboriginal communities is relatively recent, beginning in the 1940s and not coming to public notice until the 1960s.

The child welfare period. Johnston (1983) describes a rapid expansion in government funding and operation of social agencies in the late 1940s.[14] This was an accepted extension of the increase in government's role in society which had occurred during the Second World War. At the same time, the profession of social work was also moving beyond previous roles and experiencing increased confidence and credibility. In this climate, in 1947, the Canadian Association of Social Workers joined with the Canadian Welfare Council to submit a brief to a House of Commons and Senate committee appointed to consider changes to the Indian Act. The brief was critical of the system of social service delivery to Aboriginal populations because the quality of these services was inferior to that of services available to other Canadians (Johnston, 1983). Special mention was made in the brief that decisions about adoption of Indian [sic] children, made by Indian Agents, lacked "careful legal and social protection afforded to white children" (as cited in Johnston, 1983, p. 3). The conclusion of the brief was that extending provincial services in health, welfare, and education to reserves would improve services. Rather than recommending that the federal government develop a service system parallel to the provincial one, however, the brief urged the federal government to consult with the provinces (Johnston, 1983). Although Johnston accepts that the "best of intentions" underlay the CWC/CASW brief, he criticizes it for paying too little attention to the question of potential incompatibility between provincial services and the needs of Indian communities (Johnston, 1983). Transferring services developed in an urban context to remote rural communities added to the difficulties of implementing the extension of provincial services (Armitage, 1993). Recommendations by the federal government's Hawthorn Inquiry (1964–1966) for Indian initiation of and participation in development of services to their communities were not followed (Armitage, 1993). As a result, services were often initiated by non-Native authorities, children were frequently removed to non-Native foster homes, and the adoption process often proceeded with the requirement for voluntary consent waived through the courts (Armitage, 1993).

Parallels have been drawn between the residential school system and the child welfare system that supplanted it (Armitage, 1993; McKenzie & Hudson, 1985; McKenzie & Morrissette, 2002). Armitage (1993) argues that, in some ways, the child welfare system may actually have been more damaging than the residential school system because the children were rendered more vulnerable in the former, because they were cut off not only from their families but from their First Nations peers as well.

Inadequate funding arrangements also contributed significantly to what transpired through the extension of services to Aboriginal communities. Johnston (1983) notes that although revisions were made to the Indian Act in 1951 that allowed for extending provincial child welfare services, there was no accompanying authorization for funding to support this; as a result, "over the ensuing years only some provincial child welfare programs were extended to residents of some reserves in some provinces" (p. 3). Thus, for example, in provinces providing only (federally funded) child-in-care services, provincial social workers were called "only when conditions had deteriorated to the point that no alternative to apprehension was possible" (Timpson, 1993, p. 39). No funding was available for follow-up services that might have returned an apprehended child to his or her family. Since federal funds paid for the cost of children in care, there was no incentive for provinces to develop preventive services and avoid apprehensions (Timpson, 1993). Prior to the development of the federal funding formula introduced in 1991, funding of First Nations Child and Family Services agencies was "inconsistent and often inequitable" (McDonald & Ladd, 2000, p. 9). Even that formula, however, was recently deemed by the Joint National Policy Review to be inadequate to address the dramatic changes that have taken place in First Nations child and family services during the past decade (McDonald & Ladd, 2000).

A publication of the Awasis First Nation (Awasis Agency, 1997) states that when "Manitoba first extended child welfare legislation into First Nations communities ... the only services that were provided were basic crisis intervention services, and then only in life threatening situations" (p. 17). Because government policy funded children in care rather than preventive services and/or support of families and communities, placement of children outside the family was the preferred approach. Willingness to pay child-in-care costs, along with federal and provincial governments' resistance to supporting preventive services, family counselling, or rehabilitation, were major factors in making apprehension and permanent removal of children the preferred solution in problem situations (Timpson, 1993).

Johnston (1983) describes continuing arguments between federal and provincial authorities about whose responsibility it was to fund child welfare services to reserves. Whereas child welfare reserves were in the provincial domain, matters affecting Natives and lands reserved for them fell within the federal domain. When the two domains intersected to provide child welfare services to First Nations on reserves, however, provincial and federal governments each tended to place the responsibility on the other party. To complicate matters, different provinces took various positions on the issue. Although some saw the provision of child welfare services to First Nations people on reserves as an entirely federal responsibility, others have been willing to extend their services if the federal government provided funding. The result of this jurisdictional wrangling and disparity was that many reserves continued to receive funding only for services inferior to those available to other Canadian families.

This period includes what is now referred to as the "sixties scoop," a term coined by a provincial employee in British Columbia to convey the manner in which social workers "would, quite literally, scoop children from reserves on the slightest pretext" (Johnston, 1983, p. 23). The Awasis agency (1997) states:

> Between 1960 and 1980, three thousand aboriginal children were removed from their homes in Manitoba and exported out of the province for adoption, mostly by non-Native families. In the early 80s, "[...] For Canada as a whole, five Native children were removed from their families for every non-Native child placed" (Corrigan and Barkwell, 1991, p. 123). At the time, First Nations and Métis made up approximately six percent of the population [of Canada]. (p. 17)

The period since 1980: Drive toward self-determination. Although active protest by First Nations communities against removal of their children had occurred throughout the period of colonization, the move to form First Nations child welfare agencies began in the mid-1970s and reflected the growing desire for self-determination (Johnston, 1983; Koster, Morrissette, & Roulette, 2000; McKenzie, Seidl, & Bone, 1995). Both the growing recognition of overrepresentation of Native children in the child welfare system and the passage in the United States of the Indian Child Welfare Act of 1978 contributed to the rising demands and the changes that began in the early to mid-1980s (McKenzie, 1989). The experience of the Spallumcheen band of British Columbia is illustrative. In 1980 the band had 300 members, and 150 children had been removed and placed in non-Native homes over a 25-year period. The band passed a by-law giving itself jurisdiction over child welfare proceedings on reserve and exempting itself from the applicable provincial legislation. Although this step was initially disallowed on the basis of jurisdictional and legal issues, such as liability, and, despite some resistance from the province and the Department of Indian and Northern Affairs Canada (INAC), the province eventually agreed, and the band became the first to take control of its own child welfare services, with federal funding (Johnston, 1983; McKenzie, 1989). The jurisdictional issue between federal and provincial authorities has been dealt with differently in different parts of the country as Aboriginal peoples have continued to struggle for more authority in child welfare.

In Ontario, a 1981 resolution of band chiefs forbade Ontario and Manitoba to remove Native children from reserves and demanded the return of children previously removed. The chiefs also declared their intention to create their own child welfare laws and services within the context of Native culture. Ontario's first joint initiative between the First Nations and the local children's aid society, with provincial funding, had come about in 1979. It led to the hiring of the first Native child welfare prevention workers in two northwestern Ontario Aboriginal communities and was intended to promote needed care in the community and reduce the need for children to come into the care of the children's aid society. Soon after, the program was expanded to all First Nations communities in the province. In 1984, the newly enacted Child and Family Services Act provided official recognition of the rights of Aboriginal people, including the right to develop child protection agencies of their own. Under the Act, a band or Native community is permitted to designate a particular body as a Native child and family service authority; the Ministry is then obligated to enter into negotiations for the provision of services with this authorized group if requested to do so by the community. Results include agreements allowing the Aboriginal authority to provide services, and the designation of the authority as a Children's Aid Society under the Act, if the authority itself agrees. Currently, there are five Aboriginal agencies so designated in Ontario, serving 55 of Ontario's 136 First Nations (Association of Native Child and Family Services Association of Ontario (ANCFSAO, 2001); Koster et al., 2000). This number is low compared to other parts of Canada; British Columbia, for example, currently has 19 First Nations Child and Family Service Agencies, five of which are fully delegated agencies with full child protection authority.

Systemic Problems, Individual Tragedies

Around the same time that new models of Aboriginal child welfare were evolving in the early 1980s, there was an increasing awareness that apprehension might have even more traumatic effects on an Aboriginal child than a non-Aboriginal child (Johnston, 1983). Johnston refers to the Aboriginal child as being in "triple jeopardy" (p. 59), since removal from parents also entailed removal from a network of extended family, who were an important potential source of support, and removal from their accustomed cultural context, which was grounded in their local community. Just how traumatic these cumulative effects could be was highlighted through two highly publicized tragedies. Cameron Kerly, a Manitoba First Nations child, was placed in an unsupervised international adoption with a single man. After enduring sexual abuse throughout the years spent in this placement, 19-year-old Kerly brutally killed his adoptive father. The story of abuse did not emerge until he had been imprisoned early in the 1980s. There had been no efforts made by social workers to keep Cameron with his extended family, nor was a social work assessment made of the suitability of the placement or the adoptive father, in spite of Cameron's declining achievement at school (Monture, 1989). In discussing Cameron Kerly, First Nations legal scholar Patricia Monture (1989) states that the boy himself must be held morally responsible for the murder he committed, but also poses the question: "When social institutions and legal processes fail, where do we place the responsibility?" (p. 2).

The second tragedy involved Richard Cardinal, an Alberta Metis teenager who committed suicide in June 1984. His personal diary offers disturbing insights into the child welfare system (Bagley, 1985). A case review revealed that Richard had been removed from his parents for reasons of "neglect," which essentially meant "extreme poverty." Social workers involved failed to make supportive or preventive interventions, such as income provision or housing support, nor did they consult with Richard's extended family. "Yet members of this extended family might have cared for the children given a modicum of material support" (Bagley, 1985, p. 68). Richard received extremely poor care in the child welfare system, suffered numerous moves from foster home to foster home, and was treated as "slave labour" by some. In spite of several suicide attempts, a child psychiatrist who assessed Richard "made no recommendations for treatment" (Bagley, 1985, p. 68).

Richard was not an isolated case. A review of child welfare case files at the time of his death revealed that 20% of children in the care of child welfare authorities were considered to be suicidal. In the previous year, 15 of the 15,657 children in care under the Alberta government took their own lives (Bagley, 1985).

These stories not only emphasize the effects on children of their removal but also represent signs of the widespread troubling social breakdown in Aboriginal communities against a backdrop of systemic oppression. Richard Cardinal's diary explains his isolation and despair in his own words: "I had been hurt too many time [sic] so I began to learn the art of blocking out all emotion. I shut out the rest of the world out [sic] and the door would open to none" (Bagley, 1985, p. 64).

Protests by Manitoba Aboriginal people against international adoption of children like Cameron Kerly from their communities resulted in a public inquiry in the early 1980s. The ensuing report by family court judge Edwin Kimelman (1985) was strongly critical of the child welfare system. Judge Kimelman concluded that the Aboriginal community was justified in asserting that the child welfare system was practising "cultural genocide." This position is reflected in the following two excerpts:

> Cultural bias in the child welfare system is practised at every level from the social worker who works directly with the family, through the lawyers who represent the various parties in a custody case, to the judges who make the final disposition in a case. (p. 185)

> In 1982, no one, except the Indian and Métis people, really believed the reality—that Native people were routinely being shipped to adoption homes in the United States and to other provinces in Canada. Every social worker, every administrator, and every agency or region viewed the situation from a narrow perspective and saw each individual case as an exception, as a case involving extenuating circumstances. (pp. 272–273)

In response to the question of where responsibility lies, the Kimelman report identified the lack of sensitivity of the child welfare system. When families approached agencies for help, they found they were unsupported. Child welfare agencies saw "the child's best interests" as separate from the family's best interests, a separation which is incongruent with Aboriginal peoples' beliefs. This failure to recognize fundamental differences in value systems regarding children and families reflects cultural bias and an imposition of the dominant culture's values. The report notes that social workers were not trained to deal with cultural patterns that varied from their own; they were put into the field with the expectation that somehow they would learn it on the job (Kimelman, 1985). Further, Kimelman states:

> The appalling reality was that everyone believed they were doing their best, and stood firm in a belief that the system was working well. Some administrators took the ostrich approach to child welfare problems. They just did not exist ... The road to hell was paved with good intentions and child welfare agencies were the paving contractors. (p. 276)

Although cultural bias was clearly part of the problem, another dimension was the rapid economic and social change taking place in Aboriginal communities. The economic and psychological pressures that this precipitated
were unknown in any other cultural group in Canada to that time. Families
desperately attempted to deal with these changes, which threatened their own
value systems. Initially, they sought support from outside agencies, but the
structure of Eurocentric agencies, the nature of the agency workers' professional training, and their own value systems and life experience mitigated
an adequate response. The inadequate preparation and cultural biases that
Kimelman speaks of were played out against this backdrop of overwhelming social disruption and systemic biases (Carlson, 1994; McKay & Clouston
Carlson, 2003; Timpson, 1995). By the 1980s, Canadian child welfare experts
publicly acknowledged that the system did not operate in the best interests
of Aboriginal children or families (Johnston, 1983).

The following two sections present more detailed perspectives on how
these oppressive conditions reached such a point without being recognized
or prevented.

Analyses of Issues in Aboriginal Child Welfare

Child displacement and dis/memberment from their families was occurring at a rapid rate in the 70s when I was doing 'summer relief' in a child
welfare agency. The mandate of the agency I worked for was clear: I was
required by law to remove a child neglected under the definition provided in the Child Welfare Act. The grief in the life of that young woman
and her children is symbolic of shattered hopes and dreams of Aboriginal families, and especially of children. Increasingly I became aware that
the job I was doing represented a collision between child welfare and
Aboriginal people—a collision of values, a collision that resulted in the
tremendous tearing apart of the fabric of the family.[15]

In 1995, Timpson published a review called "Four Decades of Literature
on Native Canadian Child Welfare: Changing Themes," which gives a helpful analysis of developments in the responses to Aboriginal child welfare
issues from academic and non-academic child welfare sectors, both in Canada
and in the United States. Timpson's main thesis is that the trends in the literature from the 1960s reflected their respective "contemporary political
climate" (p. 525). She finds that the early literature focused primarily on
the challenges for non-Native agencies of providing services (especially
adoption and foster care) to Native communities. Later, a critique of those
services began to appear but failed to recognize conditions that gave rise to
those difficulties. Those underlying conditions were masked by a focus in the

literature on the politics of relations between Native people and non-Native agencies, and Native people and the government. Timpson's conclusion is that the "polemic presentation" (p. 539) of child welfare issues in the literature contributed to the demand from Aboriginal groups for control of child welfare services in their own communities. Timpson notes an increase in academic and Aboriginal contributions to the child welfare literature as a result of the frank examination of Native child maltreatment issues in their historical and structural context. Timpson's political analysis should be borne in mind as the literature from child welfare, legal, and Aboriginal sources is discussed below.

Child welfare officials and academics have produced a variety of explanations for the crisis in Aboriginal child welfare. Hudson and McKenzie (1981) conducted an influential review of the contemporary literature addressing the overrepresentation of Aboriginal children in the child welfare system. They grouped the literature into three conceptual approaches to explaining the problem, each of which sees it "as a reflection of the higher incidence of familial disorganization, breakdown and neglect within the native population" (Hudson & McKenzie, 1981, p. 64). The first approach understands the underlying problem of neglect from the standpoint of psychosocial development theory, and thus identifies the lack of adequate "organized personal services" as the immediate problem to be solved. In a later version of this review, the authors add that this approach to explaining the high rate of neglect views child neglect as a matter of "individual deviation" (McKenzie & Hudson, 1985, p. 127) without taking into account the systemic differences between Native and non-Native contexts.

The second group of explanations in the original Hudson and McKenzie review (1981) takes an anthropological perspective, focusing on cultural difference and recognizing that differences in cultural values between Aboriginal and white societies give rise to conflict. A study by Zentner (cited by Hudson and McKenzie, 1981) acknowledges that Aboriginal parents may be "caught" between two cultures and reject both. These explanations tend to conclude that the solution lies in helping Aboriginal people acculturate to the ways of the dominant society. This would be counter to the approach suggested by Michael Chandler's research, which finds that the greater the degree of Aboriginal community self determination as expressed by Aboriginal child welfare agencies, women in government, health programs, cultural programs, education, and fire and police services—the lower the rate of Aboriginal youth suicide. In some cases the rates were lower than those experienced in mainstream society (Chandler, 2002).

The third approach is grounded in the belief that the poor socioeconomic status of Aboriginal peoples interferes with their ability to parent adequately. Although class issues are recognized, McKenzie and Hudson (1985) point out that this perspective does not adequately account for how issues related to poverty in Native communities are connected to other differences between Native and non-Native societies. In addition, attempts to deal with poverty (such as training and relocation programs) as proposed in the third explanation tend to have as their aim the preparation of Native people for active engagement with the mainstream capitalist system. McKenzie and Hudson add that no explanations found in the child welfare literature to that point addressed the issue of Native children experiencing poorer outcomes in care.

The authors note that the three major explanatory approaches in the literature, despite their theoretically different perspectives, have in common an "ideological commitment to an assimilationist ideal of Native–white relations" (McKenzie & Hudson, 1985, p. 128). This results in policies encouraging conformity to Canadian society and a failure to honour important historical realities.

Armitage (1993) categorizes the explanations found in McKenzie and Hudson (1985) as follows: the psychosocial argument, the cultural change argument, the economic deprivation argument, the historical argument, the racial argument, and the colonial argument. He concludes that the authors favour the colonial argument; that is, the position that the child welfare system was part of a deliberate assault on Native society designed to make changes in Native people. Colonialism is characterized by Hudson and McKenzie (1981) as involving "the process of creating dependency among a nation or group, the objective of which includes the extraction of benefits by the dominant group" (p. 65). Power, decision-making, and the assumption of superior culture reside in the dominant group.

Timpson (1993) criticizes McKenzie and Hudson's colonial argument on the grounds that it emphasizes cultural colonialism at the expense of attention to structural colonialism. This places the focus "on the interaction between the Native and non-Native society front-line service workers" (p. 31) who practised cultural colonialism but leaves unaddressed larger issues of the structural colonialism underlying those individual acts. Timpson (1993) argues that the child welfare system was originally created to deal with issues that did not include the tremendous social breakdown and economic disadvantage facing Native people; rather, such social agencies were set up to deal with individual problems in individual families. The great differences in values around child care and family life were also not taken into account (Timpson, 1993).

In the period since the early 1980s (and in a few cases, the late 1970s), child welfare legislation has remained under the control of the provinces, but Aboriginal communities have developed initiatives and negotiated or implemented programs that are designed to fit with their needs as they identify them (Armitage, 1993; McKenzie & Morrissette, 2002). There are considerable variations among these initiatives and in the role that First Nations now play in child welfare, partly due to variations among First Nations communities themselves and partly to differences in historical relations between First Nations and local governments, as well as differences in provincial policies (Armitage, 1993).[16] Armitage details the differences, for example, between the relatively comprehensive approach in Manitoba and the ad hoc approach of British Columbia. A gradual shift in awareness has led to less aggressive intervention on the part of social workers than was the norm in the 1960s and 1970s and to an increasingly respectful and collaborative way of working with Aboriginal communities (Armitage, 1993). Many Aboriginal communities, however, aspire toward a very different kind of arrangement, as we shall see.

What emerges from the child welfare literature focusing on Aboriginal communities is the complex nature of the underlying issues and politics and, consequently, the failure to date of any attempted solutions. The emergent themes focus on overwhelming social problems, structural disintegration, and systemic constraints along with inappropriate policy responses. Racism and colonialism are interwoven in all of these.

Interconnection of Child Welfare and Justice Systems

> Failing [increased control over the ways in which their children are raised, taught and protected] we are convinced that we will see more, not fewer Aboriginal people in our correctional institutions in the future. We will see more young Aboriginal people falling into a pattern that is all too familiar. It takes them from institution to institution, from foster home facility to young offender facility and finally, on to adult jails. (Aboriginal Justice Inquiry, 1991, p. 509)

The issues for Aboriginal people in the child welfare system cannot be appreciated fully without understanding what effect the justice system has had on Aboriginal people. The patterns that have evolved between the justice system and Aboriginal people are strikingly similar to the patterns in the child welfare system, such as overrepresentation and the effects of colonialism. Judge Murray Sinclair, a co-author of the Manitoba Aboriginal Justice Inquiry (AJI), noted that prior to the Second World War, Aboriginal people were represented in the jail system in the same proportion as in the population (that is, they were incarcerated at the rate of about 12%). At the turn of the century, they had actually been underrepresented in the justice system. By the early 1990s, however, 66% of the men in Manitoba jails and

90% of the women were Aboriginal. Just over 70% of boys and 80% of girls in the youth justice system were Aboriginal (Aboriginal Justice Inquiry–Child Welfare Initiative, 2002; Canadian Broadcasting Corporation, 2000). Incarceration rates for youths 15–19 are nine times higher among First Nations people than among non-First Nations and seven times higher for those age 20–24 (McDonald & Ladd, 2000). Research by the Manitoba Métis Federation in 1989 determined that "the single most determinant factor of Métis people becoming offenders was their experience in the Child and Family Services system (Corrigan & Barkwell, 1991)" (as cited by Awasis Agency, 1997, pp. 1–2). In Ontario, this correlation is reflected in the fact that 40% of the offenders in the Aboriginal justice program in Toronto in the late 1990s were found to have been adopted or to have spent their adolescence in foster care (Koster et al., 2000).

The AJI explored what had happened since the 1950s to create the striking overrepresentation in the jail system. Reasons identified included changes in the province's liquor laws, new policing agreements that stationed the RCMP closer to Native communities, and the demoralization of native war veterans who, after serving in the war, found themselves treated as second-class citizens. Indeed, at that time, Natives did not have even the right to vote. The cumulative effect of these policies was found to have contributed to undermining Aboriginal culture (CBC, 2000). Many Aboriginal people who appeared before the AJI drew the Inquiry's attention to the interconnection of the child welfare system and the justice system, arguing that the removal of children and disruption of communities and their value systems ultimately led to the breakdown of traditional social behaviour patterns (AJI, 1991). In turn, these behaviours put children at risk. McKenzie and Morrissette (2002), for example, connect the existence of widespread violence against Aboriginal women—a justice matter—with the prevalence of family breakdown and child care problems—a child welfare issue.

The justice literature argues that historical governmental–Aboriginal relationships and the deliberate undermining of Aboriginal culture are at the source of the mistrust that Aboriginal people have for the justice system. This mistrust leads to Aboriginal people's "under-involvement" or reluctance to engage with Canadian civil and family law systems on a voluntary basis (Sinclair, 1994). According to the Royal Commission on Aboriginal Peoples (RCAP, 1996a), much of the mistrust of the legal system among Aboriginal peoples harks back to changes in the intent of the original agreements between the Crown and Aboriginal people in Canada. Respect for the coexistence of the two cultures was formalized in a Royal Proclamation of 1763; it offered autonomy and protection to the indigenous peoples. The RCAP suggests that, over time, "respectful coexistence" was eroded through reinterpretation of the word "protection" from help to preserve the integrity of lands and culture to a paternalistic stance that entailed domination and lack of respect (p. 12). The Confederation of 1867 was negotiated between the French and English without consultation with Aboriginal peoples. Sir John A. Macdonald declared his government's intention to fully assimilate Indian people into white society. Under the British North America Act, Parliament replaced traditional Aboriginal governments with relatively powerless band councils and imposed European and Christian forms of governance, marriage, and parenting. A series of amendments to the Indian Act instituted residential schools in the 1870s and, in the 1880s, forbade Native spiritual practices and established the restrictive pass system. Governments relocated Aboriginal communities arbitrarily for a variety of reasons (RCAP, 1996a). Because the Canadian justice system arises from institutions and laws that have been a source of oppression, Aboriginal people have come to see it as corrupted by those origins (Monture-Okanee, 1994).

In the same way that mainstream child welfare solutions are not deemed to be applicable to Aboriginal communities, neither are mainstream legal solutions seen as appropriate. Certain legal concepts that are fundamental to the Canadian justice system are not shared by Aboriginal cultures. Monture-Okanee (1994) says, "In the Mohawk language when we say law ... it means: 'the way to live most nicely together'" (p. 227). This different understanding of "law" leads to different ways of treating people who offend. Monture-Okanee claims that the very word "guilt" has no exact translation in Aboriginal languages (1994). The concept of pleading "not guilty" when one has, in fact, committed a wrong, is permissible within a justice system that artificially separates moral and ethical values from daily life, but it is not acceptable within a traditional Aboriginal frame of reference. Conventions in Canadian law thus give rise to inner tensions for Aboriginal people because the plea "not guilty" implies avoiding responsibility and undermines the central community value of attempting to reconcile relationships rather than to punish or exculpate. The adversarial system of justice is antithetical to the Aboriginal paradigm of healing and reconciliation (Sinclair, 1994), of restoring community balance through accountability and learning.

In summary, the justice literature establishes parallels between the justice and child welfare systems with regard to cultural differences, assimilationist roots, institutionalized racism and colonialism, and economic and cultural disruption. In addition, there is a recursive interaction between the effects of the child welfare system and the justice system on Aboriginal people. The demand for recognition of Aboriginal law and control over child welfare have therefore been closely linked for several decades (Zlotkin, 1994).

Jurisdictional Models for Delivering Child Welfare Services in Aboriginal Communities

The extension of child welfare services has occurred at varying paces across the country, with many inconsistencies and with varying degrees of acceptance by First Nations communities. These inconsistencies and variations make it difficult to attain a comprehensive view of the field of Aboriginal child welfare. Added to the jurisdictional and legislative differences are the variations among Aboriginal communities themselves, including rural versus urban differences, remote communities versus those in accessible areas close to other regional services, degrees of acculturation versus traditional identification, and so on. These issues complicate the development and delivery of child welfare services that are in the best interest of all Aboriginal peoples.

Zlotkin (1994) classifies Canadian legal models for child welfare systems in two broad categories: tripartite agreements and the statutory model. Tripartite agreements are between a First Nations government or tribal council, the federal government, and a provincial government and enable First Nations child welfare agencies to administer provincial, but not First Nations, law in matters of child welfare. Federal funding is guaranteed during the term of an agreement. The model Zlotkin refers to as "statutory" is that used in Ontario. The term "statutory" refers to the enablement of this model's development by provincial child welfare legislation in 1985. We discuss this pre-mandated model below.

The range of jurisdictional models is expanding as increasing numbers of Aboriginal communities and First Nations operate child and family service agencies. We have identified five models currently in operation or in development across the country. As with any program, the jurisdictional model of child and family service delivery has important implications for funding regimes, and therefore references to various funding methodologies are included in this discussion. It is important to understand that, currently, the Department of Indian and Northern Affairs Canada (INAC) only accepts financial responsibility for funding First Nations child and family service agencies that provide services to eligible children resident on-reserve. This funding is provided pursuant to a national funding formula known as *Program Directive 20–1 (Chapter Five)*, 1989 (amended 1995), commonly termed INAC Policy Directive 20–1.[17] In Ontario, First Nations child and family service agencies are exempt from Directive 20–1, because they are funded by the province of Ontario in accordance with the *Memorandum of Agreement Respecting Welfare programs for Indians between Canada and Ontario*, known as the 1965 *Indian Welfare Agreement*. Off-reserve service delivery is typically funded by the provinces/territories.

The following section describes the five main models and the relevant funding methodologies.

The delegated model. This is the most common model of jurisdiction, partly because the INAC funding formula, Directive 20-1, requires First Nations child and family service agencies to operate pursuant to this model in order to receive funding for child welfare service delivery on-reserve. In this model, the provincial or territorial provincial child welfare authority delegates Aboriginal child and family service agencies to provide services to Aboriginal peoples either on- or off-reserve pursuant to the child welfare statute(s). The mechanism for delegation varies from province to province, but in all cases the delegation is formalized either through an agreement or by an Order in Counsel. Delegation can include *full authority* (operating with full child protection and prevention authority) or *partial authority* (providing support and prevention services to families but with the provincial child welfare authority providing child protection services). While the delegated model provides an opportunity for Aboriginal peoples to care for their children and families, it is not without significant challenges. One common concern is that the provincial/territorial child welfare statutes are often founded on the individual-rights philosophy of British common law. This philosophy, as we have seen, can be diametrically opposed to the interdependent, communal, and holistic basis of Aboriginal concepts of justice and traditional means of caring for children, youth, and families. Managing the disconnection between traditional values and beliefs and the legislation is a significant challenge for most Aboriginal agencies.

An additional challenge for First Nations child and family service agencies funded for on-reserve service delivery under Directive 20-1 arises from the fact that this national funding formula does not adjust for differences in provincial/territorial legislation. This can result in gaps between what the First Nations child and family service is delegated to do and the funding levels intended to provide resources for such efforts (McDonald & Ladd, 2000). In addition, inadequate emphasis is placed on supporting community development and preventive services required to support First Nations families in caring for their children at home. In June 2000, the Assembly of First Nations and INAC published a report reviewing Directive 20-1 and providing 17 recommendations for improvements to the current policy (McDonald & Ladd, 2000). These recommendations include the establishment of mechanisms to coordinate provincial jurisdiction with federal funding, the increase of funding for "least disruptive measures" programs, and recognition of First Nations jurisdictional models. As we write this chapter, the implementation of these recommendations has not yet been realized.

Off-reserve Aboriginal child and family service delivery is funded by provincial/territorial agreements. The nature and extent of these agreements vary from province to province. The Aboriginal Justice Inquiry Child Welfare Initiative in Manitoba provides a promising model for the funding of off-reserve service delivery that recognizes both the right of Aboriginal peoples to care for their children and the diversity that exists within the Aboriginal community. The model provides for the formation of four child welfare authorities, two of which are First Nations, one Metis, and one for Non-Aboriginal clients. The model includes Aboriginal peoples in the design and decision-making in drafting child welfare legislation, standards, and funding mechanisms (AJI-CWI, 2001).

Many Aboriginal organizations, particularly those working with communities involved in active self-government processes, regard the delegated model as an interim model of governance pending recognition of Aboriginal laws. In this light, delegation is seen as a capacity-building measure while active exploration continues for more meaningful, culturally and community-based paradigms and mechanisms. Brown et al. (2002) conclude that the best thing about the delegated model may be the resistance it defines in First Nations communities as they empower themselves to sustain their traditions and values.

Pre-mandated child and family services. Aboriginal and First Nations child and family service agencies operating as pre-mandated child and family service organizations provide prevention and family support services pursuant to agreements, including licensing agreements, with the provincial/territorial government. These agencies, which are principally located in Ontario, are incorporated as non-profit transfer payment agencies with their own boards of directors (Koster et al., 2000). Their goal is to ensure that families have access to culturally appropriate preventive and foster care resources. The 1984 Child and Family Services Act, which provides the legal basis for the establishment of child welfare agencies by First Nation bodies (i.e. governments and organizations) in Ontario, also permits the exemption of a First Nation child and family service authority, band, or native community from any provision of the Act or its regulations. These exemptions are a potential mechanism for allowing the delivery of culturally appropriate services that might not meet certain requirements of the legislation (Koster et al, 2000). Six Nations of the Grand River in southern Ontario, for example, recently reached an agreement under the Child and Family Services Act that allows children placed in customary care to *not* be considered in the care of the province, yet still receive funding to support the customary care arrangement (Six Nations of the Grand River, 2002). The First Nations agencies of Ontario have called for clearly defined guidelines for achieving full mandated status (ANCFSAO, 2001). As mandated agencies, they would offer the "full range of child protection services" (ANCFSAO, 2001, p. 73) to Native children.

The self-government model. This model recognizes the jurisdictional authority of Aboriginal peoples in the area of child and family services. This authority is often based on treaties, such as the Nisga'a Treaty, which includes provisions for the development of Nisga'a laws governing child and family services so long as those laws meet provincial standards. Although at the time this draft was written the Nisga'a operated a delegated child and family service agency as a capacity-building measure, plans were under way to draft and implement tribal laws. The model of self-government has the benefit of being based on the world view, cultures, and histories of Aboriginal peoples and affirms traditional child and family caring processes rather than competing with them (Nisga'a Lisims, 2002). The government of Manitoba is in the process of transferring substantial authority over child welfare practice to regional authorities, including First Nations authorities. It remains unclear how much discretion these First Nations authorities will have to create policies and procedures that deviate from provincial ones (Department of Family Services, 2006; Hardy, Schibler, & Hamilton, 2006).

Many First Nations and Aboriginal groups across Canada have actively expressed an interest in moving in the direction of establishing self-government models of child welfare, and this is likely to be a growing area of development in the coming years. The drive for self-determination in issues of child welfare is clearly bound with broader issues of self-determination seen as crucial to sustained socioeconomic development.[18]

The band by-law model. The Indian Act allows for Indian Band Chiefs and Counsels to pass band by-laws that apply on-reserve. As described above, the Spallumcheen First Nation of British Columbia passed a by-law establishing sole jurisdiction for themselves over child and family services on reserve. The Minister of INAC at the time resisted signing the by-law, but did so after much advocacy on the part of the Spallumcheen. Funding and provincial support eventually followed after additional advocacy. The Minister of INAC has refused to recognize any further by-laws associated with child welfare, and thus the Spallumcheen First Nation continues to be the only agency operating pursuant to this model (Union of BC Indian Chiefs, 2002).

The tripartite model. Under this model of governance, the provincial and federal governments delegate their law-making authority to a First Nation, usually with the requirement that provincial standards of child welfare be followed (the name of this model refers to the three parties involved).

Although this model affords a greater degree of recognition of tribal-based authority than the delegated model, it is still administered in the context of delegation from the province/territory and federal government, giving First Nations child welfare agencies the authority to administer provincial law, but not First Nations law (Zlotkin, 1994). Thus, some First Nations and Aboriginal groups prefer to pursue models that recognize in full their jurisdictional authority to care for children, youth, and families. One example that is a step in this direction is the model adopted by the Sechelt First Nation in British Columbia. Pursuant to the tripartite agreement, the provincial government delegates its law-making function to the Sechelt First Nation with certain limits. Sechelt has authority to develop and implement tribal authority for child and family services. Consultations have begun with community Elders, leadership, and members to design the child and family services justice model. Although Sechelt operated according to the delegated model, the implementation of the new jurisdictional model is expected within the next couple of years (N. Simon, personal communication, December, 2002). Because this model relies on the delegation of law-making authority from the provincial government, this is seen as one step toward self-government but not full recognition of Sechelt law-making authority.

Issues in the Development of Culturally Appropriate Practices

Child welfare services to Aboriginal people designed, administered, and delivered by mainstream agencies under laws that are not Aboriginal can, at best, aim to be "culturally sensitive." As Rooney & Bibus argue (1996), "while cultural sensitivity is useful with recent immigrants who have not had extended contact with the dominant culture, work with historically oppressed minorities requires a perspective which recognizes the power differences between representatives of the dominant culture's agencies and members of oppressed groups" (p. 64). Understanding the historical relations between groups can enable child welfare practitioners "to look beyond their own backgrounds or training in cultural sensitivity to recognize that they represent a powerful, potentially hostile threat to families" (p. 64). Morrissette, McKenzie, and Morrissette (1993) draw a crucial distinction between "culturally sensitive" and "culturally appropriate" practice in order to emphasize their preference for the latter: "While culturally sensitive service advances awareness of issues in the Aboriginal community in the context of involvement with an ethnic minority, culturally appropriate service integrates core Aboriginal values, beliefs and healing practices in program delivery" (p. 101). Even when First Nations agencies have had the authority to deliver and administer some services, limitations to their mandate and to their role in developing the services has meant constraints on the cultural appropriateness of those services. Brown and colleagues' (2002) review of a British Columbia First Nations agency confirms that full empowerment of First Nations communities is not possible in the context of power imbalances inherent in paradigms such as the delegated model.

The needs of First Nations communities are not comparable to those of non-Aboriginal communities. In some communities, unemployment, poverty, substance use, child abuse and neglect, violence against women, youth suicide, and communal disintegration are widespread (ANCFSAO, 2001; Koster et al., 2000). Poverty and marginalization increase stress on families and contribute to their involvement in child welfare systems. This is the reality that Timpson's (1995) analysis finds largely missing from the child welfare literature, for what she deems political reasons, until quite recently. According to McDonald and Ladd (2000), 50% of First Nations children living on- or off-reserve live in poverty. In 2000, over 55% of First Nation children in Manitoba and approximately 35% of Metis children lived in poverty (Social Planning Council of Winnipeg, 2002). In some remote communities with limited infrastructure in Northern Ontario, the ANCFSAO (2001) claims that the application of Ontario's new risk-assessment instrument would likely find most or all of the children to be at risk; yet the services to respond to these conditions are absent. The Tikanagan agency in Northern Ontario, for example, identifies the following services as not existing within its catchment area: psychological assessment, residential treatment, intensive child and family intervention, day treatment programs, mobile crisis response programs, professional children's mental health counselling, early intervention and prevention, suicide prevention and response programs, programs for autism, attention deficit hyperactive disorder, and fetal alcohol syndrome, sexual abuse treatment programs, residential services for children and youth with serious developmental challenges, Special Services At Home, speech and language assessment and therapy, Healthy Babies, Healthy Children, Better Beginnings, Better Futures, and regular medical services (ANCFSAO, 2001).

The major issues at stake in considering the various models of delivering Aboriginal child welfare services are the right to self-determination and the optimal suitability of services to meet the unique needs of Aboriginal communities in ways that further the aims of community healing, capacity building, and child well-being. Adaptations of social work practices and education to the needs of Aboriginal communities have been attempted, with mixed results (Castellano, Stalwick, & Wien, 1986; Morrissette, et al., 1993). Because of the combination of unique needs and conditions, the delivery of mainstream services is bound to be less cost-effective in First Nations communities, less culturally suitable, and more difficult with regard to meeting provincial and territorial standards or reconciling them within the cultural framework of community. If full consultation and collaboration are not in place, and policy requirements are not flexible, the result can be "devastating" (MacDonald, 2002; Association of Native Child and Family Services Agencies of Ontario, 2001). No conventional model has yet been able to adequately address these needs (Morrissette et al., 1993). Organizational practices, accountability requirements, centralized control, political interference by band councils, interventive practices, and staff development and training are all issues that are inevitably problematic when services and the agencies that deliver them "operate within legislative and policy frameworks created by the dominant society" (Morrissette et al., 1993, p. 103).

The realization of such constraints has involved a painful developmental process, partly because the extension of child welfare services began in some communities before a fully informed dialogue about it had taken place. The importation of existing mainstream models in the early development of an Aboriginal child welfare system meant that structures, policies, and practices designed for another culture were being transposed uncritically (RCAP, 1996c). The response of the Association of Native Child and Family Service Agencies of Ontario (2001) to the provincial government's Child Welfare Reforms of 1999 indicate how destructive the consequences of this practice can be.

The Awasis agency (1997) cites the work of Thomas (1994) and Shields (1995) in outlining mainstream approaches to social work that "inhibit growth and development in children and families, particularly First Nation families" (p. 24). These approaches include a focus on deficit reduction rather than the promotion of capacities; the reliance on a categorical approach to service delivery; considering cases outside of their larger context; failure to incorporate holistic healing; the lack of power-sharing in the system; family powerlessness combined with agency reluctance to share power, and the barriers created by language. Morrissette et al. (1993) identify as problematic conventional approaches to direct practice, funding, and organizational structure that are incompatible with traditional ways of helping and healing. Even when new policies are family oriented and community based, prevailing practice nevertheless continues to emphasize individualized understandings of causation and counter-cultural interventions, especially placement of children outside communities (Morrissette et al., 1993).

Structural issues. Jurisdictional issues are very significant insofar as they are linked to standards and requirements, funding, and the degree of autonomy agencies actually have over policy, programs, and practices. Without jurisdictional control, the development of culturally appropriate services is impeded (McKenzie & Morrissette, 2002). Despite some measure of control over policy development within a given agency, an ongoing problem exists in relation to provincial child welfare laws and standards and the accountability issues that arise from these (ANCFSAO, 2001; Koster et al., 2000; McKenzie et al., 1995). The fundamental issue revolves around the cultural differences in conceptualizing what child welfare involves and what the priorities in promoting it will be. Since the 1999 Ontario Child Welfare Reforms, for example, practice, training, and funding have given priority to child safety based on risk assessment and protection. The emphasis is on competency, goals, and "business-plan objectives" (Koster, 2001, p. 3), in contrast to the holistic value-based approach on which practice in Ontario First Nations agencies is based. This results in a poor fit between training, funding, and technology and the current capacities and resources of the First Nations communities involved (ANCFSAO, 2001). Standards establish levels of child well-being and safety that the state can then legitimately enforce; standards are the foundation for criteria for intervention in families in the interests of children at risk. In order for these criteria to be culturally appropriate, the standards must be culturally specific (McKenzie et al., 1995).

In an attempt to identify such standards among First Nation communities, McKenzie and his colleagues (1995) conducted a series of focus groups with a broad range of representatives from eight communities. The topics addressed included the definition of a family, indicators of abuse and neglect, preferences regarding placement of children for alternate care, and how culture should shape the provision of child and family services. After outlining the themes discussed in the focus groups, the authors conclude that the emergent principles reflect a "holistic, family-and community-focused foundation for child welfare services" (p. 648). The authors note that many of the ideas expressed by the participants about what constitutes good child welfare practice are also consistent with mainstream standards. McDonald and Ladd (2000) indicate that only in British Columbia have First Nations standards been incorporated into provincial standards. In several provinces, First Nations are in various stages of developing and implementing their own standards.

Funding is a particularly thorny problem (ANCFSAO, 2001; McKenzie, 1989). The ANCFSAO (2001) identifies funding benchmarks and funding formulas related to programs—and to most aspects of organizational costs—as being inadequate or limiting at best, and at worst being in conflict with the visions, law, and values held by First Nations communities. Particularly problematic are funding formulas primarily directed at supporting children in care and that do not allow the flexibility to provide the services deemed necessary by the communities themselves. In the context of an Aboriginal vision and cultural imperative to keep families together and children in their communities, the problem is obvious. Block federal funding offers the significant advantage of affording agencies the flexibility to develop innovative programs and set their own administrative priorities (McDonald & Ladd, 2000; McKenzie & Flette, 2001; McKenzie, 2002). McKenzie and Flette's evaluation of one five-year block funding project at West Region Child and Family Services in the mid 1990s provides an example of how such funds have been used to develop accessible and culturally appropriate community resources. The funding was used to develop alternate programming (for example, a therapeutic foster home program for children with special needs), add treatment support services to each local community team, and to co-ordinate and host other community services (such as family violence and day care programs). New positions within the agency were also funded to develop new initiatives (for example, a community program for children and families struggling with fetal alcohol syndrome and its effects was developed by a co-ordinator for children with special needs). Partnership with education authorities led to a program for youth who had dropped out of school, and another offering life skills, computer training, and support services for young parents with children in care or at risk. The goal of balancing protection with prevention led to the development of programs providing resources to families and children, such as groups for mothers in which they learn and receive support from Elders and other women. Decentralized management of such programs is emphasized and supported. Nevertheless, block funding also has some disadvantages from the First Nations agencies' perspective, insofar as the agreements lack specific criteria for adjustment of funding and for establishing the subsequent starting budget base (McDonald & Ladd, 2000).

Other system issues identified in the literature are agency development and the relations between Native and non-Native child welfare authorities, which are troubled by mistrust (ANCFSAO, 2001), differing research and evaluation methods (ANCFSAO, 2001; Koster et al., 2000; Morrissette et al., 1993), and power imbalances (ANCFSAO, 2001; Awasis, 1997). Recruiting, training, and retaining staff who can meet mainstream standards for social work education, English literacy, and technological competence under these conditions (ANCFSAO, 2001; Castellano et al., 1986; McKenzie, 1989), coupled with negotiating the internal and external politics involved (ANCFSAO, 2001; McKenzie, 1989; McKenzie et al., 1995; Morrissette et al., 1993), pose an enormous challenge.

Finally, there are issues within First Nations communities themselves that contribute to the complexity of developing and delivering culturally appropriate services. Issues of internal politics related to divisions and power struggles within communities have already been alluded to. In addition, the communities are often quite small, with many or most of their members related to each other. The social worker may be related to the families she or he investigates (ANCFSAO, 2001). Where there is still a general lack of awareness about child abuse and sexual abuse (ANCFSAO, 2001), "denial and minimizing" on the part of family and community members may require interventions against their wishes, making it difficult to implement the principle of respecting parental rights (McKenzie et al., 1995). There are inherent challenges in balancing individual and collective rights in a way that promotes child, family, and community well-being. On one hand, the principle of restoring harmony to a family or community may lead to responses that ultimately fail to protect victims from abuse (La Rocque, 1997; Morrissette et al., 1993). On the other hand, there are significant potential benefits to the less formal and less structured ways of working in small, closely knit communities, such as those described by Brown et al. (2002) and MacDonald (2002). Within a Euro-Western paradigm, it is difficult to fully comprehend how to address the inseparability of children's, parents', and community's rights and the inevitable permeability of professional boundaries. This difficulty may in itself underscore the lack of cultural fit between mainstream child welfare and the needs of Aboriginal communities.

Direct practice issues. Culturally sensitive practice essentially refers to the adaptations effected by mainstream services to deal with cultural minority groups, Aboriginal and otherwise. It involves the education of workers about values, customs, and practices that may differ from those of the dominant culture in order to establish a co-operative relationship and avoid inappropriate judgments and interventions. It may involve specially designed programs, outreach, and hiring of staff who are themselves members of the cultural group being served. It was initially assumed, understandably, that the hiring of Aboriginal workers for First Nations child welfare service would significantly further the delivery of culturally sensitive practice. This has not turned out to be as simple a solution as it seemed, particularly given the structural constraints. The lack of knowledge and appreciation of Aboriginal traditions among non-Aboriginal and some Aboriginal workers has been identified as an impediment to the development of culturally appropriate services (Castellano et al., 1986; McKenzie & Morrissette, 2002). This is complicated by the diversity in "cultural identification" among Aboriginal people (Morrissette et al., 1993). The nature of mainstream social work education contributes further to the difficulty.

Conventional social work training for mainstream child protection work often emphasizes the assessment of individual deficits and control over individuals and families, rather than a broader analysis of community and structural problems affecting children's well-being (RCAP 1996c). Aboriginal peoples do not deny widespread family dysfunction—on the contrary, Aboriginal peoples recognize and are actively engaged in confronting the social problems they see in their communities regarding child welfare—they understand them as signs of larger social and historical consequences of colonialism rather than as individual deficits (Timpson, 1995). Conventional training also emphasizes confidentiality and clear professional boundaries that do not always fit with ways of life in Aboriginal communities (See Brown et al., 2002).

Since basic approaches to the client–worker relationship are shaped by cultural values, they differ among cultural groups. In the mainstream Western context, the relationship between worker and client is "uni-directional" (RCAP, 1996c, p. 40) rather than multi-faceted, as in traditional communities. This is antithetical to Aboriginal traditions of mutual aid (RCAP, 1996c, Castellano et al., 1986).

The mainstream principle of "best interests of the child," which is a cornerstone of Canadian child and family law, has been identified as being at odds with Aboriginal values and perspectives. In Aboriginal communities, the best interests of the child are not considered separately from the best interests of the community (RCAP, 1996c, p. 52), yet the "best interests" principle assumes they are separable. This conflict between individual and community interests tends to be manifested in decision-making about placement outside the home, when there is a need to balance the child's need for stable parenting with the need for community support in developing an Aboriginal identity (McKenzie et al., 1995; RCAP, 1996c). The Awasis Agency of Northern Manitoba (1997) draws on the work of Monture to suggest that "the [best interests] test is racist and further perpetuates the already severe over representation of children caught in the child system [sic] of Manitoba" (p. 28).

Aboriginal Visions of Child Welfare

Tikanagan's Vision
The Creator has entrusted us with the sacred responsibility for protecting our children, developing and sustaining strong families, and building healthy communities. The future of our communities is our children who need to be nurtured within their families and communities.

Our Goal
The sacred responsibility for developing and sustaining our families takes us as Aboriginal people back to the past to prepare ourselves for the future. The concepts, principles, and the values practised are the strengths we need now to encourage and ensure healthy families, which in turn will be the foundation of strong and healthy communities.

Principles

The primary responsibility for the safety and well being of our children is with the family. If children cannot be cared for within the family, then the extended family should care for the children. At the community level, the safety and well being of children is everyone's responsibility and anyone who is aware of children in need of protection should ensure that their families receive the assistance needed. The primary purpose of service to families is to keep them intact and ensure that children are safe and well. Service should be family focussed, community based, First Nation controlled, and First Nation delivered. (Association of Native Child and Family Service Agencies of Ontario, 2001, [i])

The foregoing is the statement of the Tikanagan Child and Family Services included in the report entitled "Child Welfare Reform Initiatives: Issues and Recommendations." In addition to the protection of children, "Native agencies have the added responsibility to change the outcomes of the past" (ANCAFSAO, 2001 p. 10) through practices that give high priority to supporting families and communities in caring for their children rather than focusing primarily on mainstream concepts of protection.

The Awasis Agency of Northern Manitoba (1997) provides another example of an Aboriginal agency's approach to child welfare work congruent with the context of Aboriginal communal and family life. As stated by Elder Sandy Beardy, that goal is:

To promote the best interests of children within the context of their families, communities, and culture, we cannot continue to view situations of pycho-social risks as act-specific and individually focused. We need to look at how we impact families and communities when we intervene in their lives. We must question treatment approaches that increase the power of workers rather than the power of First Nation families. Radical sharing of power in the family-worker constellation consists of more than techniques for increasing family skills or even family self-determination. It involves power sharing and power shedding, a professional stance that implies transformative changes in how our work is evaluated and rewarded (Gutierrez, Glenmaye & Delois, 1995). We must be able to sit down together as equals in trying to resolve a common problem. (p. xii).

The Aboriginal Justice Inquiry–Child Welfare Initiative (2001) offers as its vision "[a] child and family service system that recognizes and supports the rights of children to develop within safe and healthy families and communities, and recognizes that First Nations and Métis peoples have unique authority, rights and responsibilities to honour and care for their children" (p. 1). The goal is an agreement between the Government of Manitoba, the Assembly of Manitoba Chiefs and the Manitoba Métis Federation that would lead to a plan for the development of province-wide delivery of Aboriginal child welfare services by First Nations and Métis communities.

Taken together, the goal statements cited above reflect the range of elements found in the literature of an Aboriginal vision for the safety and strength of children and their communities. Strengthening the family is seen not only as a social issue but as a political one central to the ongoing negotiations of Aboriginal people for self-government.

Frameworks for Culturally Appropriate Practice and Education

What had happened to bring the young woman and her children to this place? What had happened to bring me—a person who entered social work to try to be "helpful"—to a place of representing an agency which intended to support families and protect children, but that has instead been hated and mistrusted, labelled an agent of domination and genocide by First Nations and Métis people? As I recall my encounter with the young woman, I see now two women, almost the same age, in a room with two children—hers. I was just a little older than she. She was new to "the city" and so was I. I was from a small Métis community outside the city, a community I left to seek education and opportunity. She probably left a small community for similar reasons. As a social worker, I felt helpless— but my helplessness was nothing in comparison to hers. The contrast in our lives was stark. It was painful to have been part of the system that had caused so much destruction. At the time I did not know how to respond differently. As a young social worker, I was attempting to do "work" defined by an agency in a certain way. I was unsure of myself, lacking in confidence. I was deeply troubled—our experience was connected in a way I could not name. Later, there was shame attached to admitting that I had been a child welfare worker. I wonder to this day, what might I have done differently? What might an individual social worker have been able to do to make a difference in the life of that young woman and her children?[19]

Given the role that the profession of social work has played in the relationship between Aboriginal people and the child welfare system, can it now contribute to transforming that relationship? Adaptation of mainstream services to meet the needs of most non-dominant ethnic or racial groups is known to be fraught with difficulties (see, for example, Tsang & George, 1998; Fletcher, 1997; McGoldrick, 1998); this is further complicated with regard to First Nations because of historical relationships and unique assets and needs. Coupled with cultural differences, the implications of colonization and systemic racism are crucial for social work practice, education, and training in general, and particularly in the area of child welfare.

There are several models of practice in the academic literature, and some that can be inferred from the writing of First Nations agencies that outline frameworks for culturally appropriate child welfare services. Morrissette et al. (1993) posit a framework for Aboriginal social work practice that shares the principles of being grounded in an Aboriginal world view and a developing consciousness about colonialism. In addition, they add the principles of "cultural knowledge and traditions as an active component of retaining Aboriginal identity and collective consciousness, and empowerment as a method of practice" (p. 91), and an understanding of the range of cultural identification among Aboriginal people. A continuum of cultural identification has been elaborated to aid in this understanding (McKenzie & Morrissette, 2002). The framework presumes the fundamental elements of a structural approach to social work; that is, the connection of individual experience to conditions of oppression. Also important is the *strengths* perspective that affirms the resilience of Aboriginal peoples and their ability to develop the best solutions to community challenges.

Morrissette et al. (1993) argue that culturally appropriate practice would go beyond "cultural sensitivity" to include using Elders and healers for traditional teaching and healing (for example, the healing circle) and a community-based approach to the development and delivery of services. This would require flexibility in funding and in accountability regarding service requirements. To accommodate these goals, agency services would need to be restructured at the administrative and direct-service levels. Social work education would need to change to support these new approaches to practice, and indeed to re-evaluate and reshape current mainstream approaches to practice. The intention of such a prescription is not to create a parallel system, but to transform mainstream services.

McKenzie et al. (1995) endorse a framework for child welfare services in First Nations communities under legislation and standards that make the provider agencies responsible for prevention and family support services (as opposed to more narrowly defined mainstream child protection practices). A child's attachment to parents and caregivers, extended family, community, and culture are all seen as important, so that preferences for out-of-home care, when necessary, give priority to keeping the child within the community. In the study upon which this model is based, the authors found that the participating communities view a child-centred approach as necessary when a child might otherwise be subject to abuse, and recognize out-of home placement as required at times. Access to trusted caregivers and counsellors may necessitate placement outside the community and this, too, is acceptable when necessary.

The Awasis Agency of Northern Manitoba (1997) is an agency with 99% Aboriginal employees whose explicit intention is a radical change in the way

child welfare practice and training of Aboriginal social workers is conceptualized. Instead of emphasizing "prevention of child abuse and neglect,"
the agency stresses "well-being within families and communities" (p. 94). The
"developmental framework" for practice merges adult education and community development, emphasizing "learning in the context of political
involvement" (p. 92).

Following are the services and systemic conditions we have culled from
the literature that are required to ensure the provision of culturally appropriate services to Aboriginal people. At the level of larger systems, First
Nations and Aboriginal ways of knowing in child welfare need to be affirmed
through legislation and resource allocations in order to augment the cultural fit and efficacy of child welfare services. At the organizational level,
the necessary features are decentralized structure, recruitment and retention of a stable core of properly trained staff, funding benchmarks and outcome measures that are suitable to the context, and participatory research
to continue development of innovative, effective programs. In order to be consistent with holism, healing, and strengthening of families and communities,
service delivery must be structured to include traditional healing, the inclusion of Elders in supportive and preventive services, the repatriation of children who have previously been removed, the use of customary care or custom
adoption whenever possible, cultivation of resources for foster care and
adoption when needed, alternatives to an adversarial legal process between
families and child welfare authorities, and a focus on the family as a unit, as
opposed to the child alone. Specific services at the community level include
community capacity building, community service teams, group programs,
and preventive/supportive service. These could include recreational programs for youth and families and education about substantive and procedural
issues regarding child abuse and neglect, sexual abuse, alcohol and substance use, suicide prevention, and so forth. At the level of families and individuals, services should include family support services (for example, in-home
services, respite care) and individual and family counselling as needed. The
need for access to mental health and child development services within the
community, or funding to gain access to them outside the community, spans
structural and service issues.

Changing practice approaches such as those described above requires
changing social work education and training as well. The Royal Commission
(1996) emphasizes the need for professional education to include cultural
issues relevant to Aboriginal people. Differences between "Aboriginal ways
of helping" and non-Aboriginal ways are exacerbated when the helping person is non-Aboriginal (RCAP, 1996c, p. 41). The problem is not simply
solved, however, by substituting Aboriginal workers with mainstream social
work education for non-Aboriginal workers. In the mid 1980s, Castellano

and colleagues (1986) cautioned Aboriginal leaders lest "a new crop of social workers, shaped in the same mould prove equally noxious [as previous social workers had been]" (p. 176). Although it recognized some aspects of existing undergraduate programs as being very helpful, the Royal Commission supports the position that the programs fall short of the needs of Aboriginal counsellors (RCAP, 1996c).

There have been systematic efforts to foster cultural sensitivity, the appreciation of diversity, and knowledge of cross-cultural practices in Canadian schools of social work in recent years. Castellano and colleagues' (1986) review of early adaptations made by schools of social work to meet the needs of education for Aboriginal students and their communities finds that the need to develop training programs quickly in areas where child welfare was being transferred to communities provided a certain impetus that was helpful. Unfortunately, in their haste to develop programs, schools have sometimes undertaken cross-cultural training before fully comprehending what that entails. In encouraging awareness of and sensitivity to cultural difference, Castellano and colleagues (1986) caution that generalizations taught in a social work program cannot adequately "prepare an outsider to understand the unique culture of a particular community at a particular point in its history" (p. 172) nor is a Native student's ancestry sufficient to ensure she or he will be aware of culturally appropriate ways of helping. In fact, they say, spending extended time in the mainstream educational system is likely to bring about attitudinal and behavioural shifts that create, rather than solve, problems for those who then go out to work with Aboriginal people. In programs where sponsoring Aboriginal communities and organizations select candidates for professional education, they indicate a preference for mature individuals with a demonstrated commitment to the community, rather than focusing primarily on academic prerequisites as academic institutions would otherwise do.

A number of issues have been identified as emerging from early attempts to adapt social work education programs to various Aboriginal communities. First, it is important to consider the contexts in which the students will be working. Second, the characteristics of the students themselves must be considered. Third, it is necessary to adapt programs to students' needs while meeting the requirements of mainstream educational standards. Finally, there must be involvement of the communities for whom the programs are intended in determining the content and process (Castellano et al., 1986). These caveats are in the revisions to the education policy statements of the Canadian Association of Schools of Social Work (CASSW/ACESS; 2000), which emphasize training that prepares students for work with "populations of diverse cultural, racial and ethnic backgrounds in different regions." They also recommend the accountability of social work schools to the communities they serve through recognition of diversity in terms of the programs of study, admissions, removal of systemic barriers, and allocation of financial and human resources toward these goals (see Appendix E of the CASSW policy statement). More specifically, the accreditation manual identifies the ways in which schools of social work are expected to address and accommodate the needs of Aboriginal communities and Aboriginal students through inclusive planning processes, curriculum design, program structure, admissions, and so forth (see Appendix D of the CASSW policy statement).

Outside the educational institutions, the problem of inadequate funding undermines efforts to develop and implement more appropriate training in the field. According to the RCAP (1996c), there were, at the time of its report, no plans or funds set aside for the training of new Aboriginal workers (despite the establishment of new Aboriginal child and family service agencies or change of personnel in existing agencies). The RCAP therefore recommends that the development of integrated services to children and families under Aboriginal control include funding for multidisciplinary training of Aboriginal personnel (1996c). The Caring for First Nations Children Society (CFNCS) Aboriginal Social Worker Training program in British Columbia is a promising model for such training (CFNCS, 2002). It is based on three central features: First, it was developed at the request of First Nations child and family service agencies; second, the competency-based curriculum integrates cultural context, best practice, and legislative requirements through processes established by First Nations and the province; third, the practice model, built on principles of holism and interdependence, reflects the diversity among First Nations communities.

Finally, funding, training materials, and methods must take into account differing levels of formal education, technological competence, English literacy, and difficulty accessing educational centres (ANCFSAO, 2001).

Summary and Conclusion

Aboriginal children are over-represented in Canada's child welfare system, just as Aboriginal youth and adults are in the justice system. At the same time, child welfare services available to Aboriginal communities are often inferior and culturally inappropriate for their unique needs. Canada's indigenous people are distinguished from other Canadians by a history of colonization, which has irrevocably altered their traditional culture as well as their economic and political context. The erosion of traditional livelihoods, soaring unemployment, the impact of residential schools, and the depth of pain suffered by those affected by child welfare and justice systems have been described by many Aboriginal peoples and have been documented by numerous research papers, policy papers, and governmental inquiries. Whereas other groups have sought Canada out as a refuge or a place of new beginnings, Aboriginal peoples have seen this—their home for thousands of years—as the place in which their oppression originated once the Europeans arrived and began the process of colonization. The oppression and assimilation experienced by Aboriginal peoples has been enacted and administered by the very institutions that have claimed to be their benefactors. The profession of social work, central as it has always been in the field of child welfare, has been an active participant in these processes.

This history has established a relationship of marginalization that makes it extremely difficult for incremental changes from within the same framework to be effective. Efforts at reform have sought solutions in changing the Aboriginal people themselves, rather than the institutions. Meanwhile, Aboriginal claims to the historical right of self-determination and self-government pose challenges to mainstream institutions. Although the goal of Aboriginal-controlled child welfare services has been identified and receives significant support among First Nations peoples and some governments, primary efforts today have focused on adapting mainstream services to provide culturally sensitive services and on developing in piecemeal fashion alternative models for culturally appropriate services. There are no simple and obvious solutions, but solutions are clearly necessary and are actively demanded by Aboriginal people.

The development of new models has had mixed success to date. Although the assumption of child welfare authority by Aboriginal peoples has increased the options for culturally based services, they are often predicated on Euro-Western legislation. This means the lack of a cultural fit between child welfare ideology, law, and services delivered. In addition, Aboriginal agencies often work with Aboriginal communities that have not experienced significant socioeconomic improvements, and the multidimensional impacts of colonization that underly child maltreatment and neglect—such as poverty, disruption of traditional parenting, and substance misuse—are yet to be redressed. It is clear in the literature that essential elements of any new model must be congruent with an Aboriginal world view regarding community strengthening, traditional ways of healing, and the aim of addressing the effects of colonialism. Appropriate hiring practices, culturally appropriate social work educational programs, adequate and flexible funding, and administrative structuring are also crucial.

Relations based on marginalization, power imbalances, and racism will need to be transformed to make these elements possible. Given some fundamental common ground between the value base of Aboriginal people and that of the social work profession, it may be possible that with openness to critical reflection and genuine respect for Aboriginal self-determination, the profession can contribute to the development of truly appropriate new systems of child welfare, not only for Aboriginal communities but for the many communities that constitute Canadian society. Establishing such systems, however, requires more than lip service to differences among world views or the adaptation of mainstream models based on child protection principles; it must take into account economic and cultural realities and the larger context of existing and historical inequities at all levels. The agenda must be driven by the needs, wishes, capacities, and structures of Aboriginal communities.

Notes

1 Terminology set out by the Royal Commission on Aboriginal Peoples (RCAP) (1996b) established *Aboriginal peoples* as the term referring to political and cultural groups considered original in North America; this includes *First Nation* (replacing the term *Indian*), *Inuit* (replacing *Eskimo*) and *Metis* peoples of Canada. First Nation people who lose their status when they leave the reserve are also included by the term Aboriginal. This terminology is not followed consistently in the literature. Different terms may be used in different parts of the country and by authors of varying backgrounds. It is a confusing issue, but we have chosen to err, when in doubt, on the side of inclusiveness. We have therefore tried to keep our use of the terms as close to the RCAP formulation as possible; but when referring to the literature, we stick to the author's own choice of term whenever appropriate. See also guidelines developed by the Department of Indian and Northern Affairs Canada (INAC) at www.ainc-inac.gc.ca/pr/pub/wf/index _e.html.

2 All four authors have worked at one time or another in the field of child welfare in Canada and all of us have worked with Aboriginal families. The personal commentary inserted in this paper comes from the one among us (Joyce Clouston Carlson) who is of Metis heritage from Manitoba and who worked in child welfare during the 1970s. The remaining authors are Gitanmaax First Nation (Cindy Blackstock) and Eastern European Jewish descent (Marshall Fine and Deena Mandell). Cindy continues to administer and develop programs in First Nations child welfare and has published in the field; Joyce has worked with Aboriginal leaders to assist in publication of oral cultural stories. Marshall and Deena are involved in various child welfare studies and teach about child welfare in multicultural contexts as part of their graduate courses on social work practice with families.

3 At the time of writing, a valuable new comprehensive resource has emerged. The First Nations Child and Family Caring Society of Canada, through the First Nations Research Site of the Centre of Excellence for Child Welfare, has compiled over 850 published and unpublished works of relevance to researchers, policy makers and practitioners (Bennett & Blackstock, 2002). While the primary focus is on Canadian work, some references are included from the United States and abroad.

4 The personal commentary inserted in this paper comes from Joyce Clouston Carlson.

5 The title Department of Indian and Northern Affairs Canada (INAC) is used interchangeably with Department of Indian Affairs and Northern Development (DIAND). See INAC/DIAND website, www.ainc-inac.gc.ca.

6 Accurate and consistent statistical information is connected to several factors. First, since terminology has varied considerably over time, statistics cited in the literature are sometimes misleading or confusing. For example, some sources use broad terms such as "Native" and "Aboriginal" when they are in fact referring to specific groups. In incorporating statistical information, we have therefore made every effort to clarify the intended group. Second, as the RCAP (1996) notes, accurate statistics are available only for First Nation people, registered under the Indian Act, and ordinarily resident on reserve; funding for services to these communities flows from the federal government. On the other hand, statistics for non-status First Nation persons, the Metis, and status First Nation persons living off reserve, as well as for Inuit persons outside the Northwest Territories, are not gathered separately from the general population; statistics are based on estimates made by service agencies. Since these agencies have used differing methods of data collection, accurately reporting and comparing statistical findings is difficult. Attempts have been made to clarify statistical references wherever the information was available.

7 The variation in the Maritime figures is thus attributable in part to variable inclusion/exclusion of non-status, off-reserve and Metis children. Similarly, the lower Manitoba and Alberta figures refer to status children only, while the higher Saskatchewan figure includes non-status, off-reserve and Metis children. The Ontario figures include the latter groups, while the Yukon figures do not.

8 Armitage refers here to Status First Nation children; Timpson, on the following page, uses the term Native to describe all categories of Aboriginal persons—status First Nation (registered under the Indian Act), non-status First Nation, Metis, and Inuit persons.

9 It is important to note that many Aboriginal ceremonies and communal structures have existed for millennia and inform social and cultural order in the community as a whole, rather than being established for specific current goals or purposes.

10 The importance of a connection to the land is expressed in the following excerpt from a submission to RCAP by the Assembly of First Nations: "Our songs, our spirits and our identities are written on this land, and the future of our peoples is tied to it. It is not a possession or a commodity for us—it is the heart of our nations. In our traditional spirituality, it is our Mother ... It is our life" (Assembly of First Nations, 1993, p. 1).

11 Stanley McKay's story was transcribed by Joyce Clouston Carlson; Mr. McKay is the author of his story.

12 These variable effects have not been well studied. One can speculate that they may be attributable to mediating influences such as positive relationships that may have been formed with teachers or schoolmates, or to families "back home" whose own histories (communal and individual) enabled them to be more supportive of their children in the schools (S. McKay, personal communication, Sept. 2002). In general, however, the issue of what role the residential schools played in the lives of individuals, communities and cultures is a highly complex one (CBC, 2000); the polarization around it does little to further our understanding of the

complexities and variables involved. It is likely that some children's experience of the schools was neither entirely harmful nor entirely beneficial. Communities were likely differently affected as well. It is also important to consider the effects of the schools in the broader context of the overall disruption of First Nations economy, social structure, customary practices, ways of living on the land, and so forth, rather than as an isolated variable.

13 The death rate in residential schools in BC ranged from a low of 11% to a high of 40% at the Kuper Island residential school throughout its 25 years of operation. These staggering death rates were due, in large part, to the substandard care and housing provided to the children (Fournier and Crey, 1997).

14 Despite this expansion, sustained funding for First Nations child welfare agencies throughout Canada was not available until the early 1990s.

15 Refer to note 4.

16 The First Nations Child and Family Services' *Joint National Policy Review* (McDonald & Ladd, 2000) contains several tables comparing key aspects of provincial child and family services legislation, delegation of statutory child and family services, and provincial and first nations service standards across Canada.

17 See www.tbs-sct.gc.ca/rma/account/sufa-ecus/fncfs-sef_e.pdf.

18 Research on the question of why some First Nations communities in the United States and Canada prospered socioeconomically—while others continued to struggle—indicates that substantive community improvement in social and economic well-being is preceded, rather than followed, by First Nations self-determination and sovereignty (Cornell & Kalt, 2002).

19 Refer to note 4.

References

Aboriginal Justice Inquiry. (1991). *Volume 1: The justice system and Aboriginal people: Public inquiry into the administration of justice and Aboriginal people.* Winnipeg: Province of Manitoba.

Aboriginal Justice Inquiry–Child Welfare Initiative. (2001). *Conceptual plan for the restructuring of child welfare in Manitoba.* Manitoba: Aboriginal Justice Inquiry Child Welfare Initiative Joint Management Committee.

Aboriginal Justice Inquiry–Child Welfare Initiative. (August 2002). *Promise of hope, commitment to change: Child and family services in Manitoba.* Retrieved January 5, 2003, from AJI-CWI website: http://www.aji-cwi.mb.ca/

Armitage, A. (1993). Family and child welfare in First Nation communities. In B. Wharf (Ed.), *Rethinking child welfare in Canada* (pp. 131–171). Toronto, ON: Oxford University Press.

Assembly of First Nations (1993). *Reclaiming our nationhood: Strengthening our heritage.* Report submitted to Royal Commission on Aboriginal Peoples. Ottawa, ON: Assembly of First Nations.

Association of Native Child and Family Services of Ontario (2001). *Child welfare reform initiatives: Issues and recommendations.* (Final draft).

Awasis Agency of Northern Manitoba. (1997). *First Nations Family Justice: Mee-noo-stah-tan Mi-ni-si-win.* Thompson, MB: Author.

Bagley, C. (1985). Child abuse by the child welfare system. *Journal of Child Care, 2*(3), 63–69.

Bennett, M., & Blackstock, C. (2002). *A literature review and annotated bibliography on aspects of Aboriginal child welfare in Canada.* Retrieved January 7, 2003, from First Nations Child and Family Caring Society of Canada website: http://www.fncfcs.com/

Blackstock, C. (November 28, 2006). Help make a difference in First Nations child welfare. Ottawa, ON: First Nation Child and Family Caring Society of Canada. Retrieved from http://www.fncaringsociety.com.

——. (2001). Restoring peace and harmony in First Nations communities, In K. Kufeldt & B. McKenzie (Eds.), *Child welfare: Connecting research policy and practice* (pp. 331–341). Waterloo, ON: Wilfrid Laurier University Press.

Brown, L., Haddock, L., & Kovach, M. (2002). Watching over our families: Lalum'utul' smuneem child and family services. In B. Wharf (Ed.), *Community work approaches to child welfare* (pp. 131–151). Peterborough, ON: Broadview Press.

Canadian Association of Schools of Social Work (2000). *Standards of Accreditation.* Retrieved September 18, 2002, from CASSW website: http://www.cassw-acess.ca/

Canadian Broadcasting Corporation. (June, 2000). *Ideas: To hurt or to heal.* Toronto, ON: Canadian Broadcasting Corporation.

Caring for First Nations Children Society (2002). *Aboriginal Social Worker training project.* Retrieved January, 13, 2003, from CFNCS website: http://www.fernweb.com /cfncs/training-program.html

Carlson, J. (1994). *Journey from Fisher River: A celebration of the spirituality of a people through the life of Stan McKay.* Toronto, ON: United Church Publishing House.

Carlson, J. (1995). *Dancing the Dream: The First Nations and the church in partnership.* Toronto, ON: Anglican Book Centre.

Castellano, M. B., Stalwick, H., & Wien, F. (1986). Native social work in Canada: Issues and adaptations. *Canadian Social Work Review, 4,* 167–184.

Chandler, M. (2002, November). *Stabilizing cultural identity as a hedge against suicide in Canada's First Nations.* Paper presented at the Aboriginal Research and Policy Conference, Ottawa, Ontario.

Connors, E., & Maidman, F. (2001). A circle of healing: Family wellness in Aboriginal communities. In I. Prilleltensky, G. Nelson, & L. Peirson (Eds.), *Promoting family wellness and preventing child maltreatment: Fundamentals for thinking and action* (pp. 349–416). Toronto, ON: University of Toronto Press.

Cook, G., & Carlson, J. (1997). Gladys Taylor Cook. In J. Carlson & A. Dumont (Eds.), *Bridges in spirituality: First Nations Christian women tell their stories* (pp. 102–144). Toronto, ON: Anglican Book Centre and United Church Publishing House.

Cornell, S., & Kalt, J. (2002). Reloading the dice: Improving the chances for economic development on American Indian reservations. Retrieved January 13, 2003, from Harvard Projecton American Indian Economic Development website: http://www.ksg.harvard.edu/hpaied/res_main.htm

Courtney, M. E., Barth, R. P., Duerr-Berrick, J., Brooks, D., Needell, B., & Park, L. (1996). Race and child welfare services: Past research and future directions. *Child Welfare, 75*(2), 99–137.

Department of Family Services and Housing. (October 13, 2006). *Changes for children: Strengthening the commitment to child welfare.* Winnipeg, MB: Author.

Fletcher, B. J. (1997). Same-race practice: Do we expect too much or too little? *Child Welfare, 76,* 213–237.

Fournier, S., & Crey, E. (1997). *Stolen from our embrace: The abduction of First Nations children and families and the restoration of Aboriginal communities.* Vancouver, BC: Douglas and McIntyre.

Hardy, M., Schibler, B., & Hamilton, I. (September 29, 2006). *Strengthen the commitment: An external review of the child welfare system.* Winnipeg, MB: Department of Family Services and Housing.

Hodgson, M. (2002). Rebuilding community after residential schools. In J. Bird, L. Land, & M. MacAdam (Eds.), *Nation to nation: Aboriginal sovereignty and the future of Canada* (pp. 92–108). Toronto, ON: Irwin Publishing.

Hudson, P., & McKenzie, B. (1981). Child welfare and Native people: The extension of colonialism. *The Social Worker, 49*(2), 63–88.

Johnston, P. (1983). *Native children and the child welfare system.* Toronto, ON: Canadian Council on Social Development.

Kimelman, E. C. (1985). *No quiet place: Review committee on Indian and Metis adoptions and placements.* Winnipeg: Manitoba Department of Community Services.

Korbin, J. (1994). Sociocultural factors in child maltreatment. In G. Melton & F. Barry (Eds.), *Protecting children from abuse and neglect: Foundations for a new national strategy* (pp. 182–223). New York: Guilford Press.

Koster, A. (2001, June). *Child welfare philosophy paper.* Discussion paper prepared for Ontario Association of Children's Aid Societies. Ontario: OACAS.

Koster, A., Morrissette, V., & Roulette, R. (2000, May). *Aboriginal Child Welfare Review: Comprehensive Report.* Ontario: Ministry of Community and Social Services.

La Rocque, E. (1997). Re-examining culturally appropriate models in criminal justice applications. In M. Asch (Ed.), *Aboriginal and treaty rights in Canada: Essays on law, equity, and respect for difference* (pp. 75–96). Vancouver: University of British Columbia Press.

MacDonald, K. (2002) *Missing voices: Aboriginal mothers who have been at risk or who have had their children removed from their care.* Vancouver: National Action Committee on the Status of Women, British Columbia Region.

McDonald, R. J., & Ladd, P. (2000). *First Nations child and family services joint national policy review: Final report, June 2000.* Ottawa, ON: Assembly of First Nations and Department of Indian and Northern Development.

McGoldrick, M. (Ed.). (1998). *Re-visioning family therapy: Race, culture and gender in clinical practice.* New York: Guilford Press.

McKay, S., & Clouston Carlson, J. (2003). Stanley McKay: Growing up in family and community the traditional way. In J. Clouston Carlson & A. Dumont (Eds.), *Bridges in understanding: Aboriginal Christian men tell their stories* (pp. 73–122). Toronto, ON: Anglican Book Centre.

McKenzie, B. (1989). Child welfare: New models of service delivery in Canada's Native communities. *Human Services in the Rural Environment 12*(3), 6–11.

McKenzie, B. (2002). *Block funding child maintenance in First Nations child and family services: A policy review (Final Report).* Winnipeg: Child and Family Services Research Group, Faculty of Social Work, University of Manitoba.

McKenzie, B., & Flette, E. (2001). Community building through block funding in Aboriginal child and family services. In K. Kufeldt & B. McKenzie (Eds.), *Child welfare: Connecting research, policy and practice* (pp. 343–353). Waterloo, ON: Wilfrid Laurier University Press.

McKenzie, B., & Hudson, P. (1985). Native children, child welfare and the colonization of Native people. In K. Levitt & B. Wharf, *The challenge of child welfare* (pp. 125–140). Vancouver: University of British Columbia Press.

McKenzie, B., & Morrissette, V. (2002). Social work practice with Canadians of Aboriginal background: Guidelines for respectful social work. In A. Al-Krenawi & J. Graham (Eds.), *Multi-cultural social work practice in Canada* (pp. 251–282). Toronto, ON: Oxford University Press.

McKenzie, B., Seidl, E., & Bone, N. (1995). Child and family service standards in First Nations: An action research project. *Child Welfare 74*, 633–653.

Monture, P. (1989). A vicious circle: Child welfare and the First Nations. *Canadian Journal of Women and the Law 3*, 1–17.

Monture-Okanee, P. (1994). Thinking about Aboriginal justice: Myths and revolution. In R. Gosse, J. Youngblood Henderson, & R. Carter (Eds.), *Continuing Riel and Poundmaker's quest: Presentations made at a conference on Aboriginal peoples and justice* (pp. 223–232). Saskatoon, SK: Purich.

Morrissette, V., McKenzie, B., & Morrissette, L. (1993). Towards an Aboriginal model of social work practice. *Canadian Social Work Review, 10*(1), 91–108.

Nisga'a Lisims Government Information. (2002). Retrieved January 6, 2003, from Nisga'a Lisims Government Information website: http://www.nisgaalisims.ca/welcome.html

Owen, M., & Farmer, E. (1996). Child protection in a multi-racial context. *Policy and politics, 24*, 299–313.

Rooney, R. H., & Bibus, A. A. (1996). Multiple lenses: Ethnically sensitive practice with involuntary clients who are having difficulties with drugs or alcohol. *Journal of Multicultural Social Work, 4*, 59–73

Royal Commission on Aboriginal Peoples. (1996a). *People to people, Nation to nation: Highlights of the Royal Commission on Aboriginal Peoples.* Ottawa, ON: Canada Communication Group.

Royal Commission on Aboriginal Peoples. (1996b). *Volume 1: Looking forward, looking back.* Ottawa, ON: Canada Communication Group.

Royal Commission on Aboriginal Peoples. (1996c). *Volume 3: Gathering strength.* Ottawa: Canada Communication Group.

Saulteaux, J. (1997). Jessie Saulteaux. In J. Carlson & A. Dumont (Eds.), *Bridges in spirituality: First Nations Christian women tell their stories* (pp. 38–71). Toronto, ON: Anglican Book Centre and United Church Publishing House.

Sinclair, M. (1994). Aboriginal peoples, justice and the law. In R. Gosse, J. Youngblood Henderson, & R. Carter (Eds.), *Continuing Poundmaker and Riel's quest: Presentations made at a conference on Aboriginal Peoples and Justice* (pp. 173–184). Saskatoon, SK: Purich.

Six Nations of the Grand River. (2002, May). *Customary care policy and procedures.* (Draft). Under review for passage by Band Council of the Six Nations.

Social Planning Council of Winnipeg. (2002). *The Manitoba child poverty report card: Children, an overlooked investment.* Winnipeg: Author

Timpson, J. (1993). *Four decades of child welfare services to Native Indians in Ontario: A contemporary attempt to understand the "sixties scoop" in historical, socio-economic and political perspective.* Unpublished doctoral dissertation, Wilfrid Laurier University, Waterloo, Ontario, Canada.

Timpson, J. (1995). Four decades of literature on Native Canadian child welfare. *Child Welfare, 74*(3), 525–546.

Tsang, A. K. T., & George, U. (1998). Towards an integrated framework for cross-cultural social work practice. *Canadian Social Work Review 15*(1), 73–93.

Union of BC Indian Chiefs. (2002). *Calling forth our future: Options for the exercise of indigenous people's authority in child welfare.* Retrieved December 14, 2002, from Union of British Colombia Indian Chiefs website: http://www.ubcic.bc.ca/welcome.htm

Zlotkin, N. (1994). Aboriginal control over child welfare: Canadian and American approaches. In R. Gosse, J. Youngblood Henderson, & R. Carter (Eds.), *Continuing Poundmaker and Riel's quest: Presentations made at a conference on Aboriginal Peoples and Justice* (pp. 185–191). Saskatoon, SK: Purich.

|4|

Using Intermediary Structures to Support Families
An International Comparison of Practice
in Child Protection

Nancy Freymond

The relationship between private family matters and State authority is complex, value laden, and firmly rooted in the historical, cultural, political, and economic foundations of society. A balance that satisfies all stakeholders in the debate between the maintenance of family privacy and the degree to which the State exercises its authority to intervene in this domain is difficult, if not impossible, to achieve and sustain. Because child maltreatment often occurs within the privacy of a family yet simultaneously involves State interests, the debate about the proper balance between family privacy and State intervention emerges in relation to this issue. This debate is often differentiated along the broad dimensions of legalism and welfare.

Advocates of a legalistic response to child maltreatment press for models of intervention that emphasize child protection through intense investigation, narrow definitions of child maltreatment, and the criminalization of abuse and neglect (Costin, Karger, & Stoesz, 1996). Advocates of a welfare response to child maltreatment prefer models that emphasize assessment, broad definitions of child and family well-being, and intervention for the purposes of maintaining and strengthening the family. The child welfare debate is polarized by these two different responses, which to some extent functions to limit and obscure possibilities.

The focus of this chapter is on possibilities that might emerge for Ontario's system of child protection if the intermediary space between the legalistic domain, where responses to situations of child maltreatment centre on coercion, and the welfare domain, where responses centre on family support, were broadened. Drawing on the international literature, particularly the work of Hetherington, Cooper, Smith, and Wilford (1997) whose research compared England's child welfare system with those in Continental Europe, this chapter examines how particular structures and roles that inhabit this intermediary space function to allow systems of child protection to appropriately assess and intervene in complex situations of risk to children. It examines how roles and structures currently relegated to the fringes of mainstream protection work in Ontario might become central to child protection services if intermediary spaces are established.

This exploration relies on cross-cultural comparisons to illuminate the legalistic emphases that currently dominate our own thinking and approaches to child welfare. Child welfare systems are constructed within a web of values, beliefs, and cultural identities steeped in history and tradition. There is a relationship between assumptions about society and the effectiveness of particular methods of responding to child maltreatment (Freeman, 2000). The methods of Continental European child and family service systems may not be directly transportable into our culture; however, examining the responses of other cultures to child maltreatment might stimulate alternative visions that move beyond the limitations of arguments for the merits of either the legalistic or welfare models of intervention.

Our strategies for responding to child maltreatment are not inevitable but socially constructed. The conceptualization of responses to child maltreatment as either being welfare-oriented or having a legalistic emphasis is an invention that allows us to organize and make sense of systems that address child maltreatment. Inventions that organize experience lie against a backdrop of "shared understandings, practices, [and] language" (Schwandt, 2000, p. 198). Social constructionist epistemologies emphasize the historical, political, economic, and cultural aspects of the backdrop as well as the social aspects of knowing (Payne, 1997). For theorists like Gergen (1999), constructionism acknowledges that multiple constructions are possible in any situation, and therefore a continuous posture of reflection is desirable. "With each move in discourse a myriad of possibilities are abandoned, meanings suppressed and life forms threatened" (p. 221). The polarized child welfare discourse suppresses alternate possibilities. Social constructionism invites possibilities for responses to child maltreatment from within and extending beyond the prescribed boundaries of welfare and legalism.

The discussion opens with a discussion of the social and political backdrop against which child protection in Ontario is currently viewed and evaluated. This is followed by an exploration of the nature of intermediary structures and roles. The discussion then moves to an examination of intermediary judicial roles in France and Scotland and how these contrast with the role of the Family Court Judge in Ontario. The roles and structures found in Ontario's child welfare system that resemble those of an intermediary nature found in Europe are also discussed.

Recent Social and Policy Contexts
for Child Protection in Ontario

The end of the 1990s brought some of the harshest public criticisms ever levied against Ontario's child welfare system. Media coverage implicated this system in a number of child deaths, citing the system's failure to protect children as a key factor (Welsh & Donovan, 1996). Criticisms of child welfare systems tend to be rooted in concerns about the acceptable level of state intervention into families, and, therefore, the outcome is often a restructuring of policies and practices that govern that level. It is in this social climate of intense, public criticism, centred on the sensitive and provocative issue of child deaths, that reforms to the child welfare system pointed toward increased state intervention.

The government of Ontario responded to these criticisms by convening a committee of government-appointed members to examine particular child fatalities (Hatton et al., 1998). Additionally, a review of child abuse and neglect files was initiated to assess compliance with established standards for child abuse investigation and management (Schwartz, 1998), and an independent evaluation was conducted to determine how the government fulfills its obligations under the child welfare legislation (The ARA Consulting Group Inc., 1998). The outcome of these assessments for the child welfare system was a number of changes to practice and legislation. These included: the introduction of risk assessment instruments and standardized procedures for child abuse investigation; the expansion of the definition of a child in need of protection to include a "pattern of neglect" (Child and Family Services Act (CFSA), Section 37 [2] a); lowered thresholds for the definition of a child as being "in need of protection"; and accelerated legal processing of permanent placements for younger children. Policies and procedures that govern the level of state intervention into the private lives of families were restructured, with the outcome being a shift to an intense emphasis on a legalistic model of intervention.

As highlighted in chapter 1, the shift to legalism has translated into new procedures for Ontario's child protection workers. The primary technique used in child protection is now investigation, into which substantial resources are poured (Wharf, 2002). Child protection workers utilize a risk assessment model, which is a formalized method of assessment that provides uniform structure and criteria for determining risk (Dawson, 2001) and seeks to give the appearance of empirically validated instruments, although its validity as a predictive measure is much debated (see Goodard, Saunders, Stanley, & Tucci, 1999). Front-line child protection workers are overwhelmed with accountability procedures and paperwork (Swift & Callahan, 2002). They report that, under the new reforms, their role has become one of case managing and policing, rather than counselling or providing support to families.

The focus on legalism has also led to an overall increase in the number of families that qualify for child protection services. Since 1998 and 2002, the number of cases in Ontario that met the eligibility requirements of a child in need of protection and needed a response by a child protection worker increased by 47%, while the number of children in substitute care increased by 40% (Ontario Association of Children's Aid Societies, 2003).

In Ontario, a front-line child welfare worker was charged with criminal negligence causing death in one of the highly publicized child deaths (Quinn, 1997), although the managers above her were not similarly charged. After a seven-month preliminary hearing, the charges against the social worker were discharged. Regardless of the outcome, this event caused considerable distress among front-line child protection workers, who are afraid that they will be held personally responsible when tragedies occur (Gilroy, 1999; Regehr, Bernstein, & Kanani, 2002).

Given that front-line child protection work now comprises stringent procedural requirements, increased case management and policing duties, increased caseloads, and the possibility of civil or criminal liability in the face of tragedies, staff recruitment and retention have been problematic. Concerns about employee shortages, high turnover rates, and worker dissatisfaction are frequently expressed (Coulthard et al., 2001). These factors point to a significant decrease in the ability of front line protection workers to make discretionary judgments. The use of professional confidence and authority to legitimate and guide interventions with families has been usurped by the reliance on legal authority and formal service-delivery regulations. Under these new practices, child protection agencies in Ontario have reported a substantial increase in the percentage of cases in which a court order was sought.

The move to an intense focus on legalism led to the abandonment of interventions that emphasize family support. As discussed in chapter 1, the service-delivery challenges that emanated from the increased emphases on legal procedures and formal service-delivery regulations have led to considerations of shifting Ontario toward a differentiated-response model of child and family welfare, following the lead of other North American jurisdictions.

Other Approaches to Child Welfare

The emphasis on legalism found in Ontario's child welfare system is not shared universally. Research examining Western post-industrial child welfare systems in Europe indicates that they share the concerns of Anglo-

American countries about the well-being of children and families. To that end, they have mechanisms whereby the state may intervene in family life. These systems also encompass complex relationships between professionals (generally social workers), families, and the judiciary. A key difference, however, is that the focus of many European child protection systems is on strengthening, rather than diminishing, parental rights and responsibilities (Pires, 1993). Another key difference is the emphasis of European systems on co-operative relationships between service providers and families. Embedded structures and professional roles exist to restore voluntary involvement whenever it becomes compromised. When social workers are unable to negotiate voluntary assistance to families and children, more coercive methods, such as securing a court order, may be applied. However, coercion is considered to be both an undesirable and an inferior method of intervention.

In the countries of Norway, Sweden, Finland, Denmark, Belgium, France, Germany, Italy, Greece, Luxembourg, and the Netherlands, child and family welfare structures are organized around a family-service orientation (Gilbert, 1997; Hetherington et al., 1997) in which interventions that emphasize assessment, parental involvement in decisions, voluntary participation, and relationship-building with the family are central. In contrast to legal processing, the key strategy for minimizing the risks of child maltreatment is the negotiation of appropriate supports to strengthen families. Resources are poured into intermediary service delivery structures that mediate between voluntary helping relationships and legal coercion.

What Are Intermediary Structures?

The tension between welfare and legalism is fundamental to the child and family welfare debate. Rather than arguing for the return to a welfare orientation, which is seen by some to be the cause of the problems that led to the present legalistic emphasis, Hetherington and colleagues (1997) propose broadening socially protected space, which in the context of child and family welfare exists between the role of supporting families and the role of the law. Social institutions that act as buffers or filters through which cases must pass before reaching more coercive legal involvements inhabit this space. Within these spaces, the worker authority is strengthened in the negotiation and facilitation of voluntary services to families, with the intention to circumvent the use of the law in a coercive manner. In England, the ability to negotiate services for families in a flexible manner has been eroded under conservative political agendas, which has led to a marked decrease in the breadth of these spaces (Hetherington et al., 1997). Under the influence of neo-conservative policies in Ontario, intermediary spaces for negotiation have also been reduced.

The fallout for child and family welfare when intermediary spaces diminish is enormous. As intermediary spaces deteriorate, fewer strategies and solutions are available to child welfare workers for responding to families, so that the child welfare role becomes increasingly procedural in nature and more closely resembles that of an agent of State control (King & Piper, 1995). It is in intermediary spaces that "everyone—children, parents, professionals—find[s] room to breathe, think, negotiate, plan, in the middle of the intensely complex and often long-term process of working out optimum solutions in cases of child abuse" (Hetherington et al., 1997, p. 7). Without such space, state intervention into private family matters is more likely to be perceived as intrusive and imposed solutions to existing problems seen by families as largely irrelevant to their daily living realities.

Contrasting Judiciary Roles in European Countries with the Role of Ontario's Family Court Judge

The underlying assumption in supporting reforms to the child and family welfare system that seek to broaden social spaces is that voluntary and co-operative relationships between child and family welfare service providers and the families and children that they serve are desirable. However, there are situations where, regardless of the options available for negotiating voluntary involvement, the use of coercion is necessary in order to ensure the protection of children. Broadening social spaces does not eliminate coercive options but rather provides access to a range of options that may increase the likelihood of engaging a family in a co-operative manner. This would decrease the dependency of child and family welfare systems on coercion to provoke change in families where risks to children are identified. Judicial involvement remains a feature of systems where broader social spaces are evident. There are countries where the judicial role itself has an intermediary function in addition to final authority. The following discussion looks at the role of France's *Juge des Enfants* and Scotland's Children's Panel. It then contrasts the key features of the judicial roles in these countries with the role of the Family Court Judge in Ontario.

Engaging the Judiciary in Continental Europe

There is an important distinction between inquisitorial and adversarial judicial systems. Jurisdictions in Anglo-American countries tend to operate on adversarial principles, in which there is an emphasis on legalism, formality, and concern for rights. Jurisdictions in continental Europe and Scotland tend to have inquisitorial judicial systems that operate on the basis of inquiry rather than legal briefs from competing parties.

In many Continental European countries, and in Scotland, evidence of harm or abuse in relation to parental responsibilities is not a prerequisite for judicial involvement. The judiciary responds to broad issues pertaining to well-being. The legal system is seen as having final authority, but the emphasis is on a consensual style where the goal is a facilitated or negotiated justice. Negotiation and deliberation involving the judge can occur either outside formalized legal proceedings or in a setting where all parties recognize that, although the judge has and could exercise formal power, the use of this power produces the least desirable result.

France's *Juge des Enfants*. France's system of child welfare is rooted in the spirit of the Fifth Republic (the French Republic established in 1958) in which there is a symbolic alliance between the State and the family in the rearing of children. The role of the *Juge des Enfants* (JE) has traditionally personified this alliance, with the JE being responsible for instituting "educational, social, psychological, and material resources to restore failing or vacant parental authority" (Grevot, 2002, p. 27). Although some European countries are very engaged in deterring families from judicial involvement, France has a much different understanding of the relationship between the judiciary and the well-being of families. Hetherington and colleagues (1997) report that judicial engagement was more prevalent in France than in any of the other seven European countries they studied, including Belgium (Flemish Community), Belgium (Francophone Community), Germany, Italy, Netherlands, England, and Scotland.

The JE has considerable status within the French judicial system; only appeals are heard at a higher level (Baistow, Hetherington, Spriggs, & Yelloly, 1996). The JE is expected to be skilled in communicating with children, and is expected to understand child development, family dynamics, and other issues that face families and children who appear in this setting. The JE is expected to attend lectures and workshops relevant to these subject areas as an ongoing part of the work (King & Piper, 1995).

This well-rounded knowledge base assists the JE in hearing cases in which child maltreatment is a concern, as well as cases where child behaviour, such as delinquency, is problematic.[1] The JE orders interventions designed to protect children in danger. There are five possible judicial orders, including:

- no further action, if the referral and first hearing leads the JE to think that no judicial decision is useful;
- a social inquiry order, where family functioning is studied and after which a plan is presented to the JE;
- an *investigation et orientation éducative* order: this is implemented by multidisciplinary teams and includes an average of ten contacts with

family members, a psychological assessment for the child, and a paediatric assessment when necessary, after which a report is presented to the JE;

- an *action-éducative en milieu ouvert* (AEMO) order: this involves family supervision and treatment implemented primarily by social work teams, involving psychologists and psychiatrists as necessary; and
- a care order, in which parental rights may be restricted but parents cannot be definitively separated from their children.

The AEMO is the most often used of the judicial orders (Grevot, 2002).

The JE, who is seen as a resource by many French families, invites social workers and family members to come together for the purpose of negotiating agreements. Individual legal representation is very limited; families interact and negotiate directly with the JE. Despite the JE's attempt to create space for dialogue, the meeting may be unbalanced due to families having little information about the system and fearing that their child will be removed (Grevot, 2002). Although a meeting with the JE can be compulsory, as is any resulting judicial order, considerable effort is made to find a level of acceptability to the parents. The JE seeks to invite consent of the family to the court-ordered measures, to re-establish any authority of the parent that may have been assumed by the state, and to mobilize state resources in order to facilitate these outcomes (King & Piper, 1995; Luckock, Vogler, & Keating, 1996). Baistow and her colleagues (1996) found that, despite the compulsory nature of the involvement, parents were readily agreeable and often requested a renewal of an AEMO.

It should be noted that the role of the JE has recently been questioned. Grevot (2002) indicates that in 1981, the central government decentralized many State powers, which resulted in the shifting of the main responsibility for child protection to the weakest level of the French Democracy. This eroded the traditional symbolic alliances between state and family in child rearing. In response, child protection practitioners began to rely more heavily on judicial orders to legitimate their work. Later, as Anglo-American ideas about risk and danger to children began to permeate French society, and child protection practitioners began losing confidence in their right to work with families in which there was concern about child safety, reliance on the judicial orders again increased. Judicial proceedings are now criticized for being "too constrained and specific" and there are official documents recommending that the JE's involvement in child protection work be limited (Grevot, 2002).

Scotland's Children's Hearing System. Established in 1971, the Scottish Children's Hearing is unique within the United Kingdom (UK) and is known throughout the world for its response to children (King, 1995). This system is based on the belief that the welfare of children is paramount, and its key features are its flexibility and informality (Dale-Risk & Cleland, 2002; King, 1995). The panel that conducts the Children's Hearing consists of three lay members, who are appointed and who work on a voluntary basis. Lay representation reflects the hearings' informality and its emphasis on sympathetic consideration of the welfare of the child (Dale-Risk & Cleland, 2002). Like the *juge des enfants*, appointed members of the Scottish Children's Panel have specialized training in the area of children's issues (King & Piper, 1995). An official called the reporter decides whether the referrals to the Children's Hearing from the social work department have legal grounds and whether the child is in need of compulsory measures of supervision. The reporter's information is based largely on social work assessments and on police reports, where applicable.

The Children's Panel is concerned with the welfare of the child and does not deal with cases in which there are disputes over the facts. There are legal grounds for the referral with which the parents and the child (where the child can understand) must agree before the hearing proceeds. Legal grounds exist if there is a lack of parental care, the child is a victim of a sexual offence, has failed to attend school without reasonable excuse, or has committed an offence, for example. If there is no agreement on the legal grounds, the case goes to the Sheriff's Court. In this court, legal aid is available for each party. The standard of proof is the balance of probabilities or, in situations of a criminal offence, beyond reasonable doubt.

After the grounds are established in the Sheriff's Court, the case returns to a Children's Hearing. The child, the parents, the reporter, and the social worker attend this legal meeting. The Children's Panel develops a plan for the care of the child in question. They may discharge the referral or make a supervision requirement. The panel works intensively with social service departments to evaluate the merits and terms of a period of care (Hetherington et al., 1997). In situations where immediate protection is required, an emergency court order may be sought, which is a temporary measure until longer-term solutions are arranged.

The Children's Hearing is often understood as having a mediating role between social workers and the family in an attempt to find solutions for the child's difficulties (King, 1995). Some social workers report that the panel provides them with confidence and support for their decisions, enabling them to take risks with their families. Some also report feeling confident that a hearing will reinforce a welfare approach, but also provide authority in involuntary situations (Hetherington et al., 1997).

At the Children's Hearing, the child is given a range of opportunities to express views, either by speaking directly to the panel, or in writing, through audio- or videotape or through a "safeguarder" who accompanies the child to the hearing. Despite these avenues for gaining an understanding of the child's views, the Children's Panel has been successfully challenged under the European Convention on Human Rights (ECHR) for not making legal representation available at this level. This challenge has resulted in the availability of appointed legal representation, but only where it appears that the child requires assistance in order to effectively participate in the hearing.

Proponents of this system argue that excessive legal representation could erode the system. Dale-Risk and Cleland (2002) suggest that "the welfare of the child is not something which can best be determined by applying legalistic formulae ... excessive legal intervention could erode the system whereby both lay members and the children appearing in front of the panel are alienated and disadvantaged" (p. 9). For now, the Scottish Hearing remains largely informal (Hallett, 2000) although broad trends, such as the legalistic approach to protecting children (see King, 1995) and the global emphasis on due process in the legal sphere, are potential threats to the informality of this system.

Engaging the Judiciary in Ontario

In Ontario, where the liberal State tradition separates the family and the state, the law settles disputes in an adversarial manner. Each party to a court action is expected to present as fully and convincingly as possible the argument for that party, so that the court will be well informed of all relevant considerations before it reaches a decision. The adversarial process focuses on justice between the parties.

Within this adversarial context, family law is distinctive. Bala (1995) writes: "Under the adversarial system, the system works because each party, in theory, will attempt to put its best foot forward. In family law, by contrast, this assumption is not always tenable" (p. 30). There is acknowledgement that often the party most affected by the outcome of a judicial proceeding is the child, who usually does not have independent representation. There is therefore some recognition that the judge may assume a more inquisitorial role in certain respects, however the latitude of France's *juge des enfants* or Scotland's Children's Panel is not evident in Ontario.

In accordance with the adversarial nature of Ontario's legal system, child welfare issues are primarily a contest. Generally, lawyers employed by child protection agencies represent the position of the child welfare authority, and parents secure independent legal representation. The role of legal counsel is to apply arguments constructed within a framework of legal rules and procedures. The role of the judge is to rule in favour of the most legally sound presentation. The energies and resources of the child welfare system tend to be focused on legal procedure.

Most Anglo-American adversarial systems have tightened procedures so that legal responses to child maltreatment have become narrowly focused on protection. In Ontario, there has been a marked decrease in judicial discretion (Walter, Isenegger, & Bala, 1995). Where, for example, the term "best interests of the child" was once deliberately vague, it is now defined by a set of specific criteria judges consider when making rulings. If the criteria are overlooked, the ruling may be vulnerable to appeals (Walter et al., 1995).

Ontario's Family Court Judge. The flexibility and informality found in the intermediary roles of France's *juge des enfants* and the Scottish Children's Panel contrasts with the role of an Ontario Family Court judge, which is not intermediary in nature. The role of the Family Court judge is largely reactive. Judges can take action only when rights, responsibilities, or duties have been somehow mismanaged, and this mismanagement has been drawn to the attention of the courts. In child welfare matters, the Family Court judge takes action when there is evidence of harm or abuse, generally in relation to parental responsibilities, and this harm or abuse is brought to their attention by the child welfare authority.

The judge, who tends to be appointed based on skills and reputation in the legal community, adjudicates according to legal rules and procedures. As opposed to achieving mutually agreeable solutions between social workers and families, the judge listens to both sides and is the sole arbiter and decision maker in the process. Success in Ontario's child welfare courts is understood as "winning" the case through adherence to the definitions and procedures.

When a child has been apprehended, or voluntary arrangements to support the family have been unsuccessful in protecting the child, an application for an order of protection is made to the court by the children's aid society. If the court finds that the child is in need of protection, one of four court orders may be made. The court order must fit with the criteria for best interests of the child (CFSA, 37 [3]).

Under a Supervision Order, the child is placed, remains with, or is returned to the parent or a relative or other member of the child's community under the supervision of a CAS. The court may specify terms and conditions regarding the child's care and supervision to the guardian, the child, the CAS, or other party to the court proceeding. The duration of a Supervision Order is from 3 to 12 months and may be extended indefinitely.

A Society Wardship Order places a child in the care and custody of a CAS for up to 12 months. The parent relinquishes guardianship of the child to a CAS for the full term of the order. For children six and over, the 12-month term may be extended for a period that does not exceed 24 months in temporary care by order and/or agreement. When a Society Wardship order is made, parents are often required to fulfill certain conditions that seek to address the concerns that rendered the child in need of protection, before legal consideration is given to restoring parental guardianship. Failure to comply with the specified conditions may lead to permanent wardship. A Supervision Order for a specified period may follow a Society Wardship Order, if the parents are successful in securing the child's return.

A child may be made a permanent ward of the Crown under a Crown Wardship Order when the need for protection that justifies the order is unlikely to change within 24 months. A Crown Wardship Order permanently transfers care, custody, and control of the child to the Director of Child Welfare, effectively transferring the role and responsibilities of the parent to the director. In situations where Crown wardship leads to the adoption of the child, parental access to the child is terminated. Society and Crown Wardship orders end automatically when the child reaches age 18 years of age or marries.

Contrasting Intermediary Structures and Roles in Child Welfare

The child welfare systems of Belgium and the Netherlands provide examples of how intermediary structures facilitate interventions in matters of child maltreatment. In Ontario, there are programs linked to child welfare, such as mediation and children's mental health services, that resemble the intermediary structures of Continental Europe, although at present they function at the margins of the system. In Ontario, these programs do not represent intermediary structures as defined by Hetherington and her colleagues (1997; i.e. preserved spaces between administrative and judicial spheres— the state and civil society); nonetheless, they are valid attempts to preserve voluntariness between the state and the family and to temper the dominance of the legalistic approach.

Contrasting Intermediary Structures

Belgium's Mediation Committees An intermediary structure that provides an alternative to judicial involvement consists of established procedures for engaging in the process of mediation. Mediation, by definition, is an intervention whereby an impartial third party, who has no decision-making power, assists the parties to a dispute to voluntarily reach a mutually acceptable settlement (McNeilly, 1997). It is a widely used intervention for divorcing couples, particularly in relation to custody disputes. In child welfare, mediation is intended to prevent the hostility that can arise between parents and child welfare authorities, particularly when legal action is taken. It aims to bring together the parties in a positive atmosphere to develop a plan to meet the child's needs.

The Belgian Flemish community makes more extensive use of mediation in child welfare cases than do other European nations, making it an integral and mandatory part of service delivery. When the voluntary relationship between service providers and the family becomes compromised and/or when attempts to motivate the family to change prove futile, it is mandatory that social workers and families avail themselves of the mediation services of a six-member panel of volunteers, each of whom have child welfare backgrounds. This politically sanctioned body has a dual purpose; it is a structure understood as an alternative to judicial processing and a mediating structure, protecting families from state intrusion (Hetherington et al., 1997).

The deliberate selection of community volunteers for this role extends the responsibility for child welfare matters beyond that of the legal and the professional, although some critics question the ability of such a committee to grasp the complex family dynamics in some abusive situations (Luckock, Vogler, & Keating, 1997). This committee has no authority beyond that of attempting to achieve, by means of its own mediation skills, a voluntary and co-operative working relationship between social workers and families. If there is a failure to reach agreement, the committee refers the family, via the public prosecutor, to the Judge for Children. As only the mediation committee can initiate referral to the legal system, it has a central and a responsible position in the delivery of child welfare services (Hetherington et al., 1997). However, the public prosecutor who assesses the legal grounds has the final authority in activating the referral.

Ontario's Mediation Centre In contrast, mediation services for child welfare cases in Ontario have not developed momentum. In the mid 1980s, June Maresca, a lawyer for the Catholic Children's Aid Society in Toronto, began discussions with American counterparts about a model of mediation for child welfare. She and her colleagues were concerned by the excessive preparation and delays that judicial processing required (Maresca, 1995). In addition, critics contend the legal strategies involved in "winning" a case, by their very nature, create an institutionalized antagonism that decreases dialogue and hampers helping relationships (King & Piper, 1995; Luckock et al., 1996; McNeilly, 1997; Palmer, 1989).

In 1989, mediation was initiated for ten child welfare cases, marking the beginning of what was to become the Toronto-based Centre for Child and Family Mediation. By 1994, an agreement was made whereby Legal Aid Ontario[2] and the Children's Aid Society of Toronto each agreed to pay 50% of the costs associated with the mediation of child welfare cases at the

Centre. Other communities have initiated similar mediation programs, but no legal aid funding has been made available for these projects (J. Maresca, personal communication, October 23, 1999).

Despite reports from social workers of high compliance rates with the agreed-upon terms of mediated settlements, as well as reports of virtually universal user satisfaction, mediation is not an intervention that has gained significant momentum (Maresca, 1995). Maresca suggests that the demonstration of its cost-saving abilities, which is a prime consideration for funding bodies, is hampered by insufficient research data. Furthermore, it is difficult for social workers, who are both overworked and confined to a culture characterized by formal bureaucratic expectations, to deviate from their standard procedures and daily routines. Of the hundreds of child protection cases that were legally processed in Toronto in 1998–99, approximately a dozen were mediated at the Centre (J. Maresca, personal communication, October 23, 1999). The Child and Family Services Act does not recognize mediation. It does, however, in its Declaration of Principles, indicate that intervention should be provided on the basis of mutual consent. At the same time, it ensures provision for legal representation for all parties.

The 1998 Report of the Panel of Experts on Child Protection: Protecting Vulnerable Children, whose recommendations were followed in most of the amendments in 2000 to the Child and Family Services Act, recommended that the legislation require courts to consider mediation in appropriate circumstances. The report described the legal system as "adversarial, complex, costly, and time consuming" (Hatton et al., 1998). More recently, changes to the child protection legislation in Ontario, as part of a broader agenda, have included a requirement to consider the use of alternative dispute resolution procedures (formal mediation services, family group counselling) instead of a court application (Legislative Assembly of Ontario, 2005; Ministry of Children and Youth Services, 2005).

Belgium's Confidential Doctor Centres   Based on research conducted in the late 1970s and early 1980s that identified confidentiality as the key aspect of non-repressive help and protection, Confidential Doctor Centres were developed in Flanders. The centres are well known for their commitment to family support and play a leading role in child protection. The centres are committed to a philosophy that understands families in which child maltreatment occurs as being in need of support, rather than coercion, to facilitate meaningful changes in functioning (Pringle, 1998). The philosophy underlying this approach also includes an emphasis on "respecting confidentiality instead of implementing control, emphasizing solidarity instead of reporting, mobilizing the family's own resources instead of maintaining their passivity, and encouraging collaboration among professionals instead

of competition" (Marneffe & Broos, 1997, p. 182). The centres are committed to changing public opinion, in order to rescue the child abuse issue from
what they see as a reductionist understanding that blames parental pathology without taking into account the complexities of the issues (Marneffe &
Broos, 1997).

In keeping with this philosophy, a clear separation from the judiciary is
a prerequisite to establishing trusting relationships. Judicial intervention is
seen as interfering with trust building in helping relationships, although it
may be necessary in situations where parents are unable to question their
own behaviour in relation to their children (a situation that is common
among those addicted to substances, with intellectual disabilities, or with serious mental illness). Initially, the centres worked in conjunction with the
judiciary but have since abandoned these arrangements (Luckock et al.,
1997). Therapy teams provide intensive therapeutic intervention with families and couples, who may be self-referred or referred by another professional,
as well as consultation to professionals such as social workers or physicians.
One source of data reports an increase in self-reporting from 2% to 38%
since the system was modified, and parents are encouraged to ask for help,
a change attributed to the parents' confidence that their requests for help will
not be met with judicial control (Marneffe & Broos, 1997). Hence, the Confidential Doctor Centres figure prominently in creating space between the
families and more coercive or legal interventions and have a leading role in
child protection.

It has been argued that the stance of the Flemish Doctor Centres on confidentiality may not free therapeutic alliances from the possibility of judicial
involvement in cases where families reject treatment (Luckock et al., 1997).
There are also questions about the nature of working consensually, particularly when authority may be exercised in a subtle manner in order to secure
participation of families under a voluntary status (Luckock et al., 1997). For
instance, parents have been reportedly offered a choice between accepting
assistance from the Doctor Centre or legally mandated interventions from
elsewhere (Luckock et al., 1997). Authority exercised in such a manner may
be seen as intruding on civil liberties.

Ontario's Children's Mental Health Services   Confidentiality is not formally possible in Ontario to the degree to which it is in the Belgian Doctor
Centres. Ontario's children's mental health services employ many professionals qualified for the task of co-ordinating and providing treatment services
to families where children may be at risk. The Child and Family Services
Act [CFSA] however, requires all professionals to inform child welfare authorities of any situations in which there is a suspicion that a child may be in need
of protection (CFSA Section 72(4)). Moreover, the 2000 amendments to

the CFSA lowered the threshold for reporting child abuse, requiring professionals to report suspicions, in addition to beliefs, that child abuse may have occurred. It is incumbent on the legal system to verify the report. The professional who has the suspicion is legally obligated to report those concerns directly to the child welfare authority (CFSA Section 72(3)). This procedural change places those who work with families in children's mental health settings in the difficult dual role of requiring a strong therapeutic alliance to facilitate assisting families with change, while simultaneously being required to report all suspicions, adding further pressure to stressed and vulnerable families and children.

Child welfare workers, who must meet the requirements of their own investigative protocols, may be hampered in their ability to work either jointly or flexibly with children's mental health professionals. Particularly in situations where apprehension is being considered, child welfare interventions may cause heightened concerns that information revealed during the mental health processes of assisting families with change will become available to child welfare authorities, hampering the ability of children's mental health professionals to create an optimum climate for intervention. The result is a gap created between the work of the children's mental health professional and the responsibilities of the child welfare system for responding to children deemed at risk.

Additionally, the stringent reporting measures enacted to further increase the safety of children in Ontario require consideration. Families often struggling with very complex issues become increasingly vulnerable to unwarranted suspicions and unnecessary stressful investigations when professionals have a diminished ability to apply discretion in assessing risk. The alienation of vulnerable families from potential sources of help is a probable and an undesired outcome of more stringent reporting measures.

Confidential Doctor Offices The Confidential Doctor Offices in the Netherlands were, until 1998,[3] intermediary structures that played a much different role than the Doctor Centres in Belgium. Four Confidential Doctor Offices were established in 1972. Suspicions of child abuse could be reported, and medical professionals found opportunities to share child abuse findings with colleagues without violating professional codes of confidentiality. The Doctor Offices substantiated concerns and co-ordinated treatment efforts for families. Voluntary working relationships were encouraged, and the Doctor Offices were generally seen as compassionate (Baartman & de Mey, 2000; Roelofs & Baartman, 1997). Treatments included parenting counselling from the school or family doctor, regular social work visitation, and individual or family therapy (Roelofs & Baartman, 1997). More extensive intervention included voluntary out-of-home placement.

If the family voluntarily embraced the planned interventions, the Confidential Doctor Offices provided a follow-up assessment after a six-month period to evaluate the level of progress for the family and to make alterations to the plan, if required. If the family was responding to treatment, the involvement of the Confidential Doctor Offices would cease at this point. Their efforts in establishing a comprehensive plan with families made their role in the prevention of child abuse extremely important. In their intermediary position, they attempted to persuade families to respond voluntarily.

Twelve Confidential Doctor Offices were established as an alternative to the Netherlands' Child Care and Protection Board that was established in 1905 and became the legal intervention sector of the child and family welfare system (Hetherington et al., 1997; Roelofs & Baartman, 1997). The Confidential Doctor Offices received all child abuse reports, including the most severe, which were then usually referred to the Child Care and Protection Board and brought to the attention of the court. The government-managed Child Care and Protection Board employed primarily social workers invested with statutory authority to investigate families and to seek judicial involvement to limit parental rights. This Board has been compared to child protection services in the United States (Roelofs & Baartman, 1997) and the Social Services Department in Great Britain (Baartman & de Mey, 2000), systems that bear many resemblances to Ontario's child protection system. Unlike the Confidential Doctor Office, the Board does not have an explicit role in persuading families to respond voluntarily or in deflecting them from more authoritative judicial intervention.

Under current reforms proposed for the Netherlands, the Child Care and Protection Board would remain separate from voluntary child and family service units. There is an interest in amalgamating youth services, child and family welfare, and youth mental health services into a Youth Services Office. The child and family welfare emphasis in this reorganization would remain on offering supportive and therapeutic services to children and families. If families cannot be voluntarily and safely engaged, then a referral to the Child Care and Protection Board would be made. The former Confidential Doctor Offices are now called Advice and Report Centres for Child Abuse. They try to connect with the family and motivate them to accept voluntary assistance. In contrast with Confidential Doctor Offices, the Advice and Report Centre is legally obliged to inform the family there has been a child maltreatment report and to open a file. Debate continues in the Netherlands about finding an appropriate balance between offering practical assistance to families and not weakening the protection of children (personal communication, Mia Lamers, February 21, 2003).

Ontario's Children's Aid Societies Ontario's CAS's provide services to families in which children are assessed to be in need of protection. The services may be mandatory, regardless of a family's willingness for intervention. Families enter the system via a demerit accounting system, whereby children must score sufficient points to be classified as at risk of maltreatment before ongoing services are provided. An overwhelming portion of the available resources is directed toward families who require legal processing and/or child placement.

Families who fit the criteria and are prepared to engage voluntarily in interventions are most likely to be referred for treatment outside the child welfare system, while the child welfare worker continues to monitor the situation until the protection concerns are satisfied. During the period when a family is voluntarily involved with the child welfare system, overworked social workers are often required to respond to a number of crises that arise with other families on their caseloads, many of which will take precedence over the needs of families whose participation is voluntary. Once the protection concerns are satisfied, there is no comprehensive process whereby follow-up assessment and further planning is conducted; families return to the child welfare system should their circumstances deteriorate sufficiently again.

Contrasting Intermediary Roles

Belgium's *Conseiller* One of the individual structures that fulfills an intermediary function in European child welfare systems is the Belgian *conseiller*. While the Flemish community of Belgium favours structures such as mediation committees and Confidential Doctor Centres, the Francophone community's intermediary functions are accomplished through the role of the *conseiller*. This legally trained individual is appointed by the government and receives referrals when there is a breakdown of the voluntary arrangement between the family and the service provider. The *conseiller* activates all referrals to the legal sphere, but not without first attempting to reach or renew a voluntary agreement for services. The services of the *conseiller* may be requested by family members, including children, and social workers.

Scotland's Reporter In Scotland, the Reporter to the Children's Panel has a pivotal intermediary position which, like the Belgian *conseiller,* diverts family situations from the judicial sphere. The reporter decides on whether there are sufficient grounds for a hearing, whether further voluntary services are required, or whether no further action is warranted (Hetherington et al., 1997). A reporter may opt to refer a family for mediation. They are accessible to professionals, parents, or children for consultation. Reporters are selected from a range of disciplines including law, social work, and education. Diversion is central to the philosophy of the Scottish system; if the reporter refers a family to the judicial sphere, decision-making may be deferred at the judicial level while further intervention at another level is attempted.

Ontario's Wraparound Co-ordinator This position is relatively new in Ontario's social services network and shows considerable promise in terms of its possibilities for engaging families in an intermediary role. Child welfare workers are recognizing the need for treatment programs that are tailored to the needs of the family (Brown & Debicki, 2000). Traditionally, treatment services in Ontario have been delivered via referral to existing programs that may or may not be appropriate for the particular needs of the family. A wraparound strategy is designed to bring together resources from family, community members, and professional helpers in an effort to build on the strengths of the family and assist with identified needs; in essence, to "wrap" services and supports around the family (Brown, 2000). Wraparound generally focuses on children who may require out of home placement, although its merits in assisting families before they come to the attention of the child welfare authorities are also being considered (Brown & Debicki, 2000).

Since 1998, seven communities in Ontario have implemented wraparound, and those whose implementation has been most successful have secured funding for a co-ordinator's position. This person is able to be neutral in relation to social service agencies by reporting to a team consisting of community representatives, professionals, parents, youth, and former consumers of service (Brown & Debicki, 2000). The co-ordinator's role is essential to the success of the wraparound process and, in a sense, functions in an intermediary capacity. Although, to date, this position does not have the authority of formalized linkages to the judicial sphere, there is considerable potential for the wraparound co-ordinator to relieve pressures from child welfare workers through planning service needs for families, linking families to resources, and evaluating service plans on an ongoing basis. There is also considerable potential for the wraparound co-ordinator to become active in diverting families away from expensive, time consuming, and often unhelpful judicial involvement. Government funding has been made available for a co-ordinator in each of the communities where the project was initiated.

Conclusion

The ability to engage least intrusive solutions, which remains a requirement under the CFSA, becomes less and less meaningful in a system where minimal intermediary structures and roles restrict options. There are a number of reasons why the state of child welfare in Ontario is concerning, not only to those who deliver child welfare services but also to policy-makers and to the public. As ideologies about what is best for children intersect and overlap, it is abundantly clear that the complexities of child maltreatment defy simplistic solutions. Ontario has reacted to media concerns about child deaths by increasing its reliance on legalism, decreasing flexibility in systems design, and minimizing opportunities to apply discretion. Child welfare workers and judges alike have been reduced to applying particular and predictable responses, regardless of the needs of the family. With the lowering of thresholds that define child abuse, the addition of an expanded definition of child neglect to the legislation, accelerated legal processing, and attempts to standardize procedures for the assessment of risk to children, these reforms clearly signalled increased emphases on legal authority and formal procedures as the foundation for child protection interventions.

Intermediary structures and roles have not received attention in Ontario's model of child welfare service delivery, despite their potential for creating co-operative working relationships with families. In addition, intermediary roles and structures have potential for decreasing expenses involved in the legal processing of families.[4] Although there are complications in comparing statistics on the incidence of child maltreatment and the effectiveness of intervention across cultures, there is no sense from the literature that countries stressing intermediary structures and voluntary engagement have disproportionately high rates of child maltreatment. There is also no sense that methods of responding to child maltreatment in Ontario are in any way more effective than those of our international counterparts. What seem certain are the advantages that intermediary roles and structures offer to families in need that are overlooked in a system dominated by a legalistic approach.

Child welfare systems reflect values and principles that are steeped in historical and cultural traditions. Engrained in Ontario's child welfare history is a focus on individual responsibility. Several critics have argued that this focus holds mothers accountable while ignoring the effects of a plethora of social ills that contribute to child maltreatment (see Callahan, 1993; Swift, 1995; Wharf, 1993). In Ontario's history, the child welfare system has seen periods with increased possibilities for intermediary roles and structures (see the discussion in chapter 1).

However, the system has never shifted sufficiently to establish different values (for example, understanding child abuse as a community responsibility) or to allow intermediary roles and structures to become embedded in the service delivery system. Over the past century, Ontario's child welfare system has continued to focus its service delivery narrowly on individuals, while economic and social factors remain in the background (Swift, 1998). We have a system that may periodically restrict the level of intrusion into families at risk of child maltreatment, while simultaneously continuing to uphold the values consistent with individual reliance and autonomy.

Increasing possibilities for intermediary spaces in Ontario's child welfare system shows promise for resolving some of the problems of the current system. I have argued that these opportunities could be provided through the recognition and enhancement of professional roles such as the wraparound co-ordinator, or existing programs like mediation, as well as through recognition of the potential value of ensuring confidentiality in children's mental health settings. For families and children, intermediary spaces would provide more opportunities for access to the co-ordinated services required to resolve issues that contribute to child maltreatment. Intermediary spaces would also provide possibilities for establishing less adversarial working relationships, which could, in turn, increase possibilities for access to, and identification of, our most vulnerable children. Furthermore, these intermediary spaces have the potential to establish more favourable circumstances for meaningful change.

For those who do the work of responding to child maltreatment, intermediary structures and roles would allow for a recovery of professional discretion; social workers, whether in a child welfare setting or a mental health setting, could apply their skills in a reasoned way, while recognizing that the optimum response to each family is a planned and comprehensive intervention strategy designed to complement and respond to the family's unique needs. For the social work profession, it would be an opportunity to address the incongruence between the nature of the profession and the duties required of social workers in Ontario's children's aid societies:

> Traditionally, social work's place and function in society centred on the creation of social peace, to be established, not primarily by coercive means, but through the considered, informed and professional negotiation of differences and inequalities ... [it belongs] to the self regulatory structures of modern society which mediate between individual and state. (Lorenz, 1994, pp. 4–5)

It is difficult for promising alternatives that lie outside the philosophical boundaries of current child welfare practice to gain credibility (Swift, 1997). These ideals seem very distant from the realities of Ontario's current child welfare system, but there is reason for optimism. Moving toward the creation of intermediary spaces does not involve a total revamping of philosophies and structures. Mediation programs, children's mental health services, and wraparound co-ordinators already exist. To varying degrees, their merits have captured government attention. Our task as a profession is to resist the tendency to become absorbed in the day-to-day requirements of mandated, legislated practice. We must recognize that embracing services outside mainstream child welfare increases possibilities for intermediary roles and structures to gain recognition and for families and children to find solutions. Our task as advocates and researchers is to continue to nudge forward those components of our social service systems that show potential for creating the philosophical and structural shifts required for a society that supports vulnerable families.

Notes

1 In Ontario the Juvenile Delinquents Act (1908–1984) required that child offenders be dealt with as children "needing aid, encouragement, help and assistance." In practice, juvenile judges were strongly influenced by notions of punishment. In 1984 the Young Offenders Act, which replaced the Juvenile Delinquents Act, legally separated child welfare and young offenders and placed a strong emphasis on rights and due process, marginalizing legal responses to crime based on welfare (Bala, 1999). In France, Belgium, Italy, Netherlands, and Scotland, children's judges work in both juvenile justice and child protection.

2 Ontario's Legal Aid Plan was first established in 1951 under the guiding principle of equal access to justice for poor people. Under the plan, private lawyers represent clients who have legal aid certificates. Lawyers are reimbursed for services via the provincial government. Applicants are assessed according to their financial situation, and all, or a portion of, their legal costs may be covered, based on eligibility. Between 1980 and 1990 the plan, which originally focused on criminal matters, expanded to include family matters as well. As of 1998, the provincial government introduced legislation to create an independent agency called Legal Aid Ontario. Lawyers whose fees are covered by legal aid represent the majority of child welfare clients in court.

3 For an expanded discussion of the recent child and family welfare reforms in the Netherlands, see Freymond and Cameron (2006). These reforms are intended to increase coordination between family support and child "protection" sectors while maintaining a priority of voluntary engagements with families and the provision of helping services.

4 Brown and Debicki (2000) cite data (Brown & Hill, 1996) that suggests considerable potential for wraparound to save money. They report that, based on 28 cases, the cost of providing wraparound services was one sixth of the average cost for all out of home placements combined (Brown & Debicki, 2000). June Maresca indicates that the demonstration of cost effectiveness for mediation has been a challenge given the lack of necessary research money for this exploration.

References

The ARA Consulting Group Inc. (1998). *Child welfare accountability review: Final report*. Toronto, ON: Ministry of Community and Social Services.

Baartman, H. E. M., & de Mey, L. (2000). Protecting, supporting and reporting: Child abuse and assessment in the Netherlands. In M. Freeman (Ed.), *Over-*

coming child abuse: A window on a world problem (pp. 281–304). Aldershot, UK: Ashgate.

Baistow, K., Hetherington, R., Spriggs, A., & Yelloly, M. (1996). *Parents speaking: Anglo–French perceptions of child welfare interventions, a preliminary report*. London: Brunel University.

Bala, N. (1995). *Mental health professionals in child related proceedings: Understanding the ambivalence of the judiciary*. Paper presented at the National Judicial Institute Program for Family Court Judges, Vancouver, BC.

Bala, N. (1999). *Reforming Ontario's child & family services act: Is the pendulum swinging back too far?* Retrieved January 29, 2001, from http://qsilver .queensu.ca/law/papers/ cfsareforms1999.htm

Brown, R. (2000). The wraparound process. In N. F. Coady & P. Lehman (Eds.), *Theoretical perspectives in direct social work practice: An eclectic-generalist approach* (pp. 347–365). New York: Springer.

Brown, R., & Debicki, A. (2000). The "wraparound" process: Strength-based practice. In M. Callahan, S. Hessle, & S. Strega (Eds.), *Valuing the field: Child welfare in an international context* (pp. 81–97). Aldershot, UK: Ashgate.

Callahan, M. (1993). Feminist approaches: Women recreate child welfare. In B. Wharf (Ed.), *Rethinking child welfare in Canada* (pp. 172–209). Toronto, ON: Oxford University Press.

Costin, L., Karger, H. J., & Stoesz, D. (1996). *The politics of child abuse in America*. New York: Oxford University Press.

Coulthard, C., Duncan, K., Goranson, S., Hewson, L., Howe, P., Lee, K., et al. (2001). *Report on Staff Retention*. Toronto, ON: Children's Aid Society of Toronto.

Dale-Risk, K., & Cleland, A. (2002). *Can Scotland's children's hearing system survive ECHR?* Paper presented at the International Society of Family Law, 11th World Conference, Copenhagen and Oslo.

Dawson, R. (2001). Debate: Risk assessment in child protection services. Yes: "an integral part of casework practice." *Canadian Social Work Review, 18*(1), 151–154.

Freeman, M. (2000). Child abuse: The search for a solution. In M. Freeman (Ed.), *Overcoming child abuse: A window on a world problem* (pp. 1–14). Aldershot, UK: Ashgate.

Freymond, N., & Cameron, G. (Eds.). (2006). *Towards positive systems of child and family welfare: International comparisons of child protection, family service, and community care models*. Toronto, ON: University of Toronto Press.

Gergen, K. (1999). *An invitation to social construction*. London: Sage.

Gilbert, N. (Ed.). (1997). *Combatting Child Abuse: International Perspectives and Trends*. New York: Oxford University Press.

Gilroy, J. (1999). Critical issues in child welfare: Perspectives from the field. In L. Dominelli (Ed.). *Community approaches to child welfare: International perspectives* (pp. 25–44). Aldershot, UK: Ashgate.

Goodard, C. R., Saunders, B. J., Stanley, J. R., & Tucci, J. (1999). Structured risk assessment procedures: Instruments of abuse? *Child Abuse Review, 8,* 251–263.

Grevot, A. (2002). *The plight of paternalism in French child welfare and protective policies and practices.* Waterloo, ON: Wilfrid Laurier University, Partnerships for Children and Families Project.

Hallett, C. (2000). *Where do we go from here? The International Context: Trends in Juvenile Justice and Child Welfare.* Retrieved, February 2, 2001, from http://www.scotland.gov.uk/cru/documents/ech4-02.asp

Hatton, M. J., Campbell, G., Colarftoni, H., Ferron, R., Huyer, D., Ortiz, T. J., et al. (1998). *Protecting vulnerable children.* Toronto, ON: Ministry of Community and Social Services.

Hetherington, R., Cooper, A., Smith, P., & Wilford, G. (1997). *Protecting children: Messages from Europe.* Dorset, UK: Russell House.

King, M. (1995). Law's healing of children's hearings: The paradox moves north. *Journal of Social Policy, 24*(3), 315–340.

King, M., & Piper, C. (1995). *How the law thinks about children* (2nd ed.). Brookfield, VT: Ashgate.

Legislative Assembly of Ontario Bill 210, Child and Family Services Statute Law Amendment Act, 2005 (Government Bill). Retrieved January 8, 2006 from http://www.ontla.on.ca/Library/bills/382/210382.htm

Lorenz, W. (1994). *Social work in a changing Europe.* London: Routledge.

Luckock, B., Vogler, R., & Keating, H. (1996). Child protection in France and England—authority, legalism and social work practice. *Child and Family Law Quarterly, 8*(4), 297–311.

Luckock, B., Vogler, R., & Keating, H. (1997). The Belgian Flemish child protection system—Confidentiality, voluntarism and coercion. *Child and Family Law Quarterly, 9*(2), 101–113.

Maresca, J. (1995). Mediating child protection cases. *Child Welfare 74*(3), 731–742.

Marneffe, C., & Broos, P. (1997). Belgium: An alternative approach to child abuse reporting and treatment. In N. Gilbert (Ed.), *Combatting child abuse: International perspectives and trends* (pp. 167–191). New York: Oxford University Press.

McNeilly, G. K. (1997). Mediation and child protection: An Ontario perspective. *Family and Conciliation Courts Review, 35*(2), 206–222.

Ministry of Children and Youth Services. (June 2005). Child welfare transformation 2005: A strategic plan for a flexible, sustainable and outcome oriented service delivery model. Retrieved December 9, 2006, from http://www.children.gov.on.ca/NR/CS/Publications/CWTrans2005.pdf

Ontario Association of Children's Aid Societies. (2003). *CAS facts: April 1, 2002–March 31, 2003.* Retrieved Nov 18, 2003, from http://www.oacas.org/resources/CAS%20Facts%20Ap02Mar03.pdf

Palmer, S. E. (1989). Mediation in child protection cases: An alternative to the adversary system. *Child Welfare, 68,* 21–31.

Payne, M. (1997). *Modern social work theory* (2nd ed.). Chicago: Lyceum Books.

Pires, S. A. (1993). *International child welfare systems: Report of a workshop.* Washington, DC: National Academy Press.

Pringle, K. (1998). *Children and social welfare in Europe.* Buckingham, UK: Open University Press.

Quinn, J. (1997). Caseworker charged in baby's death: Infant died of starvation while under supervision of Catholic Children's Aid. *Toronto Star:* p. A1.

Regehr, C., Bernstein, M. M., & Kanani, K. (2002). Liability for child welfare social workers: Weighing the risks. *OACAS Journal, 46*(1), 32–39.

Roelofs, M. A., & Baartman, H. E. (1997). The Netherlands: Responding to abuse—Compassion or control? In N. Gilbert (Ed.), *Combatting child abuse: International perspectives and trends* (pp. 192–211). New York: Oxford University Press.

Schwandt, T. A. (2000). Three epistemological stances for qualitative inquiry: Interpretivism, hermeneutics, and social constructionism. In N. K. Denzin & Y. S. Lincoln (Eds.), *Handbook of qualitative research* (2nd.ed., pp. 189–213). Thousand Oaks, CA: Sage.

Schwartz, P. (1998). *Report of the 1997 child protection file review.* Toronto, ON: Ministry of Community and Social Services.

Swift, K. J. (1995). *Manufacturing "bad mothers": A critical perspective on child neglect.* Toronto, ON: University of Toronto Press.

Swift, K. J. (1997). Canada: Trends and issues in child welfare. In N. Gilbert (Ed.), *Combatting child abuse: International perspectives and trends* (pp. 38–71). New York: Oxford University Press.

Swift, K. J. (1998). Contradictions in child welfare: Neglect and responsibility. In C. T. Baines, P. M. Evans, & S. Neysmith, M. (Eds.), *Women's caring: Feminist perspectives on social welfare* (pp. 160–190). Toronto: Oxford University Press.

Swift, K. J., & Callahan, M. (2002). *Problems and potential of Canadian child welfare.* Waterloo, ON: Wilfrid Laurier University, Partnerships for Children and Families Project.

Walter, B., Isenegger, J. A., & Bala, N. (1995). "Best interests" in child protection proceedings: Implications and alternatives. *Canadian Journal of Family Law, 12*(1), 367–439.

Welsh, M., & Donovan, K. (1996, September 18). They died despite signs of abuse. *Toronto Star,* p. A1.

Wharf, B. (Ed.). (1993). *Rethinking child welfare in Canada.* Toronto, ON: Oxford University Press.

Wharf, B. (2002). Building a case for community approaches to child welfare. In B. Wharf (Ed.), *Community work approaches to child welfare* (pp. 181–198). Peterborough, ON: Broadview Press.

|5|

Service Participant Voices in Child Welfare, Children's Mental Health and Psychotherapy

Marshall Fine
Sally Palmer
Nick Coady

Introduction and Overview

This chapter gathers the viewpoints of service participants[1] from the literature on child welfare, children's mental health, and psychotherapy services. These voices have traditionally been unheard; however, recently, professionals have more actively sought their thoughts and ideas about their experiences with service. It is likely that, until recently, service participants did not imagine that their views should be heard; such was the power of the professional gaze (Foucault, 1979).

Although the focus of the volume is clearly on child welfare and children's mental health services, there is an essential overlap between these service sectors and that of psychotherapy. It is important to note at the outset that we construe the term psychotherapy broadly to include all approaches to individual, family, and group counselling. Because psychotherapy/counselling principles are integral aspects of children's mental health services and there are fundamental elements of counselling/relationship-building in child welfare practices, we thought it critical to include this body of literature in our review.

The twentieth century introduced the idea of experts on the human condition—particularly the "abnormal" human condition. Professionals in social work, psychiatry, psychology, and related disciplines developed and refined skills for observing and diagnosing human beings. These professional discourses were sanctioned by society, thereby giving professionals the authority not only to judge what was acceptable but also to isolate and treat what was not (Gergen & Kaye, 1992; Illich, 1977; Wilson & Beresford, 2000).

Foucault suggested that this authority was sanctioned primarily because of society's need for order and control (1979). Deviancy was controlled through normalizing professional judgments and practices (Farber, 1990; Foucault, 1979; Illich, 1977). The knowledge and power gained by these professionals became sufficiently encompassing that society assumed they knew best (Wilson & Beresford, 2000) and did not question them. The professional had the answers and the cure (Payne, 2000).[2]

Given the "scientific" certainty bestowed on experts during this period, it was deemed unnecessary to query the experience or opinion of service participants, the assumption being that their opinions would be distorted and flimsy, at best (Gergen & Kaye, 1992). Service participants were considered the benefactors of the cutting edge of benevolent professional discourse—they were not seen as having a scientific perspective. Postmodern thinkers question the certainties and universal truths that emanated from professional conversations in the era of modernity (Anderson, 1995). Indeed, professional knowledge is now questioned regularly (Atkinson & Heath, 1990; Hartman & Laird, 1998).

We do not intend this introduction to portray helping professionals as uninterested, uncaring, and unhelpful toward service participants. Indeed, the studies cited in this review attest to the overall positive effects of the service experience. Our position is that professionals are genuinely concerned about the welfare of service participants. Professional concern, however, is influenced by the paradigms of the times. Modernity brought with it a paternalistic concern, focused on the expertise of the professional. Therefore, most theories concerning assistance to service participants were formulated without consulting service participants about what might work best for them.

This chapter turns the gaze toward professionals and their services. The service participant becomes the "story creator"—the one who knows best how service impacts him or her, and what professional practices are most, and least, helpful. We review the literature from children's mental health, child welfare, and psychotherapeutic services—literature that expressly explores and invites service participants' voices—to reveal what participants say about the services they experience.

For the purpose of this chapter we define "voices" as documented feedback from service participants who are given the formal opportunity to add their opinions regarding the services in which they have participated. We are aware, however, that there is another definition of consumer voice not highlighted in this chapter—the direct privileging of service participant feedback in the shaping of their ongoing social work service. Professionals with postmodern, social-constructionist, or feminist views most often promote this definition of voice. It is interesting to note, however, that, with few exceptions, even the literature on social-constructionist models of therapy (which advocates for "the client as expert" and the service provider[3] stance of "not knowing"; Anderson & Goolishian, 1992), represents primarily the views of service providers, not service participants (Bowman & Fine, 2000).

The literature in each of the three areas of service delivery captures the notion of voice differently, and, as such, the style and documentation in each section varies in accordance with the context of the literature reviewed. A number of studies in child welfare have used in-depth qualitative interviews with participants as a way of including their voices. In order to emulate the nature of the literature, therefore, the child welfare section includes some participant text. In contrast, the literature on children's mental health has a quantitative bias and focuses primarily on gathering information regarding service participant satisfaction with, and outcome of, services. Although many of these studies include findings based on service participant responses to open-ended questions, participant text, as voice, is not reported in the reviewed studies and does not therefore appear in the children's mental health section of this chapter. The psychotherapy literature has produced research somewhat mixed in methodology, though the majority of studies use some form of qualitative methods aimed largely at the process and outcome of therapy. Participant text is not used consistently and is noted only occasionally in the psychotherapy section. Regardless of methodology, the basic intent of all studies in this review is to hear from service participants— to give them voice in one form or another.

Each of the three main sections of the chapter—child welfare, children's mental health, and psychotherapy—introduces the reader to the area of service and identifies, by means of a table, the studies used in the section. Although there are variations in the headings used in the three main sections of the chapter, each section focuses on what service participants have to say about positive and negative aspects of their relationships with service providers, service-provider interventions, and broader aspects of service. Following the review of the literature in each of the three sections we summarize the findings across sections and discuss implications for practice. Finally, we note methodological limitations of studies on service-participant voice and make suggestions for future research.

Voices of Parents and Children Participating in Child Welfare Services

Introduction

Involvement with child protective services (CPS) can be expected to be a stressful experience for parents. Usually their involvement is involuntary—

initiated because someone believes they are not caring adequately for their children. This tells them that the community, or someone in the community, does not approve of them as parents. Because many families who become involved with CPS are poor and socially marginalized, the shock of agency involvement may be just one more signal that they are not accepted members of their community. Added to that stress is the fear created by CPS involvement—that their children may be taken away from them, perhaps forever. It is important to understand the viewpoints of parents and children so that service providers can respond sensitively to them at these crucial times. This review consolidates the findings of the few research studies (see Table 1) that have asked parents and children about their experiences with CPS agencies.

Parents' Perceptions of Agency Programs and Decisions

Positive perceptions. Most parents in the published studies spoke more negatively than positively about their experiences with CPS, but they did speak positively about individual workers. The most enthusiastic reports came from non-traditional programs that focused more on family support than on protecting children from their families. For example, an innovative action-research project in British Columbia placed parents and CPS workers into groups, in which parents were encouraged to describe their daily lives and their experiences with CPS to the workers. These parents reported increased self esteem: "This project has given me my self esteem back and has helped me realize that I am an intelligent person with good ideas" (quoted in Callahan & Lumb, 1995, p. 808). Mothers taking part in a self-directed group-work project in the United Kingdom reported that the project helped them to recognize that "social and life circumstances, violent men, inadequate parenting, and workings of public authorities had conspired against them and yet [they] had always blamed themselves" (Mullender & Ward, 1993, p. 77).

First Nations caregivers, parents, and grandparents who were interviewed at a First Nations child and family service agency staffed by Aboriginals spoke very positively about their experiences with this agency. It is relevant, however, that this agency did not have the authority to provide child protection services, and many of the comments compared the First Nations agency favourably with CPS agencies the caregivers had experienced. They valued the First Nations agency because it placed high importance on extended family, community, and the rights of Aboriginal people to self-determination (Anderson, 1998). They also appreciated receiving help in a way that was consistent with First Nations values of consensus and co-operation, as opposed to the force and coercion they felt when dealing with

Table 1: Overview of Studies of Voices of Parents and Children in Child Welfare

Authors	Purpose	Sample	Recruitment	Data Collection
Anderson, 1998	Find out how to maintain participants' trust and comfort when providing child protection services (CPS)	4 mothers and 2 grandmothers receiving counselling from a First Nations agency (Toronto)	First Nations (FN) caregivers who were presently receiving services from a FN family and child agency (not CPS)	Semi-structured interviews in FN agency
Anglin, 2003	To uncover the essential elements of residential child and youth care, to enhance quality of care	39 youths in 10 staffed group homes (British Columbia)	Gained access to group homes through government support of study; used theoretical sampling to get a range of homes and youths	Personal interviews in group homes
Baistow, Hetherington, Spriggs, & Yelloly, 1996	To compare parents' experiences with CPS and family support agencies in England and France	13 families in England and 13 families in France	Approached parents already involved with the agencies	Personal interviews in agencies or homes
Barth, 1990	To develop program and policy initiatives for older children in long-term foster care	55 youths formerly in foster care (San Francisco)	Multiple methods used to identify respondents, e.g. foster carers, social workers, programs for youth	Personal interviews in youths' homes, some by telephone
Callahan & Lumb, 1994	To use mothers' views to guide intervention; to educate workers about lives of families in poverty; to facilitate workers and mothers sharing common feelings of powerlessness in a climate of scarce resources	CPS managers, social workers, and mothers receiving services (numbers not specified), in two district CPS offices (British Columbia)	Invited individual, government-run CPS offices to submit proposals for action research involving single mothers receiving services; then invited mothers and social workers to participate in small groups on action projects	Focus groups combining managers, social workers, and mothers, coordinator's notes on group sessions, and journalling by mothers

Table 1 (*continued*)

Authors	Purpose	Sample	Recruitment	Data Collection
Callahan, Dominelli, Rutman, & Strega, 2003	To explore the lived experiences of young mothers in/from care and what explains variations in their experiences	11 young mothers formerly in foster care; had become pregnant between ages 13 and 18 (British Columbia)	CPS agencies identified mothers willing to participate	Personal interviews in CPS agency
Chalmers, 1996	To allow graduates of group care to provide advice to practitioners working with youths in care, and to youths entering care	11 youths formerly in foster care (Minnesota)	Mailed invitation to youths who completed an "independence" program and indicated willingness to participate	Personal home-based interviews to give their views of foster care and independence program
Drake, 1994	To identify competencies central to effective relationships in CPS practice	23 parent participants in CPS and 34 CPS workers (Missouri)	Approached parents who were randomly drawn from families who had completed services within previous 6 months	Focus groups: 5 composed of parents and 4 composed of CPS workers
Festinger, 1983	To find out how young adults are doing after leaving long-term foster care	277 former foster children in New York	Recruited through 30 foster care agencies in New York State	Structured interviews in Structured interviews in own homes
Gardner, 1998	To explore perceptions of family held by adults who spent time in out-of-home care as children	39 adults formerly in foster care vs. 39 adults from intact families in Melbourne, Australia	Advertisements (newspapers and radio), personal contacts, and six foster care agencies who contacted respondents	Structured interviews in participants' own homes
Jenkins & Norman, 1972	To explore feelings of filial deprivation in parents of children in foster care	297 mothers and 49 fathers whose children had entered foster care in previous 10 months	CPS workers identified mothers and fathers willing to participate	Personal interviews in participants' homes
Jenkins & Norman, 1975	Follow-up from 1972 study five years later	186 mothers who had been part of 1972 study	Outreach to identify mothers who took part in initial study	Personal interview in participants' homes

	Purpose	Sample	Recruitment	Method
Kufeldt, Armstrong, & Dorosh, 1995	To find out how young people in care view their own and their foster families	40 children in foster care, aged 9 to 15	CPS agencies identified respondents	Questionnaires administered by social workers or foster carers
Kufeldt, Simard, & Vachon, 2000	To use a structured tool to assess the progress of children in foster care	263 children, aged 10 to 19, in foster care (several Canadian provinces)	CPS agencies identified respondents through personal contacts (purposive sampling)	Questionnaires administered by social workers or foster carers
Leslie & Hare, 2000	To explore the experiences of youths who were involved with child welfare services and moved on to seek support from a street youth program	16 youths formerly in foster care and 21 youths with other CAS contacts (Toronto)	Youths in street youth facility with prior CPS contact invited to participate	Questionnaires administered by staff at street youth facility; focus groups at facility; some in-depth personal interviews
Mann-Feder & White, 2003	To find out how youths experience emancipation from care, the course of their transition, and their perception of preparation for exit	18 youths at 3 different stages in the transition to independent living (Montreal)	CPS social workers identified youths	Focus groups at CPS agency
McAuley, 1996	To extend knowledge and theory about children in long-term foster care, their wishes, feelings, and perception of family relationships	16 children, aged 8+, recently moved to long-term foster care (Northern Ireland)	CPS co-operated to access all children who met criteria	Personal interviews in university office; semi-structured questionnaire, child-oriented tools to elicit feelings
McCallum, 1995	To explore parents' views of CPS involving removal of their children because of abuse or neglect	McCallum (1995) interviewed 6 mothers and 4 fathers whose children had been removed (Waterloo, Ontario)	Identified parents by placing posters in the CPS agency, referrals from CPS workers, then used snowball technique	Repeated in-depth interviews in parents' home, to facilitate trusting relationships

Table 1 (continued)

Authors	Purpose	Sample	Recruitment	Data Collection
McCurdy & Jones, 2000	To evaluate several long-term programs for the prevention of child abuse	69 parent participants in prevention programs in Philadelphia	Child prevention programs helped the researchers to identify the participants	Parent participants were interviewed early in their program involvement and several years later
McGee, 1998	To identify needs for child protection as perceived by children and mothers experiencing domestic violence	54 children aged 5–17 years, who received CPS services re. domestic violence (England and Wales)	Publicity in agencies and staff inviting women and childen to participate	Semi-structured personal interviews for children as young as 5, plus questionnaires for older children
Packman, Randall, & Jacques, 1986	To evaluate the process and outcomes of placing children in agency care	270 families whose children were in the care of two Local Authorities in Southern England	CPS (Local Authorities) co-operated to recruit families	Home interviews
Raychaba, 1993	To discover the life experiences, concerns, and opinions of youths in/from care	24 youths in/from care (across Canada)	Contact through informal youth networks; and CPS agencies	Semi-structured personal interviews in place chosen by youth
Richey, Lovell, & Reid, 1991	To examine the effectiveness of a group training program to improve attitudes and skills of at-risk mothers	6 low-income mothers, aged 25 to 42, who were caring for neglected and abused preschoolers	Mothers whose children had been referred by CPS to a therapeutic day nursery were invited to participate	Self-administered questionnaires; administered pre and post training; telephone and inperson probes at pre, post, and one follow-up
Rutman, Barlow, Alusik, Hubberstey & Brown, 2000	To provide youth in/from care with a voice about their experiences of transition from care; and strengthen peer support through sharing	20 young people, in/from care, age 16–29 (Victoria, BC)	Victoria Youth-in-Care Network	In-depth personal interviews by researcher–youth pair

Saskatchewan, 2000	experiences and action planning and implementation To develop recommendations for government to change practice, policy, and legislation related to children and youth in care	164 youths in/from foster care, age 8–24, (Saskatchewan)	Identified youths through CPS agencies	Personal interviews; some group interviews
Silva-Wayne, 1995	To learn from youths who are successful graduates of foster care	19 successful graduates, age 16–26, (Toronto)	Identified youths through CPS workers and an adolescent resource centre for foster care graduates	Personal interviews in agency offices or respondents' homes
Wedeven, Pecora, Hurwitz, Howell, & Newell, 1997	To assess how the foster care experience has impacted the lives of its alumni, to target program refinement	69 alumni, age 17–35, of private foster care program (Casey Family Program) in Idaho	Identified alumni through foster care agency	Mailed questionnaire
Wilford & Hetherington, 1997	To compare parents' experiences with CPS and family support agencies in England and Germany	14 families in Germany and 13 families in England (English families from Baistow et al.)	Same as Baistow et al.	Same as Baistow et al.
Winefield & Barlow, 1995	To examine the helping relationship between parents and CPS workers in a multi-disciplinary child protection agency	24 parents and 24 CPS workers in Adelaide, South Australia	Requested involvement from parents who had been receiving services for at least 10 months	Structured interviews & standardized questionnaires for both parents and CPS workers

a CPS agency managed by non-Aboriginal staff. They reported that the First Nations agency had taught them to be better parents and, as an outcome of service, their children displayed less violent behaviour and had more friends (Anderson, 1998).

Many parents in a New York City study expressed positive feelings about the placement of their children, although these were often mixed with negative feelings and worries (Jenkins & Norman, 1972). Remembering the day of placement, 40% of mothers and 42% of fathers said they felt "relieved," while 42% of mothers and 57% of fathers were "thankful" to the agencies for placing their children in substitute care.

Negative perceptions. Some parents found child protection services agencies unresponsive when they asked for help, while others experienced agencies as demanding or intrusive. First Nations caregivers recalled that traditional CPS agencies had been very supportive of their children, but not of them as parents: "I would be crying out for help [re addictions], and there would be no one listening to me" (quoted in Anderson, 1998, p. 446). Unresponsiveness was also noted by parents in England, who said it took great effort for them to get help from CPS agencies (Baistow, Hetherington, Spriggs, & Yelloly, 1996). In another study, parents in both England and Germany were critical of "having to ask again and again" for help in managing their children (Wilford & Hetherington, 1997, p. 65). Moreover, some parents reported that agency agendas differed from their own (for example, a mother who was taking courses toward employment reported requesting agency help with daycare so she could spend time on her studies, but said the agency was pressuring her to participate in parent training; Baistow et al., 1996).

Some parents in England complained that agencies were too demanding. They felt overwhelmed by the task of child care because of inexperience and their own troubled backgrounds (Wilford & Hetherington, 1997). In this context, they experienced the CPS agencies as oppressive: "The last thing you want when you are on the edge of a nervous breakdown is to be expected to be even more responsible than you have been in the past" (quoted in Wilford & Hetherington, 1997, p. 64). Feelings expressed by parents whose children were placed in care included anger, loss, fear, and inadequacy. Anger was widespread among mothers in a New York City study that involved large numbers and included a five year follow-up after initial placement (Jenkins & Norman, 1975). When interviewed initially (approximately 90 days after their child's placement), 40% of mothers reported being angry, and at the five year follow-up, 34% of mothers were angry. Only part of this anger was directed at CPS agencies however—25% at the initial interview and 40% at the five year follow-up; for 53% of mothers at the first interview, their anger was directed at family members—partners and relatives (Jenkins &

Norman, 1972). Two of 26 German parents indicated anger through their use of the term "theft" in connection with their children being placed in group care—a mother said she experienced her children's time in care as "theft" of their lives with her and of their lives in normal surroundings (quoted in Wilford & Hetherington, 1997); a father described "the theft of [his children's] childhood, their aspirations and hopes" (p. 66).

A sense of loss was expressed by Aboriginal parents: a grandmother said, "When the child is gone away from home for six months, that bond is taken away from you, that ... closeness and love you have for that child—it's like you're losing that child" (quoted in Anderson, 1998, p. 448). An early American study reported that parents of children in residential treatment reported feelings of isolation, loneliness, and inadequacy about the separation (Mandelbaum, 1962).

Fear was expressed as "worry" in the New York study (Jenkins & Norman, 1972), partly because the researchers approached the mothers with structured questions, asking mothers whether they had worried during placement about its effect on their relationships with their children. Over one-half the mothers responded that they had these worries. More extreme reactions were given by some families in an English study (Packman, Randall, & Jacques, 1986): they described compulsory, emergency placement of their children as "a nightmare version of state interference" (p. 14). They also felt betrayed by workers from whom they had sought advice and support, in whom they had confided, and who had then used their confidences in evidence against them.

Youths' Perceptions of Placement Experiences

Positive perceptions. Most of the youths' comments about agency services, aside from those about individual workers, were related to their placement experiences. They expressed satisfaction about understanding the reasons behind their placement, feeling they had enough contact with their parents, and being able to participate in decisions that impacted on their lives (Festinger, 1983). Regarding the necessity for placement, some youths said it was the right decision—that their lives would have been much worse without placement (Barth, 1990). One youth said, "They gave me a second chance at life" (quoted in Leslie & Hare, 2000, p. 16). Other positive aspects of placement reported by youths were relationships, safety, insight, behavioural change, and preparation for independence. Regarding relationships, 53% of foster-care alumni in the study by Wedeven, Pecora, Hurwitz, Howell, and Newell (1997) mentioned a sense of belonging as an important aspect of placement, and associated this with having a good relationship with a foster carer.

Safety was mentioned by some youths living in a staff-operated group home, usually after unsuccessful foster-home experiences (Anglin, 2003). They felt that staff were better able than previous foster carers to accept their challenging behaviour and offer them a safe environment while they worked on their problems. As one youth said, "I was going through some pretty crazy stuff, and ... I needed to be somewhere where I could be where I wasn't going to hurt anyone, lash out at the wrong people" (quoted in Anglin, 2003, p. 8). These youths also saw a positive aspect to the staff changing every four days: this gave staff a break, a chance to calm down, after which they could deal with the youths' behaviour.

Youths said being in care helped them to recognize they had been abused: "without CAS [children's aid society] I would have assumed that abuse was normal" (quoted in Leslie & Hare, 2000, p. 42). They also learned to manage their anger, rather than taking it out on others (Leslie & Hare, 2000). Some youths felt they were well prepared to leave the agency for independence (Kufeldt, Armstrong, & Dorosh, 1995; Rutman, Barlow, Alusik, Hubberstey, & Brown, 2000), although many youths did not feel prepared, as will be discussed later.

Negative perceptions. Youths reported a number of negative experiences: feeling powerless; being disrespected; being unsafe; being stigmatized or marginalized; discontinuity of homes and service providers; conflict about relationships with their families; inadequate preparation for independence; and hardship in the transition from care.

Youths felt powerless because they were not given important information about plans or decisions affecting their lives. In the Saskatchewan (2000) study, few respondents knew that a case plan had been developed for them, they were rarely given any notice in advance of a move, and they were not told when service providers were leaving or who would take their place. This last point was confirmed by service providers, who said they had no time to handle ending relationships with children. In Chalmers' (1996) research, graduates recalled they were not told how long they would be in a specific placement. They also noted they were not told why they were in care; consequently, many felt it must be their fault—that they were being held singularly accountable for the difficulties in their families of origin.

Regarding decision-making, a young First Nations mother (formerly in care) recalled she was given no choices about where she was placed, even whether she would like to live in a Native home (Callahan, Dominelli, Rutman, & Strega, 2003). This was consistent with the results of a judicial inquiry that found crucial decisions about children's futures were made without their input (Gove, 1995). In the study by Wedeven et al. (1997), 10% of youths felt they had not been listened to or provided with opportunities to participate in decision-making. In Chalmers' (1996) study, some youths felt their opinions were not valued: "You're fighting against all these adults who have more say over your life than you do ... but no one ever asks you. And when they do, you don't get believed because you're automatically this troubled kid" (p.109).

Powerlessness also centred on the restrictions of group home living. In Chalmers' (1996) study, three of 11 youths objected to group consequences as a program component, and being expected to tell on others who broke rules. Mann-Feder and White (2003) heard from a youth in transition to independence that staff, "played mind games, made decisions for me" (p. 8). Feeling disrespected by the system was mentioned by a former youth in care. He described the government (CPS) office where, "Secretaries treat everybody like crap ... names being yelled over the intercom ... people talking about private things about other kids I knew right there in the hallway" (Saskatchewan, 2000, p. 34).

Only 55% of youths reported they had felt safe while in foster care (Leslie & Hare, 2000). In Gardner's (1998) study, 15% of respondents reported being raped in foster homes, and 10% reported being victims of sexual improprieties. Many youths felt stigmatized and marginalized by having to live in foster care. Regarding stigma, Silva-Wayne (1995) concluded that "the pervasive devaluation perceived by participants because they had been in out-of-home care is the strongest and most surprising finding that emerges from interviews with participants" (p. 313). In Leslie and Hare's (2000) research, one youth spoke about the stigma: "Be prepared to be labelled and let down and treated differently" (p. 15). Regarding marginalization, it was difficult for some youths to have a sense of belonging in a foster home: "I feel I'm just some intruder in someone's house" (quoted in Anglin, 2003, p. 8). A youth expressed loneliness about being in a foster home: "I felt like I was living in other people's homes, invading their families ... I felt lonely at times" (quoted in Leslie & Hare, 2000, p. 42). This loneliness persisted during the transition (Rutman et al., 2000) from care, possibly because the youth's relationship with a foster family officially ended with formal discharge from care. A youth indicated he felt rejected when he returned to see the father of his family group home over the first six months after leaving care: "he did the same thing that the other foster parents did, pushing me back ... Every time I used to see him and the family, I used to cry" (quoted in Rutman et al., 2000, p. 11).

Discontinuity of placements was another concern for many youths (Kufeldt, Simard, & Vachon, 2000; Raychaba, 1993; Wedeven et al., 1997). This related to the sense of not belonging: as one youth recalled, he had "a sense of instability ... [I] always feared that [my] adoptive parents would abandon me at any time" (quoted in Leslie & Hare, 2000, p. 41). Discontinuity was sometimes severe: "It's no fun to make new friends every month. I had nine schools and seven placements" (quoted in Leslie & Hare, 2000, p. 15). Some youths noted that the discontinuity in foster care programmed them for instability in their subsequent lives. Several respondents said they tended to move frequently because they were used to this: "I was always trying to fit in somewhere. I got a lot of rejection" (quoted in Rutman et al., 2000, p. 6). A young mother said, "You keep getting bounced and bounced around and around ... and I continued that [when she left care] ... I didn't know what stability really was" (quoted in Callahan et al., 2003, p. 4).

Discontinuity of service providers was another common experience that youths in care disliked (Callahan et al., 2003; Leslie & Hare, 2000; Raychaba, 1993; Saskatchewan, 2000); it discouraged them in their efforts to progress with their lives (Chalmers, 1996). Researchers noted that service provider changes are often caused by "the organization of work processes according to specialization of functions and categorization of clients ... [for the young women this meant] most had experienced three service providers because of the structure of the system" (Callahan et al., 2003, p.9). Possibly because of this discontinuity, youths looking forward to the transition to independence had a fear of being let down by agency staff: "I ask myself if I can rely on them" (quoted in Mann-Feder & White, 2003, p. 8).

Many youths had conflicted feelings about their relationships with their own families. Seven of 11 graduates said they had been discouraged from maintaining family ties and would advise other youths in care to "try to keep a strong bond with your family because sooner or later no matter how much you hate your family at one time or another, you need them. Even though you go through bad times, they love you" (quoted in Chalmers, 1996, p. 108). In a study of 40 children still in foster care, 36% said they wanted more contact with their families; only one-third saw their families as frequently as once a week (Kufeldt et al., 1995). Some First Nations caregivers looked back on their own apprehensions by child welfare and spoke of their sense of loss regarding their parents: "They were so nice when they weren't drinking," said one; another said removal from family was "devastating" (quoted in Anderson, 1998, p. 444). Other children expressed sadness about the loss of family connections (Kufeldt et al., 2000); and 3 of 16 children mentioned sadness at leaving their siblings when moving to foster homes from residential care (McAuley, 1996).

Disrupted family relationships created difficulty for children's attachment and identification. Children indicated their "preoccupation and identification ... with their birth families over time" (McAuley, 1996, pp. 157–158) despite most having been abused or neglected by their parents, and some having had little contact. Still, children's identification with parent figures tended to diminish over time. After four months in foster care, 10 of 17 children said their primary identification was with birth parent(s) or grand-parent; only 2 of 17 mentioned someone in the foster family, and 1 of 17 didn't know; however, after one year in care, only 6 of 13 named their birth parent(s) or a grandparent, whereas 4 of 13 said "nobody" or "didn't know" (McAuley, 1996).

Many children expressed loyalty conflicts regarding their families, or worries about their welfare; their comments suggested an area perhaps neg-lected by agencies. A study of children (aged 4 to 11) explored their feelings after four months in care (McAuley, 1996): only 5 of 16 felt they had "emo-tional permission" from at least one parent to be in foster care; only 3 of 10 children felt it was OK to talk to foster carers about their past life with their birth parents; and only 6 of 11 who had family contact thought it was OK to discuss this with foster carers (McAuley, 1996). Some children mentioned worrying about their families: A girl whose father had died said she thought about her mother "every night in bed ... how (mother) is getting on ... worry about her ... feel sad" (quoted in McAuley, 1996, p. 100). The option of returning home seemed to fade over time for some First Nations youths in care: A young woman said she couldn't fit back into her First Nations com-munity after a year in care (Saskatchewan, 2000).

Many youths commented that there was inadequate preparation for independence. Among the street youths formerly in care, only two of eight said they had been prepared for independent living (Leslie & Hare, 2000). Regarding formal preparation, one youth said, "None whatsoever. They just said, 'Here's your stuff' ... it was like the sheet was whipped from right under-neath me. I hit rock bottom. It was a huge factor in my life" (quoted in Rut-man et al., 2000, p. 7). Another youth in this study said his only preparation for independence was to be given information about the nearest welfare office. The researchers noted that some agencies had preparation programs but the youths were not emotionally ready for independence; some youths wanted to learn life skills earlier (at age 14–15), but recognized they might not have been ready at this time (Rutman et al., 2000). Youths felt unpre-pared partly because of a concern that they did not have the education and skills to find desirable employment or affordable housing on leaving care. They wanted more help with life skills and support to accomplish tasks (Barth, 1990; Mann-Feder & White, 2003; Rutman et al., 2000). They also wanted vocational counselling and more experiential opportunities to take responsibility (Wedeven et al., 1997).

As a result of being unprepared for the job market, youths experienced considerable hardship during the transition from care; many struggled with a subsistence existence (Rutman et al., 2000). In Barth's (1990) study, nearly 30% were homeless at times. Residential workers told researchers that 40% of street youths using their services had prior contact with children's aid, and many had extensive placement histories (Leslie & Hare, 2000). Young women having difficulties with early motherhood expressed "a deep sense of fragility and unpredictability about their circumstances" (Callahan et al., 2003, p. 7). Most did not feel supported by their former agencies, and some said they had to inhibit anger to get services they needed for themselves and their children.

Relationships with Service Providers

Positive perceptions from parents. Many parents who become involved with child protection services were abused or rejected as children. Often feeling marginalized by society as adults, they have difficulty forming trusting relationships. Accordingly, parents valued service providers who were caring, respectful, trustworthy, accepting, responsive, and supportive. All 10 parents in McCallum's (1995) study mentioned the importance of service providers showing caring, compassion, and commitment toward families in their case load. In Wilford and Hetherington's (1997) study, respect was mentioned by both English and German parents: "All I ask is to be treated like a human being and not a number" (p. 62).

Trust was mentioned by several parents in McCallum's (1995) study: "a person they can count on, even if they are a bad parent, somebody who they can trust is going to do the right thing for themselves and their children" (p. 77). Interestingly, this parent did not view trust just in terms of his own self interest but, more broadly, in terms of the service provider doing "the right thing."

Respondents in Winefield and Barlow's (1995) study placed the most importance on service providers' friendliness, responsiveness, and supportiveness. In a study by George, Jones, and McCurdy (1992), young, single, low-income mothers, who were assessed as being a high risk for abusing, appreciated service providers who were kind and went "the extra mile" for them. They valued the social contact that reduced their extreme social isolation more than the parenting training they received. First Nations mothers and grandmothers also looked to service providers for support, describing them as allies, advocates, and friends; they were referring to their experiences with a First Nations child and family support agency, however, rather than to a CPS agency (Anderson, 1998).

Acceptance was viewed as an important part of the relationship (Drake, 1994; McCallum, 1995). Several fathers who had been charged with sexually abusing their daughters described their appreciation of service providers who accepted them as people: "she was giving me credit for trying to be different ... and that was encouraging" (quoted in McCallum, 1995, p. 63). Parents interviewed by Drake (1994) liked workers who avoided prejudging them. Parents also felt better about the balance of power with service providers who disclosed their own failings; a mother who had trouble managing her son's behaviour said she felt better when her service provider admitted that he sometimes yelled at his kids (McCallum, 1995). Participants in several Philadelphia programs aimed at reducing child abuse described their service providers as "someone they could depend on and confide in, and who never made them feel like 'bad parents'" (McCurdy & Jones, 2000, p. 111).

Negative perceptions from parents. Parents' complaints about service providers were mainly about their attitudes toward the parent; workers were described variously as judgmental, uncaring, dictatorial, and denigrating. A man who was convicted of child sexual abuse felt the service provider had labelled him and rejected him (McCallum, 1995). A single mother felt she was being unfairly judged: "It's a laugh to be told I need money management skills. You need [to have] money to manage" (quoted in Callahan & Lumb, 1995, p. 804). A First Nations caregiver felt denigrated by her encounters with child protection service providers: "Every time I meet a [CPS] worker, they're accusing me of something, trying to make me look bad or something" (quoted in Anderson, 1998, p. 448). A judgmental attitude was linked with poor results by one mother: "If I have low self-esteem, and two kids, and social workers saying things about me, it affects them badly and me too" (quoted in Callahan & Lumb, 1995, p. 804). Others criticized service providers who took a superior attitude, giving orders to parents rather than working with them: "They don't *ask* you to do the things ... they *tell* you to do it" (quoted in Drake, 1994, p. 597; emphasis in original).

Just as they appreciated warmth and acceptance, parents were unhappy when service providers seemed uncaring: "he [service provider] was just very cold, to me, uncaring ... I guess it was just the way he said it ... the tone of his voice ... like my kid didn't matter" (quoted in McCallum, 1995, p. 65).

Positive perceptions from youths. Youths repeatedly emphasized that support and relationships with staff were more important aspects of care than programming, both during placement and in the transitional period (Mann-Feder & White, 2003). In the Leslie and Hare (2000) study, 10 of 12 youths formerly in care mentioned particular workers or foster carers who had made a significant difference in their lives. Similarly, in the Saskatchewan study (2000), youths who had built relationships with a service provider said this had had a long-term positive effect on their lives.

Youths valued the following qualities in their relationships with service providers, which included both social workers and foster parents: respect, understanding, caring/supportiveness, and commitment/dependability/loyalty. In Chalmers' (1996) study, respect was mentioned by 9 of 11 graduates of care, in particular, they suggested that service providers should "be respectful of the very personal nature of many of the questions asked of young people" (p. 109).

Youths frequently mentioned service providers who made them feel cared about (Chalmers, 1996). The researcher linked this with being understood: All 11 respondents identified at least one service provider who "understood what I had to say" (p.105). With foster carers, respondents associated being cared about with feeling openly welcomed into a foster home (Chalmers, 1996). In Leslie and Hare's (2000) study, a youth said, "[My] foster mother ... treated [me] like her own children" (p. 41).

Supportiveness was also viewed as a demonstration of caring. In Chalmers' (1996) study, 3 of 11 graduates said their service providers went out of their way to offer support or stand up for them. In Leslie and Hare's (2000) study, a youth noted, "If you're past 18 you can't get certain things ... but [my worker] goes the extra mile for me" (p. 16).

Signs of commitment by service providers were also valued by youths, many of whom had been rejected by one home after another. A youth in a staffed group home said, "It was the first place they didn't kick me out of" (quoted in Anglin, 2003, p. 10), and noted that the staff showed commitment to him when he took an overdose and was in the hospital by ensuring that someone stayed with him constantly for ten days. Some service providers showed commitment by continuing their interest in youths after they left care—the youths seemed to view these service providers as a combination of parent, mentor, and friend: "After I turned 19, she helped me with my citizenship ... hired people to work with me ... I was allowed to store some of my 'stuff' in her office ... [gave me] birthday gifts and Christmas gifts" (quoted in Rutman, 2000, p. 10). Commitment was also demonstrated by dependability and loyalty, qualities valued by the young mothers interviewed by Callahan and colleagues (2003).

Negative perceptions from youths. Negative aspects of youths' relationships with service providers included mistrust, a sense of not being cared about, being disrespected, and being unequally treated. Researchers concluded that youths who were or had been in care often had difficulty trusting service providers (Anglin, 2003; Wedeven et al., 1997). Young mothers formerly in care also revealed they had scars from their experiences that affected their ability to trust (Callahan et al., 2003).

Youths in two studies felt ignored by service providers who never visited the homes where they were placed (Chalmers, 1996; Saskatchewan, 2000). In the latter study, service providers confirmed that they did not always respond to youths' phone calls; one worker said she had not seen 30% of children on her caseload for eight months because of workload (Saskatchewan, 2000). Youths in transition to independence reported "that there were no real goodbyes and that they felt they had been 'put out.'" (Mann-Feder & White, 2003, p. 8). Young mothers formerly in care expressed a sense of being alone during their pregnancies, a highly vulnerable time in their lives (Callahan et al., 2003).

Some youths who had left care reported that service providers spoke or behaved disrespectfully to them (Chalmers, 1996). A female graduate objected to staff who "were always telling me I had to be a certain way ... to feel a certain way" (quoted in Chalmers, 1996, p. 106). Some young women who had become pregnant, while in or after care, felt they were viewed as failures, although the researchers viewed these mothers as setting high expectations for themselves in caring for their children (Callahan et al., 2003).

Youths viewed stability and permanency in relationships with service providers and caregivers as a crucial precondition for trust, attachment, and commitment (Raychaba, 1993). For youths with difficulties in relationships, stability is more likely in therapeutic foster homes or group care, but youths noted that it was necessary to fail in all other levels of homes to qualify for a therapeutic foster home (Raychaba, 1993).

Youths wanted a more equal relationship with agency staff who were assigned to them during the transition to independent living: It should be a balance, with the staff to be "close but far," to provide a "push without nagging," to avoid "overpowering authority but not allow total independence" (Mann-Feder & White 2003, p. 6).

Service Provider Interventions

Positive perceptions from parents. Parents liked service providers who shared power, gave them knowledge, and listened to them. Regarding power, parents wanted service providers to be open about the limits of their power, and be willing to share it. A mother recalled being reassured by a new service provider that there was not enough reason for the agency to remove her school-aged daughter; she compared this with her two previous service providers who had left her feeling they would take her daughter if she (the mother) did not follow all their directions (McCallum, 1995). In the study by Wilford and Hetherington (1997), 50% of German parents reported a sense of working in partnership with the service providers or social pedagogues. Speaking about desired experiences, First Nations parents and grandparents wanted more information about, and input into, placement decisions: "Talk to the parents. Let them know what is going to happen to their child ... and let the child know that they're going to be leaving the home" (quoted in Anderson, 1998, p. 451). Regarding the choice of placement, "I would want myself or someone that I knew ... to interview these people [with whom my child would be placed]" (quoted in Anderson, 1998, p. 452).

Parents also liked service providers to share their knowledge (Anderson, 1998; Winefield & Barlow, 1995). A First Nations mother appreciated advice from her service provider, who had "more knowledge, more education, on how to talk to your child," as long as the worker didn't try to "tell her what to do" (quoted in Anderson, 1998, p. 457). Parents valued service providers who talked at their level, were good listeners, and demonstrated interest in them (Drake, 1994; McCallum, 1995; Winefield & Barlow, 1995). One mother described being able to talk about her problems with a worker who would "... just sit there and listen to it all and just take it all in" (quoted in McCallum, 1995, p. 63).

Negative perceptions from parents. Most parents' negative comments related to participants' sense of helplessness in the face of agency power. McCallum (1995) found that "all 10 respondents ... said they felt alienated, intimidated, threatened and/or controlled for at least part of their time with the agency" (p. 56). A First Nations mother felt she had been deceived by the CPS service provider who took her child: "[The service provider said,] 'Just for the weekend' ... that's how my child was taken ... not letting the parent know" (quoted in Anderson, 1998, p. 451). Some parents in the Wilford & Hetherington (1997) study also talked about being "coerced into collaborating" (p. 65) with CPS. They did, however, distinguish between workers; a German mother noted, "It depends very much on the people you get, some are extremely helpful and others invade your privacy as if by divine right" (quoted in Wilford & Hetherington, 1997, p. 66). In Callahan and Lumb's (1995) study, a single mother described her feeling of being controlled: "I was a puppet for three months, everybody was pulling the strings. I was told to do this and that, and I did it—I wanted my child back" (p. 804).

Some parents complained of confusion—that they were not given information about resources and about service providers' roles, often receiving directives they didn't understand without explanations for what was being done to them (McCallum, 1995). A single mother mistakenly believed, before participation in the action research project, that her provider for social assistance had the power both to cancel her cheque and take her children (Callahan & Lumb, 1995). In Germany, where CPS tended to be viewed more as a service than a threat, a mother wanted more information about her rights (Wilford & Hetherington, 1997, p. 66–67). A First Nations caregiver wanted the service provider to give her more time: "At that time [of apprehension], if she [CAS service provider] would have actually just sat down and talked with me, instead of just running off" (quoted in Anderson, 1998, p. 448).

In the New York study, over half the mothers were worried about how placement would affect their relationship with their children. A mother whose children had returned to her said, "The children had changed; I felt treated like a stranger. It took a long time for them to trust me" (quoted in Jenkins & Norman, 1975, p. 55). Another concern raised in this study was the difficulty of visiting their children: 20% of mothers said the children were placed in locations difficult to access; moreover, 20% felt the agency discouraged them from visiting, and 70% felt the agency could do more to facilitate their contacts with their children.

Positive perceptions from youths. Youths appreciated or wanted service providers who would listen to them, discuss the youth's family and/or culture, work with their families, share power and decision-making with them, let them know when they [service providers] were leaving, reinforce their self-confidence, and support them during the transition to independence. In Chalmers' (1996) study, the importance of having service providers who listened to them was mentioned by 7 of 11 graduates from care.

Youths stated that more attention should have been given to treating their families while they were in care. In Chalmers' (1996) study, 7 of 11 graduates mentioned this: one respondent said she changed a lot in care, but when she came home her parents ignored this and still did not trust her. Regarding discussion of culture, a 17-year-old male First Nations youth, who had the same First Nations service provider for seven years, said she taught him "a lot of stuff about my people" (Saskatchewan, 2000, p. 31).

Youths reported favourably on caregivers who promoted their sense of self-confidence about moving into independence (Rutman et al., 2000). They appreciated a non-authoritative approach, as was expressed by a youth seeking services from a street agency: "Some workers don't *tell* you things, they *suggest* things ... [they] don't come across as a worker but as a friend" (as quoted in Leslie & Hare, 2000, p. 16; emphasis added).

Negative perceptions from youths. Like parents, youths wanted workers to give them more information, to advocate for them with foster carers, and to work for change in their families while they were placed. Often the negative perceptions were expressed as recommendations that suggested gaps in services. Children living with domestic violence wanted service providers to take initiative in discussing this, to address their sense of being powerless (McGee, 1998). They wanted service providers to be aware of their fear, to explain what might happen if the child reported the violence, and to provide information about available help (McGee, 1998). Youths in placement wanted information that would allow them to share in decisions about their lives, and to lessen their confusion and fear (Saskatchewan, 2000). Some youths noted that more information might lessen their perceived blame: "[re incest] Tell (the kid) it's not all their fault" (quoted in Chalmers, 1996, p. 109). As a 15-year-old said, "If a kid is old enough to talk, then they should be consulted about everything" (Saskatchewan, 2000, p. 20). Youths particularly wanted to be informed when a worker was leaving and would not be seeing them again (Saskatchewan, 2000).

Some youths felt that service providers were not effective advocates for them when they had difficulties with foster families (Wedeven et al., 1997). Youths who told their service providers they were not treated well in foster care reported that service providers told the foster carers, sometimes leading to punishment and retribution for the child (Gardner, 1998).

Youths wanted more support during their transition to independence, specifically stating that agencies should continue to provide counselling and support after foster care (Barth, 1990; Wedeven et al., 1997). Youths from three studies recommended that transition should be an ongoing process, rather than an abrupt cut-off from support (Barth, 1990; Mann-Feder & White, 2003; Rutman et al., 2000). They indicated that youths could be encouraged to test out their ability to be independent, while still receiving support beyond the age of majority. Ideally, support would come from ongoing relationships with peer mentors, service providers, and/or caregivers (Rutman et al., 2000). Peer mentoring was suggested as a way of helping youths to heal past wounds and to assume adult roles (Mann-Feder & White, 2003; Rutman et al., 2000). Some graduates of care felt they had something to offer to others in transition and were willing to help with support groups or mentoring (Chalmers, 1996; Wedeven et al., 1997). Moreover, some youths wanted an opportunity to give feedback to the agency (for example, an exit interview when they were leaving the system; Chalmers, 1996).

Methodological Issues

Research that attempts to elicit the views of service participants carries some risks related to possible bias and the reliability of responses. Many of the studies in this review found their participants through the service agencies themselves; this may have biased the findings by overrepresenting those who have had relatively good experiences. On the other hand, advertising openly in an agency increases the chance of recruiting people who may be dissatisfied with services.

When seeking participants' opinions of services, researchers should be aware of a tendency of socially desirable responses; parents or children who are still involved with agencies may fear backlash if they give negative evaluations. Winefield & Barlow (1995) tried to minimize this by carefully explaining the independence of the evaluation and the confidentiality of the results. Participatory action research, as carried out by Callahan & Lumb (1995) and Mullender & Ward (1993), has the potential to strengthen respondents' self-confidence and trust in the researchers, which may encourage more openness in expressing their opinions.

The risk of socially desirable responses may be reduced when respondents are asked open questions and are given time to become comfortable with the researchers. In McCallum's (1995) research, she began with a general request ("Describe your experience"), carried out an in-depth interview, and saw each respondent as many as three times. McCallum's approach elicited some passionate descriptions of painful experiences as well as in-depth revelations about positive experiences with service providers. In contrast, the structured questions used by Winefield & Barlow (1995) elicited mainly positive responses from parents.

Researchers who used focus groups with youths noted the potential for bias from contagion within the groups. Mann-Feder and White (2003) suggested that some of their focus groups were dominated by a few youths who were angry at staff or the system. Leslie and Hare (2000) felt their groups with street youths in a shelter were at risk of contagion, because some members of an "at risk" population might lack the ability and confidence to express their opinions in a group.

Children are especially prone to give socially desirable or defensive answers to adults because of the power imbalance. Kufeldt et al. (1995) tested for the child's ability to refuse questions by using a test with subscales for social desirability and defensiveness. This identified children who were high on these dimensions so that researchers could treat their responses to other subjective questions with caution.

Some researchers noted that questions about past experience depended upon the accuracy of respondents' memories; with youths who have been in care for many years, childhood memories may be coloured by many aspects of their experience, so findings should be interpreted with caution (Leslie & Hare, 2000; Wedeven et al., 1997). Wedeven and colleagues (1997) attempted to improve the reliability of responses to open-ended questions by having more than one rater analyze the data and by testing for inter-rater reliability (Wedeven et al., 1997).

The main limitations in methodology for the studies reviewed are the tendency to recruit respondents through their service providers and the possible effects of agency power on participants' willingness to speak freely. A few researchers avoided these pitfalls with more creative methods of recruiting, and by using participatory action research or developing a relationship with respondents over several interviews. When used with parents, these methods seem to have elicited more specific and in-depth revelations about parents' concerns, fears, and desires. The main weakness of the research with youths may have been the use of focus groups, with the risk of contagion, and the use of structured questions, with the risk of limiting youths' responses.

Summary

The recency of the above literature on parents' and children's voices in child welfare suggests that we are just beginning to ask participants about their experiences and suggestions for improvement. The major theme in the studies reviewed is the desire of parents and youths to be treated in a caring, respectful way. A significant minority of parents felt that agencies had encroached on their rights and those of their children; parents and children both wanted more involvement in decision-making and more information about agency plans and the reasons for these. Parents tended to express more concern about the lack of responsiveness by CPS agencies and service providers than about unwanted intervention. The best service providers, as described by parents, were those who were compassionate toward their failures as parents, respected them as human beings, and reached out to support them in meeting their children's needs. Children and youths felt there was a gap in agency help to deal with their feelings about living in foster care, apart from their families. A major theme with youths in transition was the sense of being unprepared for independence and in need of continued support. They felt earlier help in addressing the rifts with their families might have helped to fill this gap.

Voices of Parents and Children Participating in Children's Mental Health Services

This section of the paper summarizes the literature on service participants' views of their experiences with social service providers and agencies in the field of children's mental health. We have construed the field of children's mental health broadly to include in- and out-patient treatment of the emotional, behavioural, and psychiatric problems of children, adolescents, and their families. The literature reviewed includes feedback from youth and parents about the service providers and agencies with which they were involved. Twenty-one studies that had at least a partial focus on eliciting service participants' feedback about their experiences with children's mental health services were reviewed for this part of the chapter. Although most of these studies focused on agencies that specialized in children's mental health services, it should be noted that three studies (Carscaddon, George, & Wells, 1990; DeChillo, 1993; Kirchner, 1981) focused on mental health services for a predominantly adult population and one study (Coady & Hayward, 1998) focused on a joint child welfare/children's mental health service. An overview of the purpose, sample, recruitment method, and data collection strategy of each of these 21 studies is presented in Table 2.

Table 2: Overview of Studies of Client Voices in Children's Mental Health Services

Authors	Purpose	Sample	Recruitment	Data Collection
Brannen, Sonnichsen, & Heflinger, 1996	To assess parent and adolescent satisfaction with a case-managed continuum of care model of children's mental health services	984 families with children 5–18 years of age (63% male; 72% white) who were involved in one or more of a full continuum of services	Used same sample of families that had been recruited as part of a larger evaluation project (recruitment strategy unspecified)	Interviewer administered questionnaire
Byalin, 1993	To assess parent satisfaction with a range of children's mental health services	15 parents of children and adolescents who had received in-patient or out-patient services	Non-random selection of clients at discharge	Mailed Client Satisfaction Questionnaire (CSQ) (28% response rate)
Carr, McDonnell, & Owen, 1994	To audit practice at a child and family mental health centre, including client satisfaction with services	45 families with children under 16 years of age who had terminated services	All clients who had been discharged within a given time period	Mailed questionnaire (52% response rate)
Carscaddon, George, & Wells, 1990	To examine the impact of therapy on client satisfaction and outcome in a rural community health centre	88 primarily adult clients (mean age 30 years, range 13–64, 67% female)	All clients who were served within a given time period	Self-administered questionnaires at 2 points in time (3rd session within agency; follow-up mailed)
Charlop, Parrish, Fenton, & Cataldo, 1987	To evaluate hospital-based outpatient pediatric services	100 families with children 1–20 years of age (74% male; 73% white)	First 100 clients treated in a calendar year	Brief telephone interviews at 3, 6, and 12 months post-termination
Coady & Hayward, 1998	To conduct a qualitative program evaluation of a multi-agency (children's mental health and child welfare) family preservation program for adolescents and their families	12 mothers and 12 adolescents (8 males, 4 females) who had been involved with the agency for more than one month and who had been terminated within in the last 6 months	Opportunistic sample	In-depth, individual interviews

Table 2: (*continued*)

Authors	Purpose	Sample	Recruitment	Data Collection
DeChillo, 1993	To examine collaboration between inpatient social workers and families of clients with severe mental illness, as well as client satisfaction	102 families with a member (59% female, 65% white) who had been hospitalized for 14 days or longer (mean age 35 years, range 17–52 years)	All eligible families with members admitted to the program within a 4 month period	Interview at discharge with family member most involved with client's treatment
Eppel, Fuyarchuk, Phelps, & Tersigni-Phelan, 1991	To conduct a comprehensive quality assurance program within a multi-program mental health clinic	146 clients completed the client satisfaction questionnaire	All clients who attended the clinic in a 1 week period (60% response rate)	Self-administered questionnaires at the clinic
Fairchild & Wright, 1984	To examine staff and client assessments of the social-ecological environment of 2 adolescent treatment facilities, as well as client satisfaction with the program	52 adolescents (31 males, 21 females) from 7–17 years of age (as well as 29 staff members)	Unspecified	Interviewer administered questionnaires (individually or in groups)
Fiester, 1978	To evaluate children's treatment services at a community mental health centre	64 clients (parents or youth)	Unspecified	Telephone interview at follow-up (71% response rate)
Garland & Besinger, 1996	To gather adolescents' perceptions of outpatient mental health services	33 adolescents (13–18 years of age; 51% male; 36% white) who were or had been receiving services	Unspecified	Semi-structured interviews
Godley, Fiedler, & Funk, 1998	To assess parents' and children's satisfaction with child/adolescent mental health services (home and office-based)	469 parents (88% female; 72% white) and 387 youth (56% male; 72% white)	All client families that had agency appointments during the 2 week study period	Structured interviews conducted separately with parents and youth

Citation	Purpose	Sample	Sampling	Data collection
Johnson, Cournoyer, & Bond, 1995	To gather parent feedback about mental health professionals who had worked with their children, and to compare this with professionals' concerns about ethical issues	202 parents (90% female; 94% white) whose children had received a mental health service	Modified random sampling of mailing lists of parent-support groups	Mailed questionnaires (39% response rate)
Kirchner, 1981	To assess client satisfaction with the services at a community mental health service	254 clients (63% female; majority over 18 years of age)	All clients over 13 years of age (in two different calendar years) who had terminated services within the last 3–11 months	Mailed questionnaire (48% response rate)
Kotsopoulos, Elwood, & Oke, 1989	To assess parent satisfaction with services in a child psychiatric service	101 parents of children (66% male) who had received psychiatric services	200 consecutive referrals to the service selected	Mailed questionnaire (50% response rate)
Lishman, 1978	To gather parents' perceptions of the mental health services they and their children had received	12 parents of children 3–13 years who had received children's mental health services from the author in the last year	From 19 cases the author had closed in the last year (63% agreed to participate)	Semi-structured, in-depth interviews
Plante, Couchman, & Hoffman, 1998	To assess treatment outcome and client satisfaction with children's mental health services	115 parents whose children (70% male; 64% white) were treated at the agency	Cross-section (not specified how selected) of clients treated at the agency over an 18 month period	Self-administered questionnaires and mailed questionnaires, as well as therapist questionnaires
Shapiro, Welker, & Jacobson, 1997	To assess treatment outcome and youth and parental satisfaction with services at a children's mental health centre.	150 youth (52% female; 48% white) from 11–17 years of age, and their parents, who had completed services	Clients who had completed services within the study period and who had attended at least 3 therapy sessions (57% response rate)	Telephone interview

Table 2: (continued)

Authors	Purpose	Sample	Recruitment	Data Collection
Stallard, 1995	To assess parental satisfaction with a child and adolescent psychology service	57 families who had terminated services	All families who had completed services within the 10 week study period were mailed questionnaires and contacted for follow-up interviews	Mailed questionnaire (55% response rate) and follow-up interviews (82% response rate)
Stallard, Hudson, & Davis, 1992	To assess client satisfaction with a child and adolescent mental health service	89 families who had terminated services	All families who had terminated services in the 5-month study period	Mailed questionnaire (57% response rate)
Stuntzner-Gibson, Koren, & DeChillo, 1995	To assess general satisfaction with children's mental health services, as well as satisfaction with specific services	165 youth from 9–18 years of age (mean age 13; 68% male, 72% white) and their parents	Youth who met inclusion criteria of psychiatric diagnosis, substantial limitations in major life areas, and involvement with 2 or more youth agencies	Interviews with parents and questionnaires for children to be returned by mail (66% return rate)

Expectations of Service Prior to Involvement

A few studies provided information about the service participants' expectations prior to their actual involvement with the program under study. Stallard, Hudson, and Davis (1992) found that, for many families, the uncertainty of what to expect of service involvement was problematic. These families indicated a desire for more preparatory information regarding what the first appointment would be like and what the role of the service provider would be. Similarly, Carr, McDonnell, and Owen (1994) found that only 22% of families knew what to expect when they attended a mental health clinic for the first time. Two other studies documented negative expectations by service participants. Garland and Besinger (1996) found that 39% of adolescents expected counselling to be "frightening or intimidating." Coady and Hayward (1998) found that a majority of their small sample of families had negative expectations of service based on prior experiences with helping professionals. These negative expectations included lack of understanding by professionals, insensitivity to cultural issues, and ineffectiveness of services.

Service Participant Satisfaction with Services

Overall findings. A majority of the studies reviewed (13 of 21) included some form of service participant satisfaction rating. Overall, the high satisfaction ratings of service recipients in these studies is quite striking. Most studies used a four- or five-point scale to measure service participant satisfaction, and in all of these studies the mean service participant ratings were well above scale midpoints. The percentage of service participants who reported they were either satisfied or very satisfied with services ranged between 65% and 90%, with an across-study mean of 80%. Studies that included the satisfaction ratings of youth (Garland & Besinger, 1996; Godley, Fiedler, & Funk, 1998; Shapiro, Welker, & Jacobson, 1997; Stuntzner-Gibson, Koren, & DeChillo, 1995) also indicated relatively high levels of satisfaction, although they were always somewhat lower than parental ratings. This finding is consistent with the consensus in the broader literature that agreement between youth and parental ratings can vary significantly, and that both have a place in comprehensive evaluation (Godley et al., 1998; Shapiro et al., 1997; Stuntzner-Gibson et al., 1995). Unfortunately, "although the recognition of consumer satisfaction as a major focus of program evaluation is nothing new, the extension of this recognition to children's satisfaction has curiously lagged behind" (Stuntzner-Gibson et al., 1995, p. 623). It should also be noted that the findings of high levels of service participant satisfaction with children's mental health services are in keeping with those in the broader literature on service participant satisfaction. Stallard et al. (1992) have noted "the almost inevitable high rate of reported satisfaction" (p. 292) produced by consumer satisfaction surveys (see end of this subsection for discussion of limitations of service participant satisfaction measures).

Association between service participant satisfaction and outcome. A number of studies investigated the association between service participant satisfaction and service participant improvement or level of distress. In their study of a rural community-health clinic that served a predominantly adult population, Carscaddon et al. (1990) found that, after three sessions and at three-month follow-up, lower levels of service participant satisfaction were associated with both higher self-reported levels of symptoms and higher levels of distress. In a study of outpatient mental health services for youth, Shapiro et al. (1997) found that higher levels of youth satisfaction were associated with a number of positive outcome indicators rated by parents and therapists. Unexpectedly, youth satisfaction was not related to self-reported behavioural change. Although Godley and colleagues' (1998) study of child/adolescent mental health services did not assess outcome per se, it determined that parents who rated their child's problem as extremely serious at various points in the treatment process were least satisfied with services, and that problem severity also predicted youth's satisfaction. The authors note that a number of other studies have also found that higher levels of service participant distress are associated with lower ratings of satisfaction with services.

The positive associations between service participant satisfaction and service participant improvement or lower level of distress found in these studies make intuitive sense. One would expect that satisfaction with services would be intertwined, to some extent, with service participant outcome. In a factor analysis of their measure of youth service participant satisfaction, Shapiro et al. (1997) found "two readily interpretable factors" (p. 92): a "relationship with therapist" factor and a "benefits of therapy" factor. These two factors each accounted for about one-third of the variance in the measure, and they were strongly related. Garland and Besinger (1996) had adolescents rank the relative importance of seven different domains of satisfaction. The three top-rated domains, in order, were "meeting needs" (the extent to which the service matched perceived needs), "the quality of the interpersonal relationship with providers," and "perceived effectiveness of the interventions" (Garland & Besinger, 1996, pp. 371–372). Clearly, the top- and third-rated domains of satisfaction in this study both relate to the benefits of therapy, whereas the second-rated domain relates to the therapeutic relationship. Thus, together, these studies not only support the idea that service participant satisfaction and outcome are intertwined but also suggest that the two main factors in service participant satisfaction are the perceived benefits of the interventions and the quality of relationship with the service provider.

Despite the evident overlap of service participant satisfaction and service participant outcome, the consensus in the literature is that these are "nonredundant parameters for evaluating the quality of children's mental health services" (Shapiro et al., 1997, p. 88), and that both are valuable. It is important to note that a number of studies reviewed suggested that service participant satisfaction may be less closely associated with behavioural than with emotional outcomes. The findings of Shapiro et al. (1997) suggested that "client satisfaction measures may place less weight on improvement in public, behavioural aspects of adjustment" (p. 96). Plante, Couchman, and Hoffman's (1998) study of service participant satisfaction and outcome in children's mental health services demonstrated that parents' satisfaction with services remained high over a period of time, even though ratings of problematic behaviours and symptoms did not improve. The authors conclude that "stable reports of symptoms, combined with high satisfaction, may indicate that important 'care' (as compared with 'cure') is occurring" (Plante et al., 1998, p. 54). Similarly, Godley and colleagues (1998) reinforce the importance of "care" irrespective of "cure" by arguing that "consumer satisfaction does not have to be directly related to treatment outcome to be an important goal of service providers" (p. 44).

Association between service participant satisfaction and other variables. The most common demographic variables investigated as potential predictors of youth and/or parental satisfaction with services are gender, age, and race/ethnicity. Consistent with the overall findings in the broader literature, there is little evidence that such demographic factors are related to ratings of satisfaction (Brannan, Sonnichsen, & Helfinger, 1996; Garland & Besinger, 1996; Godley et al., 1998). Brannan and colleagues (1996) have stated that "correlational analyses reported in the literature challenge the notion that satisfaction with services is more closely related to service participant characteristics (e.g., education, income, race, and emotional state) than to service or program characteristics" (p. 140). Non-demographic factors associated with satisfaction ratings in some studies included length of service provision (higher parental satisfaction with longer service provision; Brannan et al., 1996) and degree of service participant–rated collaboration (higher satisfaction with higher levels of service participant–service provider collaboration; DeChillo, 1993). An interesting and unexpected finding in one study (Garland & Besinger, 1996) was that adolescents' perceived choice of whether to seek services was not associated with their ratings of satisfaction.

Limitations of service participant satisfaction measures. The typically high levels of consumer satisfaction with children's mental health services, as with most social services, must be viewed cautiously due to numerous methodological issues. First, studies that rely on mailed or telephone questionnaires have a significant rate of non-response, and this likely skews the results in a positive direction (Stallard, 1995). Second, most studies do not include dropouts, which probably has the effect of under-representing dissatisfied service participants and biasing the results toward higher satisfaction ratings (Shapiro et al., 1997). Third, social desirability could also inflate satisfaction ratings. Still, the overall high levels of service participant satisfaction with children's mental health services cannot be dismissed.

Another common critique of studies of service participant satisfaction is that they are too general. Two studies (Godley et al., 1998; Stuntzner-Gibson et al., 1995) investigated satisfaction with specific services, the association between these ratings, and ratings of global levels of satisfaction with services for both parents and youths. Across these two studies, although both parents' and youths' global satisfaction were correlated significantly with their satisfaction with many specific services, there were a number of services for which there was no such correlation. In addition, agreement between parents' and youths' satisfaction with specific services varied greatly, depending on the type of service. The findings of these studies suggest the importance, not only of separate measures of satisfaction for youth and parents, but also of service-specific measures to examine satisfaction. Stuntzner-Gibson and others (1995) also argue that, ideally, service participants' satisfaction with a wide-range of variables (for example, characteristics of the service provider, duration and frequency of services, accessibility and convenience of services) should also be measured. They acknowledge, however, that an instrument that adequately measures satisfaction with such a broad range of factors would be lengthy and time-consuming to administer.

Critiques based on the positive response bias and the overly general nature of service participant satisfaction measures identify the value of supplementing such measures with open-ended questions. Many of the studies reviewed included open-ended questions and it was common that "overall general ratings on fixed-choice questions tended to mask and overshadow specific negative comments to open-ended questions" (Stallard et al., 1992, p. 295). Qualitative questions thus appear to be essential for obtaining more detailed feedback from service participants about their positive and negative perceptions of various types and aspects of services, particularly to problematic aspects of service that should be addressed through efforts to improve quality (Godley et al., 1998). More specific positive and negative feedback from service participants in the studies reviewed, which was garnered from both open-ended questions and other survey-type responses, is presented below under the headings of "service providers' way of being," "service provider interventions," and "broad aspects of services."

Service Providers' Way of Being

Positive perceptions. Many of the studies reported a high percentage of positive comments from service participants about service providers, not surprising given the generally high ratings of service participant satisfaction. In their study of parent satisfaction with a hospital-based child psychiatry service, Kotsopoulos, Elwood, and Oke (1989) found that 92% of parents perceived service providers as genuinely interested in helping. Similarly, Kirchner (1981) found that, in two separate samples, only 13–14% of adolescent and adult service participants of a community mental health centre were dissatisfied with therapists' level of interest in them. Also, the most common response to the question of what service participants liked best about the service was "staff interest and concern." Similarly, in a study of a hospital-based outpatient pediatric psychology service (Charlop, Parrish, Fenton, & Cataldo, 1987), when asked what they liked most about the service, most responded either simply "the therapist," or more specifically, "someone to talk to who understands." Carr and colleagues' (1994) study found that more than two-thirds of their sample of parents perceived their service providers in a rural, English child and family centre to be understanding, sympathetic, fair, and helpful.

Some studies yielded more in-depth feedback about positive service participant perceptions of service providers and helping relationships. Johnson, Cournoyer, and Bond (1995) conducted a mailed survey that asked parents to report their views of either the "most helpful" or "least helpful" mental health professional who had worked with them and their child. The most common descriptors for the most helpful professionals included: understands parents' burdens and cares about how they feel; is courteous; is well-informed about the child's problems; values and listens to parents' opinions; and believes parents are doing their best for their children and doesn't blame them (see below for descriptions of least helpful professionals). The latter two points are reinforced by findings from DeChillo's (1993) study of collaboration between inpatient service providers and families of service participants with mental illness. This study, which found an association between level of service provider–service participant collaboration and service participant satisfaction, noted that higher levels of collaboration were predicted by a positive service provider attitude toward family involvement (for example, valuing and listening to parents' opinions) and by service providers ascribing to a biological versus a psychogenic explanation for mental illness (that is, not blaming the family or the individual). In addition, DeChillo's study documented an association between high levels of service provider–service participant collaboration and both service providers' positive attitude toward the family's intelligence/awareness and shared goals with regard to the service participant functioning.

Coady and Hayward's (1998) small-sample, qualitative program evaluation of an in-home, family preservation–type service for adolescents and their families yielded descriptions of how the service providers in this type of service were different, in a positive way, from most of the service providers previously encountered by the parents and adolescents. Service participants were very positive about how service providers carried out their helping role in a personal, human, and friendly way. They described these service providers as being down-to-earth, casual, and like a friend. Service participants said that these service providers cared more and listened and understood better than service providers from more traditional services.

Negative perceptions. Not surprisingly, negative service participant perceptions about service providers and their relationships with them were often the direct opposite of the positive perceptions. In Johnson et al.'s (1995) study, common parent descriptors of the "least helpful" professionals included: did not listen to or value parents' opinions (thus not involving them in decision-making processes), blamed the parents for the child's problems, and did not understand or care about how the parents felt. In the Coady and Hayward (1998) study, service participants characterized previous service providers with whom they did not get along as people who talked down to them and did their job without really caring. Lishman (1978) found that service participants who were dissatisfied with child psychiatric services perceived a clash in perspective between the service provider and themselves with regard to goals, felt blamed and criticized, and did not feel supported. In Garland & Besinger's (1996) study of adolescent perceptions of outpatient mental health services, the most common negative perception was feeling overly directed by service providers (that is, "being told what to do").

Service Provider Interventions

Positive perceptions. Parents appreciated "pragmatic suggestions" (Charlop et al., 1987), "specific advice" (Johnson et al., 1995), or "practical assistance" (Coady & Hayward, 1998) about how to help their child or find other services. Service participants in the Coady and Hayward (1998) study said that what differentiated practical assistance from "being told what to do" was being consulted about their ideas and given choices. Johnson and colleagues (1995) also found that parents said the most helpful service providers gave clear information about the benefits, risks, and costs of treatment. In their study of youth satisfaction with a wide range of services, it was not surprising that Stuntzner-Gibson and colleagues (1995) concluded that youths "clearly favored leisure and less formal activities compared with educational and treatment-focussed services" (p. 621). In a study of a narrower range of traditional therapeutic services, Godley and colleagues (1998) found that youth gave the highest satisfaction rating for social skills training, and that both youths and parents were more satisfied with individual than with family counselling.

Negative perceptions. Two studies (Fiester, 1978; Johnson et al., 1995) documented that a common parent complaint was that service providers did not explain to them, or teach them, how to help their children. Relatedly, in one study where parents were given suggestions for behavioural interventions, they commented that service providers underestimated the difficulty in implementing such suggestions consistently (Charlop et al., 1987). Another problem identified was that counselling was not comprehensive enough, particularly with regard to helping parents find services to meet non-psychiatric needs (Byalin, 1993; Johnson et al., 1995). Service participants also reported problems around the process of termination. Parents sometimes complained that service providers did not prepare them adequately for termination (Kotsopoulos et al., 1989) or that they had a difference of opinion with service providers about when to terminate (Brannan et al., 1996).

Broader Aspects of Services

Positive perceptions. With regard to broader issues regarding the environment of the agency, Fairchild and Wright (1984) documented an association between service participant satisfaction and service participant perceptions of an agency's "order and organization" and "program clarity." With regard to broader service issues, service participants' comments about the best features of a mental health centre included quick appointments, service providers always being available, the convenience of the clinic location, and the fee being based on income (Kirchner, 1981). Coady and Hayward's (1998) study of an intensive, family-preservation service found that service participants were very positive about service providers coming to their homes (versus requiring them to go the agency) and being flexible in scheduling appointments at times that were convenient to them.

Negative perceptions. The high rate of global service participant satisfaction in the studies reviewed did not preclude service participants offering numerous criticisms about the services they received. With regard to the early stage of agency involvement, service participants identified problems with the waiting period for a first appointment (Eppel, Fuyarchuk, Phelps, & Tersigni-Phelan, 1991; Stallard, 1995; Stallard et al., 1992); the lack of explanation around the potential benefits, risks, and financial costs of service explained (Johnson et al., 1995); and not being adequately prepared for what the first appointment would be like and what the role of the service provider would be (Stallard et al., 1992). Service participants also had a variety of complaints about the amount of service they received. Related to the finding reported earlier that longer service provision was associated with higher service participant satisfaction (Brannan et al., 1996), some service participants felt they had not had enough appointments (Stallard, 1995; Stallard et al., 1992). Service participants also complained that appointments were not frequent enough (Eppel et al., 1991) or long enough (Kirchner, 1981).

A number of other common service participant complaints related to more structural aspects of agency services. Service participants complained about inconvenient appointment times (DeChillo, 1993; Eppel et al., 1991; Kotsopoulos et al., 1989); the inconvenient location of the agency (Eppel et al., 1991); the difficulty and expense of transportation in getting to the agency (Charlop et al., 1987); the stigma associated with the setting (for example, the psychiatric department in a hospital; Kotsopoulos et al., 1989) or with sitting in a waiting room with others (Kirchner, 1981); the difficulties in changing therapists; and the cost of counselling sessions (Kirchner, 1981).

Summary

A number of tentative conclusions can be drawn from this review of studies of youth and/or parent views of and satisfaction with their experiences with children's mental health services. There appears to be an overall high level of service participant satisfaction with these services, and the main factors influencing satisfaction seem to be the quality of the relationship with the service provider and the perceived benefits of counselling. Feedback from service participants about the valued aspects of the service provider-service participant relationship confirm the generally accepted importance of support, understanding, caring, and collaboration. Another relationship factor that seems to be particularly important to parents in children's mental health is that service providers believe parents are doing their best for their children (versus blaming them). With regard to perceived benefits of counselling, there is evidence to suggest that service participant satisfaction may have a stronger association with emotional outcomes than with behavioural outcomes and that feeling "cared for" can be important independent of "cure."

Studies also suggest that high rates of global service participant satisfaction commonly mask specific dissatisfactions best elicited through qualitative, open-ended questions. In addition to the importance of relationship factors, some of the main implications for practice that stem from negative service participant feedback include the importance of: (a) preparing service participants about what to expect in an initial contact with a service provider, including clarifying roles, purposes, and costs/benefits of counselling; (b) negotiating and coming to agreement on the goals and process of intervention; (c) focusing on practical skills to help parents and youth cope; (d) considering and addressing the broader needs of the individual and family beyond psychological treatment; (e) taking service participant needs into account when scheduling times and places of meetings; and (f) negotiating termination of services and preparing service participants adequately for this.

Voices of Parents and Children in Psychotherapy

> Even when clients are directly included in therapist texts, they are not cited or quoted. They are inserted as interview data, anecdotes, interpretive themes, or case studies. (Conran & Love, 1993, p. 3)

> Beyond the indirect drowning of client voices in the cacophony of therapists building their credibility with one another, clients are overtly silenced in therapist literature. (Conran & Love, 1993, p. 3)

Much has been written by professionals about the therapeutic process (see reviews by Jacobson & Addis, 1993; Lebow & Gurman, 1995; Newfield, Joanning, Kuehl, & Quinn, 1991; Shilts & Knapik-Esposito, 1993). However, only recently has research explored how service participants perceive their therapy experiences (Conran & Love, 1993). A majority of the service participant–based research emanates from individual psychotherapy, although increasingly researchers are exploring service participants' experiences regarding couple and family therapy (Pinsof & Catherall, 1986; Wark, 1994). This section of the chapter will explore the research related to service participant voice and therapy. Table 3 documents a brief overview of the studies reviewed in this section. The studies found for this review were from the individual, group, and family therapy literature.

Expectations of Service Prior to Involvement

A number of research studies explored the kinds of expectations people had prior to their actual service experience. Some of the families who were going to therapy to deal with the drug misuse of their adolescent children expected family therapy to be sombre, with lots of interrogation, particularly directed

Table 3: Overview of Studies of Voices in Psychotherapy

Authors	Purpose	Sample	Recruitment	Data Collection
Bachelor, 1995	To examine the therapeutic alliance form the client's point of view; to compare client and theoretician's view of alliance	34, primarily single university students	Self-referred	Qualitative open-ended self-report inquiry
Bennun, Hahlweg, Schindler, & Langlotz, 1986	To assess therapists' perceptions of clients and clients' perceptions of therapists in behaviour therapy	115 inpatients in a German hospital for neurotic and psychosomatic individuals and 16 behaviourally oriented therapists	Opportunistic	Scale developed to measure perceptions of clients and therapists
Bischoff & McBride, 1996	To determine what clients found helpful and not helpful about the treatment they were receiving and how treatment could be improved	28 clients involved in either family, couple or individual therapy	Not stated—presume convenience sample	Interviews with clients at various points in therapy regarding helpful and unhelpful aspects
Bowman & Fine, 2000	To examine client perceptions of what is helpful and unhelpful in couple therapy	5 Caucasian couples in couple therapy at a university-based training clinic	Opportunistic; volunteers requested by letter given by therapist to clients	Qualitative, discovery oriented; semi-structured, in-depth interviews
Cohen, 1998	To explore worker and client perceptions of power in the client/worker relationship	24 homeless psychiatric survivor clients & 22 providers	Self-selected from non-profit agency servicing the homeless	Qualitative, open-ended and participatory structured
Elliott & Shapiro, 1992	To demonstrate how client and therapist can be enlisted as collaborators in the analysis of their own significant therapy events	1 client and 1 therapist	Not stated; client was of one of the authors	Completed the Helpful Aspects of Therapy Questionnaire at the end of each of his sessions. Researcher played video for client where most

Study	Purpose	Sample	Selection	Method
Johnson, Cournoyer, & Bond, 1995	To examine how parents view therapeutic relationship in terms of compliance with ethical standards	198 mainly white female parents of children with a range of psychological, behavioural, emotional, and cognitive impairments	Parents selected by modified randomization from mailing lists of regional branches of 3 parent support groups	helpful event was located, and described and then played for therapist alone who commented on event; Completed Helping Behavior Check List
Kuehl, Newfield, & Joanning, 1990	To initiate the construction of a client-based description of family therapy	12 families (37 individual members) predominantly white middle-class families with adolescent drug users	Opportunistic; ask clients in service to volunteer to participate	Ethnographic interviews
Lietaer, 1992	To determine which therapy processes clients and therapists experience as being either helpful or hindering	41 clients and 25 therapists in the Flemish Society for Client-Centered Therapy	Therapists identified clients for researchers to contact—convenience	Questionnaire comprising both rating scales and open-ended questions; given after every other session for a maximum of ten sessions
Llewelyn, Elliott, Shapiro, Hardy, & Firth-Cozens, 1988	To compare clients' experiences regarding the impact of helpful and hindering events	40 clients referred to psychologists for depression; clients were professional or managerial workers with score of 8 or higher on General Health Questionnaire	Not stated—assume convenience	Used the Helpful Aspects of Therapy Questionnaire after each session and at end of two forms of treatment
Maluccio, 1979	To explore and compare client and worker views regarding three phases of interpersonal	Mostly white middle-class women clients seeking help with personal or interpersonal	Randomly selected clients and their social workers	Qualitative analysis; in-depth, interviews

Table 3: (*continued*)

Authors	Purpose	Sample	Recruitment	Data Collection
Maluccio, 1979 (continued)	helping (getting engaged, staying engaged & becoming disengaged) as well as outcome	issues, and social workers at a family-service bureau		
McConnell & Sim, 2000	To evaluate the Children's and Young People's counselling services regarding mothers and children's satisfaction with counselling	24 children of divorce in therapy	Opportunistic; from counselling service	Semi-structured, in-depth interviews with mothers and children at beginning, end of therapy and post-termination
Newfield, Joanning, Kuehl, & Quinn, 1991	To uncover clients' views of, and provide feedback to, therapists about their family therapy experiences	12 families (12 mothers, 8 fathers, 17 adolescents)	Opportunistic sample	Ethnographic interviews—from general questions to specific categories
Rennie, 1994	Examine clients' perspectives of individual counselling	14 university student clients (6 men, 8 women) in university-based counselling centre	Opportunistic; clients asked to participate	Grounded theory; recollections of therapy experience stimulated by tape replay
Roberts, 1993	To explore what the experience of a mandated-therapy client was like	1 client interviewed by her therapist	Opportunistic	Qualitative interview, no coding
Sells, Smith, Coe, Yoshioka, & Robbins, 1994	To analyze couple and therapist perspectives regarding the use and process of reflecting team practice	7 couples and 5 therapists were interviewed twice over a 4-month period of therapy	Opportunistic sampling strategy	Ethnographic design; qualitative interviews after first reflecting team session and several weeks later

Author & date	Aim	Participants	Sampling	Method
Shilts & Knapik-Esposito, 1993	To hear about the utility of family therapy through the voices of the client system	A mother, daughter and their therapist were interviewed about their experience of family therapy	Opportunistic	Qualitative, in-depth interview of one family system
Smith, Yoshioka, & Winton, 1993	To determine client perspectives on reflecting teams	11 clients interviewed in university-based family therapy centre	Opportunistic sampling	Ethnographic design using three interviews; open-ended interviews & iterative process
Stith, Rosen, McCollum, Coleman, & Herman, 1996	To hear from children who were participating in family therapy re: their experiences so that therapists could enhance their effectiveness with children and families	12, families (16 children), mainly single-parent white mothers	Convenience sample of those having at least 4 sessions of family therapy	Grounded theory; 2 interviews per child and one per parent; interviews semi-structured
Telfair & Gardner, 2000	To examine reasons why adolescents attend Sickle Cell Disease support groups and to determine the level and type of help received and satisfaction with the groups	12 Sickle Cell Disease support groups (79 members) completed questionnaires	Mailed questionnaire to group participants	Questionnaires looking at attendance, satisfaction with group, reason for attending or not, and group help
van Ryn & Fine, 1997	To explore client perceptions of the process of collaborative meaning-making in couples therapy	2 couples in university-based couple and family therapy centre	Couples selected from letters given to clients by therapists	Case study approach—in-depth interviews, open-ended style; couple members interviewed first individually and then together
Wark, 1994	To examine the perspectives of client couples and their therapists on therapeutic change	5 couples and 5 therapists in a university-based family therapy training centre	Not stated—convenience presumed	Qualitative, in-depth interviews after therapy sessions

at the adolescents' drug use. These parents expected quick answers to their problems, because they were working with "experts" in the area of drug misuse (Newfield et al., 1991). "A good counselor can sit and listen and then ask you just the right things that makes the lightbulb go off" (quoted in Newfield et al., 1991, p. 287).

In another study, Stith, Rosen, McCollum, Coleman, and Herman (1996) noted that children often did not understand why they were coming to therapy. In addition, Mayer and Timms (1970) and Kuehl, Newfield, and Joanning (1990) remarked that many service participants simply did not know what to expect. Maluccio (1979) reported that a number of service participants expected treatment to solve their problems quickly. In addition, they thought that service providers would help them more actively by expressing opinions, giving advice, and offering suggestions. Mayer and Timms (1970) also found that some service participants thought that service providers would listen to their stories and reach a decision about who was right or wrong. They reasoned that after the service provider had made this decision, she or he would offer them advice regarding what to do about the problem. Finally, a service participant in the Shilts and Knapik-Esposito (1993) study expected to be preached to.

Service Provider's Way of Being

Positive perceptions. The importance of service provider caring was noted by service participants in a number of studies (Bowman & Fine, 2000; Kuehl et al., 1990; Newfield et al., 1991): "I felt that she was legitimately concerned about the two of us and our relationship. It wasn't just a job to her" (quoted in Bowman & Fine, 2000, p. 299). Newfield and others (1991) reported that service participants were more open and trusting when they thought they had established a caring relationship with the service provider. A non-judgmental attitude was another significant service provider trait commonly cited by service participants (Bachelor, 1995; Bowman & Fine, 2000; van Ryn & Fine, 1997). Newfield and colleagues (1991) found similarly that service participants liked service providers who were impartial.

The service participants in Lietaer's (1992) study liked service providers who were authentic and personal. Many studies found that service participants felt positively about service providers who seemed genuinely understanding, empathetic, interested, and concerned about them (Bachelor, 1995; Bennun, Hahlweg, Schindler, & Langlotz, 1986; Bischoff & McBride, 1996; Lietaer, 1992; Maluccio, 1979; Newfield et al., 1991; van Ryn & Fine, 1997): "the reason why I'm more open to him is not because of trust, it's more of understanding. He understands me" (quoted in van Ryn & Fine, 1997, p. 25).

Other important service provider characteristics noted by service participants included being a real person (Llewelyn, Eliot, Shapiro, Hardy, & Firth-Cozens, 1988); fun, easy-going, friendly, open, patient, enthusiastic, and interactive with children (Stith et al., 1996; Wark, 1994); streetwise (Newfield et al., 1991); friendly (Bachelor, 1995; Bennun et al., 1986); and open and flexible (van Ryn & Fine, 1997).

Newfield and colleagues (1991) also found that service participants tended to like service providers who had had similar experiences in life. This last characteristic is similar to what Maluccio (1979) found, in that service participants appreciated service providers who were close in age, as well as in family status and gender.

Negative characteristics. In three studies (Lietaer, 1992; McConnell & Sim, 2000; Stith et al., 1996), service participants said that they did not like service providers who were patronizing, condescending, or disapproving. Stith and colleagues (1996) found that service participants did not appreciate service providers who seemed distant. Similarly, Lietaer (1992) noted that service participants did not like service providers who lacked warmth, involvement, and understanding, and Mayer & Timms' (1970) found that service participants did not like service providers who appeared uninterested in what the service participant had to say. Kuehl and colleagues (1990) noted that when a family thought that the service provider was just doing his job, the family felt less likely to participate in the process. Newfield and colleagues (1991) noted that service participants did not like service providers who were provocative, hurtful, or who did not seem to care: "He would just ask questions like he really didn't care ... just ask you questions and make it hurt" (quoted in Newfield et al., 1991, p. 293).

Service Provider Interventions

Positive perceptions. A number of studies found that service participants liked service providers who offered them suggestions with the underlying implication that these suggestions would not be imposed (Johnson et al., 1995; Kuehl et al., 1990; Mayer & Timms, 1970; Newfield et al., 1991; van Ryn & Fine, 1997). Bachelor (1995) and Bowman and Fine (2000) found that service participants appreciated service providers who had good listening skills. Bachelor (1995) also noted that service participants thought positively about service providers who were able to facilitate their understanding of their issues. Lietaer's (1992) participants, while mentioning the importance of understanding, also included the facilitation of self-exploration and self-acceptance. Service participants in two studies pointed out that respectful behaviour from the service provider was an important characteristic (Bachelor, 1995; Maluccio, 1979). Wark (1994) noted that couples valued service providers who were able to give both partners equal time. Maluccio (1979) and Bennun and colleagues (1986) found that service participants appreci-ated service providers who seemed competent in the practice of their pro-fession. Llyewlyn and colleagues (1988) noted that service participants liked service providers who reassured them—made them feel supported and hope-ful. A service participant in the Shilts and Knapik-Esposito (1993) study said that it was beneficial when the service provider helped her appreciate the little things that would happen in therapy—the small changes that she was making. Likewise, Wark (1994) and Lietaer's (1992) participants liked service providers to validate the changes they were making in therapy. Wark (1994) found that service participants liked hearing the opinions and per-spectives of their service providers. Bennun and colleagues (1986) noted that service participants valued service providers who were organized, deci-sive, and clear.

Bowman and Fine's (2000) participants thought that rules around ver-bal abuse were important to general safety in the therapy room. They also found that service participants liked sessions to end on a positive note and appreciated being able to talk about what was important to them, rather than what was important to the service provider. McConnell and Sim (2000) noted that knowing the relationship was considered confidential helped child service participants feel safe with their service provider. Wark (1994) and Lietaer (1992) noted that service participants appreciated service providers who were able to provide them with new viewpoints. Sells, Smith, Coe, Yoshioka, and Robbins (1994) found a reflecting team (supporting ther-apists who observe therapy sessions and provide observations to the family and their therapists) to be useful, in that the team acts as a buffer when anger or fear is being played out in the couple session. Couples also appre-ciated being able to sit back and listen to the team. They found that this took the pressure off and allowed them to dissect information: "You can tell if she's not saying it [anger] because of the possible consequences from the husband. She might regret saying it later, but it has to be said. The team can maybe notice that and say that for her" (quoted in Sells et al., 1994, p. 258).

Negative perceptions. Service participants in the Kuehl and colleagues (1990) and Lietaer (1992) studies stated that they did not like service providers who were on "too strict a program" and could not take into account preferences of service participants. Service participants in Lietaer's (1992) study disliked intrusive service providers. Bowman and Fine (2000) noted that service participants had problems with service providers who competed with them for talk time: "I almost find like I'm in competition with her ... We want to get out what we all feel is important. We both talk over each other sometimes" (p. 304).

Rennie (1994) and Lietaer (1992) noted that some service participants thought that service providers controlled the conversations, were critical, and talked about things that were not relevant or accurate. Newfield and colleagues (1991) found that parents tended to want service providers to be more direct—to question their adolescents and give them advice. Some service participants did not feel satisfied, because they found the service providers' questions to be redundant, irrelevant, and improper (Mayer & Timms, 1970). In addition, service participants wanted more action and advice, but were hesitant to challenge the "expert." These service participants tended to drop out of counselling (Mayer & Timms, 1970).

Mayer and Timms (1970) found that service participants were uncomfortable with service providers who were inactive and indecisive, or who misinterpreted what service participants were saying. Bischoff and McBride (1996) and Lietaer (1992) gleaned that service participants were frustrated if their service provider did not seem in control of the direction of therapy, or if the service provider was too passive or non-confrontational (Lietaer, 1992). Wark (1994) found that service participants were upset when the service provider did not find an immediate solution, did not give them what they wanted out of therapy, or did not understand them.

McConnell and Sim (2000) reported that some mothers in their study felt that the service provider did not communicate enough with them about the job the service providers were doing with their children, which had a negative effect on their relationship with the service providers. Cohen (1998) noted that when a service provider acted in an authoritarian way it typically upset service participants and weakened relationship bonds: "We were always on the same level. That's the kind of relationship that helps me. The worker I had before had to be in charge; she always had to be right about everything. She did me a lot of harm" (quoted on p. 438). Service participants reported withdrawing from the relationship and services when they experienced unresolvable differences with their service providers (Maluccio, 1979). Lietaer's (1992) study found that service participants did not appreciate service providers who interpreted too quickly, or were discouraged by, the lack of service participant progress.

Some couples in the Sells and colleagues (1994) study thought that introducing the reflecting team too early in therapy was intimidating. With respect to reflecting team interventions, they also noted that some service participants believed that some team members behind the mirror were critical and judgmental, and that the team was not effective in the beginning of therapy.

Finally, McConnell and Sim (2000) found that some children felt their confidentiality had been compromised by the service provider, and this made them feel less trustful of the therapist. In this vein, some service participants were concerned about service providers who were not up to "ethical standards," such as not explaining the specifics of what was needed to help their child (Johnson et al., 1995).

Satisfaction with Service

Only a few studies sought to determine how satisfied service participants were with their therapy service. In general, service participants reported satisfaction with services. McConnell and Sim (2000) revealed that 46% of children and 50% of mothers felt that the counselling service had helped. Telfair and Gardner (2000) state that 67% of group members in the Sickle Cell Disease groups reported satisfaction with the group.

A few additional studies did not quantify service participant satisfaction results, but stated them qualitatively. Llewelyn and colleagues (1988) found that problem solving had a positive impact for service participants receiving prescriptive therapy. Studies by van Ryn and Fine (1997), Bowman and Fine (2000), and Lietaer (1992) found that service participants thought they gained self-knowledge and had additional options and possibilities to deal with their problems: "There's always a different option so he's [the therapist] made me more aware that there are other options" (quoted in van Ryn & Fine, 1997, p. 27).

Bowman and Fine (2000) noted that the therapeutic sessions helped service participants come to new understandings about the relationships they were in. Llewelyn and colleagues (1988) and Wark (1994) found that increases in service participant awareness (for example, of behaviour and past emotions) was a positive aspect of therapy. The service participant in the Shilts and Knapik-Esposito (1993) study came to the realization that she was the only one that could change her behaviour—that she had to help herself. Wark (1994) noted that service participants found gaining insight into solutions for their problems helpful. Similarly, Elliott and Shapiro (1992) and Lietaer (1992) found that service participant insight was very important in the delivery of therapeutic services. Finally, Stith and colleagues (1996) discovered that children thought that family therapy made positive changes in their families and in their ability to solve problems.

Some comments were associated specifically with reflecting team interventions. Sells and colleagues (1994) noted benefits to the reflecting team process: providing more insight into problems, allowing people alternatives so that they could think differently about their issues, and acting as a buffer when the tension in sessions gets high. Smith, Yoshioka, and Winton (1993) found that the single most important aspect of reflecting teams mentioned by service participants in their study was the opportunity to have multiple perspectives on their issues. They particularly appreciated looking at the dialectic between the different perspectives, because this helped them clarify which was the best fit for them: "It was good for me. It helped to give me some insight into different ideas and things I may not have thought of. To actually see what's happening ... that was so important to me" (p. 280).

Dissatisfaction with Service

Service participants in most studies suggested that they were dissatisfied with some aspects of therapy service. Bowman and Fine (2000) noted that some service participants in couple therapy did not feel that there was a strong enough link between sessions and real life. In addition, some felt unacknowledged, because the service providers seemed more preoccupied with their partners:

> I remember at times feeling like, "hmm, you know, what I think and feel doesn't count here." ... I think it felt like that because there was a lot of discussion happening between [the therapist] and Peter and there were times when I probably said maybe two or three sentences the whole session. (quoted in Bowman & Fine, 2000, p. 303)

Regarding family therapy, Kuehl and colleagues (1990) found that families would have liked individual as well as family sessions.

Maluccio (1979) observed that service participants who left therapy prematurely did so for reasons such as not having made an emotional connection with the service provider or having left the first session with only a vague and uncertain idea about future therapy plans. Maluccio (1979) found that service participants wanted more flexibility in relation to the timing and location of interviews and access to more diverse treatment modalities. Finally, some service participants were dissatisfied with service, because they found the agency environment to be negative (Maluccio, 1979).

Adolescents in the groups studied by Telfair and Gardner (2000) noted that they would have preferred focusing on learning skills and strategies for dealing with life experiences. Newfield and colleagues (1991) found that some adolescents thought counselling was unnecessary, embarrassing, and an invasion of privacy. In the Stith and colleagues (1996) study, some children stated that they did not like one-way mirrors and videotape recorders. In addition, they did not like sitting in the waiting room for parts of a family session.

Bassett, Lampe, and Lloyd (1999) observed that parents wished that services were accessible and available at all times and that reaching an answering machine instead of a human being in a time of stress was very upsetting. These parents also wanted to be linked to other community resources and to have services not only in times of crisis but when they were feeling well. In addition, they wanted more sympathy from mental health service providers and more community education toward understanding mental illness.

Research Methodology

The majority of studies in this section used some form of qualitative data collection and coding methodology. This is not surprising given that therapy is viewed as a complex systemic process requiring research methodologies that can tap this complexity (Moon, Dillon, & Sprenkle, 1990). Qualitative research methodologies typically have the capacity to capture complexity, unlike many quantitative measures (Steier, 1985). On the other hand, qualitative research findings typically cannot be generalized, due to small sample sizes and convenience sampling strategies that are not representative of a population.

Particular concerns with the qualitative research done in a number of these studies need to be mentioned. Researchers note that service participants can be hesitant to talk about the more negative aspects of their service providers (Bowman & Fine, 2000; Hill, Thompson, Cogar, & Denman, 1993; Rennie 1992). For this reason, it is helpful if information given by service participants is done at arms length from their therapist. Nonetheless, some studies in this review did use service providers as researchers (Bischoff & McBride, 1996; Roberts, 1993; Shilts & Knapik-Esposito, 1993).

Given the imbalance of power and the preference for service participants to avoid saying negative things to and about their service providers, it is likely that information collected will be skewed in a positive direction. Bischoff and McBride (1996) also note that some of the service providers doing the interviewing were novices at research interviewing and were attempting to make the interviews both therapeutic and research oriented. This double purpose might confound the openness and inquisitiveness of the interview (Bischoff & McBride, 1996). In addition, this can complicate the exploration of many issues that need to be explored and addressed concretely, such as boundaries, limitations, power, and so on (Daly, 1994). A final point that can be made about qualitative research in therapy practice is that, if research interviews are conducted during the process of therapy, there can be an interactive effect between the research and the therapy (Wark, 1994). Wark's (1994) research participants stated that the research interviews made a difference in the quality and outcome of their therapy; they increased its effectiveness. This interactive effect is intriguing and needs to be factored into studies investigating ongoing therapy process.

Summary

It is worth noting that the service providers' way of being appears to have important effects on the experiences of service participants. One of the main overall findings relates to the importance of core therapeutic conditions and issues of respect and validation. Indeed, the cumulative results of psychotherapy research suggest a positive therapeutic alliance is the best predictor of successful outcome (Horvath & Symonds, 1991; Lambert & Bergin, 1994; Orlinsky, Grawe, & Parks, 1994).

Although positive ways of being are essential to the therapeutic alliance, interventions also provide a crucial element for change. Service participants felt positively about service providers who were good listeners and who could facilitate the understanding of their issues. They liked being encouraged about the change they were making and appreciated service providers who were organized and clear and who supported and reassured them.

Service participants also described aspects of service provider interventions that they did not like. For example, service participants did not appreciate service providers who were indecisive, too controlling or authoritarian, or who became discouraged by lack of service participant progress. They also did not favour service providers who were too passive or competed with them for talk time.

The Choir

In this section we bring all the voices of service participants together. Given the sizeable variety of terms participants used to describe their experiences, we resolved to collapse ideas under themes that represent, as closely as possible, the main thoughts of the participants. In order to do this, several iterations of the findings from all three service sectors were needed to reduce and group them into categories and themes. We hope this effort does justice to the meanings of the participants, making the cacophony of voices interpretable by the reader. Below, we organize the ideas from all sectors into five categories of findings with two themes in each.

Category 1—Relationship-Enhancing Aspects of the Service Provider

The themes in this category describe characteristics of the service provider that were important to service participants and that enhanced their experience and willingness to work with the provider.

Theme: Caring ways of being. Many of the ideas expressed about the characteristics of service providers were similar to each other. Under this theme we place the following characteristics: courteousness, friendliness, warmth, compassion, understanding, showing interest, listening well, dedication, kindness, empathy, sympathy, being dependable, and showing concern.

Theme: Service provider as human. Service provider characteristics identified by participants suggested the importance of them feeling that the service provider was a "real" and humane person who was similar to them in some way. Participants described "good" service providers as authentic and personal, easy going, patient, enthusiastic, open, flexible, fun, interactive with children, and low-key and streetwise with youth. In addition, service participants commented on the importance of self-disclosure by the service provider and of having some similarity in values and experiences (for example, age, family status, gender).

Category 2—Helpful and Change-Enhancing Actions of the Service Provider

Themes under this category address aspects of service provider interventions or actions that were seen as positive and helpful by service participants.

Theme: Helpful actions. Participants found the following actions by service providers helpful in the process of service provision: facilitating self-exploration, validating changes, providing new viewpoints, offering opinions and perspectives, teaching, giving pragmatic suggestions and specific advice, offering social-skills training for youth, and advocating for the service participant.

Theme: Validating actions. This theme represents service providers' actions that helped the participants feel validated and respected as human beings. Ideas that fit in this theme were are as follows: fairness, sharing power, being an ally, not imposing provider views, including participants in the planning of their service, accepting service participants for who they are, involving service participants in decision-making (being collaborative), sharing knowledge, talking at their level, being supportive, showing loyalty, being responsive, and facilitating self-acceptance and self-exploration. In addition, providers were appreciated for helping participants to see the small changes that they were making, and believing that the parents were doing the best they could for their children.

Category 3—Unhelpful and Change-Discouraging Aspects of the Service Provider

Themes under this category address aspects of service provider interventions, actions, and ways of being that were seen as negative and unhelpful to service participants. These actions had the effect of discouraging change for the service participants.

Theme: Unhelpful or negative actions. Participants identified a number of service provider behaviours as unhelpful and having negative effects on them. These actions were: talking about irrelevant things, being too quick to interpret service participant behaviour, competing with service participants for talk time, misinterpreting what the service participant is saying, not being in control of direction of service, and lacking clarity and preparation. Other actions were: asking redundant and irrelevant questions, giving orders, not being able to find timely solutions to problems, underestimating difficulty in participants implementing suggestions consistently, lacking preparation for and agreement about termination, not linking sessions with real life, and indicating discouragement with lack of service participant progress.

Theme: Unhelpful or negative ways of being. Participants viewed some service providers as conducting themselves in ways that felt unhelpful, negative, or invalidating of them as people. These experiences occurred when service providers were seen as being distant, provocative, inactive, critical, judgmental, uncaring, patronizing, condescending, controlling and overtly directing, disapproving, unsupportive, authoritarian, and rigid in their approach to service. Other unhelpful ways of being involved showing no interest in participants' opinions, showing a superior attitude, not including participants in decision-making, and conveying an attitude that the service provider was "just doing the job."

Category 4—Professionalism

There were findings across areas that spoke to what we term professionalism. These are personal characteristics or actions that indicate competence or incompetence with regard to the behaviour expectations of professional associations.

Theme: Professional competence. Certain issues identified by service participants spoke to the competence of the service provider. Participants described competence with words such as well-informed, helpful, knowledgable, organized, decisive, clear, open to the limits of his/her power, and ethical regarding issues of confidentiality.

Theme: Professional incompetence. Some participants noted service provider characteristics and actions that were clearly unprofessional. Terms used about the service provider included hurtful, uninformed about resources and service provider's roles, and not being up-to-date on ethical standards.

Category 5—Organization Features

These themes relate specifically to issues experienced by service participants regarding the larger agency or organization from which they sought help.

Theme: Organization-friendly features. Some participants talked about characteristics of organizations that made them seem more friendly and welcoming. Participants noted such features as quick appointments, easy availability of service providers, easy accessibility to the clinic, program clarity, a well-developed organization, and income-based fees.

Theme: Organization-unfriendly features. Participants identified a number of features that made certain organizations unwelcoming. These features were: a generally negative environment, long waits for first appointments, inconvenient appointment times, too few and too infrequent sessions or services, difficulty with transportation to the agency, stigma associated with being involved with the organization, the high cost of counselling sessions, difficulty in switching service providers, and being exposed by sharing a waiting room.

The Echo

This chapter has explored the voices of service participants in three service sectors: child welfare, children's mental health, and psychotherapy. The emphasis has been on service participant voices, even when studies included the perceptions of service providers. This was done to highlight and privilege the ideas and opinions of the participants in these services—voices that have not typically been heard and sometimes not even welcomed.

The findings in this review blend together across service sectors. There is strong support over all three sectors for the importance of a good relationship between service provider and service participant. Aspects of the relationship are identified in the themes *caring ways of being* and *the service provider as human*. There is also support for the significance of particular service provider interventions. These are demonstrated by the themes *helpful actions* and *validating actions*. Service participants are also aware of what they think should constitute professionalism, and these ideas are expressed in the themes *professional competence* and *professional incompetence*.

Service participants were able to identify attitudes and behaviours that can damage the therapeutic alliance. These were pointed out in the themes *unhelpful ways of being* and *invalidating actions*. These themes, in addition to the theme of *professional incompetence*, should be examined in more detail by researchers and service providers, because they ultimately lead to the demise of relationship and, as such, they are the antithesis of the service provider's charge and concern.

Service participants identified themes that were pertinent specifically to service organizations. The themes, *organization-friendly features* and *organization-unfriendly features*, identify important factors for organizations to weigh. Although some aspects, such as stigma and intrusiveness, may be difficult to alter, especially in child welfare, other factors can be changed. Potentially important strategy adjustments include making services more accessible to service participants (for example, developing local satellite services) and providing some supportive services to service participants who are on long waiting lists. In addition, more consideration could be given to the issue of privacy in the waiting room—which is certainly ethically relevant. These issues seem to be significant to service participants, and we recommend that researchers and agencies explore organizational features that lead to more or less comfort for consumers.

Methodological Issues

There are a number of issues to consider with regard to developing research methodology when investigating service participants' views of social services. Service participants, particularly in child welfare situations, may be reluctant to give frank responses, or their responses may be of the "socially desirable" type, if they suspect that the information could be used against them, or if the information is critical of their service providers—the professionals upon whom they have been so dependent. In the same view, service participants who are fearful of possible repercussions may choose not to participate in research, and, therefore, the sample of persons who do participate may be biased in a positive direction. For these reasons, the issue of confidentiality is highly important. We recommend that researchers have minimal or no association with the agencies or service providers under study and that they identify clearly how the information will be used, how it will be reported, who will have access to it, and how the information will be protected.

Children are particularly vulnerable to issues of power imbalance, thus their responses may be of a socially desirable nature in order to please the adult researchers. We have made a few suggestions in this paper to deal with social desirability in children (that is, use subscales that measure social desirability and defensiveness, and only include children who have the ability to refuse to answer a test question). We emphasize, however, that perhaps the most important aspects of interviewing children or giving them questionnaires, is to be sensitive and respond appropriately to their potential concerns, fears, the contexts of the interviewing, and to their developmental/language and comprehension levels (Aldridge & Wood, 1998; Bourg, Broderick, Flagor, Kelly, Ervin, & Butler, 1999; Breakwell, 1990).

Issues relating to studies of service participant satisfaction have been raised in this chapter. We suggest, in light of the literature on the differences between youth and parent responses, that separate measures of satisfaction need to be developed for each. In addition, satisfaction measures should be service-specific and cover as wide a range of variables as is feasible. Finally, satisfaction measures are enhanced when they are combined with open-ended questions that put flesh on the bones of quantitative-type data.

Another issue raised relates to the fact that qualitative research conducted during the therapeutic process has been shown to have an influence on the actual therapeutic relationship being investigated, which confounds the study of the relationship. This interpenetration, which is reported as enhancing the therapeutic relationship, needs to be investigated further. Researchers also need to determine the impact on the findings of using the therapists of participants to collect information. Given service participants' tendency not to want to be critical of their service providers, and their belief that service providers know what they are doing, their responses are bound to be incomplete.

Summary

The voices of service participants in the diverse service sectors of child welfare, children's mental health, and psychotherapy clearly and loudly endorse the importance of service providers being respectful, understanding, caring, and supportive. As other chapters in this volume point out, however, there is not always a clear correspondence between service participants' wants and needs and service responses. Although the critical importance of a good helping relationship and humane ways of being are long-standing service provider principles, it is clear that the service responses in each of the service sectors reviewed sometimes fall short of such ideals. It is possible that these principles seem so basic that service providers overlook them in favour of loftier therapeutic interventions or because of the increasing demands on their time. More research should be focused on the factors that facilitate or impede the development of a good helping alliance, particularly in an area such as child welfare, where a working relationship can be complex to build and maintain given the circumstances and social control role of the service provider. Investigation should also be conducted at the organizational level, because factors such as lack of privacy, inconvenient location, long waiting periods, and inadequate explanations of the service can contribute or detract considerably from the helping relationship and overall sense of trust of the service.

Service participants' ideas need to be sought and factored strongly into the service delivery equation on all levels. A clear need remains to continue the recent trend of inviting service participant voice in child welfare, children's mental health, and in psychotherapy. This chapter, as stated at the outset, is an attempt to hear the voices of service participants. Let us listen, learn, and join with service participants in the pursuit of respectful and effective service provision.

Notes

1 We use the phrase, "service participant" throughout to stand for such terms as client, patient, consumer, customer, and so forth.
2 It should be acknowledged that there have always been exceptions to the dominant discourse within the helping professions—those that have attempted to promote a more humble and collaborative approach to helping (e.g., Carl Rogers' client-centered therapy and other humanistic models of counselling).
3 For the sake of clarity we use the term "service provider" throughout to mean any type of helping professional (therapist, psychologist, social worker, etc.).

References

Aldridge, M., & Wood, J. (1998). *Interviewing children: A guide to child care and forensic practitioners*. New York: John Wiley and Sons.

Anderson, H., & Goolishian, H. A. (1992). The client is the expert: A not knowing approach to therapy. In S. McNamee & K. J. Gergen (Eds.), *Therapy as social construction*. Newbury Park, CA: Sage.

Anderson, K. (1998). A Canadian child welfare agency for urban Natives: The clients speak. *Child Welfare 77*(4), 441–460.

Anderson, W. T. (1995). Introduction: What's going on here? In W. T. Anderson (Ed.), *The truth about the truth: De-confusing and re-constructing the postmodern world* (pp. 1–11). New York: G. P. Putnam & Sons.

Anglin, J. (2003). *Staffed group homes for youth: Towards a framework for understanding*. In K. Kufeldt & B. McKenzie (Eds.), *Child welfare: Connecting research, policy, and practice*. Waterloo, ON: Wilfrid Laurier University Press.

Atkinson, B. J., & Heath, A. W. (1990). Further thoughts on second-order family therapy—This time it's personal. *Family Process, 29*(2), 145–155.

Bachelor, A. (1995). Clients' perception of the therapeutic alliance: A qualitative analysis. *Journal of Counseling Psychology, 42*(3), 323–337.

Baistow, K., Hetherington, R., Spriggs, A., & Yelloly, M. (1996). *Parents speaking: Anglo-French perceptions of child welfare interventions: A preliminary report*. Unpublished report. London, UK: Brunel University, Centre for Comparative Social Work Studies.

Barth, R. P. (1990). On their own: The experience of youth after foster care. *Child and Adolescent Social Work, 7*(5), 419–440.

Bassett, H., Lampe, J., & Lloyd, C. (1999). Parenting: Experiences and feelings of parents with a mental illness. *Journal of Mental Health UK, 8*(6), 597–604.

Bennun, I., Hahlweg, K., Schindler, L., & Langlotz, M. (1986). Therapist's and client's perceptions in behaviour therapy: The development and cross-cultural analysis of an assessment instrument. *British Journal of Medical Psychology, 59*, 275–283.

Bischoff, R. J., & McBride, A. (1996). Client perceptions of couples and family therapy. *American Journal of Family Therapy, 24*, 117–128.

Bourg, W., Broderick, R., Flagor, R., Kelly, D. M., Ervin, D. L., & Butler, J. (1999). *A child interviewer's guidebook.* Thousand Oaks, CA: Sage.

Bowman, L., & Fine, M. (2000). Client perceptions of couples' therapy: Helpful and unhelpful aspects. *American Journal of Family Therapy, 28*(4), 295–310.

Brannan, A. M., Sonnichsen, S. E., & Helfinger, C. A. (1996). Measuring satisfaction with children's mental health services: Validity and reliability of the satisfaction scales. *Evaluation and Program Planning, 19*(2), 131–141.

Breakwell, G. M. (1990). *Interviewing.* New York: Routledge, Chapman and Hall.

Byalin, K. (1993). Assessing parental satisfaction with children's mental health services: A pilot study. *Evaluation and Program Planning, 16*(2), 69–72.

Callahan, M., Dominelli, L., Rutman, D., & Strega, S. (2003). Undeserving mothers: Perspectives of young mothers in/from government care. In K. Kufeldt & B. McKenzie (Eds.), *Child welfare: Connecting research, policy, and practice.* Waterloo, ON: Wilfrid Laurier University Press.

Callahan, M., & Lumb, C. (1995). My cheque and my children: The long road to empowerment in child welfare. *Child Welfare 74*(3), 795–819.

Carr, A., McDonnell, D., & Owen, P. (1994). Audit and family systems consultation: Evaluation of practice at a child and family centre. *Journal of Family Therapy, 16*(2), 143–157.

Carscaddon, D. M., George, M., & Wells, G. (1990). Rural community mental health consumer satisfaction and psychiatric symptoms. *Community Mental Health Journal, 26*(4), 309–318.

Chalmers, M. L. (1996). Voices of wisdom: Minnesota youth talk about their experiences in out-of-home care. *Community Alternatives: International Journal of Family Care, 8*(1), 95–121.

Charlop, M. H., Parrish, J. M., Fenton, L. R., & Cataldo, M. F. (1987). Evaluation of hospital-based outpatient pediatric psychology services. *Journal of Pediatric Psychology, 12*(4), 485–503.

Coady, N., & Hayward, K. (1998). *A study of the Reconnecting Youth Project: Documenting a collaborative inter-agency process of program development and client views of the process and outcome of service.* Waterloo, ON: Wilfrid Laurier University, Faculty of Social Work.

Cohen, M. B. (1998). Perceptions of power in client/worker relationships. *Families in Society: The Journal of Contemporary Human Services, 79*(4), 433–442.

Conran, T., & Love, J. (1993). Unknowable experiences. *Journal of Systemic Therapies, 12*(2), 1–19.

Daly, K. J. (1994). Using qualitative methods to study families. In G. Handel & G. G. Whitchurch (Eds.), *The psychosocial interior of the family* (pp. 53–68). New York: Aldine de Gruyter.

DeChillo, N. (1993). Collaboration between social workers and families of patients with mental illness. *Families in Society, 74*(2), 104–115.

Drake, B. (1994). Relationship competencies in child welfare services. *Social Work, 39*(5), 595–602.

Elliott, R., & Shapiro, D. A. (1992). Client and therapist as analysts of significant events. In S. G. Toukmanian & D. L. Rennie (Eds.), *Psychotherapy process research: Paradigmatic and narrative approaches* (pp. 163–186). London: Sage Publications.

Eppel, A. B., Fuyarchuk, C., Phelps, D., & Tersigni-Phelan, A. (1991). A comprehensive and practical quality assurance program for community mental health services. *Canadian Journal of Psychiatry, 36*(2), 102–106.

Fairchild, H. H., & Wright, C. (1984). A social-ecological assessment and feedback intervention of an adolescent treatment agency. *Adolescence, 19*(74), 263–275.

Farber, S. (1990). Institutional mental health and social control: The ravages of epistemological hubris. *The Journal of Mind and Behavior, 11*(3&4), 285–299.

Festinger, T. (1983). *No one ever asked us. A postscript to foster care.* New York: Columbia University Press.

Fiester, A. R. (1978). The access system: A procedure for evaluating children's services at community mental health centers. *Community Mental Health Journal, 14*(3), 224–232.

Foucault, M. (1979). *Discipline and punishment: The birth of the prison.* New York: Springer-Verlag.

Gardner, H. (1998). The concept of family: Perceptions of adults who were in long-term out-of-home care as children. *Child Welfare 77*(6), 681–700.

Garland, A. E., & Besinger, B. A. (1996). Adolescents' perceptions of outpatient mental health services. *Journal of Child and Family Studies, 5*(3), 355–375.

George, S., Jones, E., & McCurdy, K. (1992). *The William Penn Foundation Prevention Initiative: An in-depth study of high risk mothers.* Chicago: NCPCA.

Gergen, K. J., & Kaye, J. (1992). Beyond narrative in the negotiation of therapeutic meaning. In S. McNamee & K. J. Gergen (Eds.), *Therapy as a social construction* (pp. 166–185). Newbury Park, CA: Sage.

Godley, S. H., Fiedler, E. M., & Funk, R. R. (1998). Consumer satisfaction of parents and their children with child/adolescent mental health services. *Evaluation and Program Planning, 21*(1), 31–45.

Gove, Justice T. (1995). *Report of the Gove Inquiry into Child Protection.* Victoria: British Columbia Ministry of Social Services.

Hartman, A., & Laird, J. (1998). Moral and ethical issues in working with lesbians and gay men. *Families in Society: Journal of Contemporary Human Services, 79*(3), 263–276.

Hill, C. E., Thompson, B. J., Cogar, M. C., & Denman, D. W. III (1993). Beneath the surface of long term therapy: Therapist and client reports of their own and each other's covert processes. *Journal of Counseling Psychology, 40,* 278–287.

Horvath, A. O., & Symonds, B. D. (1991). Relation between working alliance and outcome in psychotherapy. *Journal of Counseling Psychology, 38,* 139–149.

Illich, I. (1977). Disabling Professions. In I. Illich (Ed.), *Disabling Professions* (pp. 11–39). London: Marion Boyars.

Jacobson, N. S., & Addis, M. E. (1993). Research on couples and couple therapy: What do we know? Where are we going? *Journal of Consulting and Clinical Psychology, 61,* 85–93.

Jenkins, S., & Norman, E. (1972). *Filial deprivation and foster care.* New York: Columbia University Press.

Jenkins, S., & Norman, E. (1975). *Beyond placement: Mothers view foster care.* New York: Columbia University Press.

Johnson, H. C., Cournoyer, D. E., & Bond, B. M. (1995). Professional ethics and parents as consumers: How well are we doing? *Families in Society, 76*(7), 408–420.

Kirchner, J. H. (1981). Patient feedback on satisfaction with direct services received at a community mental health center: A two-year study. *Psychotherapy: Theory, Research and Practice, 18*(3), 359–364.

Kotsopoulos, S., Elwood, S., & Oke, L. (1989). Parent satisfaction in a child psychiatric service. *Canadian Journal of Psychiatry, 34*(6), 530–533.

Kuehl, B., Newfield, N. A., & Joanning, H. (1990). A client-based description of family therapy. *Journal of Family Psychology, 3*(3), 310–321.

Kufeldt, K., Armstrong, J., & Dorosh, M. (1995). How children view their own and their foster families: A research study. *Child Welfare, 74*(3), 695–715.

Kufeldt, K., Simard, M., & Vachon, J. (2000). *Looking after children in Canada.* Unpublished report. Fredericton, NB: University of New Brunswick, Murial McQueen Fergusson Centre for Family Violence Research.

Lambert, M. J., & Bergin, A. E. (1994). Psychotherapy outcome research: Implications for integrative and eclectic therapists. In A. E. Bergin & S. L. Garfield (Eds.), *Handbook of psychotherapy and behavior change* (4th ed., pp. 143–189). New York: Wiley.

Lebow, J. L., & Gurman, A. S. (1995). Research assessing couple and family therapy. *Annual Review of Psychology, 46,* 27–57.

Leslie, B., & Hare, F. (2000). *Improving the outcomes for youth in transition from care.* Toronto, ON: Report of Working Group, Children's Aid Society of Toronto.

Lietaer, G. (1992). Helping and hindering processes in client-centered/experiential psychotherapy. In S. G. Toukmanian & D. L. Rennie (Eds.), *Psychotherapy process research: Paradigmatic and narrative approaches* (pp. 134–162). London: Sage.

Lishman, J. (1978). A clash in perspective? A study of worker and client perceptions of social work. *British Journal of Social Work, 8*(3), 301–311.

Llewelyn, S. P., Elliott, R., Shapiro, D. A., Hardy, G., & Firth-Cozens, J. (1988). Client perceptions of significant events in prescriptive and exploratory periods of individual therapy. *British Journal of Clinical Psychology, 27*, 105–114.

Maluccio, A. N. (1979). *Interpersonal Helping as Viewed by Clients and Social Workers*. New York: The Free Press.

Mandelbaum, A. (1962). Parent–child separation: Its significance to parents. *Social Work, 7*(4), 26–34.

Mann-Feder, V., & White, T. (2003). *The transition to independent living: Preliminary findings on the experiences of youth in care*. In K. Kufeldt & B. McKenzie (Eds.), *Child welfare: Connecting research, policy, and practice* (pp. 217–225). Waterloo, ON: Wilfrid Laurier University Press.

Mayer, J. E., & Timms, N. (1970). *The client speaks: Working class impressions of casework*. New York: Atherton.

McAuley, C. (1996). *Children in long-term foster care: Emotional and social development*. Avebury, UK: Ashgate Publishing.

McCallum, S. (1995). *Safe families: A model of child protection intervention based on parental voice and wisdom*. Unpublished doctoral dissertation. Waterloo, ON: Wilfrid Laurier University.

McConnell, R., & Sim, A. J. (2000). Evaluating an innovative counselling service for children of divorce. *British Journal of Guidance and Counselling, 28*(1), 75–86.

McCurdy, K., & Jones, E. (2000). *Supporting families: Lessons from the field*. Thousand Oaks, CA: Sage.

McGee, C. (1998). *Children's and mothers' experiences of child protection services following domestic violence*. Unpublished paper delivered at International Conference of Program Evaluation and Family Violence Research. Durham, NH: University of New Hampshire.

Moon, S. M., Dillon, D. R., & Sprenkle, D. H. (1990). Family therapy and qualitative research. *Journal of Marital and Family Therapy, 16*(4), 357–373.

Mullender, A., & Ward, D. (1993). The role of the consultant in self-directed groupwork: An approach to supporting social action in Britain. *Social Work with Groups, 16*(4), 57–79.

Newfield, N. A., Joanning, H. P., Kuehl, B. P., & Quinn, W. H. (1991). We can tell you about "Psychos" and "Shrinks": An ethnography of the family therapy or adolescent drug abuse. In T. C. Todd & M. D. Selekman (Eds.), *Family therapy approaches with adolescent substance abusers* (pp. 277–310). Boston: Allyn and Bacon.

Orlinsky, D. E., Grawe, K., & Parks, B. K. (1994). Process and outcome in psychotherapy: Noch einmal. In A. E. Bergin & S. L. Garfield (Eds.), *Handbook of psychotherapy and behavior change* (4th ed., pp. 270–376). New York: Wiley.

Packman, J., Randall, J., & Jacques, N. (1986). *Who needs care? Social work decision about children.* Oxford, UK: Basil Blackwell.

Payne, H. (2000). Introduction. In H. Payne & B. G. Littlechild (Eds), *Ethical practice and the abuse of power in social responsibility: Leave no stone unturned* (pp. 7–15). London: Jessica Kingsley.

Pinsof, W. H., & Catherall, D. R. (1986). The integrative psychotherapy alliance: Family, couple, and individual therapy scales. *Journal of Marital and Family Therapy, 12*(2), 137–151.

Plante, T. G., Couchman, C. E., & Hoffman, C. A. (1998). Measuring treatment outcome and client satisfaction among children and families: A case report. *Professional Psychology: Research and Practice, 29*(1), 52–55.

Raychaba, B. (1993). *Pain, lots of pain: Family violence and abuse in the lives of young people growing up in care.* Ottawa, ON: National Youth in Care Network.

Rennie, D. L. (1992). Qualitative analysis of the client's experience of psychotherapy: The unfolding of reflexivity. In S. G. Toukmanian & D. L. Rennie (Eds.), *Psychotherapy process research: Paradigmatic and narrative approaches* (211–233). London: Sage.

Rennie, D. L. (1994). Clients' accounts of resistance in counselling: A qualitative analysis. *Canadian Journal of Counselling, 28*(1), 43–57.

Richey, C. A., Lovell, M. L., & Reid, K. (1991). Interpersonal skill training to enhance social support among women at risk for child maltreatment. *Children and Youth Services Review, 13*(1–2), 41–59.

Roberts, M. F. (1993). Day in "court." *Journal of Systemic Therapy, 12,* 55–67.

Rutman, D., Barlow, A., Alusik, D., Hubberstey, C., & Brown, E. (2000). *Supporting young people's transitions from government care.* Unpublished manuscript, Victoria, BC: University of Victoria.

Saskatchewan. (2000). *Children and youth in care review: Listen to their voices.* Regina, SK: Saskatchewan Children's Advocate Office.

Sells, S. P., Smith, T. E., Coe, M. J., Yoshioka, M., & Robbins, J. (1994). An ethnography of couple and therapist experiences in reflecting team practice. *Journal of Marital and Family Therapy, 20*(3), 247–266.

Shapiro, J. P., Welker, C. J., & Jacobson, B. J. (1997). The Youth Client Satisfaction Questionnaire: Development, construct validation, and factor structure. *Journal of Clinical Child Psychology, 26*(1), 87–98.

Shilts, L., & Knapik-Esposito, M. (1993). Playback of the therapeutic process: He said, she said, they said. *Journal of Systemic Therapy, 12,* 41–54.

Silva-Wayne, S. (1995). Contributions to resilience in children and youth: What successful child welfare graduates say. In J. Hudson & B. Galaway (Eds.), *Child welfare in Canada: Research and policy implications* (pp. 308–323). Toronto, ON: Thompson Educational Publishing.

Smith, T. E., Yoshioka, M., & Winton, M. (1993). A qualitative understanding of reflecting teams I: Client perspectives. *Journal of Systemic Therapies, 12*(3), 28–43.

Stallard, P. (1995). Parental satisfaction with intervention: Differences between respondents to a postal questionnaire. *British Journal of Clinical Psychology, 34*(3), 397–405.

Stallard, P., Hudson, J., & Davis, B. (1992). Consumer evaluation in practice. *Journal of Community and Applied Social Psychology, 2*(4), 291–295.

Steier, F. (1985). Toward a cybernetic methodology of family therapy research: Fitting research methods to family practice. In L. L. Andreozzi (Ed.), *Integrating research and clinical practice* (pp. 27–36). Rockville, MD: Aspen.

Stith, S. M., Rosen, K. H., McCollum, E. E., Coleman, J. U., & Herman, S. A. (1996). The voices of children: Preadolescent children's experiences in family therapy. *Journal of Marital and Family Therapy, 22*(1), 69–86.

Stuntzner-Gibson, D., Koren, P. E., & DeChillo, N. (1995). The Youth Satisfaction Questionnaire: What kids think of services. *Families in Society, 76*(10), 616–624.

Telfair, J., & Gardner, M. M. (2000). Adolescents with sickle cell disease: Determinants of support group attendance and satisfaction. *Health and Social Work, 25*(1), 43–50.

van Ryn, E., & Fine, M. (1997). Client perceptions of collaborative meaning-making in couples' therapy. *Journal of Collaborative Therapies, 5*, 22–29.

Wark, L. (1994). Client voice: A study of client couples' and their therapists' perspectives on therapeutic change. *Journal of Feminist Family Therapy, 6*, 21–39.

Wedeven, T., Pecora, P. J., Hurwitz, M., Howell, R., & Newell, D. (1997). Examining the perceptions of alumni of long term family foster care: A follow-up study. *Community Alternatives: International Journal of Family Care, 9*(1), 88–106.

Wilford, G., & Hetherington, R. (1997). *Families ask for help: Parental perceptions of child welfare and child protection services in an Anglo-German study.* London, UK: Brunel University, Centre for Comparative Social Work Studies,

Wilson, A., & Beresford, P. (2000). Surviving an abusive system. In H. Payne and B. G. Littlechild (Eds.), *Ethical practice and the abuse of power in social responsibility: Leave no stone unturned* (pp. 145–174). London: Jessica Kingsley.

Winefield, H. R., & Barlow, J. A. (1995). Child and worker satisfaction in a child protection agency. *Child Abuse & Neglect 19*(8), 897–905.

|6|

Placement Decisions and the Child Welfare Worker
Constructing Identities for Survival

Nancy Freymond

Child welfare workers manage a fundamental tension between maintaining family privacy and using state authority when intervening in situations of child abuse and neglect (Esposito & Fine, 1985). In daily practice, this tension compels workers to make difficult, emotionally laden decisions between child removal and family preservation. The removal of a child from a family due to abuse or neglect is the most intrusive intervention used by child welfare workers (Wiehe, 1996). The permanent removal of a child from biological parents is one of the most extreme representations of the tension between child removal and family preservation.

In Ontario, a crown ward refers to the legal status of a child who has been permanently removed from parental care. Research has tended to focus on the effects of short-term and long-term separation and loss for the child (see Kufeldt, Vachon, Simard, Baker, & Andrews 2000; Palmer, 1995; Steinhauer, 1984). Research is absent, however, regarding the effects of the crownwardship process on child welfare workers. This chapter examines how workers experience one of the most extreme representations of the tension between child removal and family preservation when they are required to make crown-ward decisions. It further explores how child welfare workers survive emotionally by constructing particular identities to manage the emotional strains associated with making children crown wards.

Current Climate of Child Placement in Ontario
In the past decade, child welfare workers have faced unprecedented pressures in their work environments. As discussed in chapter 1, Ontario's child protection system has come under scrutiny in response to media coverage about

the deaths of children known to the child protection system. A series of reviews of Ontario's child welfare system resulted in expanded definitions of child abuse, lower thresholds of intervention, and the introduction of a risk assessment model to guide decision-making (Swift & Callahan, 2002). Inside child protection agencies, a climate of fear has emerged, as workers fear that they will be held liable in cases of child death. Gilroy (1999) writes:

> Social workers recognise the need for accountability, but they fear that they may become scapegoats in tragic deaths of children, that courts and the public will hold them responsible without knowing the case, while the insufficiency of funding for child welfare and other basic services needed by families, and the difficult conditions under which child welfare workers do their jobs, will be ignored. (p. 35)

In daily practice, the changes in child protection procedures have led to shifts in how child welfare workers experience their responsibilities (see the discussion in chapter 7). Child welfare workers make critical decisions about apprehending children, often against the parents' wishes, fearing that by leaving children in the home they will be blamed civilly or criminally should further injuries or fatalities occur (Regehr, Bernstein, & Kanani, 2002).

In response to public concerns about indecisive planning around permanent arrangements for children (Welsh & Donovan, 1997; Hatton et al., 1998), the provincial child welfare reviews also resulted in amendments focusing on the length of time that elapses before a permanent placement decision for a child considered "at risk" occurs. Former legislation stipulated that a child could be in temporary foster care for a maximum continuous period of 24 months before the child either had to be returned home, or made a crown ward. This meant that a child could, theoretically, be moved in and out of foster care for the duration of his childhood years, as long as no single period of foster care was longer than 24 months. In order to promote earlier and more decisive planning, the current legislation and regulations stipulate that children under the age of six must now have a permanent placement after 12 months of temporary foster care has accumulated from the date of the first placement. In daily practice, not only are child protection workers placing more children into substitute care, they are making permanency plans at a much earlier point in the process. These factors point to a likely increase in the number of crown wardship decisions that individual workers will face.

Methodology

In order to understand the experiences of child welfare workers when making decisions to permanently remove children from biological parents, we conducted individual interviews, two to three hours in length, with six workers from Ontario's child protection system. Three of the workers were supervisors of staff who provided ongoing child protection services. Two workers provided ongoing services to families and children, and one was employed as an investigator of child abuse allegations. One of the participants was a new graduate and had worked in child welfare for less than one year. The others had a minimum of five years of experience.

The interviews used the same strategy, beginning with what Spradley (1979) refers to as a grand tour question, namely, "tell me your experience of crown wardship decision making." The interview allowed for flexibility so that the respondents could organize their account in a manner consistent with their own conceptualizations of this experience. Each of the interviewed workers subsequently participated in a group discussion, where further reflections on the experience of the placement process were elicited, and preliminary research findings were discussed. One group involved the supervisors, and the second group involved the front-line staff. This separation occurred at the request of the front-line workers.

In the individual interviews, each worker spoke specifically about how they manage emotionally when confronted with the permanent removal of children from their birth families. Workers recounted their experiences by telling stories of their involvements with particular parents whose children eventually became permanent wards. The organization of these stories highlights the processes involved in permanent placement.

Methods of Analysis

Three analytic strategies were applied to the data. Grounded theory focuses on social processes and fosters the identification of connections among events (Charmaz, 2000; Ryan & Bernard, 2000; Strauss & Corbin, 1990, 1998). This analytic strategy, when applied to the data, was instructive in developing an understanding of how workers think about and cope emotionally with crown wardship decision making. Examples from the transcripts of workers' statements about the placement process, and how they cope emotionally with the strains of their work, were identified through a process referred to as open coding by grounded theorists (Ryan & Bernard, 2000). Key concepts from these statements were categorized, and the themes that emerged were compared across the data. Relationships among these concepts were noted through additional coding and links to a substantive model about coping processes developed.

A second analytic strategy was applied specifically to the sections of the interview in which workers told stories of involvement with particular mothers in the permanent placement process. According to Riessman (1993), narrative analysis is concerned with seeing the world from the perspective of the person interviewed, by analyzing how stories are told. She suggests that people are likely to tell narratives about the experiences in their lives, particularly if there has been a "breach between ideal and real, self and society" (p. 3); in this study, between ideas about saving children and the actual work of doing so. The story metaphor emphasizes that we create order and construct texts in particular contexts, which, in turn, allows us to claim identities and construct lives (Riessman, 1993). In the sections of the interview where stories were told, recurring themes clustered at various junctures of the stories, revealing a consistent story structure. The structure of the worker stories about permanent-placement experiences was instructive for developing an understanding of the process and the child welfare context in which it unfolds.

A third analytical strategy involved a process of personal reflection, a process that Alvesson and Skoldberg (2000) refer to as turning "attention 'inwards' towards the person of the researcher" (p. 5). I approached the data with a certain pre-understanding that originated from personal experiences as a front-line child welfare worker. Given that all research can be seen as a fundamentally interpretative activity (Alvesson & Skoldberg, 2000), I acknowledge that my assumptions have had an inevitable impact on the data analysis. Narration or storytelling is an avenue through which we can identify ourselves (Gergen, 1999). Therefore, in order to clarify and reflect on my own experiences with the placement of children, I was interviewed by a child welfare worker who did not participate in this study but is familiar with the topic area. This record of personal experience was then subjected to the same analytic processes as the other individual interviews. The personal interview helped to identify my biases and provided a backdrop against which the voices of others could be considered. The result was an ongoing, critical self-exploration of my interpretations. None of the quotations cited in this paper are drawn from this interview.

Together the three analytical methods allowed for a multi-level interpretation of the data. The first level focused on the emotional coping processes of individual workers, where coding patterns revealed consistencies in how child welfare workers conceive of their work. This focus led to the development of a substantive model of worker coping. At the second level of interpretation, the narrative approach provided a broad lens where workers, through the sharing of stories about permanent placement, effectively illustrated the context in which the work of making permanent-placement decisions is conducted. At the third level of interpretation, personal reflection heightened the emphasis on my interpretation of the data. An ongoing process of self exploration led not only to the acknowledgement of personal biases but also to the emergence of new self-understanding in relation to child welfare experiences.

Study Findings

The presentation of the findings is divided into two major sections. The first section describes the worker's perspectives of the various stages of the crown wardship placement process. The second examines how workers cope with the emotional strain inherent in the work of severing relationships between mother and child. This is followed by my personal reflections on my child welfare experiences and the new understandings that have emerged for me as a result of this research. The discussion concludes with questions that arise about the nature of this work and the implications for children and families.

The Crown Wardship Process

Crown wardship is a process that is managed through the relationships among child welfare service providers. The service providers told stories about their experiences with the process that were similarly organized. Analysis of the structure of the stories indicates that each story can be divided into three sections, and that each of these sections corresponds to a particular phase of the crown wardship process. The first phase of the process is the identifying phase. Correspondingly, the story opens with a description of the mother's attributes that signal the potential for a crown wardship outcome. The second phase of the crown wardship process is chance giving, which becomes the plot of the story. Reissman (1993) refers to the plot as the section of the story that details unexpected twists or complicating actions. In these stories, the plot included descriptions of service provider angst about the process. The final phase of the crown wardship process is the formalizing phase, which corresponds to the resolution of the story. During this phase, workers attempt through negotiation to secure the consent of the client to the legal request for crown wardship. Regardless of the outcome of the negotiations, the stories all have the same resolution. There is a judicial ruling granting the crown wardship order and the worker anxiety, which occupies the story's plot, gives way to reliance on administrative and legal procedure. Each of the phases of the crown wardship process and the corresponding story section is presented in greater detail in the following sections.

Identifying. The introduction of each of the stories consists of statements containing two main points that identify the parents whose children eventually became crown wards. The first point distinguishes the parents along gender lines. The parents who are central to the stories are mothers. Three fathers are mentioned. One has been incarcerated for a murder conviction; the other two are described as physically abusive. No father is considered central to the parenting issue in question. The most involved father participated with the mother in counselling and in attending access visits. The worker described the relationship between the parents as one where:

> There was some mutual violence but clearly he was the one that had the power in the relationship. He was released from jail. She [meaning the mother] initially agreed that she would not allow him to move back into the home but turns out she did. At that particular point in time I considered taking it to court.

The focus of this worker's evaluation is on the mother's actions (that is, letting him back into the home) and not on the father's violence, despite the acknowledgement of the power imbalance.

Ensuring the well-being of children has historically been the responsibility of mothers. Although the interviewees made continual references to their work as involving the assessment of "parenting," and although "parenting" generally is a term used in reference to both fathers and mothers, the crown wardship process focused primarily on the evaluation of mother–child relationships. This is consistent with literature that identifies a primary focus on mothers in the child welfare system (Miller, 1991; Callahan, 1993; Swift, 1995; 1998; Roberts, 1999). Fathers tend to be mentioned in relation to the mother and, more specifically, to demonstrate the mother's inadequacy around choosing a suitable partner (Polansky, Chalmers, Buttenweiser, & Williams, 1981) or around curbing male violence (Frost & Stein, 1989).

The second component of the identifying stage consists of statements that categorize the mother's particular attribute and/or parenting deficit that causes concern for the child welfare authority. Examples include statements such as: "she functioned around a six-year-old level, so there was no question that she could really handle the child" or "she was alcoholic and there was domestic violence" or "mom tried a lot of different things. She tried to change her lifestyle. She tried to get rid of her addiction habits." According to Swift (1995), clients are processed in the child welfare system according to their particular categorization. Implicit in this type of categorization are values about parenting which underlie the rationale for child welfare involvement.

Categorizations shift as parental deficits are discovered. At the inception of child welfare services, the emphasis was on problems such as neglect and cruelty (Jones & Rutman, 1981); in the 1960s the focus shifted to physical abusiveness (Costin, Karger & Stoesz, 1996) and the psychological immaturity of the parent (Young, 1964; Katz, 1971). The 1980s saw child sexual abuse come to the forefront, and the past decade has seen an emphasis on the dilemmas associated with the parenting abilities of addicted mothers. A

13-year veteran of child welfare reflects on the categorizations: "it's unbelievable. We used to have things like discipline problems, domestic violence, sexual abuse—that was a big one ... [now] ... every worker I supervise probably has 3 or 4 on their caseload that is addicted."

In addition to the prevalence of the addiction category, a history of child welfare involvement is also an identifying category that causes concern. One worker identified this category as consisting of "the kind of things the Children's Aid has been involved in prior to myself and ... what kind of progress has been worked on, [and] what kind of issues have come up." Workers often used adjectives like "terrible" or "bad" in relation to this history. Finally, mental illness of the mother is another categorization that was routinely mentioned during the interviews. One worker describes mental illness as a category that is often a more "clear-cut" example of the necessity of crown wardship, particularly when the illness is chronic in nature.

There was substantial suggestion that crown wardship is underway at the identifying stage of the process. Workers use language such as "the writing was on the wall" or "having a sense" from the beginning about the crown wardship outcome. One worker says "sometimes it's quite clear, especially in the beginning because the mom has the history she has, or the baby is born with drugs in her system." Of the mentally ill mother, where the crown wardship application is "clear cut," the worker wonders: "how many more will there be; we've heard that she is pregnant again?" The categorization that occurs at the outset sets the tone for the nature of the child welfare involvement, and shapes the outcome for involved families.

Chance giving. The plots of the worker's stories consist of description of the second phase of the crown wardship process, during which mothers are given chances to prove parenting ability. For workers, one of the chief tasks of the chance-giving stage is the observation of the mother's ability to comply with terms, which have been established by the worker and are often sanctioned by a supervision order. Also, during chance giving, workers describe an emotional response that often produces internal conflict. Although the level of discomfort for each worker varies, it is this emotional response that creates a need for workers to develop beliefs about their role in relation to the crown wardship process in an attempt to soothe their discomfort. These beliefs will be discussed later in the chapter.

During the chance-giving stage, mothers are required to attend therapies relevant to their categorization, such as counselling, addictions treatment, or parenting classes. They are expected to participate in regular, often supervised, visits with their children, who may be in foster care. If addiction is an issue, parents may be required to submit to regular drug screens. One worker speaks of the prospect of an identified mother attending parenting courses:

> We have to demonstrate that we offered it to her ... we as an agency are supposed to offer people parenting courses etcetera to help them, to assist them, to a point where they would actually be able to parent so ... I filled out the form.

She continues with description of the futility of the action:

> She had been to every parenting course that had happened here. She had been to mother–child things. She had been to, what they call, group access, where parents actually have access to their children who are in foster care, in a group setting, she made no progress whatsoever.

Chance giving is not always a mandatory step. It may be bypassed, generally in situations where the mother has been categorized as having a "terrible history." It is from this history that evidence is drawn for the legal proceedings. One worker speaks of the struggle to comply with an agency decision to draft an immediate crown wardship application:

> She had never been evaluated as a parent. We had never had any contact with her while she was in charge of children. So we were really basing this on history, on who she had been historically as opposed to who she was as a parent ... we were making a huge leap ... that was difficult.

In another instance a worker describes how, early in her career, she made a decision to return a baby to the mother's care rather than proceeding directly to a crown wardship application based on the history. She describes that decision as follows:

> That was a situation where, I think, I know, that my own supervisor didn't agree whole-heartedly with myself. There was a little bit of naiveté on my part, being brand new. I think a little bit of what was going on was that feeling that you want to see people change. The mom is giving the best effort that she possibly could. There's no doubt in my mind that she was and we, myself, supported that. She got some treatment. She had some support. The baby went home and the baby was probably home for about two weeks ... She phoned me while she was drunk, while she was getting drunk with her own mom, and we went back out and apprehended the baby and went to crown wardship from there. And I think that was a little bit more difficult on a personal level because you have this feeling, you know, she's doing great, she's doing wonderful, maybe this mom is finally going to make a change in her life. Ten years later I look back on it and I wouldn't have made the same decision.

At the chance-giving stage in the crown wardship process, the worker knows the parent's categorization and is anticipating the outcome; as one worker says, "we're building our case right from the beginning." The worker's stories suggest that the outcome for the family depends on the identifying category. One worker speaks of an exception, a case in which the crown wardship plan was abandoned. This seasoned worker, based on her own observations of the family, and a thorough reading of the file, presented a case for misidentification that culminated in her colleagues acknowledging that they had mistakenly "just got on a roll with what the other worker was saying about adoption and went with it." To thwart the established crown wardship plan, the worker had to overturn the mother's original categorization.

The workers frequently mentioned the emotional strain associated with the contradictions that arise during the chance-giving stage. Child welfare workers are confronted with the difficulties of balancing the needs of the identified family, the child welfare bureaucracy, and the legislative system. In reference to the impossibility of achieving a balance that meets the needs of the various parties to the process, one worker describes this position as a "thoroughly no-win situation." On one level, workers consider the needs of the family and wrestle with the questions that arise. One worker asks:

> Should we give her [the mother] one more chance? How many chances do you give? What is right for the children? That's one part of the struggle ... you know she's a good mom when she's clean ... should this child watch this while this child is still young? Should this child have to say goodbye to this person they have lived with all their lives?

The intensity of the emotional struggle varies. A worker speaks of situations where:

> you know that this is what you absolutely have to do. There is no choice. This child needs to be made a crown ward. There are no relatives. This Mom absolutely can't do it. So it's more clear-cut. Others are much more of a struggle, when you have a mother that you really like, when you see her with her children and you really, really know she cares.

Child welfare organizations are also large bureaucracies in which procedures are specific. When a parent is identified as a crown wardship client, there is an implicit expectation that workers will adhere to the procedures appropriate to the initial categorization. One worker speaks of how she feels "furious" when the procedures are not followed:

> I just really think that if the family service worker doesn't agree with the [crown wardship] decision we need to contain that within our walls. We can't allow that discrepancy to be seen by the client or by the community ... [she] made us look like fools in the community and has told mom that maybe there is a chance that we are backing off here ... She was a new worker. She had only been here for five weeks and really felt badly for mom, as did everybody else.

This worker continued by describing how agreement about the crown ward-ship categorization was achieved. An internal meeting was held with all workers connected to the case to clarify the plan for the baby, a process referred to as bringing the worker "on board." Although internal agreement is expected, workers are not always able to bring other community profes-sionals "on board" with crown wardship plans. They described criticism from the community as a difficult aspect of the crown wardship process. As one worker says, in light of the lack of support from the community profes-sionals, "betrayal from one of our own" is almost more than we can bear.

Chance giving appears to be primarily a process of collecting evidence, in situations where there is an insufficient historical account, for the purpose of satisfying legal requirements. In all likelihood, the emotional intensity for workers is heightened as they are required to give chances to the mother and simultaneously deny that the purpose of this chance giving is to satisfy legal requirements for the demonstration of parental failure. The worker who filled out the parenting form provides one of the many examples from the stories of how workers struggle with finding balances that satisfy needs at the legislative level. She speaks of her failure to respond to the legal needs saying: "At the beginning I didn't know what I was doing. I got onto a mov-ing train. Even the part about offering them parenting courses, I didn't know that, and I should have known that. I didn't know what crown wardship really meant." The confusion arises for the worker who seems to know that insisting on another parenting course for the mother is a questionable inter-vention from the perspective of the needs of the identified family. Because chance giving appears to be a vehicle for the legal demonstration of parental failure, the needs of the identified family may be secondary in this process.

Finally, workers must also find ways to reconcile discrepancies that arise regarding their knowledge of human nature and the expectations for change during the chance-giving stage of the crown wardship process. Question-ing the expectations for change placed on the mothers, one participant says:

> We expect a lot. Take a mom with four kids who is alone and has to meet all of the demands of the kids and all of the demands of the CAS ... now add depression to the mix and it is just so hard ... could I really be a client and do it? The answer is probably not.

Another worker speaks to this discrepancy:

> you have parents that are struggling, that need some support whether that be [from] the children's aid, or a mental health facility, or whether that be a drug addiction agency or what have you ... You can't expect people to deal with all of these issues. Deal with what all the research out there tells us about all of these issues and how much time, and how much treatment and how much effort they take.

Despite these rather profound doubts about the fairness of chance giving for identified families, the child welfare worker must find ways to cope with the emotional demands of their position; in essence, to know where the crown wardship process is leading but to simultaneously deny this knowledge while the chance-giving stage unfolds.

Negotiating. The resolution of the story involves the final stage of the crown wardship process where, after a period of negotiation, judicial assent is obtained. Negotiating appears to be an attempt to strike an agreement with the mother, whereby she consents to the crown wardship application. Negotiation may be motivated by the belief that proceeding with the mother's consent is preferable to a conflict culminating in a lengthy and stressful trial.

The stories contain many references to a negotiating phase. At the point of negotiation, the worker is clear, usually in writing, about the intention to request crown wardship. As one worker says "the lines are drawn." The negotiation phase is described in various ways. One worker says:

> As the family service worker, it is that worker's responsibility to start speaking with the mom about what are the plans—what is it that is the Children's Aid's view of the situation and ... try to negotiate or deal with her about what it is that we have planned and the gulf, the vast gulf that is in between the mom and the Children's Aid.

This worker repeatedly applied the phrase "chipping away at the gulf" to conferences where professionals would meet with the mother in a show of public support for the crown wardship plan. Another worker referred to a script she follows:

> The way I do it is to start very early. I guess I normalize a lot of things and then it's a matter of playing it out. Often I have to send the child home because I know I don't have enough to prevent the child from going home ... and then eventually the kid acts out enough that they [meaning the parents] say OK it's fine ... that's what I mean about the script. I have to sort of [pause] well I'm leading them with some things.

Another worker is much more blatant about the negotiating tactics:

> It [referring to a crown wardship application] was a bargaining chip with this young woman ... it was easier to say to her "if you sign you still get to see [name of mother's oldest son]. And your other child, well, she's younger and we're doing her a big favour by making it possible for her to be adopted."

In order to maintain a level of acceptability with their work, social workers must necessarily shield themselves from descriptions framing their actions as exploitive or manipulative (Margolin, 1997). Justification for negotiating a crown wardship settlement is found in the belief that a trial is a painful ordeal for mothers that workers should avoid when possible. As one worker says:

> I had a lawyer say to me once that a crown wardship trial in child welfare is like a murder trial in criminal court and I really believe that; that the stakes are so high and we are just doing the ultimate. We are taking somebody's child away from them and in that process what we end up doing is taking the witness stand, talking about all of the deficits of this and that. I think it is just so tragic.

Obtaining judicial assent formalizes the crown wardship process. The court order represents the conclusion to a negotiated settlement or to a trial. One worker reflects on the prospect of their request for crown wardship being denied:

> I think that by the time we get to a crown wardship hearing the parent doesn't really have much of a side to present. I think we lose very few crown wardships. I think that's because the agency takes that step so seriously and we really don't make those decisions unless we feel we have to.

The worker stories contained limited references to court with the exception of that of the newest worker, who had applied for crown wardship based on the mother's "terrible history." She speaks to her beginning experience with the family court system:

> I wish she [referring to the mother] had a lawyer that was fifteen times better than our lawyer; that would give us a run for our money; that would make us look under every rock and stone and make sure beyond a shadow of a doubt that this is the right decision ... I wish I could say prove me wrong. I want to be proven wrong but I know he can't. After I left court the last time I couldn't come back into the office. I went home and cried for three hours because I felt terrible.

As the above worker so poignantly describes, the crown wardship process is laden with emotion for workers. The process unfolds amid extreme pressures and in the absence of mechanisms for proving "beyond a shadow of a doubt" that the correct decisions have been made, even though procedures may have been followed flawlessly.

New workers are presented with a number of statements that can be embraced as tools for managing emotions associated with the work of separating children from their mothers. The degree to which workers are able to integrate these statements into their own belief systems impacts their ability to remain in the child welfare system. As one worker says of the crown wardship process:

The whole thing is sad. It's not that you become jaded or hard, but after a while you develop ways to protect yourself. It's something that has to be done so you have to be strong, not just for yourself but for the mother too ... at the beginning it [is] more emotional. At the beginning it takes hours of your time. But also at the beginning you just get drawn into how this is part of your work. Like breathing. It's just a part of every day life. It's just a part of every six months at least.

The worker who is new to the field of child welfare, reflects on her beginning experience:

I wanted to work for an agency that had some power to get these kids out of these horrific situations. This is the place to do it, but I never dreamt it would be like this. I never dreamt it would be such a draining experience. I thought I would feel good about it. I thought I would feel like I had rescued someone ... I'm not a quitter. I don't want to be one of those people [who says], you know, I did it for eight months and I couldn't deal with it and I left. I keep thinking there's some magical hump I need to get over where I say: ok, I'm not new anymore. I know what I'm doing. Now I like the job.

This worker expresses her longing for a way to think about her work that distances her from the emotional strain; that, as she says, gets her over the magical hump and to a place where she likes the job.

How Workers Cope: Strategies and New Identities for Getting Over the Magical Hump

To cope with the magnitude of being responsible for the crown wardship process, which on two occasions was referred to as "playing God," workers cannot think of themselves as the sole decision maker. An important strategy for workers is to assign responsibility for crown wardship decisions to another source, a process that de-individualizes and distances workers emotionally from responsibility for the outcome. As workers shed the identity of an autonomous decision maker, space is created for the establishment of new identities and, conversely, as new identities gain ground, workers become increasingly de-individualized. Workers become agents of a source to which responsibility for the crown wardship process can be attributed. The following discussion explores the new identities that workers may develop. The strategies for de-individualizing are italicized and included within the context of this discussion.

An agent of society. Child welfare workers frequently use the term "the Society" in reference to the decision maker. This term is ambiguous. It may refer to the name of the child welfare authority (that is, the specific children's aid society), or it may refer to a society of Canadians in general. The newest worker recounts her reaction to a supervisor's advice about de-individualizing:

> My supervisor says don't say 'I,' say 'the society.' Ok, 'the Society' doesn't think you can parent and she hears, 'I' don't think you can parent. What a message to give to a first time mother ... you know, there is so much talk around here about [how] *you don't own the decision. The Society owns the decision.* That's a bunch of bunk. It is. I own the decision.

Conversely, a supervisor with several years of experience says: "you work with the worker so *everyone validates what you are doing* all the way along. *You're never really alone with it.* It just sometimes feels like you're all alone with it. But you're not. There's always some collaboration." And another supervisor says, "if the bureaucracy is really working, then it is a decision that is not left for one person. It is a decision that is shared by the agency. And for the most part, it is my experience that that works very well."

One worker speaks of "Society," in reference to the broader society of Canadians:

> We never used to ask for drug tests. We used to think that was too intrusive. Now it's just routine. We used to feel a bit embarrassed to look in our client's cupboards. We used to get so many calls saying there is no food in the house. And we would be criticized for not being intrusive enough. I think Society wanted us to be family oriented, not do those kinds of things, but now it seems like expectations are different.

This worker acknowledges that she understands her role as being in relation to the broader society of Canadians. Her role involves responding to the expectations of Canadians, whose expectations influence the methods deployed to accomplish the work.

An agent of the client.   Sometimes, workers think of themselves as accomplices with the mother in facilitating the crown wardship process. In these situations, *the worker believes that some mothers inwardly desire the removal of their children.* An accomplice interprets certain behaviours as signals that crown wardship is the mother's secret desire. One worker says:

> Sometimes it comes right down to the wire and then there is a slip up. It's almost like they let us know on purpose ... I do think slip-ups are on purpose ... they [in reference to an addicted mother] know the routine. They have to be tested regularly. They have to come regularly for access visits to maintain the relationship with children. So they know very well. They should be aware, really aware.

Another says: "the writing is on the wall again because I get a sense. You learn what the parents want. They sort of know too. I feel that they often already know what's going to happen." Another says, in reference to apprehending a baby who eventually became a crown ward, "it was probably one of the easiest apprehensions I ever did because mom actually was crying and upset but did get the baby ready, and I could see that she really wanted this." The implications of acting with the understanding that crown wardship is what a mother truly wants, despite the mother's outward protest, reassures the worker that she is someone who helps others, someone who serves the client's wishes.

An agent of a higher force. Acting as an agent of "the Society" or as an agent of the client helps to disperse and deflect responsibility for the crown wardship process away from the worker, but the existential question of why we live in a society where crown wardship is required still remains. Some child welfare workers find answers at the existential level by developing fatalistic beliefs. As one worker says, "it's like there is something out there making sure that things happen the way they should." This worker seems to find comfort from the idea that crown wardship is an ordained process, controlled by a higher force. Another worker says:

> I have decided to think of everything in terms of karma. You know, it's this child's karma ... the child didn't make a good decision prenatally to choose these people as parents ... I have to comfort myself in some way but I'm uncomfortable and I don't know what the solution is.

This worker searches for answers at an existential level, although she suggests that self-comfort remains a challenge. Embracing the identity of an agent of a higher force allows child welfare workers to assign responsibility for crown wardship decisions to an omnipotent source.

When the child welfare worker is acting as an agent of "the Society," as an agent of the client, or as an agent of a higher force, she is not required to face the family as an individual. Supervisors seem to have a direct role in encouraging the development of new identities. They do so by suggesting that there is a *separation between the "making" and the "owning" of decisions*, which, in turn, assists workers with the acceptance of their work as representatives of another source. There is *repeated validation for workers* that the crown wardship process is right. There is also the reassurance that *you're never alone with the decision*, that you are supported by others who understand. And finally, *when parental failure is established, it may be interpreted as an expression of the mother's innermost desire for crown wardship*, rather than evidence of a child welfare failure. This interpretation is a technique that assures that workers continue to see themselves, not only as rescuers of children, but also as assisting mothers to accomplish what they "really want."

The quote from the new worker, who struggles to maintain her individual autonomy by using "I" in reference to a decision about parenting ability, is the same worker who never dreamed that the crown wardship process would be "such a draining experience." Becoming de-individualized may de-emphasize a worker's identity as a thinker and as a decision-maker; it may also cause individual identity to become obscured as the worker becomes an agent of another source. In order to find refuge from the emotional strains associated with a monumental decision like crown wardship, it may be that workers' must discard individual autonomy and embrace the comforts associated with emotional distance from the realities of this work.

The identity of a doubter. Even though child welfare workers develop new identities to assist them with the emotional strains of the crown wardship process, they continue to express considerable doubt about the work that they do. Child welfare workers are not oblivious to the criticism of their practices, nor are they unaware of the potential negative outcomes of foster placement and adoption. One worker speaks to the issue of negative outcomes for crown wards:

> As good as a foster mom can be, we are still taking them away from their parents. I think there is an inherent sense of belonging, even if it's a dark hole of a relationship with the parents and, most of the kids, I find, have insecure attachments.

The doubt about the appropriateness of their work is a persistent theme in the stories. Statements like "there isn't enough information out there to suggest that what we do is right" or "I want to be convinced that there is a best way, but I think that is a fantasy" express a common theme of doubt about the merits of crown wardship. When I asked a participant how she could know the crown wardship outcome two years prior to its occurrence, she responds with:

> Well we use intuition rather loosely but I think that's the way it is for me. I think I had a sense back then but wasn't as confident. But every now and then I'll doubt myself, but that's my nature. I still believe in doubting myself. Like don't be so sure of yourself. Look at the big picture. And I think you always have to have that. I try never to be so rigid. I don't think I am.

It is puzzling that workers, despite some strong expressions of doubt, continue to do work that involves separating children and mothers. Margolin (1997), in his critical examination of the social work profession, states that social workers are able to cure doubts about their practice by acknowledging the legitimacy of those very doubts. Child welfare workers can "know and not know" simultaneously; that is know enough about a mother's ability to permanently remove her child while, at the same time, be uncertain about the appropriateness of this intervention.

Traversing the magical hump. Participants acknowledged that to remain in child welfare they must reach a level of acceptance of the merits of the crown wardship process. Workers "have to come around because there is no choice ... it's acceptance of the system that we work in ... there is a structure to follow," declares one of the supervisors. "Getting over the magical hump" or "coming around" is demonstrated by the willingness to follow established procedures. The significance of adhering to the structure is verified by another worker who says, "If this system is working the way it should, this stuff [the crown wardship process] should be straightforward."

.   "Getting over the magical hump" also requires belief. In reference to an older child's wishes about adoption the worker says, "They don't know what's in their best interest. They don't know yet. But we believe, somehow, that it will be ok, well, we have to believe that it will be." Acceptance of the system, as evidenced by adhering to established procedures, and belief in an outcome that "will be OK" appear to be the necessary ingredients for workers to remain in the system and participate repeatedly in the crown wardship process.

Overview of Findings

Figure 1 provides an overview of the conceptual model that emerged for this analysis. The formal structure of the child welfare system comprises the legislative/legal requirements and the organizational structures and procedures. This structure is the context in which crown wardship stories unfold. Each of the stories consists of an introduction, a plot, and a resolution, which correspond respectively to the identifying, the chance-giving and the negotiating and formalizing stages of the crown wardship process. It is also within this formal context that workers construct new identities to cope with the emotional demands of participating in the crown wardship process. Strategies for de-individualizing lead to the construction of new identities and to an acceptance of their role within the child protection system.

Child welfare workers construct identities to soothe the conflicting emotions that arise when this tension comes to the fore. The child welfare worker's experience of the crown wardship process reveals that workers must embrace a specific system of beliefs in order to manage their emotions in relation to this process. Part of the socialization of new workers involves the development of an almost standardized set of beliefs about the crown wardship process. Workers who deviate from these beliefs are branded by their peers as "new" or "immature" and are subjected to meetings designed to "bring them on board with the plan," all of which are powerful messages about conforming. It seems untenable that a worker could maintain an individual identity as a decision maker in the context of the crown wardship process.

Figure 1: Relationships between the Narrative Structure, Phases of the Permanent Placement Process, and Worker Coping

I suspect that those who make such an attempt are forced by workplace pressure, and by emotional discomfort, to leave.

Reflections

This research was motivated by a need to understand my experience of participating in making permanent-placement decisions. At the beginning of my involvement with child welfare, I believed that the work of saving abused children, through placement in loving, nurturing environments, would be challenging but ultimately satisfying. Instead, I discovered that the work of placing children in foster care was deeply troubling and the feelings associated with the process were confusing.

At the outset of this research project, I was troubled by my child welfare experiences, and confused and angered by workers who were able to remain in child welfare settings. As I listened and reflected on my own work, this confusion and anger seemed to give way to a new compassion. I began to see how child welfare workers are in a "no-win situation," and how there is a prevailing need to find comfort when the work is emotionally exhausting and deeply troubling. I began to see how I too was caught in a web of intense contradiction. Like the workers that I interviewed, the child welfare identities that I had constructed emerged in my stories about mothers and the crown wardship process. I can recall how these identities helped me to manage emotional conflicts, and how painful it was when the identities were not sustaining.

Now, as I position myself as an autonomous decision maker, dilemmas about how I managed the emotions of the work give way to concerns about how the child protection system continues to reinforce and maintain environments where emotional distance from parents is a requirement for survival. I ask myself why the child protection system continues to create situations for workers where the pressures to conform are intense, and why in permanent-placement situations a shield of constructed identity is necessary for survival. I ask myself, what were the costs to the mothers and to the children on my caseloads when the processes of de-individualizing and constructing a new collective identity became central to my socialization as a child protection service provider? How did these processes colour my understanding of their needs and impact my decisions?

Conclusions

The strategies that workers use for emotional coping may not be sufficient in the current climate of child protection in Ontario. Child welfare workers are conducting more investigations[1] and placing an increased number of children into substitute care.[2] Worker dissatisfaction, employee turnover, and burnout persist in systems of child protection (Cameron, Freymond, Cornfield & Palmer, 2001; Daley, 1979; Teram, 1988). A recent study from one of Ontario's child welfare agencies shows that, in 1999 and 2000 combined, 79% of family service workers transferred or terminated, as did 93% of intake workers. These authors suggest that these retention problems are not related to market influences such as a strong economy and more mobile workforce but rather to "specific stresses, expectations and job design of the protection positions" (Coulthard et al., 2001, p. 5).

Gilroy writes that child welfare workers are "working at enormous costs to their own health and the integrity and effectiveness of the jobs they do" (1999, p. 30). The inherent complexities of child welfare work, coupled with difficult working conditions, cause concern that decisions may become grounded in the necessity of managing the strains of the work, as opposed to responding to the needs of the families in question. Although this study is limited to the views of six workers in an agency in Ontario, it does point to the need for further research into the experiences of front-line child welfare workers and how they cope with the strains inherent in their work.

At the heart of the crown wardship process is the tension between preserving families and child removal. Child welfare workers need strategies to cope emotionally with their work. Placing children in substitute care is, and should be, an emotional event. However, the intense processes that workers undergo in order to cope emotionally with the contradictions of their work colour the relationships they are able to develop with families and children. The needs of vulnerable families and children become defined and shaped in a context of worker coping. The coping processes of workers, likewise, colour interventions with families and children. To keep the needs of families and of children central to the work of child welfare, workers must be able to hear and to respond creatively and flexibly to the needs of children and families. They require workplaces where they are encouraged to develop supportive helping relationships with families and to maintain their identity as individual decision makers, rather than pressured to conform to standardized beliefs.

Child welfare systems require sustaining processes of communication in which front-line workers can share experiences and find emotional validation. Meaningful dialogue may lead to new understanding of worker experience and the profound dilemmas that they are required to manage in their daily practices. Child welfare families require processes of communication in which they can share their experiences of child welfare involvements, and likewise find validation. And service users and service professionals need mechanisms to build relationships where the needs of families can not only be known but be central to the development of positive and meaningful practices of child welfare.

Viable alternatives to our current system of child protection do exist. In many non-Anglo-American nations and First Nations cultures, child welfare practices, and the nature of the relationships between workers and families that ensue, are different from what we find within our system. Workers are encouraged to use their professional talents in developing creative and proactive interventions in response to child maltreatment concerns (Cooper, Hetherington, Baistow, Pitts, & Spriggs, 1995; Hetherington, Cooper, Smith, & Wilford, 1997; Marneffe & Broos, 1997). Within these systems, relationships between child welfare workers and families may not be as intensely impacted by contradictions. Worker morale and turnover were not reported to be central issues.

Although particular methods may not be directly transportable across systems, cross-cultural comparisons are useful for stimulating awareness of alternate possibilities and for prompting the rethinking of emphases that currently dominate our system. The knowledge that child welfare workers in other systems may be able to effectively respond to issues of child maltreatment in an emotionally sustainable work environment generates interest in further research and hope for a different future for our present system. The work of child welfare can and must be accomplished within morally and emotionally sustainable work environments where workers can respond flexibly to the needs of families and children.

Notes

1 In Ontario, between April 1, 2002, and March 31, 2003, child welfare organizations responded to a total of 236,430 calls, 34% of which met the eligibility requirements of a child in need of protection and would be responded to by a child protection worker. This figure represents a 47% increase since 1998 (Ontario Association of Children's Aid Societies, 2003).

2 In Ontario, substitute care was provided to 30,291 children during the 12-month period of April 1, 2002–March 31, 2003. This represents a 28% increase from 1998–1999. On March 31, 2003, there were 18,126 children in substitute care. This is a 40% increase in the number of children in care since March 31, 1998 (Ontario Association of Children's Aid Societies, 2003).

References

Alvesson, M., & Skoldberg, K. (2000). *Reflexive methodology: New vistas for qualitative research.* London: Sage.

Callahan, M. (1993). Feminist approaches: Women recreate child welfare. In B. Wharf (Ed.), *Rethinking child welfare in Canada* (pp. 172–209). Toronto, ON: Oxford University Press.

Cameron, G., Freymond, N., Cornfield, D., & Palmer, S. (2001). *Positive possibilities for child and family welfare: Options for expanding the Anglo-American child protection paradigm.* Waterloo, ON: Wilfrid Laurier University, Partnerships for Children and Families Project.

Charmaz, K. (2000). Objectivist and constructivist methods. In N. K. Denzin & Y. S. Lincoln (Eds.), *Handbook of qualitative inquiry* (2nd ed., pp. 509–535). Thousand Oaks, CA: Sage.

Cooper, A., Hetherington, R., Baistow, K., Pitts, J., & Spriggs, A. (1995). *Positive child protection: A view from abroad.* Lyme Regis, UK: Russell House.

Costin, L. B., Karger, H. J., & Stoesz, D. (1996). *The politics of child abuse in America*. New York: Oxford University Press.

Coulthard, C., Duncan, K., Goranson, S., Hewson, L., Howe, P., Lee, K., et al. (2001). Report on staff retention. Toronto, ON: Children's Aid Society of Toronto.

Daley, M. (1979). Preventing worker burnout in child welfare. *Child Welfare, 58*, 443–450.

Esposito, G., & Fine, M. (1985). The field of child welfare as a world of work. In J. Laird & A. Hartman (Eds.), *A handbook of child welfare: Context, knowledge and practice* (pp. 727–740). New York: Free Press.

Frost, N., & Stein, M. (1989). *The politics of child welfare: Inequality, power and change*. Worcester, UK: Billing and Sons.

Gergen, K. (1999). *An invitation to social construction*. London: Sage.

Gilroy, J. (1999). Critical issues in child welfare: Perspectives from the field. In L. Dominelli (Ed.). *Community approaches to child welfare: International perspectives* (pp. 25–44). Aldershot, UK: Ashgate.

Hatton, M. J., Campbell, G., Colarftoni, H., Ferron, R., Huyer, D., Ortiz, T.J., et al. (1998). *Protecting vulnerable children*. Toronto, ON: Ministry of Community and Social Services.

Hetherington, R., Cooper, A., Smith, P., & Wilford, G. (1997). *Protecting children: Messages from Europe*. Dorset, UK: Russell House.

Jones, A., & Rutman, L. (1981). *In the children's aid: J.J. Kelso and child welfare in Ontario*. Toronto, ON: University of Toronto Press.

Katz, S. (1971). *When parents fail*. Boston: Beacon Press.

Kufeldt, K., Vachon, J., Simard, M., Baker, J., & Andrews, T. L. (2000). *Looking after children in Canada: Final Report*. Fredericton, NB: University of New Brunswick, Muriel McQueen Fergusson Family Violence Research Centre, and The Social Development Partnerships Division of Human Resources Development Canada.

Marneffe, C., & Broos, P. (1997). Belgium: An alternative approach to child abuse reporting and treatment. In N. Gilbert (Ed.), *Combatting child abuse: International perspectives and trends* (pp. 167–191). New York: Oxford University Press.

Margolin, L. (1997). *Under the cover of kindness: The invention of social work*. Charlottesville, NC: University of Virginia Press.

Miller, J. (1991). Child welfare and the role of women: A feminist perspective. *American Journal of Orthopsychiatry, 61*(4), 592–598.

Ontario Association of Children's Aid Societies. (2003). *CAS facts: April 1, 2002–March 31, 2003*. Retrieved Nov 18, 2003, from http://www.oacas.org/resources/CAS%20Facts%20Ap02Mar03.pdf

Palmer, S. E. (1995). *Maintaining family ties: Inclusive practice in foster care*. Washington, DC: Child Welfare League of America.

Polansky, N., Chalmers, M. A., Buttenweiser, E., & Williams, D. (1981). *Damaged parents: An anatomy of child neglect*. Chicago: University of Chicago Press.

Regehr, C., Bernstein, M., & Kanani, K. (2002). Liability for child welfare social workers: Weighing the risks. *OACAS Journal, 46*(1), 32–39.

Riessman, C. K. (1993). *Story analysis.* Newbury Park, CA: Sage.

Roberts, D. (1999). Mothers who fail to protect their children: Accounting for private and public responsibility. In J. Hanigsberg & S. Ruddick (Eds.), *Mother Troubles* (pp. 29–49). Boston: Beacon Press.

Ryan, G. W., & Bernard, H. R. (2000). Data management and analysis methods. In N. K. Denzin & Y. S. Lincoln (Eds.), *Handbook of qualitative research* (2nd ed., pp. 769–802). Thousand Oaks, CA: Sage.

Spradley, J. P. (1979*). The ethnographic interview.* New York: Holt, Rinehart & Winston.

Steinhauer, P. (1984). The management of children admitted to child welfare services in Ontario: A review and discussion of current problems and practices. *Canadian Journal of Psychiatry, 29,* 473–484.

Strauss, A. L., & Corbin, J. (1990). *Basics of qualitative research: Grounded theory procedures and techniques.* Newbury Park, CA: Sage.

Strauss, A. L., & Corbin, J. (1998). *Basics of qualitative research: Techniques and procedures for developing grounded theory* (2nd ed.). Thousand Oaks, CA: Sage.

Swift, K. J. (1995). *Manufacturing 'bad mothers': A critical perspective on child neglect.* Toronto, ON: University of Toronto Press.

Swift, K. J. (1998). Contradictions in child welfare: Neglect and responsibility. In C. Baines, P. Evans, & S. Neysmith (Eds.), *Women's caring: Feminist perspectives on social welfare* (pp. 160–190). Toronto, ON: Oxford University Press.

Swift, K. J., & Callahan, M. (2002). *Problems and potential of Canadian child welfare.* Waterloo, ON: Wilfrid Laurier University, Partnerships for Children and Families Project.

Teram, E. (1988). From self-managed hearts to collective action: Dealing with incompatible demands in the child welfare system. *Children and Youth Services Review 10,* 305–315.

Welsh, M., & Donovan, K. (1997, June 21). How to save children. *Toronto Star,* p. A1.

Wiehe, V. R. (1996). *Working with child abuse and neglect: A primer.* Thousand Oaks, CA: Sage.

Young, L. (1964). *Wednesday's children.* New York: McGraw-Hill.

|7|

Understanding and Preventing Burnout and Employee Turnover

Cheryl Harvey
Carol A. Stalker

When you do your job well in child welfare you are only rewarded with more. In the past year I have lost sight of the value of my life outside of my work. I have become consumed by what I can't accomplish at work. The emphasis on paperwork prevents quality interaction and actual assistance being provided to clients. I am not winning the race but I am supporting my clients as best I can within all the limitations that exist.

It's not a particular event (i.e. a crisis, death on my case load) that has led me to start a job search, it's the cumulative effect of having *way* too many details, not enough time to accomplish what I need to, and the impact the stress of overtime/deadlines has on myself. As well, it breaks my heart that this stress is obviously spilling over onto my child ... I don't always feel I have the emotional energy left over for her.

These passages are taken from comments written by two direct service workers on a survey they completed as part of a study of the workplace experience of child welfare workers in Ontario in 2002. They highlight common experiences of the emotional impact on those who work in child welfare: stress, emotional exhaustion, and burnout. The latter passage also points to one person's way of dealing with this impact—leaving the organization.

Research on burnout began with human service workers in the early 1970s (Maslach & Schaufeli, 1993). Most of the social work literature on burnout studied child welfare workers (Jayartne & Chess, 1984), and it is generally assumed that burnout is very high in child welfare settings. As will become clear in this chapter, burnout is usually understood to result from ongoing stress in the workplace that, over time, impairs functioning on the job and in the individual's personal life.

A common assumption is that burned-out workers leave their jobs. While many studies (Cordes & Dougherty, 1993; Leiter & Harvie, 1996; Lee & Ashforth, 1996; Manlove & Guzell, 1997) found that workers who score high on burnout measures are intending to leave their jobs, some studies (e.g. Manlove & Guzell, 1997), including one with child welfare workers (Drake & Yadama, 1996), have found that some workers do not quit but become cynical about their clients and distance themselves emotionally. Clearly, if cynical, emotionally detached workers stay in their positions and communicate uncaring and devaluing attitudes toward vulnerable children and families, the consequences are serious.

In addition, child welfare agencies have identified worker turnover as a particularly problematic organizational issue. For example, the Children's Aid Society of Toronto recently reported that annual turnover among its family service workers tripled from 1997 to 2000, and intake worker turnover increased from 10% to 18% during the same period. In addition, many front-line workers transferred to other positions in the organization as those became available (Coulthard et al., 2001). This same study cites reports of turnover in other child welfare agencies, identifying annual turnover at 40% and higher among family service workers.

Turnover is costly to organizations and high turnover radically escalates costs related to the money spent in recruiting, selecting, and training new staff. But there are other costs too: the costs borne by a child or a family who lose, at minimum, a sense of continuity with a worker, costs related to the impact on co-workers of seeing a valued colleague leave, the costs of the increased workloads assumed by others who must do more until a replacement is found and up-to-speed, and the costs of losing the knowledge and skills that extensive experience creates.

Certainly, both burnout and turnover have the potential to become serious concerns in child welfare organizations. This chapter begins with an overview of research on employee turnover, exploring first a simple model of turnover in organizations before discussing recent innovations in theories about how unwanted turnover occurs. Next, we turn our attention to burnout in human service workers, with an emphasis on findings relevant to social workers and other professionals in child welfare and the organizations that employ them. We describe how the concept of burnout is usually operationalized, identify the variables empirically associated with burnout and thought to be its antecedents and consequences, and summarize a theoretical model that offers an explanation of the causes of burnout and its relationship to other forms of stress, coping and organizational processes. We briefly present some findings from our workplace study of four child welfare agencies mentioned above and conclude with suggestions for preventing burnout and turnover in child welfare organizations.

The Roots of Turnover

Managers use turnover levels as indicators of organizational well-being. They assume that low turnover (in combination with other indicators such as low grievance rates and absenteeism) means that employees are satisfied with their work and their working conditions. On the other hand, managers know that high turnover generally means that something, or several things, are going wrong. Managers may examine their organization's recruitment and selection procedures, its pay and recognition practices, its design of particular jobs, its training and development systems, how its managers interact with their staff, whether people have the resources to do their jobs, and so on. Managers do this to search for the answer to a problem and sometimes err in the solution, because they assume a single cause rather than a complex interweaving of multiple factors. This section will demonstrate that turnover is a result of organizational factors, some of which managers can control and some that they cannot. The latter group includes, for example, economic factors, characteristics of individual employees, and government regulations. All these play a role in an individual's decision to voluntarily leave an organization.

We begin by briefly defining the type of turnover we are interested in. Then we describe some highlights in the history of turnover research before turning to focus on a simple model of how turnover happens that we have developed from the findings of recent reviews of this literature. We conclude this section with some current innovations in thinking about the decision processes individuals use when choosing to leave an organization.

Employee turnover is measured at the organizational level. It is defined as the number of people who leave an organization, either voluntarily or through managerial action, over the course of a year, calculated as a percentage of the number of employees in the organization. Turnover within an organization is also often measured by work unit (department, division) or by position (intake worker, receptionist, youth worker).

The research on employee turnover distinguishes between voluntary and involuntary turnover. Involuntary turnover occurs when a person is fired, laid off, or retires at the age specified by the organization or legislation. Voluntary turnover is viewed as the employee's choice, although researchers acknowledge that some "voluntary" turnover occurs when some people who leave an organization are actually responding to management pressure. Others decide to leave because they are dissatisfied in some way with their current position, or because a spouse is relocating, they return to university, have a child, and so on. Therefore, some voluntary turnover is beyond the organization's control, but some may be preventable if organizations understand its origins. We are primarily interested in voluntary turnover, or turnover initiated by the individual.

A Simplified Model of Turnover Research

Voluntary turnover research began with work on understanding the impact of job attitudes[1] on employees' behaviours at work. Steers and Mowday (1983) traced the history of researchers' interests in job attitudes. They noted that, in a 1955 review of which job attitudes might be related to subsequent employee turnover, Brayfield and Crockett (as cited in Steers & Mowday, 1983) found low job satisfaction to be correlated with higher turnover. The relationship was not a strong one, suggesting that there was a lot more leading to turnover than simply whether one was satisfied with one's job.

March and Simon (1958) moved beyond looking at simple one-to-one relationships between a job attitude and a single behaviour to examine the state of theories about the structure of organizations and how people working in organizations behave. They proposed that a person's decision to participate in an organization was the result of a complicated rational process. They concluded that a desire to leave an organization is a result of both individuals' level of satisfaction with their jobs and their perception of alternatives for creating more satisfaction within the organization. Further, they saw satisfaction as a product of (a) the fit between a person's self-image and the job's characteristics, (b) the predictability of the work environment, and (c) the compatibility of work requirements with those of other roles a person occupies. A dissatisfied person might seek to transfer within the organization to another, more attractive position, or they might want to leave. Before a person could actually leave however, March and Simon proposed that they had to find a viable alternative to their current position. This would be more likely: (a) in good economic times, (b) when many other organizations are "visible" alternatives, and (c) when the person's own characteristics make them more attractive to another organization (for example, they are relatively young or highly skilled; March & Simon, 1958).

Notice that March and Simon pointed to factors at several different levels affecting an individual's decision to stay or leave an organization. These include characteristics of the individual, the job itself, the person's nonwork life, relationships with others in the organization, the reward and decision-making systems in the organization, the external economic environment, and the labour market.

March and Simon's model of turnover set the stage for decades of research that sought to capture all factors that lead to job satisfaction and to turnover. Thousands of articles that attempt to tease out the relationships among an ever-increasing number of variables have been published. Most of this research has been done in business and large public-sector organizations, although the researchers' conclusions have generally been supported in the smaller number of studies in human service organizations.

Figure 1 shows the types of antecedents to turnover and the relationships among them that researchers have studied. This figure and Table 1 below reflect (but greatly simplify) the conclusions of several recent reviews of the turnover literature, notably the reviews by Barak, Nissly, and Levin (2001), Griffeth, Hom, and Gaertner (2000), Hom and Griffeth (1995), Irvine and Evans (1995), Kossek and Ozeki (1999), Lease (1998), Lee, Carswell, and Allen (2000), and Tai, Bame, and Robinson (1998). In addition, several recent studies focusing on human service organizations were consulted, and their conclusions are incorporated. Interested readers are encouraged to consult the original sources for the details of this research.

Figure 1 shows the antecedents of turnover organized into five categories: characteristics of individuals; factors that are a part of the job itself and how it is done; factors that relate to the organization and its practices and procedures; job attitudes (especially job satisfaction and organizational commitment) and states (job burnout) that develop as a result of the interaction of personal, job, and organizational factors; and individual behaviours and intentions viewed as more immediate, or proximal, to actual turnover.

Generally, researchers view the relationships among the types of turnover antecedents as working in the following ways. Individuals bring to their workplace a set of characteristics consisting of personality and demographic features, friendships, family, and non-work responsibilities. These provide the ingredients for both personal support and work conflict and a degree of affinity for their current occupation. People become members of a workplace that also has its own characteristics. These workplace characteristics are organized into factors related closely to the particular job an individual performs and factors that are imbedded in the organization as a whole. Job factors include the degree of freedom or autonomy that a person has to make decisions, how challenging the job is (job scope), the degree of role clarity, overload, and conflict present, and the degree of support provided to do the job. Organizational factors consist of established human-resource management policies (for example, pay and benefit rates and promotion practices) and cultural elements (for example, leadership style and justice practices), as well as some externally determined attributes such as the organization's reputation.

Some organizational factors, such as leadership style and culture, influence how specific jobs are designed, so the model shows an arrow from organization factors to job factors. For example, formal, hierarchical organizations like banks or a government departments often define their jobs in extremely clear, narrow ways—creating jobs with low autonomy, high role clarity, and close supervision. Organizations employing human-service professionals often include positions involving more autonomy and less

Figure 1: A Simplified Model of Voluntary Turnover

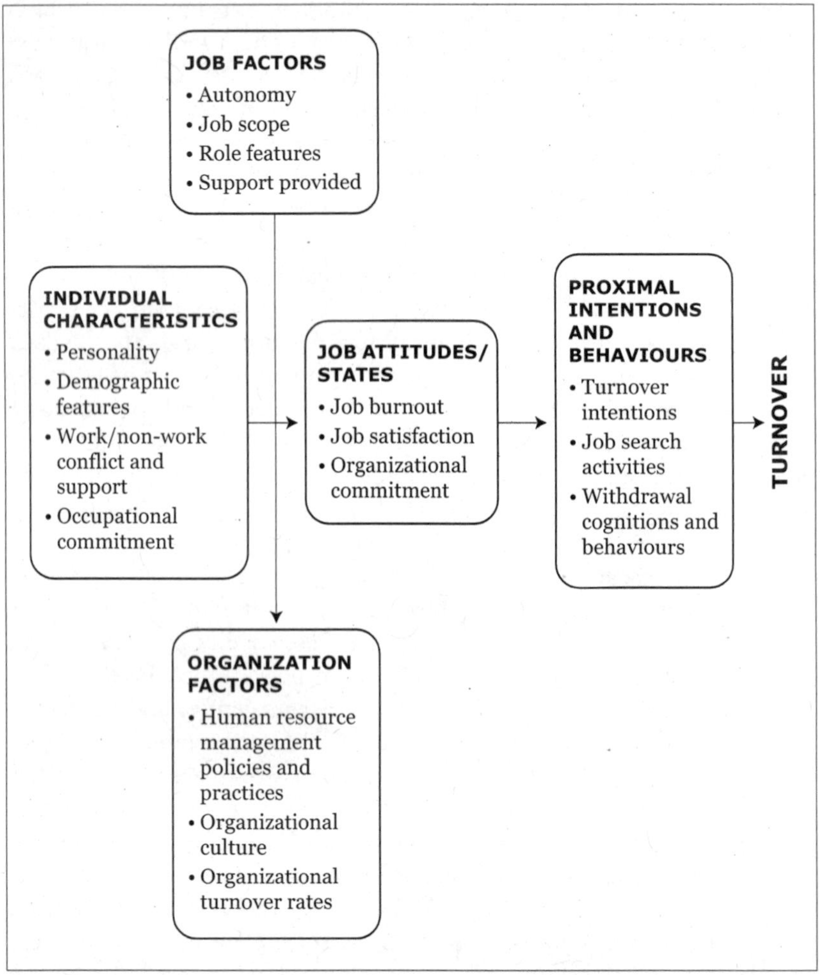

JOB FACTORS
- Autonomy
- Job scope
- Role features
- Support provided

INDIVIDUAL CHARACTERISTICS
- Personality
- Demographic features
- Work/non-work conflict and support
- Occupational commitment

JOB ATTITUDES/ STATES
- Job burnout
- Job satisfaction
- Organizational commitment

PROXIMAL INTENTIONS AND BEHAVIOURS
- Turnover intentions
- Job search activities
- Withdrawal cognitions and behaviours

TURNOVER

ORGANIZATION FACTORS
- Human resource management policies and practices
- Organizational culture
- Organizational turnover rates

supervision and rely on professionals' training and adherence to codes of ethics to regulate appropriate behaviour. Child welfare agencies are complex in that they employ professionally trained workers to provide skilled intervention with children and families but also serve a government function involving civil and human rights. This function requires close adherence to legal requirements. This complexity contributes to the challenge in understanding factors that contribute to turnover in child welfare workplaces.

As the model indicates, individuals respond to the features of their jobs and their organizations. They develop job attitudes, such as job satisfaction and organizational commitment, and psychological states, such as job burnout. When individuals feel low job satisfaction, low commitment to their organization, or high burnout, they may form high intentions to leave their jobs. This results in job search behaviours, such as preparing a résumé, beginning to look elsewhere, and, ultimately, actual turnover. Thus, the model is an overview of how individuals' experience of their job and its organizational context combine to create attitudes that may ultimately lead to turnover.

Figure 1 illustrates a simple model, because it does not include the myriad of variables, interactions, and feedback loops that researchers have pursued. Although exploring these in detail is beyond the scope of this chapter, we examined the reviews of the turnover literature to create the following table summarizing the authors' conclusions about the factors that influence turnover.

Table 1 lists the antecedents to turnover investigated by researchers, organized by the same five categories as in the earlier figure. Most of the individual, job, and organizational variables do not directly affect turnover intentions. Instead, they have their major impact on job attitudes or psychological states as the model in Figure 1 indicates. Many of these variables have a very slight impact on actual turnover, while others are more significant. In the table, an asterisk indicates variables that researchers have found to be more strongly related to turnover intentions or actual turnover.

Considerable evidence shows that, across a wide variety of occupational groups, the best predictor of actual turnover is turnover intention. Since the next best predictors of turnover are organizational commitment and overall job satisfaction (Griffith et al, 2000; Hom & Griffeth, 1995; Lease, 1998), research has focused on discovering the list of individual, job, and organizational factors that predict organizational commitment and job satisfaction. As the reader can see, there are many variables related to turnover and to job attitudes, often in intuitive ways. For example, low opportunity for promotion is related to higher turnover, as is low work-group cohesion and high work–family conflict (Hom & Griffeth, 1995). These variables are significantly related to low job satisfaction and low organizational commitment, which are, in turn, related to higher intentions to leave a job.

Researchers who have conducted their studies in human-service organizations have looked at some factors of particular interest to them. For example, Hatton and Emerson (1998) found that public respect for the job workers were doing was related to turnover. Baker and Baker (1999) concluded that perceived differences in ideology among workers affected their commitment to the organization. In human-services organizations, job stress or job burnout also may be a relatively strong predictor of turnover (Barak et al., 2001; Barrett, Riggar, Flowers, Crimando, & Bailey, 1997), although this variable has rarely been included in private sector studies.

Table 1: A Summary of Individual and Organizational Variables Related to Higher Turnover

Individual Factors	Job and Organizational Factors	Job Attitudes/States	Proximal Intentions and Behaviours

Personality Features
• positive affectivity (high)
• conscientiousness (high)
• agreeableness (high)
Demographic Factors
• dependents/kinship responsibility (high)
• tenure (high)
• career stage
• age
Conflict and Support
• work–non-work (family) conflict (high)
• supportive family and friends (low)
• community embeddedness (low)
Occupational Factors
• occupational commitment (low)
• occupational turnover intention (high)
• scripts* (see section on the unfolding model)
	Job Factors
	• autonomy (low)
	• role clarity (low)
	• role overload, conflict (high)
	• job scope (high challenge and complexity vs. routinization)
	• work group cohesion (low)
	• co-worker support (low)
	• supervisory support (low)
	Organization Factors
	• human resource management policies and practices
	  • flexibility (low)
	  • corporate day care
	  • competitive pay rates
	  • contingent rewards
	  • competitive benefits
	  • promotion practices (unfair)
	  • mentoring
	• distributive, interactional, & procedural justice (low)
	• promotional opportunity (low)
	• promotion satisfaction (low)
	• leadership culture
	• organizational turnover rates* (high)
	• public respect (low)
		• job satisfaction* (low)
		• organizational commitment* (low)
		• job burnout* (high)
		• image violation* (high)
		• job embeddedness* (low)
			• turnover intentions* (high)
			• intention to stay* (low)
			• job search activities* (high)
			• perceiving alternatives* (high)
			• withdrawal cognitions* (high)
			• withdrawal behaviours* (high) (lateness, absence, performance reduction)

Note: An asterisk (*) indicates a strong relationship of the antecedent variable to actual turnover or turnover intentions. The other variables listed here are significantly related to one or more job attitudes or states. Descriptors such as low or high refer to the variable's relationship to higher turnover intentions or actual turnover. For example, low autonomy is related to high turnover intentions.

Most research on turnover and its antecedents examines just one or two parts of the model we described above. As a result, we know quite a lot about, for example, the influence of equitable rewards on organizational commitment and about the importance of autonomy or control to professionals in determining job satisfaction, but we still cannot predict actual turnover with much certainty. In fact, a close look at the empirical findings reveals that the accuracy with which one can predict voluntary turnover is actually quite low. As Lee and colleagues (1999) point out, Hom and Griffeth's (1995) comprehensive meta-analysis demonstrated that the "proportion of variance shared by levels of satisfaction and turnover is 3.6 percent, and the proportion shared by intention to leave and actual leaving is 12 percent" (Lee, Mitchell, Holtom, McDaniel, & Hill, 1999).

Obviously, we must acknowledge that research focusing only on understanding job satisfaction, organizational commitment, and so on, is not advancing our knowledge of why individuals might decide to stay with or leave an organization. However, this research has been indispensable in improving our understanding of how managers can create workplaces in which high job satisfaction and organizational commitment are commonplace. We will use this understanding later in our discussion about how child welfare managers can prevent or reduce turnover. In this next section, however, we describe a promising new theory of the decision process people use to determine whether to leave a job. Awareness of this process can lead to more opportunities to reduce organizational turnover.

Theoretical Innovations: The Unfolding Model and Job Embeddedness

The Unfolding Model. In 1994, recognizing that current ways of thinking about antecedents to turnover were not leading to significant contributions, Lee and Mitchell proposed an alternative theory they termed the "unfolding model." According to Lee and colleagues (1999), most previous turnover theories assumed that a rational choice process precedes employee resignations. That is, the process begins with low job satisfaction, leads to searching for, evaluating, and selecting another job, and quitting only when one has accepted another job offer. The difficulty is, Lee and Mitchell (1994) observed, it doesn't always happen that way. People who are very satisfied with their jobs also leave them, prompted by some event. These events have different attributes, that is, they may be positive or negative, expected or unexpected. Some people even quit without searching for another job.

Prompted by this puzzle, Lee and Mitchell conducted informal interviews with people who had left their jobs and spent "many hours in conversation and debate" (Lee & Mitchell, 1994). The unfolding model they propose asserts that previous research on turnover had focused on only one path that people follow and that there are at least three other possible scenarios.

Two concepts or constructs are crucial to understanding the unfolding model. The first of these is "shock," which is "a particular, jarring event that initiates the psychological analyses involved in quitting a job" (Lee et al., 1999, p. 451). A shock can be positive, negative, or neutral; expected or unexpected; and internal or external to the person experiencing it. Unsolicited job offers, transfers, firm mergers, changes in marital status, a poor performance evaluation, and admission to graduate school are all examples of shocks. The unfolding model proposes that when people encounter a shock, they evaluate it in the context of their own experience and make a decision about what to do.

Some people, when reacting to a shock, find and resort to a "script" for their response. This is the second important concept in the model. A script is a pre-existing plan of action based on a person's prior experience, on observations of others in the same or a similar situation, on reading, or on perceived social expectations. It serves as a decision rule in the situation. We will use examples to illustrate these two concepts in action as we describe the four paths leading to turnover in the unfolding model.

In the first example, a social worker is responsible for the outcome of a particularly challenging and successful case conference attended by employees of several agencies. A manager from one of the other agencies approaches the worker to ask her to consider a supervisory position that has been vacant in his organization for some time. They chat about the position over a spontaneous lunch meeting. The offer flatters and shocks the worker, who thinks it over quickly and accepts later that afternoon. The worker searched her memory for any experience of similar shocks and quickly found that a similar request had led to her taking her current job. So, in this instance, there was a shock and a ready script to enact; there was no job dissatisfaction, no image violation, nor search for other alternatives. This type of turnover decision represents Lee and Mitchell's Path One in the unfolding model depicted below (Lee and Mitchell, 1994).

Path One: Shock → Script? → Yes → Quit

In Path Two, the shock leads to an image violation and reconsideration of the employee's attachment to the organization. After some thought, the employee leaves the organization without searching for alternatives. Consider this example: A social worker swears angrily and loudly after a phone conversation with a client. He is completely surprised and appalled by his reaction to his client. He has never done this before and experiences a shock at his own behaviour. When he thinks about what he has done, the image of himself as an easy-going person who can handle almost anything is violated, and he reconsiders whether he wants to work at this agency. He types his resignation, thinks about it overnight, and hands it in the next day before leaving for home.

Path Two: Shock→ Script? → No→ Image Violation? → Yes→ Quit

In Path Three, the shock and image violation lead to lower job satisfaction, which leads to a search for and an evaluation of alternatives. If this leads to the perception that another option fits with the person's image, the employee resigns. For example, a family services worker receives a call from a police officer informing her that the child in a family with whom she has been working has been killed by his mother. One result of this call is that the worker evaluates her own perception of her competence. Despite reassurance from her supervisor and others on her team, she judges herself incompetent and becomes very dissatisfied with her job. She begins to look for another position and eventually receives an offer from a community mental health organization. In this job, she would be working with adults experiencing problems in their workplaces. She feels that doing this would fit better with her goal of helping others improve their lives, and she resigns from her current position.

Path Three: Shock→ Script? → No→ Image Violation? → Yes→
Reduced Job Satisfaction → Search → Alternatives? → Yes→
Image Fit? → Yes → Quit

Path three could also be entered through a positive shock. For example, if we use the situation described in path one, in which there is an unsolicited job offer, but there is no ready script, then path three could unfold with the social worker assessing whether the position offered fits better with what she wants than does her current position or some other option. Job dissatisfaction could be relatively small in this case.

In Path Four, there is no shock, and therefore no script is engaged. Here, employees engage in a periodic evaluation of whether the job and the organization continue to meet their needs. Over time, both organizations and people change, so this sporadic check is a thoughtful assessment of whether the fit with image is continuing or not. If not, the image violation leads to lower levels of satisfaction, then to lower organizational commitment, job search, alternatives, intention to quit, and turnover. This is the path that has been extensively explored by turnover researchers (as has the part of path three from reduced job satisfaction onward). Lee and Mitchell (1994) label this path Four B. Realizing that some people behave differently once they realize they are dissatisfied with their job—they just quit, without searching for other alternatives, Lee and Mitchell designated this shorter path as Four A.

Path Four A: Image Violation? → Yes → Reduced Job
Satisfaction → Quit

Path Four B: Image Violation? → Yes → Reduced Job
Satisfaction → Search → Alternatives? → Yes → Image Fit? → Yes → Quit

The paths take different lengths of time to unfold. Paths one and two move quickly, in days or weeks, whereas paths three and four can take a very long time. In the latter case, dissatisfaction may take a long time to build. In paths three and four, the search for and evaluation of alternatives, including non-work options, can also take a long time (Mitchell, Holtom, & Lee, 2001).

Mitchell, Holtom, and Lee (2001) summarize the empirical support for the unfolding model. They report five studies (for details, see Lee et al., 1999; Mitchell, Holtom, Lee, Sablynski, & Eraz, 2001) that used a combination of qualitative and quantitative approaches. These studies found that most people leave organizations via path three (52% over three samples) or path four B (30%), taking time to search for other alternatives and assessing an image fit before quitting their current positions. Five percent left following path one, 6% path two, and 7% path four A. Notice that this means that 63% left following some initial shock, and that about 18% left without searching for an alternative. Job dissatisfaction plays a role in 95% of decisions to quit, although it is an initiating factor in just 37% of the situations examined in this collection of studies. "In combination, these data help to explain why the traditionally studied variables of job dissatisfaction and alternatives aren't strongly predictive of turnover. A lot of people leave without alternatives or as a result of some shocking event that may not be associated with job dissatisfaction" (Mitchell, Holtom, & Lee, 2001).

Hom and Griffeth (1995) called the unfolding model a "refreshing new perspective," and point out that the unfolding theory also gives greater attention to the origin of the turnover process, which had been neglected by earlier theories. Others have begun to test the unfolding model in their research. For example, Somers and Birnbaum (1999), Somers (1999), and Morrell, Loan-Clarke, and Wilkinson (2004) have found support for this new way of thinking about turnover.

Job embeddedness. Their explorations of the unfolding model to understand why and how people leave organizations led Lee and Mitchell and their colleagues to investigate the opposite—why people stay. They created the concept of job embeddedness to explain staying in organizations (Mitchell, Holtom, & Lee, 2001; Mitchell, Holtom, Lee et al., 2001; Mitchell & Lee, 2001).

Mitchell and Lee (2001) state that there are three factors influencing people to stay in their jobs:

(1) the extent to which one has strong attachments to people or groups on-the-job and in their community; (2) the extent to which they fit or are a good match with their job and community; and (3) the degree to which they would have to give up or sacrifice things if they left their job. We label these factors: links, fit, and sacrifice. (p. 35)

Links are the formal and informal connections a person has on or off the job with other individuals or groups, resulting in a "web of attachments" that range in number and importance. For example, the importance of work relationships with co-workers, management, supervisors, and unions have all been mentioned by researchers as having an effect on turnover intentions. Some reports also discuss the impact of family relationships on turnover decisions, and others say that non-family links (church, recreational) are also important. Mitchell and Lee (2001) believe the number of links put pressure on a person to stay; in addition, they believe that family and friends bring normative ("shoulds," "values") pressures to bear on a person considering leaving a job.

Fit is "an individual's compatibility with their work and non-work settings" (Mitchell & Lee, 2001, p. 37). On-the-job fit has been studied for decades. Turnover increases when people see that they do not fit their job, organization, or their occupation (Mitchell & Lee, 2001). They assess fit along a number of dimensions, including skills, climate, values, problem-solving style, and congruence with supervisors' perceptions of culture. Mitchell and Lee (2001) propose that off-the-job fit is also important and discuss ideas such as fit with the cultural and recreational life of a city.

Sacrifice is viewed as "the things that someone must relinquish or give up when leaving a job. It is the perceived loss of material or psychological benefits that currently are available or will be available in the future" (Mitchell & Lee, 2001, p. 39). They include job stability and future opportunities such as training and promotion, the investments people have made in understanding how their current organization works both formally and informally, and the extent to which people feel that others know and understand them and their strengths, weaknesses, and desires, enabling them to function more smoothly.

Off-the-job sacrifice is significant when an individual considers relocating to obtain a new position. A person might lose the community links built up over time, possessions, and investments in the community. Even if relocation is not a factor, people may need to change their work schedule, commuting time, and so on.

So, where do the unfolding model and job embeddedness connect? Mitchell and Lee say that job embeddedness affects how the unfolding model develops. For example, in an exploratory study, Mitchell and Lee (2001) found that highly job-embedded people who experience shocks have fewer plans (scripts) about leaving than those who are less embedded in their organizations.

Both the unfolding model and job embeddedness have much to offer researchers seeking to add to our understanding of how people decide to leave their organizations or to stay with them. Combined, these two advances also add ways of structuring our thinking about management strategies for avoiding the turnover of valued employees. For example, what actions can a manager take to increase the job embeddedness of a new employee, so that if this person experiences a shock he or she will be less likely to leave? Can links reduce the likelihood of burnout?

Recall that, in the simplified model of turnover presented in Figure 1, burnout is one of the psychological states produced by individual, job, and organizational factors. We next look at burnout specifically and examine its antecedents and its consequences. We begin by defining burnout and tracing the history of burnout research.

Burnout

What Is Burnout?

In the early 1970s, Herbert J. Freudenberger, a New York psychiatrist, identified burnout as a problem affecting volunteers in a health care agency. He observed that these volunteers gradually lost their initial motivation and passion for the work and began to experience a variety of mental and physical symptoms (Maslach & Schaufeli, 1993). At the same time, Christina Maslach, a social psychology researcher, was studying cognitive strategies used by human-service workers to put emotional distance between themselves and their clients. In 1981, Maslach and Jackson published the Maslach Burnout Inventory (MBI), which defined burnout as:

> a three dimensional syndrome characterized by emotional exhaustion, depersonalization ("negative, cynical attitudes and feelings about one's client"), and reduced personal accomplishment ("the tendency to evaluate oneself negatively, particularly with regard to one's work with clients"). (Maslach & Jackson as cited in Schaufeli, Enzmann, & Girault, 1993, p. 200)

The MBI has become the most widely used instrument for measuring burnout, and the way it operationally defines burnout has become the accepted definition. Although the concept of burnout was initially restricted to people who work in human-service professions, Leiter & Schaufeli (1996) and others found support for the experience of burnout across a wide range of occupations. Most researchers now agree that burnout in human services is only one type of a more general phenomenon characterized by chronic fatigue at work, attempts to distance oneself psychologically from one's career, and decreases in one's subjective experience of effectiveness (Halbesleben, & Buckley, 2004; Leiter & Schaufeli, 1996).

It should be noted that not all researchers accept the definition of burnout reflected in the MBI. Considerable evidence supports the view that the emotional exhaustion subscale of the MBI is the central component (Cox, Kuk, & Leiter, 1993). Koeske & Koeske (1993) argue that the three-component conceptualization of burnout has hindered theoretical development, and that a decision to define burnout as equivalent to emotional exhaustion would enable clearer links with the extensive empirical research on stress. Although some studies have supported the three-factor structure of the MBI, other researchers have argued that a two-factor model including only emotional exhaustion and depersonalization might be more appropriate because of inconsistent relationships between personal accomplishment and organizational variables (Halbesleben & Buckley, 2004). The MBI has also been criticized for its psychometric limitations, namely that the items in the exhaustion and depersonalization subscales are all worded negatively and those in the personal accomplishment subscale are all worded positively. A newer measure, the Oldenburg Burnout Inventory developed by Demerouti, Bakker, Vardakou and Kantas (2003), has only two scales, exhaustion and disengagement, and avoids the wording bias of the MBI (Halbesleben & Buckley, 2004).

Two reasons have been suggested for the popularity of the burnout concept and its application to many diverse fields. The first is that it does not stigmatize the person experiencing it as do the concepts of depression or work stress. The perspective from which the concept originated emphasized the social context of work as the major determining factor, and therefore did not hold the individual responsible. Second, it provided a useful, nonblaming explanation for the experiences of many human-service workers during a period of rising public expectations and decreasing resources (Cox et al., 1993).

The 1980s have been termed the "empirical phase" of burnout research as study designs were not developed from well-constructed theoretical frameworks; since the late '80s, efforts have been made to correct this shortcoming, and recent studies now refer to a theoretical model that guides the research.

Although some characteristics of individuals, including demographic and personality variables, have been studied, the primary focus has been on job and organizational factors as antecedents to burnout. Most studies have found that job factors are more strongly related to burnout than are individual characteristics. However, these findings are based on studies with methodological limitations, and, consequently, more research is required before firm conclusions can be made about all of the causes of burnout (Maslach & Schaufeli, 1993).

In recent reviews, the correlates of burnout have been grouped into two categories: the antecedents and consequences of burnout. This reflects the dominant view of burnout, namely that a variety of factors, including the experience of stress at work causes or at least contributes to burnout. Burnout is seen to lead to several consequences, including job dissatisfaction, lack of commitment to the employer, and "withdrawal behaviours" such as frequent absence and leaving the job (Cox et al., 1993). However, since most studies have been cross-sectional, the assignment of many of these variables into one of these two categories should be seen as provisional and requiring further support by means of longitudinal research.

The findings summarized below and in Table 2 have been drawn largely from four recent papers that reviewed research on burnout (Cordes & Doherty, 1993; Halbesleben & Buckley, 2004; Lee & Ashforth, 1996; Leiter & Harvie, 1996;). In addition to these four review papers, the findings reported in some recent papers (since 1995) reporting antecedents and consequences of burnout have also been incorporated. Studies that use the MBI typically distinguish which of the three subscales are most strongly related to the antecedents and consequences being examined.

Antecedents of Burnout

Cordes and Dougherty (1993) grouped the antecedent variables into three categories: (a) job and role characteristics; (b) organizational characteristics; and (c) personal characteristics (Note the similarity to the model described earlier and illustrated in Figure 1 that organizes variables related to turnover).

Job and role characteristics correlated with burnout.   In samples of human-service employees, researchers report that the characteristics of the employee–client relationship are the most critical antecedent to burnout. Leiter & Harvie (1996) state in their review of mental health workers that it is the experience of working with people, and especially with individuals who are suffering, angry, or difficult to help, that is the core of the burnout phenomenon. Cordes & Dougherty (1993) also state, based on a thorough review of studies using the MBI, "Client interactions that are more direct, frequent, or of longer duration, for example, or client problems that are chronic (versus acute) are associated with higher levels of burnout" (p. 628).

It will come as no surprise to anyone in the child welfare field that role overload (especially quantitative overload, or the perception that the work cannot be done in the allotted time) is associated with higher levels of

Table 2: A Summary of Burnout Antecedents and Consequences

Individual Antecedents	Job and Organizational Antecedents	Individual Consequences	Job Attitude and Behavioural Consequences
Personality Features • agreeableness (low) • coping strategies (passive—mixed findings) • extraversion (low) • hardiness (low) • neuroticism (high) • expectations of self and organization (high) **Demographic Factors** • age younger (mixed findings) • fit between working hours and family concerns (match) • tenure (low)	**Job Factors** • interactions with service recipients are direct, frequent, and of long duration • service recipient problems are chronic; involve aggressive or other behaviours; or involve severe mental health issues • job expectations (unmet) • job scope (challenge and complexity) (low) • role ambiguity (high) • role conflict (high) • role overload (excessive workload) • autonomy (low) • work group cohesion (low) **Organization Factors (Perceived)** • administrative support (low) • other community agency support (low) • resources for clients (low or inadequate) • decision-making process (top-down) • distributive and procedural justice (low) • leadership style (impersonal) • organizational inefficiency • punishment (non-contingent) • supervisor: high level of cynicism and emotional exhaustion; not accepting of change; perceives high levels of health risks • supervisor support (low) (mixed findings)	**Physical & Emotional** • chest pain • depersonalization (detached, cynical relationships with service recipients) • depression • gastrointestinal disturbances • headaches • helplessness and anxiety • irritability • insomnia • poor appetite **Interpersonal** • deterioration in social and family relationships • impatience and moodiness in interactions • lower marital satisfaction • withdrawal from interaction with clients	• turnover intentions (higher) • turnover higher (mixed results) • absenteeism (higher) • communication with coworkers re management (negative) • drug, alcohol and tobacco use (increase) • job satisfaction (lower) (mixed results) • job performance (reduced) • organizational commitment (lower)

burnout. Role conflict occurs when there are incompatible messages about what is expected of the individual in a particular role. Role ambiguity refers to the perception that expectations are unclear. Both of these variables are associated with higher levels of burnout, emotional exhaustion, or depersonalization. Also, significant associations between high levels of burnout and low job autonomy have been found. Lower depersonalization is correlated with higher work-group cohesion and greater skill utilization (job scope). The mismatch between what the work actually is and what a new worker expected of the job may also be associated with emotional exhaustion (Lee & Ashforth, 1996).

Organizational factors correlated with burnout. Compared to the number of studies examining the relationship between job characteristics and burnout, fewer have looked at organizational characteristics (Cordes & Dougherty, 1993). However, these have found that an affiliative leadership style, perceived support from management, the provision of structure and clear expectations, and the involvement of staff in decision-making seem to be associated with less burnout (Leiter & Harvie, 1996). In addition, Lee and Ashforth (1996) found that emotional exhaustion was lower when employees perceived opportunities to be innovative and to participate in decisions affecting their work. The perception that workers are punished regardless of their performance (noncontingent punishment) was associated with increased emotional exhaustion. An increased sense of personal accomplishment was also associated with greater participation in decisions and the perception that the organization emphasizes efficiency and good planning (task orientation). Others have found relationships between higher emotional exhaustion and the perceptions of organizational inequity, low organizational support, more "work hassles," and not being able to access resources for clients. Working in an urban (versus rural) agency has also been associated with more emotional exhaustion.

In addition, Leiter and Harvie (1997) found evidence of a significant relationship between the perspectives of supervisors and the workers they supervise. Workers whose supervisors were accepting of change scored lower on emotional exhaustion, and workers whose supervisors perceived more health risks related to the work scored higher on emotional exhaustion. Supervisors' emotional exhaustion levels were also associated with the professional efficacy scores of the employees they supervised. When taken together, 41% of the emotional exhaustion of staff could be predicted by the supervisor variables. Leiter and Harvie (1997) noted that the findings of this study support the idea that stress has mutual or transactional effects—individuals experiencing stress evoke responses from the people around them, which, in turn, can exacerbate the stress of the first person. Halbesleben and Buckley (2004) also commented on studies that suggest an element of "social contagion" may affect burnout; individuals more susceptible to emotional stimuli might be more affected by their colleagues' burnout.

Considerable research on the effects of social support on stress and burnout has revealed that perceived social support from supervisors and co-workers is associated with lower levels of burnout or its emotional exhaustion and depersonalization components (Cordes & Dougherty, 1993; Lee & Ashforth, 1996; Leiter & Harvie, 1996; Munn, Barber & Fritz, 1996; Um & Harrison, 1998; Armstrong-Stassen, Al-Ma'aitah, Cameron, & Horsburgh 1998). However, some have found conflicting findings, and Halbesleben and Buckley (2004) note that, while work-related social support may be helpful in providing needed resources, the need for this support may undermine a worker's self esteem or colleagues may tire of providing it. Cordes and Dougherty (1993) point out that most of the research has explored professional and organizational support, and neglected personal sources of social support.

Individual characteristics and burnout. Studies examining associations between burnout and such demographics as age, years of experience, gender, marital status, having children, and education have produced conflicting results. Cordes and Dougherty (1993) indicate that employees' beliefs about what they are able to accomplish with clients (achievement expectations) and their expectations about the professional system and the job (organizational expectations) have been associated with burnout. One study (Stevens & O'Neil, as cited in Cordes & Dougherty, 1993) found that less-experienced employees tended to have higher expectations of themselves and of organizational resources, and also higher burnout levels, whereas more experienced employees had apparently shifted their expectations to fit the reality and had lower burnout scores. Some studies have found that the individual's most recent training environment influenced these expectations, as did messages received from job recruiters (Gold as cited in Cordes & Dougherty, 1993; Wanous as cited in Cordes & Dougherty, 1993).

Koeske and Kirk (1995) and Rush, Schoel and Barnard (1995) report that psychological well-being or hardiness (people who respond to stress with "active" coping or a "fight" response) may protect some individuals from developing burnout, but in some cases, individuals who respond to stress with "active" coping strategies may actually become more stressed rather than less (Rush et al., 1995). Others have examined the relationship of the "Big Five" personality factors[2] and found a positive relationship between neuroticism and emotional exhaustion, whereas depersonalization was inversely associated with extraversion, openness to experience, and agreeableness (Halbesleben & Buckley, 2004). One study suggested that the relationship between number of work hours and burnout was dependent on individual differences in how working hours affected family concerns (Barnett, Garies & Brennan as cited in Halbesleben & Buckley, 2004).

Consequences of Burnout

Fewer studies have examined consequences than antecedents to burnout (Leiter & Harvie, 1996). The consequences discussed below are summarized in Table 2 on page 289.

Of all the consequences of burnout studied so far, the relationship between burnout and turnover intentions has the strongest empirical support. For example, Manlove and Guzell (1997), in a study of childcare centre staff, found that a change from low to medium or from medium to high emotional exhaustion made it two and half times more likely that the person would intend to leave their job.

Only a few studies have examined the relationship between burnout and actual turnover. One study involving nurses (Firth & Britton, as cited in Cordes & Dougherty, 1993) did not find a significant relationship between either emotional exhaustion or personal accomplishment and actual turnover, but did find a moderate association between higher depersonalization and turnover. Manlove and Guzell (1997) found that, although emotional exhaustion was related to intention to quit, it was not related to actual turnover. In a study of child welfare workers, Drake and Yadama (1996) did find that high levels of emotional exhaustion were associated with job exit within the next 15 months; however, in the same study, high levels of depersonalization did not have an effect on turnover.

Hom and Griffeth's (1995) meta-analytic review of turnover research suggested that burnout may foreshadow turnover, but because burnout has been studied primarily in human-service fields, reviewers of employee turnover across all occupations have not reported significant findings connecting burnout and turnover. As noted in our discussion of turnover earlier in this chapter, actual turnover is probably affected by perceived alternatives. This moderating variable may play a role in the conflicting findings regarding the relationship between burnout components and actual turnover.

Burnout components have been linked with a variety of mental and physical health problems, including decreased self-esteem, increased depression, irritability, helplessness and anxiety, increased impatience and moodiness, insomnia, headaches, poor appetite, chest pain, and gastrointestinal disturbances (Cordes & Dougherty, 1993). Since burnout is conceptualized as resulting from stress that continues over a period of time, it is not surprising that these well-known correlates of extended stress are also found in individuals with high levels of burnout.

A number of studies with human-service workers have supported the notion that depersonalization follows emotional exhaustion in time, and is a way of coping with it (Guerts, Schaufeli, & DeJonge, 1998; Leiter, 1993). Studies (especially with police officers) have also shown that burnout is associated with the deterioration of social and family relationships. Leiter and Durup (1996), in a longitudinal study of female health care professionals designed to understand "spillover" (the impact of work on the family domain and vice versa), found "more evidence of associations from work to family than from family to work" (p. 41). Emotional exhaustion had a negative effect on ratings of marital satisfaction; however, family problems did not obviously disrupt work unless there was active personal conflict and not simply an absence of family support. Higher levels of "consumption behaviours" (drug, alcohol, and tobacco use) have also been associated with higher burnout (Cordes & Dougherty, 1993).

The studies looking at burnout and job attitudes have found that higher burnout levels, and higher emotional exhaustion and depersonalization in particular, were associated with lower job satisfaction and organizational commitment (Cordes & Dougherty, 1993; Lee & Ashforth, 1996; Silver, Poulin and Manning, 1997). Cordes and Dougherty (1993) noted that absenteeism and lowered job performance are related to higher burnout. Others have also reported an association between lower job performance and burnout, as assessed by both workers and their supervisors (Wright and Cropanzano, 1998; Halbesleben & Buckley, 2004).

Although this review reveals some areas where the findings are conflicting, considerable empirical support exists for the idea that the variables listed in the first two columns of Table 2 contribute to the development of burnout, and that high levels of burnout lead to the consequences listed in the third and fourth columns of Table 2. Numerous theoretical models have been advanced to explain how these variables interact to cause burnout and how burnout leads to the consequences identified. We now turn our attention to discussing the one model that seems most promising in its attempt to make sense of the relative importance of these variables and the ways in which they may interact to produce different outcomes.

A Theoretical Model of Burnout

The model that has received the most attention and empirical support is the conservation of resources (COR) theory of stress (Hobfoll, 1989; Hobfoll & Freedy, 1993). Hobfoll and Freedy (1993) conceptualize burnout as a response to stressful work conditions, a unique disorder, and one that is related to the "family" of stress disorders. The basic premise of the theory is that individuals strive to obtain and keep what they value—resources.

Resources include "conditions," such as having a job, or a quality marriage; "energies," such as money, stamina, and knowledge; "personal characteristics," such as skills, good health, or high self-esteem; and "objects," such as clothing and furniture (Hobfoll & Freedy, 1993). The theory postulates that when circumstances threaten a person's obtaining and keeping resources, stress occurs. Three conditions are seen as resulting in stress: (a) when resources are threatened or inadequate to meet demands, (b) when resources are lost, and (c) when individuals invest resources and do not receive the expected return. In the workplace, examples of demands include heavy workload and pressure, stressful events, and role conflict and role ambiguity (Lee & Ashforth, 1996). Burnout develops when stress continues over a period of time.

Consider this example: a child welfare worker finds that meeting the demands of her large caseload (including several complex family situations and some very unco-operative parents) leaves her so exhausted that she has no energy in the evenings or on the weekends to enjoy time with her partner and children. According to the COR theory, she would experience stress because of the perceived loss of resources (stamina, and threat to a quality marriage or good relations with children), and if this continued for some time she would be at risk for burnout.

The major resources in the workplace include social support from co-workers and supervisors and job enhancement opportunities such as having more control over work demands, participation in decision-making, opportunity to work autonomously, and a reward system that recognizes effort and skill (Lee & Ashforth, 1996). The COR theory states resource loss leads to burnout and other consequences such as absenteeism, lateness, poor job performance, plans to quit one's job, reduced commitment to the organization, reduced job involvement, and reduced job satisfaction (Lee & Ashforth, 1996).

Three principles are also included in the COR theory; the first is "primacy of loss." Because people tend to try to protect themselves from loss of resources, they are more sensitive to loss experiences than to gain experiences. The second principle is the "secondary importance of gain." Although gain in resources is seen as less important in terms of stress outcomes than loss, gain in resources is still important, because having considerable resources decreases the chances of loss and makes it less likely that individuals will suffer additional stressful events when a loss occurs. For example, individuals with good self-esteem and a satisfying marriage will be less likely to suffer depression and marital problems if they lose their job than persons who have low self-esteem and are socially isolated. A person with a variety of skills and work experiences will be less likely to be laid off from a job or will have less difficulty finding another one. Anything that leads to a gain in resources can be seen as a protection or buffer against work stress associated with future threats or loss of resources. The third principle is that individuals invest resources to prevent loss and in the hope of gaining more resources. When the investment does not "pay off," work stress is likely to increase. For example, the employee who invests time and money in increasing her credentials (perhaps obtaining an MSW on a part-time basis), expecting that she will be promoted and gain increased status and salary, will perceive a loss if this does not happen (Hobfoll & Freedy, 1993).

Job demands and resources were postulated by the COR theory to be differentially associated with the three components of burnout. Subsequent research has confirmed that job demands are more predictive of emotional exhaustion, and resources more strongly associated with either depersonalization or personal accomplishment (Halbesleben & Buckley, 2004; Lee & Ashforth, 1996; Wright & Cropanzano, 1998;). More recently, Halbesleben and Bowler (cited in Halbesleben & Buckley, 2004) argued that the relationship of burnout to job performance can be understood in terms of a decision about the investment of resources. They found that higher emotional exhaustion in workers was associated with less investment of resources in doing the job itself (lower job performance), and with more investment in efforts that would benefit co-workers (organizational citizenship behaviours, for example, involvement in union activities). They suggest that this is an attempt to gain social support and reduce burnout.

Close examination of this model and attempts to test it reveal that many researchers equate burnout with emotional exhaustion only, and view depersonalization as one way that some individuals cope with either emotional exhaustion or work stress. The degree to which a lowered sense of personal accomplishment is a necessary component of the burnout phenomenon is unclear; the idea that it may moderate the relationship between stress and emotional exhaustion or the relationship between emotional exhaustion and outcomes such as job turnover seems plausible. Even advocates of the COR theory who continue to operationalize burnout using the three scales of the MBI recognize that the determinants of the three components differ from one another. The conclusion that we come to is that the core experience of the concept of burnout is that operationalized by the emotional exhaustion scale of the MBI. Depersonalization and a lowered sense of personal accomplishment should be seen as experiences that are sometimes associated with emotional exhaustion, but not always.

A common theme among all theoretical models of burnout is that individual factors play a relatively small role compared to that played by job and organizational characteristics. Our review indicates that a bias toward this conclusion has existed among burnout researchers since the early days.

While we suspect that less biased research may come to similar conclusions, more attention to the role of individual differences in the development of emotional exhaustion, depersonalization, and a lowered sense of accomplishment is indicated. More research is also needed to clarify how individual differences interact with organizational factors. Since most research to date has focused on specific job factors, future research should focus more on organizational factors that affect specific job factors and address such questions as: What are the indicators of a healthy organization? And, how does an unhealthy organization change to a healthy one?

We look at some answers to these questions later in this chapter when we address how burnout might be reduced or prevented. But first, we provide some results of our study of the workplace experience of child welfare workers during a time of change in Ontario to illustrate the levels of emotional exhaustion and turnover intentions in our child welfare agencies.

The Workplace Study

We began our study of employees' experience of the workplace in children's aid societies, knowing that Ontario's Child Welfare Reforms initiated strong forces for change in the child welfare system and within each child welfare agency. Essentially, the government directed its 52 children's aid societies (CAS) to adopt a narrower focus than previously (resources to be primarily devoted to child protection issues) with funding determined by the number of open protection cases and children in care. At the same time, the criteria for finding a child in need of protection was broadened to include witnessing domestic violence, a structured risk-assessment tool was introduced, and timelines for detailed documentation were shortened. As a result, children's aid societies hired large numbers of new staff to manage the large increases in service demands related to investigation, intervention, and the placement of children in care. These rapid changes created significant challenges for managers who continued to work to maintain caring service environments for children and families and, at the same time, enhance working environments that would attract and retain staff.

In this section, we briefly report on some of the results of our study during this time of shifting priorities, stress, and growth. In response to the concerns of agency managers, we focused the research on workers' reports of their levels of and antecedents to emotional exhaustion, job satisfaction, and intention to leave their organizations. We also attempted to discover what contributes to a satisfying and healthy workplace in child welfare organizations.

Method

A convenience sample of four children's aid societies in southern Ontario participated through an employee survey. Survey items were selected from preexisting valid and reliable scales measuring dimensions previously found to be related to employee turnover, job satisfaction, or to emotional exhaustion. The 254-item survey was distributed to all employees in the four participating organizations in 2001. A comment page was provided for written comments. The majority of items used a Likert scale to indicate the strength of agreement with each statement. Employees received a personally addressed envelope containing the survey through their agency's internal mail and returned completed surveys directly to the researchers. The response rate was 49.3%; 403 surveys were completed of 817 distributed.

Results and discussion

Almost 60% of survey respondents were direct service workers (DSWs). This proportion, as well as those of other positions, is roughly equivalent to the actual proportions of employees working in the four agencies. The majority of survey respondents were female (82%) and over half of DSWs had a social work degree (57.2%). Almost half (48.6%) of all employees participating in the survey, and almost 58% of DSWs, had been with their agency for two-and-a-half years or less. This is consistent with the recent, extensive growth in staffing reported by Ontario CASs and with relatively high turnover rates in child welfare (Coulthard et al., 2001). Our personal experience tells us that many new graduates take their first professional position in a CAS; perhaps this is also suggested by the 42% of DSWs who were under 31 years old.

Looking at the prevalence of emotional exhaustion as measured by the MBI, we found that almost 50% of the managers, 33% of the supervisors, 29% of support staff, and 44% of DSWs reported a high level of emotional exhaustion. Clearly, many people at every level in these child welfare agencies experienced being emotionally exhausted. The experience of emotional exhaustion did not diminish with tenure in the organization for a significant proportion of employees. More than one third of senior employees (those with more than 10 years' tenure) reported high levels of emotional exhaustion. This suggests a norm of high emotional exhaustion in child welfare and, perhaps, also acceptance of the idea that high emotional exhaustion is simply a part of working in child welfare.

When we examined emotional exhaustion in direct service workers only, we noted that DSWs in children's services were somewhat more likely than those in intake and family services to report low emotional exhaustion levels. However, there was no area of direct service work where the majority of employees were not moderately or highly emotionally exhausted.

The high levels of depersonalization found among all employees (30%) and particularly among DSWs (37%) were also a concern. While depersonalization may be a self-protective consequence of emotional exhaustion, we wondered how trusting, respectful relationships with children and families could possibly be formed under those conditions.

Considering the findings regarding levels of emotional exhaustion, we expected some negative impact on the job satisfaction of these employees. However, 47% of all respondents were highly satisfied with their jobs overall. Only 8% of employees reported low job satisfaction. Managers were most likely to be highly satisfied, with 73% of those respondents in that category. More than 50% of supervisors and support workers were also highly satisfied.

Levels of high job satisfaction among DSWs were somewhat lower than the total employee average with 42% indicating high overall job satisfaction. Family services DSWs were least likely to report high job satisfaction (only 37%), and DSWs in children's services were the most likely to have low overall job satisfaction ratings (12%). DSWs in intake were least likely to report low job satisfaction (7%) and the most likely of all DSWs to be highly satisfied with their jobs overall (48%).

With such high job satisfaction reported, perhaps it is not surprising that just 16% of DSW participants were thinking about leaving their jobs. We do not have data on how many subsequently did leave, but prior research leads us to expect that fewer than 16% would actually leave in the next year.

Our most striking finding was that, despite these high levels of emotional exhaustion, satisfaction with the work itself was quite high. How can people who are working so hard and feeling so emotionally burdened be satisfied with their jobs? We speculate that, at least to some extent, this is explained by the research literature that suggests that social workers as a group are strongly motivated to give of themselves in order to help others. This is supported by the literature on women's roles in the helping professions (e.g., Baines, Evans, & Neysmith, 1991; Callahan, 1993), and child welfare is certainly a woman-dominated field.

Regardless, we are greatly concerned about the pervasiveness of high levels of emotional exhaustion among child welfare employees and find the high levels of depersonalization a definite threat to the potential for trusting, productive helping relationships. The fact that 12% of all child welfare employees and 16% of DSWs scored highly on intention to leave suggests that, for some, their focus was starting to turn elsewhere.

To try to understand more about what may contribute to strong intentions to leave and similarly strong intentions not to leave, we examined in more detail those in the low and high categories on this scale. We looked for statistically significant differences between these two groups on responses to other survey scale scores. Both the scales on which these two groups differed significantly and those on which they did not are shown in Table 3. Here we can see that those who reported strong intentions to leave were discontented on several dimensions. As expected, they were more emotionally exhausted, more likely to distance themselves (depersonalization) from their clients than employees who did not have strong intentions to leave, and they were preparing to look for another job. They were more dissatisfied with their jobs overall and on many job satisfaction dimensions.

Among the typically identified antecedents to both emotional exhaustion and turnover intentions, we note that these participants were experiencing considerable role conflict and ambiguity in their jobs; they felt that their personal values and those of the agency did not match; they perceived that their work was negatively affecting their family life; they did not trust the organization and perceived the organization as treating employees unfairly; they did not feel as much pride in the agency as did other employees; they experienced less support from the organization in terms of training and assistance to do their work, and they felt less support from their co-workers and supervisors.

We report these results as an example of the impact on employees of the current design of the child welfare system and its agencies. Ultimately, the cumulative effect of high levels of emotional exhaustion and depersonalization among direct service workers at the front line impacts service delivery and children's and families' experiences of child welfare services.

Table 3: Turnover Intentions and Survey Scale Scores

High Intention to Leave— Higher Scores on	High Intention to Leave— Lower Scores on	No Significant Differences
• emotional exhaustion • depersonalization • image violation • intention to quit • job search—active, preparatory • perceived inequitable employment relationship • role ambiguity • role conflict • work–family conflict	• agreeableness • conscientiousness • job satisfaction—overall • job satisfaction—resource adequacy, comfort, challenge, promotions • loyalty • organizational commitment—affective, continuance, normative • organizational justice—distributive, procedural, interactional • organizational support—instrumental, affective • organizational trust • personal accomplishment • supervisor support • work group cohesion	• autonomy • family–work conflict • job satisfaction—financial

Fortunately, with so much written and discovered about the antecedents to burnout and turnover, there are many possibilities for preventive interventions, and we turn our attention now to looking first at strategies for preventing turnover in child welfare organizations and then at strategies for preventing burnout. From this review, it becomes clear that a significant proportion of the strategies advocated to prevent turnover are similar to those believed to prevent or reduce burnout.

Preventing Unwanted Turnover

Before we offer suggestions for reducing unwanted burnout and turnover, it is important to acknowledge that this goal is not easily achieved in child welfare organizations. Twenty years ago, Esposito and Fine (1985) wrote,

> [Child welfare workers] are expected to compensate for abuse and abusive families, for unjust economic distributions that inequitably limit opportunities and resources, for inadequate educational systems that deprive minority and poor youth of solid academic preparation, and for policies and institutions that punish working-class and poor families by withholding resources necessary for subsistence. Forced to negotiate with the courts, the schools, and bureaucratic service systems to improve children's chances for a "good life," Child Welfare workers often lack the structural power, tools, or resources to enforce their decisions. (pp. 728–729)

Administrators of child welfare organizations also face limits in what they can do to make their organizations healthy workplaces. They are constrained by limited budgets and restrictive funding formulas; they also work within the larger system that attempts to manage contradictory expectations. They are asked to create and maintain organizations that strengthen and support families while always acting in the best interests of the child, organizations that give parents the benefit of the doubt but also ensure that no child is abused or neglected. We see the strong emphasis on risk assessment and protection of the child in the current Ontario Child and Family Services Act coupled with the inadequate resources being directed toward supporting the well-being of families as a significant part of the problem. Administrators can and do seek change in the emphasis and direction of policy and legislation, but they do not have complete control over how these larger system variables affect their particular agency. This context needs to be acknowledged as we make suggestions in the next two sections regarding reducing turnover and burnout. On the other hand, administrators may find that suggestions based on this review of the research offer some practical ideas about changes that are under their control and which would benefit their organization.

For the suggestions we make below for reducing unwanted turnover, we have drawn on three sources: our reviews of the literature that identified antecedents to turnover; the recent work of Mitchell, Lee and their colleagues, particularly Mitchell and Lee (2001) and Mitchell, Holtom and Lee (2001) on the implications of the unfolding model and the concept of job embeddedness; and on the accumulated body of knowledge on recommended human-resource management practices. To help organize our recommendations for reducing turnover, we will use the typical human-resource management cycle that begins with the recruitment of new employees, continues through the management processes and organizational structures designed to maintain people as valued workers, and ends with the termination of an employee.

Recruitment and Selection

Let's begin with a common scenario compiled from experiences related to us by employees in child welfare organizations:

> Children's Aid Society A has had several workers leave recently and needs to hire three replacements. It advertises in the local paper for social workers (BSW or MSW) to work as direct service workers. A human-resources employee screens the applications for the quoted credentials as they come in and passes on to a supervisor the resumes of qualified applicants. As soon as the supervisor has time, she enlists a front-line worker to assist her, and the two of them sift through the resumes looking for people who stand out in some way. They search for someone with previous experience in child welfare, but most applicants are new graduates or working part-time in another sector.

> They select eight people and call them for an interview. Six weeks have passed since the ad was first placed. Two people have already secured other full-time positions, one person says he really only wants to work part-time, and five agree to interviews.

> The supervisor finds another worker to help with the interviews, because the first worker cannot take more time away from her clients to do interviews. The two of them meet over lunch and plan a series of questions to ask the applicants. They interview the candidates and put most of the questions to each. When they review their impressions, they find they can quickly agree on one person who was very talkative, confident, and pleasant. Each finds one other person that they did not like at all and agree to eliminate them. They list some pros and cons for the other two candidates and decide that they should be offered positions—other agency workers are asking when they will be getting some relief from overtime and their high caseloads.

Six months later, the first person hired has left by mutual agreement. He had overstated the depth of his experience and was reluctant to seek help when working with complex cases. Within the first three months, the supervisor knew he was not going to become competent, despite his disclaimers that he was "as good as anybody." On the other hand, the supervisor found to her surprise that one of the other hires was absolutely wonderful. The final person hired had quickly returned to her part-time position in another agency, shocked that she was immediately expected to take on new cases and handle them completely on her own.

Unfortunately, this type of scenario is too common. People who are well trained in their professions but poorly trained in how to select an employee must do hiring under immense pressure to find someone quickly to fill a position. They have an unclear picture of the type of person they are looking for and limited assistance to develop the tools needed to do this difficult task well. Predictably, the outcome is an unhappy one for many. However, an organization can take steps to improve how it chooses its new employees and reduce the turnover caused by poor recruitment and selection practices.

The hiring of a new worker ideally begins with accumulating two different types of knowledge—one about why people are leaving, and the other about the characteristics of those who stay and flourish in the position. Information about why people are leaving is best gathered through exit interviews (see the discussion in the section on termination below).

For the second type of knowledge needed before recruiting, management must devote time to understanding the attributes of workers who flourish in the position being filled (see Table 4 for a summary of our suggestions at each stage of the human resource management cycle). A good strategy is to identify two to five people who enjoy the job and do it well. The key questions are: What knowledge, skills, abilities, and personal characteristics contribute to these people being able to perform exceptionally well? Which of these are absolutely required in a new person? Which can be added through training or other means after hiring?

Once the description of the model candidate is clear, the challenge is to determine how these attributes can be assessed during the selection process. A well-designed interview, particularly a structured one,[3] is crucial, as is asking the candidate to undertake a work sample (actually do a client interview or respond in detail to a hypothetical situation). Conducting a thorough reference check is also essential. Some personality or other testing may also be done. For example, empirical evidence exists that a high level of conscientiousness is related to both higher levels of performance and lower rates of turnover (Barrick & Mount, 1991). It is certainly an important attribute in the current child welfare field and can be reliably measured.

Table 4: Avoiding Unwanted Turnover through the Design of Human Resource Management Systems

When	What	How	Why
Recruitment and Selection Before recruiting	Define the right person	• Identify current (or previous) position holders who perform the job exceptionally well. List the knowledge, skills, abilities, and personal attributes of the ideal candidate. • Determine the qualities that you absolutely must have on hiring and those that can be added through training or other means afterward. Include attributes associated with low turnover (e.g., conscientiousness, values fit) as long as these do not violate local labour regulations (e.g., hiring on the basis of marital status or the number of dependents).	• To maximize the potential for job fit • To reduce the possibility that the person hired will not be able to do the job.
Before selection	Design the selection process	• Determine how the critical attributes will be assessed—consider using personality tests, and work sample tests. • Create interview questions that will enable interviewers to evaluate critical attributes—consider using a structured interview or a standard process	• To create a process that will be a reliable and valid assessment of each candidate while avoiding a potential mis-hire.
	Train interviewers	• Review the critical attributes and how they will be assessed. • Provide an outline of the process/questions to use. • Discuss how individual evaluations will be combined if more than one interviewer is used. • Consider including, as a measure of their own performance, interviewers' hiring success.	• To minimize the potential for a "gut feeling" only decision.
During the selection process	Realistic job preview	• Describe a typical day on the job. Outline the specific tasks and interactions required in the job. Provide details about the amount of time required in different tasks. • Include a description of the amount of support available to a new, versus continuing, person in the position. Describe the organization's culture and norms. • Provide opportunities for a candidate to meet people in the job or people with whom an incumbent would interact.	• To reduce the potential for shock when the job turns out to be different than expected.

Table 4: (*continued*)

When	What	How	Why
During the selection process	Reference checks	• Use questions related to critical attributes and be sure to check any concerns that have arisen during the selection process.	• Past behaviour is the best predictor of future behaviour.
Making the offer	The offer	• Make it attractive! State any non-financial incentives that may be uniquely appealing to the candidate, for example, access to on-site day care. • Make the process easy! Set out who will do what by when to build confidence in the organization on the part of the new employee.	• To begin building the list of items that will become difficult to sacrifice on leaving the organization. • To demonstrate how formal interactions with the organization will occur
Orientation Orienting the new employee	The initial orientation	• Provide information about formal policies and procedures. Describe expectations and support, including initial training. • Introduce the new employee to co-workers, supervisors, and managers. • Assign a mentor for the initial period. • If the employee is new to the community, provide information and links to local services. • Fit the length and intensity of the orientation to the complexity of the job.	• To begin establishing the links, the fit, the sacrifices. • To develop trust in the organization and affective commitment to it. • To minimize the potential for shock that the reality of this organization does not match its promises. • To provide the new employee with scripts to use on encountering the unexpected.
	The "settling-in" phase	• Encourage the new person to ask questions and to explore the boundaries of the job. Help new people identify how their values fit with the organization. • Provide challenging, achievable tasks and supportive feedback. Identify and provide for ongoing training needs. Discuss "how things work around here" and how to solve problems that arise. • Provide opportunities to engage in team/task force activities. Facilitate links with others in the organization and community.	• To continue building links, fit, and sacrifice. • To create job satisfaction and organizational commitment.

| **Maintenance Phase** | Developing permanence through reward, recognition, development, and performance management systems | • Identify those you definitely want to stay and train, transfer, or terminate others.
• Design your human resource management systems and your organization to reduce known antecedents to turnover. | • To maximize ongoing job embeddedness.
• To minimize the potential for shock, image violation, and the development of job dissatisfaction and reduced organizational commitment. |
| **Termination** | Exit interview | • Identify the reasons for unwanted turnover, using the unfolding model as a guide for your investigation. | • To add to the list of characteristics defining the model employee.
• To improve the design of the organization and its systems, especially its human resource management systems. |

Just as important as describing the model child welfare worker is training those who will be involved in evaluating the candidates. Human-services professionals are tempted to assume that, because they interview people all the time (as clients), they know how to conduct a selection interview. When there is more than one interviewer, they need to discuss the critical attributes of the model candidate and how these will be assessed. They need to prepare or review the interview schedule and talk about how they will work together in an interview and make the decision regarding the candidate to be selected.

In our opening example, the supervisor didn't have a clear idea about the characteristics she was looking for or how she would evaluate them. She was surprised with the success of one of her hires and with the failure of another. Management needs to decide which parts of the process human-resource professionals should carry out, and which need to be done by supervisors and co-workers. Generally, the more specific and detailed the position description and the job advertisement is, the more screening can be done by a human-resource staff member.

All of this preparation takes time, but it is necessary to design effective recruitment and selection processes. In the current climate, when the need for new employees in child welfare organizations is very high, it is tempting to move quickly and "go for the warm body" who has basic qualifications. This strategy is short-sighted; it costs more in training, support, mistakes, reduced morale in others who continue to carry more of the load, and, ultimately, it costs in additional unwanted turnover.

At some point during the selection process, the candidate must be told what the job is really like and what it is like to work in the organization. This realistic job preview reduces turnover by increasing the probability that the job will match the candidate's expectations and that the organization's culture and values will match as well. The preview should outline both the positive and negative aspects of the job and working in the organization. Interviewers should describe a typical day, discuss specific tasks and types of interactions, the challenges usually encountered by new employees, and how the organization facilitates new employees' integration and learning.

Once the reference checks are done and a hiring decision made, an offer is made to the candidate. The candidate looks for signs of equity and fair dealing throughout this process. An attractive offer that highlights aspects of the work that the individual will find appealing and satisfying is recommended. Since the offer process often goes through many stages, management should try to keep the candidate fully informed and feeling welcomed throughout. Doing this has an impact on the sacrifices the individual will perceive when thinking about leaving the organization (remember the job embeddedness model described earlier, in which leaving the job would mean giving up this experience of being valued and respected by the organization). This step also begins to establish some norms around how the organization treats employees and how it expects its employees to behave during a formal interaction.

A well-designed and executed recruitment and selection process reduces shocks related to unmet expectations and ensures a better fit with the organization's values and culture, while building an initial commitment to the organization in the new employee.

Orientation

The process of integrating the new employee begins with orienting them to the policies, procedures, and practices of their new organization and their position. It also begins with introducing them and linking them to managers/supervisors and co-workers. A mentor can often help a new employee make sense of the organization. The mentor should be an experienced child welfare employee (not a supervisor/manager) who exhibits the values and attitudes that the agency wants to encourage in its new employees. The mentor helps integrate the new person by providing a sounding board, by anticipating questions, concerns, and reactions, and by letting the new hire know "how things are done around here." Learning very complex jobs is often easier when an inexperienced person has a model to observe. Mentors can perform this function, or new employees can shadow an experienced worker as part of their training before taking on their own, independent cases.

Mentors and managers can both offer organizational scripts[4] that the new worker can use when encountering new situations to avoid these being experienced as shocks leading quickly to turnover. These scripts can take the form of suggestions about what to do or sharing details of how the more experienced worker thinks when "X" happens. In child welfare, front-line workers need to be prepared for the suspicion and anger they often face when investigating allegations of child abuse or neglect. They need assistance to learn how to empathize with the anger and fear that parents feel when they have been reported to child welfare authorities; they need models for how a worker can begin to develop a relationship involving respect and trust with the client, while at the same time maintaining the role of authorized investigator. New workers often need help to identify the contradictory roles they are asked to play—to be both a helpful social worker and a person who enforces the Child and Family Services Act. They may also need help to recognize the societal contradictions that the child welfare field manages: on one hand the public sees the family as sacred and private and something in which the state should not interfere; on the other hand, abuse and neglect of children occurs and needs to be prevented or stopped (Esposito & Fine, 1985). Discussions of these contradictions may help new workers to make sense of the negative attributions they experience from the public or from the courts. Hearing how more experienced workers think about and cope with these contradictory expectations can be very reassuring. Easing new hires into their roles, and supporting them through training, mentoring, and providing opportunities to ask questions and share concerns, is essential during the initial phase of employment.

As the new person begins to settle in to the job, the manager/supervisor should be both encouraging and challenging. They need to encourage the new person to ask questions, to explore and test the boundaries of accountability and responsibility, and to identify any specific training and support needs. They need to empathically challenge the new person to perform difficult, achievable tasks, to work productively and co-operatively with others, and to solve problems that arise. The manager should provide timely, accurate feedback on performance and share the formal and informal organizational rules and norms. This is a second time when the organization's values around performance and its treatment of its employees are communicated. New employees' fit with the organization, their understanding of the sacrifices they might make if they change jobs, and their links to others in the organization are being established through this stage, and their job satisfaction and organizational commitment increase.

The Maintenance or Ongoing Phase

During this phase of employment, individuals focus on doing the job well and on the rewards they get. Here, too, is where job dissatisfaction and lower organizational commitment can intrude when their antecedents are present. During this phase, organizations require an effective design for all human-resource management systems (reward and recognition, training and development, and performance management systems). In addition, the organization's design of its own structure, the definition of jobs, accountabilities, and responsibilities, and the provision of adequate resources to do the jobs are all involved. The culture and norms of the organization, especially as these relate to the treatment of employees, come into play. Consider here the suggestions that focus on reducing job demands and increasing job resources, which are discussed in the next section on preventing burnout.

We can refer to Mitchell and Lee's models of job embeddedness and turnover and to the antecedents of burnout for advice on the design of organizations to minimize unwanted turnover. For example, we know that role conflict is associated with increased turnover. Can the job be designed to reduce role conflict? If not, can the supervisor intervene to offer better ways to deal with the conflicts before the situation escalates to the point where some new event constitutes a shock or the continued experience leads to reduced job satisfaction? If a shock is felt, can the supervisor offer an alternative script, or some other incentives to someone considering leaving?

This may be a time when the supervisor can share her or his experience with difficult case outcomes. Knowing that one's supervisor had to deal with the suicide of an adolescent in care, or the return of a child to a home that she perceived as dangerous, is important for relatively new workers. Being able to talk about how one copes with perceptions of failure or inadequate service is extremely important for the development of child welfare workers who can, over the long term, derive satisfaction from their work in spite of exposure to the trauma and despair experienced by so many clients.

This phase is rich with opportunities for management to design an organization that meets the needs of its employees while achieving its mission. Encouraging a work–life balance (Duxbury & Higgins, 2001), and strong employment relationships (Lowe & Schellenberg, 2001) increase the links that Mitchell and Lee consider important while also increasing the list of sacrifices that turnover could create. Providing professional development—for example, training that helps workers understand why children who have been abused by their parents resist being separated from those parents, or offering concrete help around working with ethnically diverse families—contributes to workers' sense of mastery and competence. Providing contingent rewards (money is not necessary, but recognition is) demonstrates that good performance is important and that strong performers are noticed. Having employee assistance programs acknowledges that the work can be stressful and that the organization wants to be helpful and supportive. Offering flexible hours, different types of employment contracts, and extended leaves can all relieve stress, work–life conflicts, and burnout. Competent, caring supervisors and managers provide role models and support. The emphasis in this, the longest stage in the human resource management cycle, is on developing and encouraging the employee's achievement as an exemplary worker, and on appropriately and personally recognizing that achievement.

Termination Phase

Exit interviews with departing employees, using the unfolding model described earlier as a guide to the type of questions to ask, can provide the organization with critical information. For example, ask the employee who is leaving questions about whether they experienced a shock or an image violation and what type it was ("Was there a particular event or experience that prompted your resignation? Have you been thinking about leaving for a long time?"). Ask whether they had a script in place and whether there was an opportunity for management to intervene with reframing the situation ("Was this an inevitable decision when "X" happened? Is there anything we could have helped you with or anything we could have done to encourage you to stay?"). Ask whether the employee had another offer, or is leaving without an alternative in place. Again, it is valuable to know whether there was an opportunity to intervene by means of some incentive to stay (more rewards, different or more flexible hours, more supervision and support, an internal transfer, and so on).

The point of the exit interview is to gain as much information as possible about how management can make internal organizational changes to affect the variables over which it has some control. For example, in the case described in the introduction to this section, where a new employee quits soon after starting, a relatively simple change might be for the agency to be clearer regarding its expectations of a new employee. The agency might decide to modify its practice of having new workers immediately take on their own cases independently.

The exit interview also provides an opportunity to gather some understanding of characteristics of individuals themselves that may be related to turnover. These latter characteristics can form the negative part of the description of a model candidate, that is, the type of candidate to avoid hiring. The overconfidence and reluctance to seek support displayed by a new hire in our example could be qualities that interviewers screen against. Some of this negative information can also be gleaned by talking to both the people who made the hiring decision and to the individual's supervisor.

Throughout these suggestions for preventing turnover, we have emphasized the creation of effective human-resource systems and processes. Our ideas may seem difficult or expensive to put into practice in child welfare organizations. However, an organization considering how to approach its own turnover issues can analyze which parts of the system might benefit the most from implementing changes. For example, by looking at the relationship between individuals' tenure and turnover, one might see that people tend to leave within the first two years of employment. In this case, the focus should be on understanding why (through exit interviews) and then making the appropriate changes to recruiting, selection, or orientation systems. Increasing understanding of why the best people stay through this period can also inform any changes.

Preventing Burnout

Although many authors have offered suggestions and ideas about how to cope with or prevent burnout, relatively few of these have been systematically implemented, and almost none have been empirically validated (Halbesleben & Buckley, 2004; Maslach & Goldberg, 1998; Schaufeli et al., 1993). Maslach and Goldberg (1998) noted that most prevention recommendations have focused on changing the individual, even though the research indicates that job and organizational factors play larger roles in burnout than individual ones. Interventions focusing on the individual include admonitions to eat a healthy diet and exercise regularly, to balance one's work and personal life, to learn time-management skills, to seek support from supervisor or colleagues, to learn stress-management techniques, and to increase self-awareness.

Many of the strategies advocated for the prevention of turnover are also relevant to the prevention of burnout. Cherniss (1993) emphasized the value of a well-planned orientation to the work, including job shadowing and structured opportunities to receive concrete feedback and support. Burnout researchers have also suggested that formal mentoring of new workers may be helpful (Blankertz & Robinson, 1997). In a series of case studies of helping professionals conducted over many years, Cherniss (1993) found that those who believed that they could effect change in their workplace and were successful in their efforts to reduce organizational sources of stress were the ones who were able to overcome early symptoms of burnout. Clearly, organizational strategies that leave employees feeling that managers listen and respond to their concerns, and that all are treated fairly and equitably, will go a long way to preventing burnout as well as turnover.

From our review of literature on burnout prevention, the most refreshing perspectives are those put forward by Halbeselben et al. (2004), Leiter and Maslach (2000), and Maslach and Goldberg (1998). They encourage a shift away from a focus on preventing or reducing burnout toward examining ways that organizations can increase workers' engagement with their work. The direct opposite of the three components of burnout are energy (rather than exhaustion), strong involvement (rather than depersonalization), and a sense of efficacy (rather than a reduced sense of accomplishment). A focus on how a child welfare organization can enhance workers' energy, involvement, and sense of efficacy may be more useful or at least add to the traditional approach that places emphasis on the individual's responsibility to balance work and personal life, and it may enhance stress-management techniques. Such a focus is clearly consistent with the work on job embeddedness (for example, Mitchell & Lee, 2001).

In ways similar to those recommended for preventing and reducing turnover, Maslach & Goldberg (1998) advocate that each organization have interventions designed to address the specific job situation in which workers are located. Recognizing the usefulness of the COR model, they postulate that certain jobs or roles in a particular organization have inherent demands and available resources. When the fit between the demands of the job and the resources available to the workers is good, burnout is likely to be low.

Burnout is therefore framed in terms of job–person mismatch. Maslach and Leiter (as cited in Maslach & Goldberg, 1998) have identified six areas in which this mismatch can take place. They are:

1) *work overload*—chronic inability to keep up with the work because there is too much to do, not enough time and insufficient resources;
2) *lack of control*—individuals constrained by policies and rigid expectations without the opportunity to innovate or be creative;
3) *insufficient reward*—insufficient salary and benefits for the work accomplished, and also not enough internal rewards, such as sense of having done something important and well;
4) *breakdown of community*—a loss of a sense of positive connection (social support) and even more importantly, chronic and unresolved conflict with co-workers;
5) *absence of fairness*—workload or pay is not perceived as fair, or there is cheating or inequity in terms of evaluations or promotions; and
6) *value conflict*—a mismatch between the requirements of the job and the worker's values or principles.

Work overload and lack of control are ubiquitous problems in child welfare organizations. Changes in these areas are not completely within the control of an agency's managers. Managers do routinely try to reduce workloads by hiring additional workers or experimenting with different ways of processing referrals and ongoing cases. The need to conform to government and court requirements for time limits on response, comprehensive risk assessment, and detailed documentation reduces the ability of the agency to provide more autonomy in many situations. However, it appears that in cases where it is feasible, reducing caseloads and allowing workers as much control over case management as possible would be beneficial.

Our study of child welfare organizations in Ontario suggests that one of the reasons burnout and turnover are not higher in many child welfare organizations is related to the sense of satisfaction that many child welfare workers derive from perceiving that they have made a positive difference in the lives of children and families. These findings imply that managers who help workers to recognize the importance of the work they are doing, and support them by identifying interventions that they have done well in spite of difficult circumstances, will reduce burnout in these workers.

Numerous studies in child welfare report that support, especially from co-workers, one's immediate work team, and from supervisors, is extremely important in feeling satisfied with the work and reducing burnout. Organizational strategies that train supervisors to facilitate supportive work groups and to provide supportive supervision are clearly important for preventing burnout. Child welfare workers repeatedly endorse the importance of being able to talk to one's supervisor about emotional reactions to the work, and of being able to trust and respect the supervisor's judgment. Given this, decisions about who is promoted to supervisor have important implications for burnout levels in the employees they supervise.

Implementing recommendations made earlier that contribute to an employee viewing the organization as fair and transparent in its treatment of workers would clearly address mismatches involving perceptions of unfairness. Organizational practices that can provide promotion or other forms of recognition for exemplary work are important for preventing burnout in child welfare. For example, workers who provide excellent mentoring need to be recognized and rewarded for their important contribution to staff training and retention. Furthermore, the suggestions discussed earlier in terms of preparing child welfare workers for "shocks" and helping them develop scripts to respond adaptively to these shocks would address possible mismatches between the worker's values and principles and the requirements of the job.

What seems to be important to an effective program for burnout prevention is involvement of employees at all levels. Leiter and Maslach (2000) have developed a very user-friendly resource titled "Preventing Burnout and Building Engagement" that includes a manual and workbook providing detailed instruction for either a small group of employees or a manager to begin an individualized assessment of the engagement and burnout experienced by employees in all parts of an organization. The resource includes an Organizational Checkup Survey that can be used to gather relevant information, suggestions about usual steps in the process, and expectable problems along the way (Leiter & Maslach, 2000). Although its effectiveness has not yet been assessed, it offers concrete step-by step help based on empirical research. The kit appears to have considerable potential for assisting organizations to design interventions tailored to their unique context and circumstances.

Halbesleben and colleagues (2004) note that the realistic job previews and expectation-lowering procedures recommended to reduce turnover should also be effective in reducing burnout by improving the fit between job demands and resources available to the worker. Similar to Leiter and Maslach (2000), they argue that action research involving workers at all levels in a systematic investigation of the concerns of a specific organization provides opportunities for employees and management to collaborate and increase social support. They point out that an action-research approach can lead to the development of an intervention customized to address the particular needs of the organization. In our view, the resource kit developed by Leiter and Maslach (2000) would provide useful materials that could be used in an action-research model. Both Leiter and Maslach (2000) and Halbesleben and colleagues (2004) seem to agree that preventing burnout requires a collaboration between management and employees, a careful analysis of the experience of workers at all levels, and an action plan tailored to the specific needs of the organization. The idea that one approach to burnout prevention will fit all situations is no longer credible.

Conclusion

As this chapter has demonstrated, our understanding of how and why burnout and turnover happens in organizations is still evolving despite a great deal of attention by researchers over the past 50 years. We know that an individual's decision to leave an organization is a result of both personal and organizational factors, and it appears both domains also contribute to employee burnout. From the research that has explored the relationships among personal, job, and organizational variables and turnover, we know that job satisfaction and organizational commitment are important determinants of individuals' intentions to leave or stay with their employer. In child welfare organizations, burnout or emotional exhaustion also seems to be a substantial factor in determining turnover intentions.

This review has enabled us to identify many of the correlates of high job satisfaction, high organizational commitment, and low burnout, and suggests several strategies that child welfare organizations can employ in the design of their organizations and in the selection, development, and ongoing interaction with their employees. The strategies described in this chapter have become recommended practices for contemporary child welfare agencies.

The recent theoretical innovations of Lee and Mitchell (1994) have added both to our understanding of how people make decisions to leave organizations and to how human service organization managers might intervene in that decision process. Their hypothesis that people often have "scripts" that indicate how to behave when positive or negative "shocks" occur suggests opportunities for child welfare managers to influence these scripts. For example, a proactive human resource department could design an orientation program that anticipated many of the shocks that a new child welfare worker might encounter and recommend ways of reacting to those shocks. New workers need to be prepared for the first time they have to apprehend a child. They need to be prepared for the possible involvement of the police and the strong emotions felt by all involved. Supervisors need to help workers think about this scenario and about how they construct their role and their responsibilities. If longer tenured employees feel "embedded" in their agencies because of the organization's support for excellence in supervision, for strong work group cohesion, and for maximizing the best fit between the job and the individual, their first resort in the face of an unexpected event will be to talk to a trusted colleague rather than hand in their resignation. In both cases, unwanted turnover can be averted. Similarly, the development of the conservation of resources (COR) model of burnout and the empirical support for its tenets has advanced our ability to better understand how burnout happens and what conditions decrease its prevalence.

While the research has taught us much about the antecedents to burnout and turnover and about prevention strategies, there is still more to learn. As we noted earlier, most studies of turnover were done outside the human-services sector, and the relationship of burnout to organizational commitment, job satisfaction, and to actual turnover requires more research. Studies are needed that focus specifically on these questions in child welfare organizations. In addition, studies that evaluate the impact of organizational intervention strategies such as those suggested by the unfolding model and by the COR model need to be undertaken.

Child welfare organizations do have an advantage over many business organizations. Their staff is typically extremely committed to the organization's mandate. Building on this commitment to purpose to the degree that it becomes commitment to the organization takes energy, time, and a reflective approach to management. The return for this effort is ultimately in benefits to the clients and to the community that the agency serves. We have demonstrated that burnout and turnover have many roots—some of these are strong contributors to high levels of burnout and turnover, and others are weaker determinants but still add to the cumulative effect. Much research has been done, but more studies, based on new ways of understanding the processes that culminate in burnout or turnover will increase our ability to reduce both these outcomes. Our hope is that this chapter has increased awareness of the conditions that lead to burnout and turnover and has stimulated readers to think about how child welfare organizations can become less fertile soil for the roots of avoidable burnout and turnover.

Notes

1 Job attitudes are evaluative thoughts and feelings about various aspects of a job or the employing organization that develop as a result of employment.
2 The five-factor model, a popular approach to the study of personality traits, comprises five personality dimensions: openness to experience, conscientiousness, extraversion, agreeableness, and neuroticism. The five factors were derived from factor analyses of a large number of self- and peer reports on personality-relevant adjectives and questionnaire items [McCrae, 1997 #121].

3 A structured interview, also known as a behavioural interview, is one that follows a predetermined set of questions designed to explore the candidate's previous experience through examples of behaviours relevant to the current position requirements. "Give me an example of a time when you sought advice from your supervisor about a difficult case," is an appropriate question whereas, "Do you ask for advice?" is not.

4 Pre-existing plans of action as described in the unfolding model.

References

Armstrong-Stassen, M., Al-Ma'aitah, R., Cameron, S. J., & Horsburgh, M. E. (1998). The relationship between work status congruency and the job attitudes of full-time and part-time Canadian and Jordanian nurses. *The International Journal of Human ResourceManagement, 9*(1), 41–57.

Aryee, S., Vivienne, L., & Stone, R. (1998). Family-responsive variables and retention-relevant outcomes among employed parents. *Human Relations, 51*(1), 73–85.

Baines, C., Evans, P., & Neysmith, S. (Eds.) (1991). *Women's caring: Feminist perspectives on social welfare.* Toronto, ON: McClelland & Stewart.

Baker, J. G., & Baker, D. F. (1999). Perceived ideological differences, job satisfaction and organizational commitment among psychiatrists in a community mental health center. *Community Mental Health Journal, 35*(1), 85–95.

Barak, M. E. M., Nissly, J. A., & Levin, A. (2001). Antecedents to retention and turnover among child welfare, social work, and other human service employees: What can we learn from past research? A review and metanalysis. *Social Service Review, 75*(4), 625–661.

Barrett, K., Riggar, T. F., Flowers, C. R., Crimando, W., & Bailey, T. (1997). The turnover dilemma: A disease with solutions. *Journal of Rehabilitation, 63,* 36–42.

Barrick, M. R., & Mount, M. K. (1991). The big five personality dimensions and job performance: A meta-analysis. *Personnel Psychology, 44,* 1–26.

Ben-Dror, R. (1994). Employee turnover in community mental health organization: A development stages study. *Community Mental Health Journal, 30*(3), 243–257.

Blankertz, L. E., & Robinson, S. E. (1997). Turnover intentions of community mental health workers in psychosocial rehabilitation services. *Community Mental Health Journal, 33*(6), 517–529.

Callahan, M. (1993). Feminist approaches: Women recreate child welfare. In B. Wharf (Ed.) *Rethinking Child Welfare in Canada* (pp. 172–209). Toronto: McClelland & Stewart.

Cherniss, C. (1993). Role of professional self-efficacy in the etiology and amelioration of burnout. In W. Schaufeli, C. Maslach, & T. Marek (Eds.), *Professional burnout: Recent developments in theory and research* (pp. 135–149). Washington, DC: Taylor & Francis.

Cordes, C. L., & Dougherty, T. W. (1993). A review and an integration of research on job burnout. *Academy of Management Review, 18*(4), 621–656.

Coulthard, C., Duncan, K., Goranson, S., Hewson, L., Howe, P., Lee, K., et al. (2001). *Report on staff retention*. Toronto, ON: Children's Aid Society of Toronto.

Cox, T., Kuk, G., & Leiter, M. P. (1993). Burnout, health, work stress, and organizational healthiness. In W. Schaufeli, C. Maslach, T. Marek (Eds.), *Professional burnout: Recent developments in theory and research* (pp. 177–193). Washington, DC: Taylor & Francis.

Demerouti, E., Bakker, A.B., Vardakou, I., & Kantas, A. (2003). The convergent validity of two burnout instruments: A multitrait-multimethod analysis. *European Journal of Psychological Assessment, 19*, 12–23.

Drake, B., & Yadama, G. N. (1996). A structural equation model of burnout and job exit among child protective services workers. *Social Work Research, 20*(3), 179–187.

Duxbury, L., & Higgins, C. (2001). Work-life balance in the new millennium: Where are we? Where do we need to go? *Canadian Policy Research Networks Discussion Paper* (p. 80). Ottawa, ON.

Esposito, G., & Fine, M. (1985). The field of child welfare as a world of work. In J. Laird & A. Hartman (Eds.). *A handbook of child welfare* (pp. 727–740). New York: Free Press.

Griffeth, R. W., Hom, P. W., & Gaertner, S. (2000). A meta-analysis of antecedents and correlates of employee turnover: Update, moderator tests, and research implications for the next millennium. *Journal of Management, 26*, 463–488.

Geurts, S., Schaufeli, W., & De Jonge, J. (1998). Burnout and intention to leave among mental health-care professionals: A social psychological approach. *Journal of Social and Clinical Psychology, 17*(3), 341–362.

Halbesleben, J. R. B., & Buckley, M. R. (2004). Burnout in organizational life. *Journal of Management, 30*, 859–879.

Hatton, C., & Emerson, E. (1998). Brief report: Organisational predictors of actual staff turnover in a service for people with multiple disabilities. *Journal of Applied Research in Intellectual Disabilities, 11*(2), 166–171.

Hobfoll, S. E. (1989). Conservation of resources. A new attempt at conceptualizing stress. *American Psychologist, 44*, 513–524.

Hobfoll, S. E., & Freedy, J. (1993). Conservation of resources: A general stress theory applied to burnout. In W. Schaufeli, C. Maslach, & T. Marek (Eds.), *Professional burnout: Recent developments in theory and research* (pp. 115–129). Washington, DC: Taylor & Francis.

Hom, P. W., & Griffeth, R. W. (1995). *Employee turnover*. Cincinnati, OH: International Thomson Publishing.

Irvine, D. M., & Evans, M. G. (1995). Job satisfaction and turnover among nurses: Integrating research findings across studies. *Nursing Research, 44*(4), 246–253.

Jayartne, S., & Chess, W. A. (1984). Job satisfaction, burnout, and turnover: A national study. *Social Work, 29*(5), 448–453.

Koeske, G. F., & Kirk, S. A. (1995). The effect of characteristics of human service workers and subsequent morale and turnover. *Administration in Social Work, 19*(1), 15–31.

Koeske, G. F., & Koeske, R. D. (1993). A preliminary test of a stress-strain-outcome model for reconceptualizing the burnout phenomenon. *Journal of Social Service Research, 17*, 107–135.

Kossek, E. E., & Ozeki, C. (1999). Bridging the work–family policy and productivity gap: A literature review. *Community, Work & Family, 2*(1), 7–32.

Larson, S. A., & Lakin, K. C. (1999). Longitudinal study of recruitment and retention in small community homes supporting person with developmental disabilities. *Mental Retardation, 37*(4), 267–280.

Lease, S. H. (1998). Annual review, 1993–1997: Work attitudes and outcomes. *Journal of Vocational Behavior, 53*, 154–183.

Lee, K., Carswell, J. J., & Allen, N. J. (2000). A meta-analytic review of occupational commitment: Relations with person- and work-related variables. *Journal of Applied Psychology, 85*(5), 799–811.

Lee, R. T., & Ashforth, B. E. (1996). A meta-analytic examination of the correlates of the three dimensions of job burnout. *Journal of Applied Psychology, 81*(2), 123–133.

Lee, T. W., & Mitchell, T. R. (1994). An alternative approach: The unfolding model of voluntary employee turnover. *Academy of Management Review, 19*, 51–89.

Lee, T. W., Mitchell, T. R., Holtom, B. C., McDaniel, L. S., & Hill, J. W. (1999). The unfolding model of voluntary turnover: A replication and extension. *Academy of Management Journal, 42*(4), 450–462.

Leiter, M. P. (1993). Burnout as a developmental process: Consideration of models. In W. B. Schaufeli, C. Maslach, & T. Marek (Eds.), *Professional burnout: Recent developments in theory and research* (pp. 237–250). Washington: Taylor & Francis.

Leiter, M. P., & Durup, M. J. (1996). Work, home, and in-between: A longitudinal study of spillover. *Journal of Applied Behavioral Science, 32*(1), 29–47.

Leiter, M. P., & Harvie, P. L. (1996). Burnout among mental health workers: A review and a research agenda. *International Journal of Social Psychiatry, 42*(2), 90–101.

Leiter, M. P., & Harvie, P. L. (1997). Correspondence of supervisor and subordinate perspectives during major organizational change. *Journal of Occupational Health Psychology, 2*(4), 343–352.

Leiter, M. P., & Maslach, C. (2000). *Preventing burnout and building engagement: A complete program for organizational renewal.* San Francisco: Jolley-Bass.

Leiter, M. P., & Schaufeli, W. (1996). Consistency of the burnout construct across occupations. *Anxiety, Stress, and Coping, 9*, 229–243.

Lowe, G. S., & Schellenberg, G. (2001). What's a good job? The importance of employment relationships. *Canadian Policy Research Networks* (p. 117). Ottawa, ON.

Manlove, E. E., & Guzell, J. R. (1997). Intention to leave, anticipated reasons for leaving, and 12-month turnover of child care center staff. *Early Childhood Research Quarterly, 12*, 145–167.

March, J. G., & Simon, H. A. (1958). *Organizations.* New York: Wiley.

Maslach, C., & Goldberg, J. (1998). Prevention of burnout: New perspectives. *Applied and Preventive Psychology, 7*, 63–74.

Maslach, C., & Schaufeli, W. (1993). Historical and conceptual development of burnout. In W. Schaufeli, C. Maslach, & T. Marek (Eds.), *Professional burnout: Recent developments in theory and research.* Washington, DC: Taylor & Francis.

McCrae, R. R., & Costa, P. T. (1997). Personality trait structure as a human universal. *American Psychologist. 52*(5), 509–516.

Mitchell, T. R., Holtom, B. C., & Lee, T. W. (2001). How to keep your best employees: Developing an effective retention policy. *Academy of Management Executive, 15*(4), 96–109.

Mitchell, T. R., Holtom, B. C., Lee, T. W., Sablynski, C. J., & Eraz, M. (2001). Why people stay: Using job emebeddedness to predict voluntary turnover. *Academy of Management Journal, 44*(6), 1102–1121.

Mitchell, T. R., & Lee, T. W. (2001). The unfolding model of voluntary turnover and job embeddedness: Foundations for a comprehensive theory of attachment. In B. Staw & R. Sutton (Eds.), *Research in Organizational Behavior* (Vol. 23). Greenwich, CT: JAI Press.

Morrell, K., Loan-Clarke, J., & Wilkinson, A. (2004). The role of shocks in employee turnover. *British Journal of Management, 15*, 335–350.

Munn, E. K., Barber, C. E., & Fritz, J. J. (1996). Factors affecting the professional well-being of child life specialists. *Children's Health Care, 25*(2), 71–91.

Rush, M. C., Schoel, W. A., & Barnard, S. M. (1995). Psychological resiliency in the public sector: "hardiness" and pressure for change. *Journal of Vocational Behavior, 46*, 17–39.

Schaufeli, W. B., Enzmann, D., & Girault, N. (1993). Measurement of burnout: A review. In W. Schaufeli, C. Maslach, & T. Marek (Eds.), *Professional burnout: Recent developments in theory and research* (pp. 199–215). Washington, DC: Taylor & Francis.

Silver, P. T., Poulin, J. E., & Manning, R. C. (1997). Surviving the bureaucracy: The predictors of job satisfaction for the public agency supervisor. *The Clinical Supervisor, 15*(1), 1–20.

Somers, M. J. (1995). Organizational commitment, turnover and absenteeism: An examination of direct and interaction effects. *Journal of Organizational Behavior, 16*, 49–58.

Somers, M. J. (1999). Application of two neural network paradigms to the study of voluntary employee turnover. *Journal of Applied Psychology, 84*(2), 177–185.

Somers, M. J., & Birnbaum, D. (1999). Survival versus traditional methodologies for studying employee turnover: Differences, divergences and directions for future research. *Journal of Organizational Behavior, 20,* 273–284.

Steers, R. M., & Mowday, R. T. (1983). Employee turnover in organizations. In R. M. P. Steers (Ed.), *Motivation and Work Behavior* (3rd ed., pp. 470–481). New York: McGraw-Hill.

Tai, T. W. C., Bame, S. I., & Robinson, C. D. (1998). Review of nursing turnover research, 1977–1996. *Social Sciences Medicine, 47*(12), 1905–1924.

Um, M.-Y., & Harrison, D. F. (1998). Role stressors, burnout, mediators, and job satisfaction: A stress-strain-outcome model and an empirical test. Social *Work Research, 22*(2), 100–115.

Wright, T. A., & Cropanzano, R. (1998). Emotional exhaustion as a predictor of job performance and voluntary turnover. *Journal of Applied Psychology, 83,* 486–493.

|8|

Pathways to Residential Children's Mental Health Services
Parents' Perceptions of Service Availability
and Treatment Outcomes

Karen M. Frensch
Gary Cameron
Gerald R. Adams
Catherine de Boer

Among the general child and youth population, rates of identified mental health problems are 14–25% (Stiffman, Chen, Elze, Dore, & Cheng, 1997). Over half these children have more than one mental health challenge, and these problems often go undetected (Children's Mental Health Ontario, 2005). Specific subgroups of children and youth, such as children involved with child welfare (Shin, 2005), have a higher prevalence of mental health difficulties. Some studies have suggested that up to 50% of children involved with child welfare have a psychiatric disorder (Knitzer & Yelton, 1990) and up to 80% have some emotional, behavioural, learning, or developmental difficulties (Burns et al., 2004). There is a significant overlap in the children served by both child welfare and children's mental health services (Cameron & Hoy, 2003). For example, at least half the available beds in children's residential mental health treatment facilities are allocated to children from the child welfare system. Mental health needs exceed service availability.

The "gateway sectors" of child welfare, juvenile justice, medicine, and education serve as multiple pathways to mental health services. Studies on the long-term mental health needs and service use of children and youth show modest use of mental health services (delivered through these "gateway" sectors) and even less use of specialty mental health services like psychiatric hospitals and community mental health centres (Burns et al., 1995; Burns et al., 2004; Farmer, Burns, Phillips, Angold, & Costello, 2003). Undoubtedly "organizations charged with the health, education, and welfare of children ... have a role to play" in the provision of mental health services (Burns et al., 1995, p. 147). However, these sectors are often limited by inadequate recognition of need, poor connections to mental health resources, and staffing and financial constraints (Knitzer, Steinberg, & Fleisch, 1991; Stiffman et al., 1997; Stiffman et al., 2000). Child welfare, in particular, faces serious challenges in recognizing and responding to the needs of children with emotional and behavioural difficulties. According to Farmer and colleagues (2003), the child welfare and juvenile justice sectors serve as gateways for the fewest children and youth, but children and youth with serious emotional disturbances (SED) are more likely to receive services through these sectors than children with other less severe mental health needs.

Children and youth with emotional and behavioural difficulties will use many different services throughout childhood and adolescence (Silver et al., 1992). Despite the policy trend toward integrated systems of care for children and youth with mental health challenges, little is known about how families experience front-line service provision across the service sectors of child welfare, general medicine, and education. Of particular interest are families' experiences with the child welfare system as they search for solutions. What are some of the challenges facing families when they approach child welfare for help in meeting the unique and often extreme needs of their children?

Research by the Partnerships for Children and Families Project offers a candid look at the experience of parents seeking services for a child with emotional and behavioural problems. From conversations with 29 parents who placed their child in a residential community mental health treatment centre, we heard about their quest for timely and appropriate services, the daily pressures of caring for a child in need of residential mental health treatment, the impact of "working with services that don't work," and the experience of finally obtaining services that addressed the needs of their child. Prior to becoming involved with residential mental health services, over 70% of these families first came into contact with the child welfare system. Although child welfare provided relief to some families in the form of an out-of-home child placement, the majority of parents described not only the inability of the child welfare system to respond adequately to the needs of their family but also the distressing experience of interacting with a system that they felt often blames parents for their child's difficulties.

A priority of this chapter is to convey the intensity of everyday life for families caring for a child with emotional and behavioural difficulties. Many families described in detail the mounting pressures of caring for their child in the home, advocating for services for their child, and managing the routine stresses of daily life. For some families, a crisis situation precipitated entry into residential treatment. For others, the parents' determination and perseverance in finding help for their child resulted in access to residential treatment.

We briefly summarize the experience of families once a child enters residential treatment. Integral to this experience are the feelings of relief and sadness at the reality of placing a child in out-of-home treatment. We report treatment outcomes for both children and families, and we conclude the chapter with some thoughts about the future of effective systems of care for children and youth.

The Study

Our study involved 29 primary caregivers who had a child or youth placed in residential treatment at one of two local children's mental health treatment centres. We interviewed 27 female caregivers and 2 male caregivers. The mean age of parents interviewed was 40.75 with a range of 30–54 years. The average number of children per family was 2.93 with a range of one to eight children. The largest portion of parents (46.4%) had two children. The marital status of the sample (at the time of the interview) was as follows: married (N=9), divorced (N=9), common-law (N=4), single (N=4), separated (N=2), and widowed (N=1). Eighty-three percent of parents indicated being born in Canada. Other countries of birth included England, Jamaica, Scotland, Portugal, and the United States. Similarly, 89.7% of parents indicated that English was their first language spoken. Other first-spoken languages included German, French, and Polish. It is likely that this demographic profile is indicative of the larger population of parents and families receiving services at these two children's mental health centres, however we cannot know for sure without comparative data.

Length of agency involvement was reported to range from one month to14 years with an average of 1.84 years of agency involvement. The two children's mental health centres in the study offered a range of services (such as intensive home-based services, family counselling, and residential treatment), and parents did not distinguish between service types when reporting length of agency involvement. Eighty-two percent of parents reported that their child had received agency services for two years or less.

Parents were visited in their homes (to assure comfort and to eliminate travel inconveniences) by an interviewer and engaged in a one-on-one dialogue that explored dimensions of their everyday lives and reflected on their service experiences. Interviews consisted of a series of open-ended questions and were approximately 1½ to 2 hours in length. All interviews were audio-taped and transcribed. Parents were given a gift of $25.00 for participating in the study. Following the interview, parents were sent a copy of their interview to keep. For our purposes, the names of family members, cities in which families live, or specific life circumstances that could be used to identify a particular family have all been changed.

Pathways to Service

Parents' conversations offer a personalized view of the challenging nature of navigating an often long and winding pathway to children's residential mental health services. Parents of children requiring residential treatment are seasoned advocates for their children. Prior to considering this extreme option, these parents have negotiated their children and themselves through a range of services explicitly and peripherally connected to children's mental health. Parents were involved with a number of service sectors along the way with varying degrees of success, including the child welfare system, medical sector, and education system.

Child Welfare

Child welfare was a service sector frequently encountered by parents in their quest for mental health services. Approximately 70% of the families in our study had previous involvement with at least one child welfare agency. This involvement ranged from a brief referral to having their child placed in out of home care. In fact, 45% of these primary caregivers reported that their child had one or more out-of-home placements in a foster home, group home, or emergency shelter. Other research by the Partnerships Project offers further evidence of a significant overlap in child welfare and children's mental health populations (Cameron & Hoy, 2003; Freymond, 2003).

Much research has documented the mental health needs of children in the child welfare system. Specifically, Burns and colleagues' (2004) study of the mental health needs of 3,803 youth, age 2–14 years and involved with child welfare, documented scores in the clinical range on the Child Behaviour Checklist (CBCL) for 47.9% of all children surveyed. They did not report on types of clinical impairment. However, according to Shin (2005), some of the most common diagnoses for children in foster care with mental health needs include conduct disorder (40%), depressive disorder (32%), adjustment disorder (32%), anxiety disorder (19%), and attention deficit hyperactivity disorder (ADHD) (13%). Despite the significant mental health needs of children involved with the child welfare system, levels of actual provision of mental health services vary widely. Only 11.7% of the children scoring in the clinical range on the CBCL had received any mental health services in the 12 months preceding the study (Burns et al., 2004). Other studies have reported higher rates of service provision; for example, Shin (2005) found that 50% of foster-care youth had received mental health services. Farmer, Burns, Phillips, Angold, and Costello (2001) reported that children with a history of foster-care placements and children involved with child welfare (but not in placement) are more likely to receive mental health services than children living in poverty and not in contact with the system. They suggest that child welfare acts as "a de facto gatekeeper of mental health services for young people" (p. 621). However, services received are not necessarily adequate. In Shin (2005), half of the youth who received services only participated in a diagnostic interview while smaller proportions of youth received actual services, such as individual therapy (49%), emergency care (33%), family therapy (29%), group therapy (25%), medication management (20%), and in-patient and residential treatment (15%).

The service mandate of child welfare agencies limits them to the provision of mental health services for children and youth of families involved with child welfare. In the Ontario Child Welfare Eligibility Spectrum (OACAS, 2000), a tool used to assist service providers in making decisions about eligibility for service, guidelines are articulated for situations involving mental health issues such as caregiver and child conflict/child behaviour, caregiver response to child's mental, emotional, and developmental conditions, and caregiver response to a child under 12 who has committed a serious act. These sections discuss the mental health needs of children; however, service provision is mandated only in situations where caregiver response is deemed inadequate; for example, the caregiver "does not provide or refuses to provide or is unavailable or unable to consent to treatment to address or alleviate the child's condition" (p. 33) or caregivers who "consent to the treatment but do not follow through and take the actions necessary to provide the treatment" (p. 33).

Mental health needs of children within the family are not easily separated from mandated protection concerns such as a parent's inability to meet the extreme emotional needs of their emotionally or behaviourally disordered child. Freymond's (2003) study of parents' experiences of having a child placed in out-of-home care by child welfare addresses the emphasis on parental inadequacy as a prerequisite for services and posits that "mothers may not realize that in order to secure assistance, the information that they provide to workers must focus on their own inabilities, rather than on their child's negative behaviours" (p. 151). One mother expressed how a domestic dispute opened up services for her son:

> I mean I needed help and nobody would do it for me. Nobody would do nothing and it was when the punch happened ... That's when people finally started to recognize me [when parent was hit by partner]. That's when I started getting help. That's when children's aid says okay, yes, we will put him [in a temporary placement] we'll try and get foster care for him, yes, we'll try and help you get him into [the residential treatment centre]. He was in ... in the snap of a finger. When I tried doing it all by myself, oh, well, there might be a year's waiting list, there might be two years, blah, blah, blah, there's no beds, there's this, there's that, there's everything.

Several parents involved with both child welfare and children's mental health in our study offered comparisons of the two systems, highlighting the obstacles to obtaining help from child welfare. Most notable were parents' perceptions that their concerns were not acknowledged by service providers and that they felt blamed for their child's difficulties. For some parents, child welfare service providers were seen as disbelieving and incapable of providing appropriate services. The following are typical comments from parents who described child welfare service providers' lack of acknowledgment regarding concerns about their child:

> It's very frustrating. Because at first, I would sit there and tell them this, and nobody would believe me. Finally we had a case conference and the first foster mother was there, and she sat there and backed me up 100% and I was like, thank god somebody's listening to me. Finally.

> The only good thing that came out of that was that F&CS foster families, anybody else that was dealing with [child] began to believe what I was saying about her. So, it was validation, no, I'm not going crazy.

In both cases, it took another service provider working within child welfare (that is, a foster mother or group home staff) to validate these parents' concerns before they were regarded as needing service.

Another sentiment expressed by many parents involved with child welfare was that they felt blamed by child welfare. For example, one parent remarked: "you ask them for help, and, you know, like, why do you need it? Can't you do it yourself? Why can't you be a decent parent? So don't look at me as if it's my fault." Similarly another parent said:

> When he was in foster care I thought I had lost him to somebody else. When he was in residence I knew that I was going to get him back. I knew. I'm not saying nothing bad about Children's Aid, but to me they pin out the parents that are bad where [residential service providers] didn't do that. They never ever put us down as bad parents.

Only a few of the families who had received services from child welfare spoke favourably about their interactions with service providers. More frequently, service providers were described by parents as disrespectful, blaming, intimidating, and threatening. One parent explained:

> I felt a lot of the times, I felt they were just trying to intimidate me, not help me. [...] Children's Aid was so disrespectful to me on the phone, it was pathetic. [...] I think at first they were trying to rule me and overpower me ...

Initial encounters with child welfare service providers typically were difficult: "He didn't want to know anything. He came in here with daggers in his eyes, ready to condemn somebody." Another said, "I didn't like her the

day she walked in my house." Maintaining communication with child welfare service providers was also highlighted by some parents as an obstacle.
More specifically, parents expressed frustration with the inaccessibility of
service providers:

> [child welfare service provider] called just when the Christmas holidays
> were coming on. So I had no way to get a hold of anybody to talk to any-
> body. So, after the holidays were over I called her office and every flip-
> ping time you called there was never anybody there to take your call. It
> was always an answering machine.

> [The Children's Aid Society] told us they would keep in contact with us
> and let us know how the child [son placed in a foster home] is doing. I have
> not heard from them. They told me they were going to have a worker
> deal with our needs because we don't have our child here ... I have not
> heard from anyone ... I got a call from [the residence] telling me that
> [son] had a new [child welfare] worker and her name was [Sherry]. I
> have not heard from [Sherry] since she is the new worker [six weeks ago].

Not all experiences with child welfare were regarded as negative by parents
of children suffering with mental health challenges. Freymond (2003)
reported that some families had exhausted the helping resources of other
community social service programs; for them, out-of home child welfare
placement was available and experienced as a welcomed relief.

General Medicine

Previous studies have reported on the use of the medical sector as a gateway
to mental health services (Burns et al., 1995; Farmer et al., 2003). In our
study, a number of parents first approached their family doctor with the
concern that something was wrong with their child. Criticisms of the medical sector from our study included parents' perceptions of having their concerns dismissed as needless worry, receiving advice that the child will "grow
out of it," or the concerns labelled as a "phase," and even misdiagnoses. One
mother in our study explained

> I almost felt sometimes like I was just banging my head against a wall.
> And I wasn't getting anywhere because I was trying to tell these doctors
> that I knew something was wrong and they were trying to tell me that I
> didn't know what I was talking about. So if they had listened to me at the
> beginning, we could have gotten all the testing done, we could have got-
> ten everything, and he could have been on his way a long time ago. So
> that was, it was awful.

Farmer and colleagues (2003) reported that only 12.9% of children surveyed as part of the Great Smoky Mountains Study (southeastern United
States) entered the mental health system through the general medical sector.

Rates of service use through a medical provider were slightly higher for children and youth involved with child welfare (36%) and those in foster care (48%) (Farmer et al., 2001). Commonly, need for service is determined by diagnoses; however, many children and youth who do not qualify or are overlooked for diagnoses have symptoms that affect functioning, and actual need may be underrepresented in the research (Angold, Costello, Farmer, Burns, & Erkanli, 1999). Furthermore, research has found that general health practitioners tend to overlook a significant proportion of existing mental health problems and diagnoses because they don't recognize the problem or have insufficient knowledge of predisposing factors (Stiffman et al., 2000). Several parents in our study spoke of their challenges in approaching the medical sector for help:

> We had no idea he had all these syndromes and everything. And so we started getting him tested in grade one. It seemed every doctor we took him too, he had something else.

> He used to scream a lot whenever he didn't get his own way. I even had a doctor tell me to lock him in his room, sit outside, and just let him scream. I found out later that that is abuse of some sort but I tried it. It didn't help. He screamed for 11 hours.

> There was one ... one pediatrician, who was able to make everything clear, and make everything make sense. But before that, like, the family doctor brushed it off as, you know, A.D.H.D. Hyperactive.

Providers in gateway sectors have a role to play in the identification and assessment of mental health problems and can be pivotal in obtaining appropriate services through referrals, consultations, and liaisons with other services (Stiffman et al., 2000). In their investigation of the role of service providers in moderating the gap between service needs and actual service provision, Stiffman et al. found that 22% of the variance in service provision could be explained by service providers' assessments and connections to resources. Moreover, 40% of the variance in referral to services was influenced by these same factors. The "perception of need (although often inaccurate) may determine the youth's pathway to services more than actual need and service availability" (Stiffman et al., 1997, p. 341). When compared to youth self-reports, service providers' reports of youths' mental health needs show poor recognition and inaccurate identification. Youth's identification of service need was not predictive of service provision (Stiffman et al., 2000).

In our research, over half (62%) of the parents first heard about residential treatment as an option for their child from professionals already involved with the family, such as doctors, teachers, and social workers. These professionals informed parents about services, discussed their suitability for their child, and provided information about how to access services. Of the 16 parents who spoke about their initial contact with the residential treatment centre, only four indicated that they had initiated contact of their own volition. In comparison, 12 parents either had professionals contact the residence on their behalf, or they did so themselves following the advice and endorsement of professionals. Although referrals for residential treatment can come directly from parents, these families relied heavily on professionals to initiate and strengthen their child's application.

Education

Many children enter into mental health services through the education sector. Burns et al. (1995) reported that 70–80% of children in their sample who had received mental health services were first seen by a service provider in the education sector. Similarly, in their study of points of entry into the mental health system, Farmer et al. (2003) reported that 60.1% of youth receiving mental health services entered the system through the education sector. This included seeing a guidance counselor and/or involvement in special education classes. Over 50% of the youth who came from education were only mildly troubled and were the least likely to meet the diagnostic criteria for psychiatric disorder. Youth who suffered from serious emotional disorders were the least likely to come into contact with mental health services based on contact with the education sector first (Farmer et al., 2003).

Parents in the Partnerships Project spoke of their efforts to obtain services for their child within the education sector. Because the children in our sample were dealing with significant emotional and behavioural challenges, most of them experienced significant difficulty at school. Approximately 33% of parents described advocating fiercely within the school system in an attempt to keep their child engaged in regular schooling. Parents articulated their tribulations in working with the school system to obtain services for their child:

> Three weeks of summer school and they're kicking him out. I had to beg the principal to please keep him. One more strike and he's out though. And I've been doing that for years with teachers. And pleading, and phoning, and hearing the messages, "and son did this" and "they gave him a 50 in both classes."

> Like I home-schooled him in grade two and then tried to get him back to school in grade three, I'm trying to get the sequence right here. They wouldn't take him back. I had to actually write letters to the MP to get [child] back in school. [...] They, I had grade five they wanted to put him in daycare. He's ... he was ten years old. They wanted to send him to daycare for the afternoons. I couldn't believe it. I said no.

> I've never felt like I could call any one at the public school and talk to them about [son] because they just don't understand. I get so frustrated because [doctor], a very busy pediatrician, offered to go to the school and talk to any one who had to deal with [son] and explain how to deal with him, what was wrong with him. They refused. The school refused. They didn't have time for that.

> But I had a very hard time with the school, a very hard time with the school. [...] They were, the [principal], sorry, was very, very upset with me because I took everything in my own hands. And [school principal] got really nasty with me and then [child's] teachers got really mean with him and he wasn't ... they weren't letting him go to the bathroom and he was peeing in his pants and all kinds of things. Yeah, it got really bad so I pulled him out of school. I pulled him out. He wouldn't go to school. He'd get sick in the morning because he didn't want to go to school and all kinds of stuff. So, and then all of the sudden I was going to be charged because my son wasn't in school.

After much effort, many parents were left frustrated and angry by their encounters with the school. Some parents, however, were more successful than others:

> I'm not quite sure when it started, you know, to be honest. I didn't, like with school, whenever I noticed anything happening, I would always be in contact with them and they were pretty good about, you know, altering his curriculum and whatever we could do. So, that would make it more interesting for him so he'd want to be there. I bent over backwards trying to help him.

Because schools are able to reach the most children in need, Farmer et al. (2001) recommend that improved screening and service delivery be provided through the school system.

The Realities of Daily Living

At least 60–70% of parents talked about the great effort they invested in advocating for their child. Efforts included researching treatment programs and new schools, pursuing diagnoses, convincing the focal child's school to "bend the rules," or placing the focal child in foster care. Parents talked about "begging" schools, professionals, family, and even friends for help:

> And that day I started rattling chains. I called people from my church who were youth workers and I knew [child] needed help. I didn't know if it was gonna be through the criminal court system or whether it was going to be through a social system. At point we had already been con-

nected with family and child services. [...] I just got every resource I could find.

But that's the point then at which we contacted [the residential treatment centre] and, you know, we tried a number of places. Like she was at the point where she was running out of friends to stay with and where was she going to go and she didn't want to come home. And so I tried to do some research as to what's available ... [...] I remember calling all kinds of people that I knew almost begging if they would take my daughter and let her live with them ...

Often having worked their way through a series of unsuccessful services, parents described feeling increasingly frustrated with the amount of effort and length of time involved to "work with people who don't work." Parents reported feeling unheard or dismissed, or they were told that there was nothing wrong with their child. One parent poignantly described her experience saying:

Nobody is helping me. Nobody will put me on waiting lists, nobody's listening. Nobody. I phoned the police. They said there's nothing we can do. Well, what do you want me to do to because if I tie her in her room or if I beat her up and say you're not going out and that's it and I physically force her to stay home, I'll be arrested and they're not doing anything. And I'm thinking you idiots. So, when you [police] come to my door and tell me my daughter is dead, then what? Then are you going to do something? Well, I'm not waiting for that and I'd say, I'm not waiting for that. I am not doing that. I'm not waiting for that knock on my door at three o'clock in the morning. I'm not doing that, or the phone call.

Fuelling parents' search for help was their experience of not knowing what to do, where to go, or whom to call. Feeling unsupported and isolated, parents in our study talked about the perception that there was no one out there to help, or that there was no one out there who *could* help:

I was tired. I was frustrated. I didn't know what to do. I figured there's got to be somebody out there to help me.

It got to the point where you think that nobody can help. You're clutching at straws, anything.

There wasn't any support. I was getting stonewalled from every agency. There just didn't seem to be any supports out there.

A growing sense of desperation compounded the situation for families already living in distress as they struggled to care for their child and carry out routine activities (for example, working, preparing meals, going to appointments), maintain other relationships with partners and siblings, care for their own physical and mental well-being, and search for services for their child:

> Two kids with special needs ... your life consists of trying to balance and manage your work, that schedule, the school schedule. But along with this, you have specialists, pediatricians, counselling. You have this whole spectrum going on at the same time as you're trying to manage your life.

> Trying to help [child] with his A.D.D. Bringing him to the best doctors. Getting him on medication, paying for all this stuff. Helping him at school. And then having [another] little one at home, working, and a husband. I don't know how I didn't have a nervous breakdown ...

> All these appointments, constantly going to doctor's appointments and then he was on probation and court and I mean it was endless, school appointments, it was just one appointment after another after another I would say for about the last three years ...

At some point the process of engaging with professionals and "the system" takes on an adversarial nature for parents. Parents in our study used terms like "war," "rattling chains," "pushing," "pressuring," and "fighting" to describe their efforts to get their child needed services. One parent reflected, "you wish you could work together with the people instead of against them." Similarly another parent remarked, "you are fighting to get what your child needs." Several parents reported an average of three to five years before the focal child was properly diagnosed and receiving helpful services. For some, it was the involvement of a professional (for example, parole officer, foster parent) substantiating the validity of what parents were saying that finally brought help to the child and the family. For others, it was their unrelenting determination and perseverance:

> There's no reason that you can't do something, so I was raised with that philosophy and my confidence has given me the ability to go out and seek help. Find the community resources to help my kids and not take no for an answer. Or if that door closed I'd find another one. So I'd always keep moving forward and I would use that experience to help other people who seemed to be struggling so much, because I've been there.... I am a mover and a shaker.

> I was beginning to think that I was crazy.... But then as a mother I still had to, because you can't give up on your kid. You still have to go with your instinct.... So, finally with all my pushing and his behaviour in the course as he got older and his dad obviously wasn't very nice to him which didn't help matters so I just was pushing, you know and I just pushed and pushed and finally now we've got a diagnosis. He's on medication to curve it and there's a difference in him.... finally when they

realized we weren't going to budge ... all of a sudden they came up with a plan ...

I kept pushing and pushing. That's what I felt they needed.... they certainly knew that I wasn't going to back down.

For other families in our study, the escalation of a child's behaviour caught the attention of a professional already involved with the family, which led to finally help. An escalation of behaviour usually referred to a serious incident such as a delinquent act or violent outburst:

She was very abusive. Verbally abusive, started to get physically abusive. I had to lay charges and stuff like that.

Getting into scraps at school. Either him getting hurt or him hurting someone else. So it started to escalate during this period of time.

At one point we called the police because she disappeared. We had absolutely no idea where she was. She packed her bags and took the bike and left home. She overdosed on Tylenol and came and told me and we rushed her to emergency ... .

He pulled a knife on me in the kitchen and I called the police and at that point they said you gotta get some help.

Twenty families in our study described gaining access to residential mental health services in response to a crisis situation. Eight families mentioned that police involvement hastened admission. Nine children were bumped up on the waiting list for residential services after another out-of-home option (for example, foster care, in-patient psychiatry, crisis bed at residence) had been temporarily secured due to a behavioural crisis. Four families indicated that an escalation in behaviour at school was the precipitating event for residential care. These were not mutually exclusive categories.

Previous research suggests that violent behaviour is the greatest precursor to hospitalization or residential treatment for youth (Gabel & Shindledecker, 1992; Garrison et al., 1990; Lyons & Schaefer, 2000) and at least half of the youth in residential treatment have histories of aggressive behaviour (Grosz et al., 1994). Garland (1995) argues that children and youth with conduct disorder, characterized by a cluster of externalizing behaviours, are more likely to receive services than children and youth with depression or anxiety disorders. Moreover, once in care, "the greater the level of dangerousness the more likely a child or adolescent would be discharged to the same or higher level of care (or [would] run away from care)" (Lyons & Schaefer, 2000, p. 72).

Residential Children's Mental Health Services

While residential treatment was a welcomed intervention for many families, it was generally regarded by parents as a treatment of "last resort." This extreme option was considered because of the tenacious and escalating nature of their child's behaviour, parents' increasing difficulties in containing and coping with it, and the gaps in service delivery in other sectors. One parent described residential treatment as her "last hope":

> I took him [son] to the family doctor, then I took him to [another doctor] who was a child psychologist. I took him to a behavioural specialist, different doctors.... he was put on medication at age three, on tranquilizers.... And again, I've had to go through the same thing with [another son], trying to get him diagnosed somewhere.... No other agency would listen to me, everybody I went to would say well you fall between the cracks ... I couldn't get any help from disability, because asthma wasn't considered a disability. [Son] was a behavioural child, learning disabilities, well okay, sure, lots of people have them. So every agency I went to just seemed to say I can really feel for you, but you kind of fall between the cracks. I didn't fall into any category. That was my last hope.

As a result of both public policy and professional preference, residential care has been regarded as a treatment of last resort since the advent of the treatment principle of least restrictive environment in the mid 1970s. The goal of deinstitutionalization and a strong normalization philosophy in public health has furthered this idea (Elson, 1996). Given that residential treatment is offered as a last resort, Elson contends that "children and adolescents who need residential treatment are the losers when they are forced to fail a variety of outpatient services prior to being referred." (p. 34) Furthermore, "much residential work has reflected ideas of children being damaged or disturbed, children possessing some problem or pathology, or parents being incompetent or deficient" (Durrant, 1993, p. 12).

According to Goldberg (1991), families experience varying levels of guilt associated with having "failed the child in the eyes of the community" (p. 1) and guilt associated with a sense of relief from having to minister to a child's excessive needs. "Sadly, children are often taken to residential programs in much the same way that cars are taken to workshops. The family understandably wants them to be repaired; however, the successful repair may confirm their lack of expertise" (Durrant, 1993, p. 13). Parents in our study talked about facing the reality of placing their child in residential treatment and coming to terms with their feelings of failure as a parent:

> I balked at sending [child] away. I, you know, it was like to me I was a failure. I have to send him away. I didn't like the fact he was in residence. I didn't like any part of it at all. Within two weeks I changed my mind.

(*Now what changed your mind?*) Just son's behaviour. What a difference in the kid. It was like night and day. [...] That's when I changed my mind. [...] I thought it was best for [child].

It was not something I was even prepared for, that was for sure. Yeah. Um ... in one sense, I felt a failure as a mom. Because, it's like, oh, I can't deal with this? But on the other, when I thought about it really, and after I spoke with several people there and what not, I realized that hey, well ... that was my choice. I couldn't let him stay home, and then ... things would have went from bad to worse.

Some parents in our study expressed worry about their young child being away from home, feeling alone and unloved, and being "tucked in" by strangers:

I was pretty distressed. My son was in basically an institution. He's my only boy, he's so dear to me and to be put in there and you can't tuck him in at night ... and then you got this lady witching at you. It was like, can you not understand? This is tearing me apart.

Other parents worried about their child feeling that the family was "giving up" on them:

It was hard because I knew we needed help, but we didn't realize how drastically they helped them, or try to help them. It was like I was putting him away. And that's the way he felt. You're pushing me away, you want me out of the family, you don't want me here.

It's scary because you know, you're going to wonder too, like how is your child going to feel? It's not, it can't be good for your child to go in and not have mom there right now, yet he's going in to total strangers, every one is a stranger to him. He gets sick in the night or he has nightmares, there's nobody that he's familiar with to be there for him.

At the same time, parents' positive reactions to placing their child in residential treatment included experiencing a sense of relief and finally feeling like there was some hope for their child. Approximately 60% of parents in our study described some positive effect from placing their child in residential treatment. The most common positive reaction to placement was experiencing a sense of relief, also described as "a big weight lifted off." Parents talked about placement being the "best thing" for their child and feeling hopeful that placement would ultimately provide the help that they needed:

You know, it was just a sigh of relief. And knowing that I can ... ah, work with these guys [service providers] here.... It's ... um ... just the burden of ... all that anger, being taken down, off my shoulders was a big one. And knowing that he's safe and happy was another one. And knowing that ...

they don't let him run the streets there ... just the burden of ... all that anger being taken off my shoulders ...

I had a lot of hope and expectations that it was really going to help with a lot of the issues. That is was really going to perhaps even alleviate some of the issues. It was an answer to a prayer absolutely.

Hooray! Finally! And you're so hopeful, like I am, anyway. I don't know if everybody. I'm always like, I always feel so hopeful, like, thank god we're going to get help. It's just like, such a big relief. It really is. It's not that, you know. It's got nothing to do with getting rid of your child, or anything. Cause I want my children with me. But ... you know, when they're like this. You can't always be there because of the behaviour. It gets so severe. But, it's like a major relief, it's like a great big weight has been lifted off your shoulder. And you're so hopeful, thinking this is going to be ... this is gonna help, this is going to be the answer, you know?

These positive sentiments continued as parents described their interactions with residential treatment service providers. Almost every parent in our study spoke favourably about their service provider. In contrast to experiences with other service sectors, in particular child welfare, families felt heard and understood by service providers in children's mental health:

Everybody that I met out there is very warm. They don't criticize you. They don't look down on you. They are willing to go to great lengths to help you out. Knowing that [son] is safe and happy, you know, it was just a sigh of relief.

Parents also identified the accessibility of residential service providers and appreciated their ability to support parents and connect them to resources. Not only did the service providers seem familiar with the challenges facing these children, they also conveyed to parents willingness and an ability to address their child's needs. These favourable impressions appeared to last throughout the duration of treatment, independent of whether or not parents reported an improvement in their child's functioning. Riley, Stromberg, and Clark (2005) reported similar parental satisfaction with service providers in children's mental health. Over 90% of parents surveyed, whose children had received mental health services (N=534), strongly agreed with a statement articulating that staff were respectful of parents and spoke to them in a way that they could understand. Similarly, Martin, Petr, and Kapp (2003) reported that parents were generally satisfied with how service providers explained their roles to parents, included parents in treatment planning, and employed family-centred treatment techniques.

Overall, rates of consumer satisfaction in mental health (70–90%) are typically high (Rey, Plapp, & Simpson, 1999; Riley et al., 2005). Reasons for such high levels of satisfaction are varied and are often attributed to measurement flaws (such as social desirability) rather than a true assessment of satisfaction. Despite this caution, consumer satisfaction in children's mental health remains a significant area of interest for those delivering services. Indeed, parental satisfaction is important, because parental attitudes can influence participation in services. Furthermore, meeting a family's needs is often a major treatment goal, and understanding what contributes to parental satisfaction can be useful in service design and delivery (Rey et al., 1999; Riley et al., 2005).

In an effort to understand factors that may be associated with parental satisfaction in children's mental health, recent studies have focused on the relationship between parental satisfaction and child treatment outcomes. However, mixed results from this research offer little clarity. Several large studies, such as the Fort Bragg Evaluation Project (Lambert, Salzer & Bickman, 1998) which was "designed to see whether an experimental continuum of care produced better outcomes and client satisfaction, as well as lower costs, compared with traditional services at two comparison sites" (p. 271), found no correlation between parental satisfaction and pathology change in children. Similarly, Rey, Enshire, Wever, and Appollonov (1998) reported a "lack of association between satisfaction with the treatment received and outcome" (p. 45) in their three-year study of disruptive adolescents treated in a day program. In contrast, a large study of all children served between 1992 and 1996 by Sydney's (Australia) children's mental health centres reported that children with a negative treatment outcome (as judged by a clinician) had significantly lower parental satisfaction scores than children rated as having a positive treatment outcome (Rey et al.,1999). Godley, Fiedler, and Funk (1998) reported that "perception of the seriousness of their child's problem" (p. 43) was the best predictor of overall parental satisfaction. That is, parents who perceived their child's difficulties as extremely serious reported being the least satisfied overall.

While the Partnerships research was not designed as an outcome study of residential treatment, the data proved to be adequate for identifying broad post-treatment outcome patterns across these 29 children and families. We also had ample qualitative information about parent's perceptions of services. Like Lambert et al. (1998) and Rey et al. (1998), we also observed parents' level of satisfaction to be independent of how their children were functioning after residential treatment. We remain cautious, however, in using the qualitative data to estimate change in functioning over time. There was no equivalent to a standardized measure in our study to gather information about a single construct across cases and across time, which would allow us to estimate degree of change. The data also did not allow us to calculate a percentage change over time or to be precise about greater or lower amounts of change among various subgroups.

In our study, 73% of parents spoke positively about residential treatment after their involvement with services. This sentiment is juxtaposed with the relatively poor outcome patterns for children after residential treatment. Most of the older children in our study continued to experience serious ongoing problems in daily living, which in many cases rivalled or exceeded their challenges prior to entering residential treatment. About 33% of these children had left home, and many had unstable living arrangements or were "on the streets." Post-treatment functioning of the younger children in our group of families was not notably more encouraging, although there was moderately more evidence of successful or partially successful adaptations. Approximately 50% of the younger children did not return to their original homes after residential treatment. Parents of both age groups of children remained concerned about major adaptation problems at school and renewed high levels of daily pressure on parents and siblings in the family.

In addition, families experienced immediate and direct benefits as a result of residential treatment. Almost 75% of parents with younger children talked about a substantial reduction in the level of tension in the home when their child was in residence. One parent described the feeling as being released from a "state of siege." About 50% of these parents highlighted benefits for other siblings in the home:

> She [sibling] became a lot calmer. Like, I was able to get her out of some of the bad habits that she'd picked up from him.

> They [siblings] were glad that he was getting help. They did feel a bit relieved because they could now walk around and not have the fear of being butchered. But they also missed him.

> For my daughter, it was just amazing because once he left and went into the school our whole home here became a sanctuary. Peace—that we needed and she blossomed.

Parents also experienced improvements in their own personal well-being. At least 50% of parents reported gains in their ability to cope with the pressures of their lives and to find some enjoyment in daily activities:

> I was functioning better. I was doing better at work. I was enjoying my work. I was a lot happier. We began sort of having fun. You know, if we wanted to go to breakfast, it was like oh, yeah, we can do that without worry that I'm going to have to stop and come back ... I stopped feeling sick all the time which was really good.

> I wasn't being threatened. I ... and I slept. I would never sleep, when he was upstairs. I was so scared he was going to beat up on [son], or ... pull through his threat of killing [daughter]. ... And I was able to relax. I was able to ... it was a totally, totally different way of living.

Other parents talked about pursuing personal goals such as returning to school:

> I haven't been in school for years. I didn't finish high school. I was like, oh my God, I've got to go back to school. I wanted to. ... But I loved it. It's so different going to school when you're older. ... there's just an at ease, feeling now, ... whereas before, it would be just panic. ... Now, I know I can handle just about anything. You know. Because it's like ... I've already been through the worst.

> You know, I'm really, really focused on work, started taking night classes and working on that degree and all of the things that I have not been able to do. And also focus on kind of my therapy so now I can actually go to therapy and deal with my issues ...

Other studies have also reported positive impacts for families involved with residential treatment (Wright, 1997), although it remains an understudied area. The role of the family in residential treatment has evolved in recent years. Families play a more active role in their child's residential treatment, and, increasingly, programs emphasize continued contact with family and community. Families are regularly invited to contribute to the formal treatment process by participating in family therapy, individual counselling sessions, and by setting treatment goals for their child and the family (Koroloff, Friesen, Reilly, & Rinkin, 1996). Psycho-educational models of residential treatment, for example, consider ways to increase the competencies of all members of a child's environment (Lewis & Lewis, 1989). Family involvement in treatment can have positive impacts on both family members and children in residence (Hatfield, 1994).

In light of the benefits to families, which include improved personal functioning and feelings of immense relief and hope, high levels of parental satisfaction with services make sense even in the face of ongoing challenges for children after treatment. Rey and colleagues (1998), in their attempt to understand why parents and youth perceive services as helpful in spite of a lack of significant improvements in psychopathology, concluded, "if the perception reflects a decrease in the level of stress for families, these programs may result in benefits not only for the children but also for parents" (p. 47). Moreover, Wells, Wyatt, & Hobfoll (1991) contended that "minimally we need to heed the often-repeated calls for the reconceptualization of residential treatment as a family support system" (p. 214).

Systems of Care

There is increasing recognition that children and youth with serious emotional and behavioural disorders have difficulties across many life domains and will come in contact with many services that will attempt to meet these needs (Farmer, 2000). Furthermore, the needs of children and families seldom occur in "neat, separate organizational boxes that represent the service delivery system" (Weber & Yelton, 1996, p. 227). Child welfare and children's mental health systems, as demonstrated in our research and elsewhere, have responsibility to service many of the same children and families, and the "increasingly complex problems facing many of the families participating in both systems require a response of a complexity unlikely to be available in a single system" (Weber & Yelton, 1996, p. 220).

In light of parents' negative experiences of seeking help from child welfare, coupled with the substantial proportion of children with serious emotional and behavioural challenges who come to the attention of child welfare, our research calls for a greater responsiveness on the part of child welfare toward families in need. Recent policy directions in child and youth services recognize the "need for better integration of child protective services with services designed to support families, children, and youth." (Ministry of Children and Youth Services, 2005, p. 13) In 2004, the Ministry of Children and Youth Services created the Partnership Strategies Office with the mandate to "explore and develop opportunities to create, support, and maintain quality cross-sector partnerships that support healthy and active children and youth in Ontario."

Service sectors like the education system can play a significant part in the provision of services within a system of care for children. Because a high number of youth first access services through the education sector, schools can play a greater role in the identification of children in need and in the provision of services (Farmer et al., 2001). Knitzer (1996) argues that involving education as a key player in systems of care is central to changing the fragmented profile of delivery systems. School-linked support services and the use of school as a "hub" for service delivery are seen as promising strategies for increasing the accessibility and use of mental health services by families. Indeed, the Partnerships for Children and Families Project's study of alternative service-delivery models in child welfare showcases the potential impact of community and school-based programs on families' experiences of service delivery. The Children's Aid Society of Halton in Burlington, Ontario, employs child protection service providers in selected schools to offer both protection and prevention services to the school community. Opinions expressed by parents, school principals, and service providers involved with the program provide support for the improved identification of children with mental health needs and greater ease of accessibility to child welfare and children's mental health services in a school-based delivery model (Cameron, Hazineh, & Frensch, 2005).

Systems of care are an increasingly popular method of delivering services to children and youth with serious mental health needs (Rosenblatt & Woodbridge, 2003). The term "system of care" was first used by Knitzer (1982), in the publication *Unclaimed Children*, in response to an absence of appropriate services for children with serious emotional disturbances. An original focus of systems of care was to explore how "services could be ideally organized and coordinated across child-serving agencies in order to provide services to children and support their smooth transition from one service to another" (Hernandez & Hodges, 2003, p. 21). Knitzer proposed several principles fundamental to systems of care, including services offered in the least restrictive setting, family involvement, cultural/ethnic sensitivity, and easy movement from one service to another. The coordination of service by child-serving sectors such as mental health, child welfare, and education allows for a system of care that can be flexible in adapting to the individual needs of children and families (Friedman, 2003; Lourie, Katz-Leavy, De Carolis, & Quinlan, 1996; Weber & Yelton, 1996).

So far, what is known about the effectiveness of systems of care has focused on system level issues. At a systems level, integral to cross-sector collaboration are similarity in the values and principles guiding each sector, working with the same groups of children and families, and striving for compatible goals (Friedman, 2003). Studies have documented that "system level reforms have consistently resulted in desired system-level changes." (Farmer, 2000, p. 629) Research on the effectiveness of systems of care as an intervention, however, has been scarce, and the results are inconsistent at the child- and family-outcome level (Hoagwood, Burns, Kiser, Ringeisen, & Schoenwald, 2001). Children and youth generally served by systems of care are a "high risk" group and this invites the question: what outcomes are realistic for these youth? The process of defining and measuring the success or effectiveness of systems of care is still in its infancy. For example, current research on the effectiveness of systems of care as an intervention has only followed youth for short time periods (6 months to 2 years), and this may be too short a time frame to document any significant changes. According to Farmer (2000), the field has not clearly specified when desired outcomes should be noted and what post-treatment environments and conditions are necessary to build on any gains made. To better understand the achievement of positive child- and family-level outcomes, more information is needed "in the intersection of system level knowledge and clinical intervention knowledge" (Hernandez & Hodges, 2003, p. 24).

Despite these criticisms, Knitzer's (1982) original conceptualization of systems of care as a way to organize fragmented services remains an attractive approach to facilitating the service experience for families with emotionally and behaviourally challenged children. Mental health and other child-serving sectors, in particular child welfare, all have significant roles to play in contributing to effective systems of care. Although the families in our study found their way to residential mental health services, a service they perceived to be helpful, their tribulations along the winding and fragmented path to children's mental health services point to continuing challenges in offering a system of care that delivers flexible, timely, and appropriate services. For example, family-centred services (a basic principle of systems of care) should involve responding to the needs of the whole family and incorporate family supports such as respite, child care, in-home assistance, and parent training (Friesen & Huff, 1996). Certainly our research supports the benefits of directly supporting families involved with residential treatment. Some research suggests that building individualized services around the unique needs of families is the next phase in the evolution of systems of care (Hernandez & Hodges, 2003; Rosenblatt & Woodbridge, 2003). An additional challenge for systems of care in the future will be to translate system-level collaboration into benefits for children and families, providing services that will make a difference to their lived experiences of caring for a child with emotional and behavioural difficulties.

References

Angold, A., Costello, E. J., Farmer, M. Z., Burns, B. J., & Erkanli, A. (1999). Impaired but undiagnosed. *Journal of the American Academy of Child and Adolescent Psychiatry, 38*(2), 129–137.

Burns, B. J., Costello, J., Angold, A., Tweed, D., Stangl, D., Farmer, E. M. Z., et al. (1995). Children's mental health service use across service sectors. *Health Affairs, 14*(3), 147–159.

Burns, B. J., Phillips, S. D., Wagner, H. R., Barth, R. P., Kolko, D., J., Campbell, Y., et al. (2004). Mental health need and access to mental health services by youths involved with child welfare: A national survey. *Journal of the American Academy of Child and Adolescent Psychiatry, 43*(8), 960–970.

Cameron, G., Hazineh, L., & Frensch, K. (2005). *Children's Aid Society of Halton: A school-based model of child welfare service delivery.* Waterloo, ON: Wilfrid Laurier University, Partnerships for Children and Families Project.

Cameron, G., & Hoy, S. (2003). *Life stories of mothers and child welfare.* Waterloo, ON: Wilfrid Laurier University, Partnerships for Children and Families Project.

Children's Mental Health Ontario. (2005). *Key Facts.* Retrieved November 25, 2005, from www.kidsmentalhealth.ca

Durrant, M. (1993). *Residential treatment: A cooperative, competency-based approach to therapy and program design.* New York: W. W. Norton.

Elson, S. E. (1996). Children's residential treatment: Last resort or treatment of choice. *Residential Treatment for Children & Youth, 14*(2), 33–44.

Farmer, E. M. Z. (2000). Issues confronting effective services in systems of care. *Children and Youth Services Review, 22*(8), 627–650.

Farmer, E. M., Burns, B., Phillips, S. D., Angold, A., & Costello, E. J. (2001, December). Use of mental health services by youth in contact with social services. *Social Services Review,* 605–624.

Farmer, E. M., Burns, B. J., Phillips, S. D., Angold, A., & Costello, E. J. (2003). Pathways into and through mental health services for children and adolescents. *Psychiatric Services, 54*(1), 60–66.

Freymond, N. (2003). *Mothers' everyday realities and child placement experiences.* Waterloo, ON: Wilfrid Laurier University, Partnerships for Children and Families Project.

Friedman, R. M. (2003). A conceptual framework for developing and implementing effective policy in children's mental health. *Journal of Emotional and Behavioral Disorders, 11*(1), 11–18.

Friesen, B., & Huff, B. (1996). Family perspectives on systems of care. In B. A. Stroul (Ed.), *Children's mental health: Creating systems of care in a changing society* (pp. 41–67). Baltimore, MD: Paul H. Brookes.

Gabel, S., & Shindledecker, R. (1992). Adolescent psychiatric inpatients: Characteristics, outcome, and comparison between discharged patients from a specialized adolescent unit and nonspecialized units. *Journal of Youth and Adolescence, 21,* 391–407.

Garland, A. F. (1995). *Teacher's identification of adolescents' need for mental health service.* Bethesda, MD: NIMH Mental Health Services Research Conference.

Garrison, W. T., Ecker, B., Friedman, M., Davidoff, R., Haeberle, K., & Wagner, M. (1990). Aggression and counteraggression during child psychiatric hospitalization. *Journal of the American Academy of Child and Adolescent Psychiatry, 29,* 242–250.

Godley, S. H., Fiedler, E. M., & Funk, R. R. (1998). Consumer satisfaction of parents and their children with child/adolescent mental health services. *Evaluation and Program Planning, 21,* 31–45.

Goldberg, K. (1991). Family experiences of residential treatment. *Journal of Child & Youth Care, 6*(4), 1–6.

Grosz, D. E., Lipschitz, D. S., Eldar, S., Finkelstein, G., Blackwood, N., Gerbino-Rosen, G., et al. (1994). Correlates of violence risk in hospitalized adolescents. *Comprehensive Psychiatry, 35,* 296–300.

Hatfield, A. (1994). The family's role in caregiving and service delivery. In H. P. Lefley & M. Wasow (Eds.), *Helping families cope with mental illness* (pp. 65–77). Langhorne, PA: Harwood Academic Publishers.

Hernandez, M., & Hodges, S. (2003). Building upon the theory of change for systems of care. *Journal of Emotional and Behavioral Disorders, 11*(1), 19–26.

Hoagwood, K., Burns, B., J., Kiser, L., Ringeisen, H., & Schoenwald, S.K. (2001). Evidence-based practice in child and adolescent mental health services. *Psychiatric Services, 52*, 1179–1190.

Knitzer, J. (1982). *Unclaimed children: The failure of public responsibility to children and adolescents in need of mental health services.* Washington, DC: Children's Defense Fund.

Knitzer, J. (1996). The role of education in systems of care. In B. A. Stroul (Ed.), *Children's mental health: Creating systems of care in a changing society.* (pp. 197–213). Baltimore, MD: Paul H. Brookes.

Knitzer, J., Steinberg, Z., & Fleisch, B. (1991). Schools, children, mental health, and the advocacy challenge. *Journal of Clinical Child Psychology, 20*, 102–111.

Knitzer, J., & Yelton, S. (1990). Collaborations between child welfare and mental health: Both systems must exploit the program possibilities. *Public Welfare, 48*, 24–33.

Koroloff, N. M., Friesen, B. J., Reilly, L., & Rinkin, J. (1996). The role of family members in systems of care. In B.A. Stroul (Ed.), *Children's mental health: Creating systems of care in a changing society* (pp. 409–426). Baltimore, MD: Paul H. Brookes.

Lambert, W., Salzer, M., & Bickman, L. (1998). Clinical outcome, consumer satisfaction, and ad hoc ratings of improvement in children's mental health. *Journal of Consulting and Clinical Psychology, 66*(2), 270–279.

Lewis, W. W., & Lewis, B. L. (1989). The psychoeducational model: Cumberland house after 25 years. In R. D. Lyman, S. Prentice-Dunn, & S. Gabel (Eds.), *Residential and inpatient treatment of children and adolescents* (pp. 97–113). New York: Plenum Press.

Lourie, I., Katz-Leavy, J., De Carolis, G., & Quinlan, W.A. (1996). The role of the federal government. In B.A. Stroul (Ed.), *Children's mental health: Creating systems of care in a changing society* (pp. 99–114). Baltimore, MD: Paul H. Brookes.

Lyons, J. S., & Schaefer, K. (2000). Mental health and dangerousness: Characteristics and outcomes of children and adolescents in residential placements. *Journal of Child and Family Studies, 9*(1), 67–73.

Martin, J. S., Petr, C. G., & Kapp, S. A. (2003). Consumer satisfaction with children's mental health services. *Child and Adolescent Social Work Journal, 20* (3), 211–226.

Ministry of Children and Youth Services. (2005). *Report on the 2005 review of the Child and Family Services Act (CFSA).* Retrieved November 24, 2005, from http://www.children.gov.on.ca/NR/CS/Publications/CFSAReview Report2005-en.pdf

Ontario Association of Children's Aid Societies. (2000). *Ontario Child Welfare Eligibility Spectrum.* Retrieved November 24, 2005, from http://www.oacas .org/resources/eligibility/

Rey, J. M., Enshire, E., Wever, C., & Appollonov, I. (1998). Three-year outcome of disruptive adolescents treated in a day program. *European Child & Adolescent Psychiatry, 7*, 42–48.

Rey, J. M., Plapp, J. M., & Simpson, P. L. (1999). Parental satisfaction and outcome: A four-year study in a child and adolescent mental health service. *Australian and New Zealand Journal of Psychiatry, 33*, 22–28.

Riley, S. E., Stromberg, A. J., & Clark, J. (2005). Assessing parental satisfaction with children's mental health services with the youth services survey for families. *Journal of Child and Family Studies, 14*(1), 87–99.

Rosenblatt, A., & Woodbridge, M. W. (2003). Deconstructing research on systems of care for youth with EBD: Frameworks for policy research. *Journal of Emotional and Behavioral Disorders, 11*(1), 27–37.

Shin, S. H. (2005). Need for and actual use of mental health service by adolescents in the child welfare system. *Children and Youth Services Review, 27*, 1071–1083.

Silver, S. E., Duchnowski, A., Kutash, K., Friedman, R. M., Eisen, M., Prange, M., et al. (1992). A comparison of children with serious emotional disturbances served in residential and school settings. *Journal of Child and Family Studies, 1*, 43–59.

Stiffman, A. R., Chen, Y., Elze, D., Dore, P., & Cheng, L. (1997). Adolescents' and providers' perspectives on the need for and use of mental health services. *Journal of Adolescent Health, 21*, 335–342.

Stiffman, A. R., Hadley-Ives, E., Dore, P., Polgar, M., Horvath, V. E., Striley, C., et al. (2000). Youth's access to mental health services: The role of provider's training, resource connectivity, and assessment of need. *Mental Health Services Research, 2* (3), 141–154.

Weber, M., & Yelton, S. (1996). The role of the child welfare system in systems of care. In B. A. Stroul (Ed.), *Children's mental health: Creating systems of care in a changing society* (pp. 215–233). Baltimore, MD: Paul H. Brookes.

Wells, K., Wyatt, E., & Hobfoll, S. (1991). Factors associated with adaptation of youths discharged from residential treatment. *Child & Youth Services Review, 13*, 199–216.

Wright, E. R. (1997). The impact of organizational factors on mental health professionals' involvement with families. *Psychiatric Services, 48*(7), 921–927.

|9|

Fundamental Considerations
for Child and Family Welfare

Nick Coady
Gary Cameron
Gerald R. Adams

The preceding chapters dramatically highlight the serious ethical and practical dilemmas facing the "Anglo-American child protection paradigm" and argue for looking beyond settings and systems already familiar to us for ideas for change. This chapter examines niches for reform within current arrangements and encourages a basic rethinking of the child and family welfare enterprise in Canada. First, we discuss several fundamental system design challenges facing Canadian child and family welfare. Second, we examine specific implications for service delivery and, third, we consider opportunities for improving helping relationships. Finally, we present reflections about future directions for child and family welfare research.

System Design Challenges

Trapped in the Language of "Protecting" Children

It is our contention that there has been a substantial impoverishment of the language dominating discussions of child welfare in Canada over the past ten years. Consequently, our frame of reference is unnecessarily constricted, limiting both what we do and what we can envision. Increasingly, all child welfare discourses, to have a chance of being heard, must defer to an exclusive frame of reference dominated by a specific conception of the interests of children. All public issues must be raised within this frame of reference and all actions justified by it. We have become trapped within an idiosyncratic language of the protection of children, largely unaware of its dubious ethical and practical consequences. Our language needs to rediscover complexity, nuance, and balance in order to amend our perceptions of appropriate relationships among children, families, communities, and the state. Child and family welfare language should enrich our thinking about positive possibilities for helping.

In the dominant child protection framework, all challenges faced by families, whether poverty; social isolation; or parental depression, anxiety, physical illness, or lack of knowledge, are relevant only to the extent of their impact on the parenting environment for children. These quintessentially human conditions are simplified and emptied of their emotional and political content. They increasingly become demerit points in a forensic balance sheet for parents. This narrow frame of reference leads to the ethically and practically untenable positions of isolating and valuing children's existence above all others in the family and community, while simultaneously only being interested in a very small portion of what children need to be safe and well.

In her discussion of child placement, Nancy Freymond (2003) locates this framework within the continuing "child-saving" tradition of "Anglo-American child protection" and the identification of the "deserving" poor, concepts that have coloured Canadian child welfare since its inception. This emphasis has been exacerbated by the neo-conservative preference for detection and retribution, rather than assistance, that has dominated politics in Ontario and other North American jurisdictions for the past ten years and more. In addition, this frame of reference focuses on individual legal rights and self-contained identities (Love, 2006), making it reasonable as a normal consequence of protecting children to separate them from their families and communities.

In marked contrast to this child protection frame of reference, many child and family welfare systems in continental Europe view healthy families as an essential foundation for a good society. Some of these systems seldom, if ever, permanently sever links between children and their families, even when children enter out-of-home care. In this more collective frame of reference, as a matter of normal everyday living, many families are offered and expect assistance from the state and community to raise their children.

The contrast between the Anglo-American child protection paradigm and the First Nations' perspective of "an interdependent web of life" is even more stark. Catherine Love (2006) contrasts the self-contained individualism underpinning colonizing processes in New Zealand, with the Maori ideal of an ensembled self, which is fluid and does not emphasize maintaining distinctions between self and others. This sense of ensembled self "may contain a number of people living and dead" (p. 17) and is located "in a field of influences that may include but is not confined to self" (p. 18). This conception of self does not make it seem reasonable as a normal consequence of "protecting children" to separate them from their families and communities. Rather, the emphasis is on maintaining connections and healing the family and community relationships that lead to difficulties.

To take the argument further, from our perspective, it is not self-evident why assisting families, maintaining family and community connections, and developing healing relationships should remain marginal considerations within mainstream conceptions of Canadian child and family welfare. A richer language and more inclusive frame of reference would place these purposes on an equal footing with the protection of children from maltreatment, which currently predominates our discussions. Our current language also obscures considerations of shared responsibilities for raising children and collective responses to concerns about their safety and well-being. It makes it very difficult to recognize and utilize the persistence under adversity, the commitment to family, and the substantial capacity to find "solutions" that exist in many families and communities (Cameron & Hoy, 2003; Freymond, 2003).

We believe that we need to move beyond the impoverished language and world view of the Anglo-American child protection paradigm. Even evaluating this system on its own terms, we have found no evidence that it is superior to other child and family welfare paradigms at protecting children from harm, its primary raison d'être. For example, a recent report for the United Nations Children's Fund about child maltreatment deaths in "rich countries" indicated that most countries with lower rates of child maltreatment deaths than Canada do not have systems that resemble the Anglo-American child protection paradigm (Innocenti, 2003). In chapter 1, Cameron and colleagues argue that in cases of less drastic forms of child maltreatment, there is no evidence that children are hurt more often, or endangered children are less likely to be detected, in more family-focused European models of child and family welfare. On the other hand, these approaches seem able to facilitate easier access to helpful resources for children and families, and there is convincing evidence that children in struggling families do better on a variety of developmental outcomes in countries with more generous social provisions in place (Hertzberg, 2003, 2004; Phipps, 1999).

A 1998 Canadian study by Nico Trocmé and colleagues of 7,672 child maltreatment investigations found that half were substantiated by child protection workers. Of these, only 18% involved physical harm to children and only 4% required any form of medical treatment (cited in Trocmé & Chamberland, 2003). These authors argue that these findings indicate that would be reasonable to allow service providers more time to offer positive assistance to more families, rather than requiring an immediate formal investigation in all circumstances. Our perspective is that we would be well served by simply recognizing the numerous obstacles facing many of these families. There is no convincing conceptual or practical reason for an appropriate system of child and family welfare to have responding to child abuse or maltreatment as its central organizing focus. It is time to create a more positive vision for children and families and to situate the specific function of protecting children within a broader purpose of maintaining healthy families, communities, and society.

The Realities of Lesser Privilege

The discussion in the introduction highlighted that, from its inception, Canadian child welfare has focused its attention on the "dangerous and immoral classes," poor families highly vulnerable to any disruptions to their sources of support. Although the rationale for intervention has changed over time—from protecting society, to reforming children, to saving children from immorality, to protecting them from physical and emotional harm—the populations targeted have not (Freymond, 2003). Poor and disadvantaged families, as well as racial and ethnic minorities, and in particular First Nations, are much more likely to have an open child protection case and to have a child apprehended and placed involuntarily in state care. Yet, these less privileged living realities shared by so many families remain at best a background consideration in the practice of child welfare in Canada.

The previously cited UNICEF report (Innocenti, 2003) also concluded that "poverty and stress along with drug and alcohol abuse appear to be the factors most clearly associated with child abuse and neglect" (p. 2). Deena Mandell and her colleagues in chapter 3 have suggested that in some First Nations communities most of the children are likely to be found "at risk" using the current standard risk assessment indicators. In the Partnerships for Children and Families Project's program of research, the parents of the families involved were almost exclusively the working poor or living on social assistance (Cameron & Hoy, 2003; Freymond, 2003; Maiter, Palmer & Mangii, 2003). In one our focus groups, child welfare service providers discussed the life stories of 16 mothers. When queried by the group facilitator why, after two hours of discussion, no one had commented on the issues of poverty so evident in the stories, one worker volunteered: "The majority of people we work with are females who are marginalized and who struggle with poverty ... You don't even question it anymore because that's what it is" (Cameron & Hoy, 2003, p. 218).

These lives of lesser privilege are dramatically illustrated by a recent study of 1,042 child protection cases open in 1995 and 2001 at a southern Ontario children's aid society (CAS) (Leschied, Whitehead, Hurley, & Chiodo, 2003a, 2003b). This research painted the following startling profile of families involved in 2001 with the child protection agency:

- More than half of the mothers involved with the CAS were victims of wife assault, and 68% of the children of these abused women were admitted to care at the time of the most recent case opening.
- 64% of the mothers involved with the CAS were on social assistance, and 80% of the children in care came from families on social assistance. 86% of cases considered to be child neglect had mothers on social assistance and 84% of the women experiencing assault were on social assistance. 83% of single mothers involved with the CAS were on social assistance.
- 42% of the children admitted to care had a parent who was involved with child welfare as a child; 71% of these parents were receiving social assistance, and 75% were unemployed.
- 29% of the cases had mothers considered to have a diagnosis of depression, and 59% of these women were unemployed.
- 79% of the children from First Nations involved with the CAS were in care.
- 20% of mothers experienced a chronic health problem, and 23% were considered to have a substance abuse problem.

Consistent with contention earlier in this chapter, all of these indicators of distressed living conditions were considered in this report almost exclusively in terms of their impact on the parenting environment for children. For example, Leschied and colleagues (2003a) point out that increasingly child protection workers have addressed women abuse in order to ensure the well-being of children (p. 43). Not surprisingly, the report concludes that the child welfare agency is fulfilling its mandate by focusing on children living in "unsafe" environments. The contributors to this book would ask whether this mandate itself is sensible in the face of such a profile of families living in difficult circumstances. We might also ask about what sort of useful assistance families received from these involvements, or whether children were better off as a result. What we do learn is that the number of children in CAS care increased 70% between 1995 and 2001, and an incredible 64% of 592 children in the 2001 random sample of open child protection cases were considered to be in need of protection and were admitted to CAS care.

As emphasized in the introduction, most children, parents, and families involved with child welfare confront the persistent challenges of, and sometimes the impossibility of, surviving severe living circumstances. These circumstances cannot be understood only as individual obstacles; they are ways of living shared by communities and sometimes generations of people. It also is clear that the overwhelming majority of children in these families, even children who enter state care, will continue to grow up in these homes. We have argued earlier that the health of these parents (particularly mothers) and these families are central to the well-being and sense of belonging of their children (Cameron & Hoy, 2003). We are unlikely to be more help-ful to these children and their parents until these understandings underpin the core conceptions of helping in child and family welfare in Canada. These perceptions move us toward bringing more helpful living resources to chil-dren and parents and engaging them in ways that they find acceptable. They require that we build upon the motivation, the persistence, the courage, and the strength in these families and their communities (Cameron & Hoy, 2003) and that we accept a shared responsibility for raising and protecting these children.

Distance between Families and Child Protection Service Providers

In chapter 5, Fine, Palmer and Coady argue that positive relationships between service providers and families are as fundamental in child welfare as they are in psychotherapy and children's mental health services. These authors argue that positive helping relationships are central to engaging child welfare clientele in making changes in their lives. Indeed, expanding trusting and co-operative relationships between most families and child welfare service providers is a necessary condition in bringing more useful assistance and resources to children, parents, families and communities.

The Partnerships for Children and Families Project's program of research underscores the magnitude of the obstacles between many child protection personnel and families. An initial gap is that the daily living realities for most child protection service providers is very different from those described previously for the clientele of a southern Ontario children's aid society. In addition, Harvey, Stalker, and their colleagues' research (Harvey, Mandell, Stalker, & Frensch, 2003; chapter 7 of this book) found that more than 89% of 402 direct service workers in four children's aid societies estimated that they spent less than half their working time working with families, and almost 19% said that they were in contact with families less than 20% of their working time. Almost 62% of direct service workers were spending more than half of their time documenting their work.

In her reflections on how child protection workers manage the strains of permanently removing children from families, Nancy Freymond (chap-ter 6) argues that "a climate of fear has emerged as workers fear they will be held liable in cases of child death." (p. 250) She states that "it may be that workers must disregard individual autonomy and embrace the comforts associated with emotional distance from the realities of this work" (p. 264). In chapter 7, Harvey and Stalker note that depersonalization, or emotional distancing from clientele, is a common sequela to high levels of emotional exhaustion in the human services. They also found that about 44% of direct service workers scored in the highest range on the Maslach Burnout Inventory's Scale for Emotional Exhaustion.

Another illustration of this emotional distancing was found in the service-provider focus groups when discussing the mothers' life stories presented in the introduction. Groups of child protection services providers from two agencies read summaries of all eighteen mothers' stories and met to discuss them. An initially perplexing pattern was that, whereas the parent focus groups quickly became engrossed in these mothers' life stories, it proved very difficult to get the service providers to talk about the mothers in the stories at all. They preferred to talk about the challenges of their work or about "clients" in general. With hindsight, we can hypothesize that this may be an illustration of emotional distancing for self protection.

Another form of distancing may be reflected in the types of disparaging comments made about mothers by some service providers in these focus group meetings, without any overt reaction from their colleagues. Although the comments surprised members of the research team, they were not indicative of many service providers' comments; nor did they necessarily reflect how any of these service providers might relate to these mothers. Our conjecture is that such characterizations may not be uncommon in private conversations among child protection workers. For example, one service provider remarked that:

> Its not unlike ... university level [service provider] talking to grade school kids [mothers] ... Imagine if you haven't any clue even that you have issues, let alone giving them a name. We're asking a lot. We're asking kindergarten people to use university coping skills." (Cameron & Hoy, 2003, pp. 217–218)

In separate focus groups, both mothers (using words like "uncaring," "guilty until proven innocent," and "unavailable" to describe service provider attitudes) and child protection service providers (using words such as "business-like," "no time," and "have to be mistrustful" to illustrate their work) talked about the gap between them. In addition, given the magnitude of the decisions being made, it concerns us that many of the service providers interviewed were the second or third or fourth child protection worker involved with a family and had only a basic familiarity with the living circumstances of the family. It also was evident that serious decisions, such as the apprehension of a child, were often being made quickly with minimal understanding of the complexities of the lives of either the children or their parents (Frensch & Cameron, 2003).

Nonetheless, with some trepidation on both sides, many mothers and service providers expressed a desire for more positive connections with each other. Both were appreciative of the times when such constructive relationships developed. When mothers understood the relevance of "suggestions" for interventions, they often were quite willing to engage in these processes, and, when they did not understand, they became "evasive" (Cameron & Hoy, 2003; Frensch & Cameron, 2003; Freymond, 2003; Maiter, Palmer, & Mangii, 2003). From our perspective, expanding the space and the support for the development of consensual and constructive relationships between members of struggling families and service providers is a fundamental consideration for improving Canadian child and family welfare.

Providing Useful Assistance to Children, Parents, Families, and Communities

Although relatively recent innovations in the Canadian child protection system, such as expanded mandatory reporting, standard risk assessment protocols, fixed service time lines, and tighter limitations on the time a child can be in care without becoming a permanent ward of the state, are just beginning to be subject to critical scrutiny, Cameron and colleagues (chapter 1) describe a consensus in the literature that Anglo-American child protection systems provide a minimal level and range of assistance to children and parents.

In the Partnerships for Children and Families Project's program of research, there was little evidence of many meaningful supports and services coming to families through their involvement with children's aid societies. (Cameron & Hoy, 2003; Frensch & Cameron, 2003; Freymond, 2003) Families are investigated, taken to court, instructed to modify certain behaviours and to participate in standard set of programs (for example, counselling, parenting, addictions, anger management), sometimes referred to other professional treatment services, and have their children taken away. In this volume's chapter about mothers' placement experiences, the authors talk about the lack of congruence between this range of interventions and the daily living realities of most mothers and their families.

The most fundamental consideration for Canadian child and family welfare is to bring more diverse types of assistance to struggling children, parents, families, and communities. Our current child protection paradigm is extremely limited both in fact and in its potential to provide this assistance. Costs continue to increase rapidly in this paradigm (meeting of Ministers of Social Service, 2003) without bringing more help to families or creating improved work environments for service providers. This child protection paradigm is overly preoccupied with finding fault and limitations, and too many families unnecessarily fear and resent their child protection involvement. Although positive changes to front-line practice are possible within the existing child and family welfare system, innovation at the system design level is paramount to escape this impasse.

Implications for Service Delivery

The shifts in child and family welfare evolving from the discussions in this volume would involve making principles and procedures long at the heart of the Anglo-American child protection paradigm (for example, formal investigations of child abuse, use of coercive state power and adversarial legal processes, mandatory supervision of families, and out-of-home placements) secondary to mutually acceptable involvements with families, where emphasis is placed on co-operative working relationships and providing supports and resources to strengthen family functioning (Cameron et al., chapter 1). Table 1 provides an overview of our suggestions for service delivery innovations and improving helping relationships in child and family welfare. This paradigm shift would involve the creation of intermediary space (chapter 4) for negotiating consensual agreements with families, while permitting the use of legal authority if and when necessary.

Although some child welfare service providers manage to create intermediary space within the current paradigm, bureaucratic controls and recording requirements make this difficult. When agencies have managed to create intermediary space for negotiation and mediation with families, it has usually been done through demonstration projects with no official mandate (chapter 2). Instituting such changes on a larger scale and in a more meaningful way would amount to a paradigm shift, requiring changes in policy, procedures, and resource allocations. This shift also would entail building supports for such changes in agency training and supervision, and building a different "ideological community" (Harvey & Stalker, chapter 7) committed to a more balanced approach to Canadian child and family welfare.

Flexible Responses and Providing Assistance

Freymond and Cameron (chapter 2) argue persuasively that a standardized investigation of every allegation of maltreatment is not only costly and unnecessary, but is also threatening to families and sets up adversarial relationships. They suggest a flexible response system, which ideally would be mandated, in which the initial response to most families would be negotiation of a voluntary involvement focused on providing resources and services to meet their unique needs. Immediate use of coercive investigation and child apprehension would be available, but would be reserved for exceptional circumstances. Formal investigative, legal, and child placement services would be specialized but ancillary services to the child and family welfare enterprise. In addition, except in emergency situations, third-party mediation would be preferred, and ideally mandated, to reach agreement between families and service providers and to avoid the need for formal court applications.

Table 1: Suggestions for Service Delivery Innovations and Helping Relationships

Service Delivery Innovations

Collaboration and provision of support and practical assistance:
- A differential response system should be used whereby the initial response to most families would be negotiation of a voluntary involvement focused on providing resources and services.
- Except in emergencies, third party mediation should be used (ideally, mandated) to reach agreement between families and service providers in order to avoid formal court applications.
- Formal investigative, legal, and child placement services should be specialized but ancillary services used only in emergencies.
- Reliance on formal bureaucratic controls over service decisions and time lines should be reduced to permit service providers to spend more time helping families.

Partnerships with social service and community organizations:
- Child welfare organizations should work closely, and ideally share the mandate for the welfare of children and families, with a wide variety of social service and community organizations.
- Children and parents should be linked with an array of formal and informal services and resources to meet a broad spectrum of needs.
- Child welfare services should be co-located with other community services and resources in disadvantaged neighbourhoods.
- Community resources and networks should be used to protect children and support parents.

Family-friendly placement options:
- Joint placements of mothers and children should be used whenever possible to reduce unnecessary separations.
- Extended family or other families within the same social network should be preferred over traditional foster placements.
- Where foster placement is the only available option, supportive connections between families and foster parents should be facilitated.

Helping Relationships

Empathic, supportive, and collaborative relationships with families:
- Service providers should endeavour to tune in to and empathize with the current and past daily living realities of families.
- Service providers should endeavour to tune in to and empathize with the fear and stigma of child welfare involvement for families.
- Service providers should push traditional professional boundaries toward a warmer, more supportive person-to-person way of being.

Going the "extra mile" for families:
- Service providers should place a primary focus on support and assistance.
- Service providers should endeavour to get to know and care about families on a personal level.

Such changes put more faith in the discretion and judgments of front-line service providers and their supervisors, and endorse a preference for welfare and social work principles in working with families (chapter 1). A prerequisite would be to reduce reliance on formal bureaucratic controls to allow more flexibility in responses and to permit service providers to spend more of their time helping children and parents. The limitations of the current system with regard to providing needed assistance are underscored by Fine and colleagues' (chapter 5) conclusion that child welfare parents "express more concern about the lack of responsiveness by CPS [child protective services] agencies and service providers than about unwanted intervention" (p. 210).

Partnerships with Social Service and Community Organizations

If the provision of useful assistance to children, parents, and families became a central focus of child and family welfare, child welfare organizations would have to work closely, and ideally share their mandate, with a wide variety of social service and community organizations (chapters 1 & 2). Protecting children and enhancing the well-being of children, parents, and families, would no longer be the exclusive responsibility of parents nor of stand-alone child protection agencies.

A particular paradox of Canadian child welfare, with its emphasis on protecting and focusing on the "best interests" of children in interventions, is that so little assistance is provided directly to children. In the Partnerships for Children and Families Project's program of research, child protection interventions focused almost exclusively upon investigating and modifying parents' behaviours (Cameron & Hoy, 2003; Frensch & Cameron, 2003; Freymond, 2003) . Occasionally, there was evidence of children being connected to childcare or remedial services for developmental delays or specialized treatment programs.

There are a range of easily accessible program strategies for children and adolescents that have demonstrated value in reducing family stress, promoting child well-being, and protecting children from physical and emotional harm (for example, see the reviews in Cameron, O'Reilly, Laurendeau, & Chamberland, 2001 and in Nelson, Laurendeau, Chamberland, & Peirson, 2001). It would be profitable to make programs for children, such as mentoring, after school clubs, homework supports, apprenticeships, nutrition enhancement, social/recreational opportunities, contact families, and daycare basic elements of helping in child and family welfare.

Similarly, parents need to be provided with a broader array of services and resources. Rather than the standard requirement for counselling that many child welfare service plans currently contain (Frensch & Cameron, 2003), more thought and effort needs to be put into connecting families with diverse services and resources. Even when personal or family issues are the focus, and counselling an appropriate response, child welfare service providers need to help families consider a range of options (from standard family service agency counselling to self-help and mutual aid groups) and to facilitate the linkage with such supports. Furthermore, depending on families' needs and preferences, efforts should be made to connect them with a much wider range of practical resources. This could include resources for food and clothing, collective kitchens, family resource centres, child development programs, in-home and respite services, education and employment programs, recreation programs, and faith groups, as well as existing informal social supports. The core principle is to "bring together resources from family, community members, and professional helpers in an effort to build on the strengths of the family and assist with identified needs" (Freymond, chapter 4, p. 179).

Beyond active partnerships between child welfare agencies and other services and resources, multiple services could be located together with child and family welfare services, as exemplified by the Shelldale Centre discussed in chapter 1. Similarly, child and family welfare service providers could be placed in settings such as schools and women's shelters, with an emphasis on establishing more helpful relationships with children, parents, families, and communities. Such innovations could help to de-stigmatize child welfare services and to link families with resources. Potentially, such changes could enhance community capacity development and increase local influence over child and family welfare services.

In the Partnerships for Children and Families program of research, for example, a study comparing service provider and family experiences in community and school-based child protection services with child protection services in traditional agency settings in Ontario (Frensch, Cameron & Hazineh, 2005) concluded that:

> School and community-based models of service delivery illustrate that, even within existing fiscal and legislative constraints, it is possible to create more a constructive and welcomed approach to child welfare without compromising the protection of children. Within these models, service providers have greater access to information about families and are more aware of community resources and strengths. In turn, families receive assistance that is more immediate and relevant to their needs. Indeed with the level of school, community, and service engagement with these families, it is reasonable to surmise that children are more protected while families receive more assistance. (pp. 30–40)

In addition, community resources and networks, including extended families, should be integral to protecting children and supporting families. The Aboriginal community healing or caring vision for child and family welfare "places helping children and families within the context of a healing process for the whole community" (chapter 1, p. 36). This type of holistic focus, which includes providing service to protect children and to strengthen families as well as to build community capacity, is potentially as relevant to disadvantaged "mainstream" communities as it is to First Nations (chapter 3).

Family-friendly Placement Options

The proposed paradigm shift for child and family welfare does not deny the necessity of temporary and permanent out-of-home placements for children, and in extreme situations, as a first response. Freymond and Cameron (chapter 2) point out, however, that in the majority of situations where foster care placement occurs, it is of short to moderate duration, and the child returns home. They argue that, given the potentially traumatic effect on both parents and children of such separations, every effort should be made to maintain continuity of parent–child relationships. Creative options toward this end include joint placement of children and parents (either with another family or, as is possible in Sweden, in small public institutions); using homes from extended family or social networks as placements (this is particularly important when culturally appropriate placements are suggested, as with Aboriginal families); short-term respite placements with a nonprofessional, stable "contact family," whose role is to support children in their families; and, where traditional foster or institutional placement is used, encouraging and facilitating supportive connections with parents and other family members. Support for the importance of maintaining the continuity of parent–child relationships when out-of-home placements are necessary is suggested by research that finds parental involvement and family support during residential treatment to be the most significant and consistent predictor of treatment progress and positive post-discharge adaptation (chapter 8).

Implications for "Troubled" Children and Youth

In the introduction, we highlighted that a significant portion of families that become involved with child welfare services have children or youth with mental health and behaviour challenges. For example, in the Quebec Incidence Study of Reported Child Abuse, Neglect, Abandonment, and Serious Behaviour Problems (Tourigny et al., 2002), 39% of the cases reported to youth protection services included serious behaviour problems in youth. The Partnerships for Children and Families research on parents with children who require residential mental health placements documents the extraordinary stress that caring for children who seriously "act out" places on families, especially on mothers, and describes these women's efforts over years, often at the expense of their own health, to get help for their children. It also shows the inappropriateness of expecting residential care to provide a short-term "cure" for these children's struggles (chapter 8; Cameron, de Boer, Frensch, & Adams, 2003). Frensch and her colleagues' discussion (chapter 8) of the need to view residential care not as a way to separate children from families but primarily as part of an ongoing system of family support, is germane in this regard, as is their argument for considering access to residential care as a first rather than only a last resort. Improving long-term life outcomes for these children and their families also requires that attention be given to a flexible continuum of educational, family, housing, and daily living supports after they leave residential care (Cameron, de Boer, et al., 2003).

Implications for First Nations Child and Family Welfare

In chapter 3, Mandell and colleagues document the horrendous impact that involvement with child protection services has had on First Nations across Canada and internationally. This must be acknowledged along with the realization that continuing with "business as usual" ravages these communities. Our framework for child and family welfare has to be broad enough to accommodate alternative notions of "ensembled selves" (Love, 2006), to foster community healing and capacity building and to support families and protect children. This requires ways of working that respect First Nations' values and traditions and that are guided by Aboriginal people themselves. Although finding an appropriate compromise between Canadian child protection authorities' mandates and the desires of Aboriginal communities to take care of their own has proven elusive thus far, it remains a priority. As mentioned earlier, the community-caring paradigm of child welfare exemplified by programs unfolding in many First Nations has much promise, both for practice with Aboriginal people and as a paradigm from which mainstream child welfare systems can learn.

Implications for Helping Relationships

Some service providers within the current child protection system are successful at negotiating mutually acceptable service agreements with families. Some place a primary focus on providing support and practical assistance to families and fashion placements to maintain parent–child connections. Similarly, some child welfare agencies locate child protection teams in community settings to facilitate linkage to supports and resources and to foster community capacity building (Frensch et al., 2005). Nonetheless, although there is capacity within the current child protection system to accommodate the two broad suggestions for improving helping relationship outlined below, system level changes in ideology, policies, resource allocations, service provider training, and supervision are critical in increasing these capacities.

Empathic, Supportive, and Collaborative Relationships with Families

One of the themes emerging from the discussions in this volume is that the child protection or threshold paradigm of child welfare too often engenders harsh attitudes toward and coercive relationships with families. Given the social-control emphasis in the threshold paradigm, the highly contentious and emotionally draining nature of child welfare work, and the substantial potential for service provider burnout, and the depersonalized attitudes towards clientele that often go with it (chapter 7), the development of constructive helping relationships with clients in the current system is no doubt easier said than done.

The literature supports the commonly held view that poor helping relationships are not uncommon in child welfare. Fine and colleagues' (chapter 5) review of 26 studies of child welfare clients' experiences with services found a high prevalence of negative relationships with child welfare service providers. They documented that parents and children involved with child protection services described some service providers as "judgmental, uncaring, dictatorial, and denigrating" (p. 203). Similarly, Freymond and Cameron's study (chapter 2) of mothers who experienced the out-of-home placement of their children by child welfare noted how these women frequently felt blamed by service providers seen as impolite and unfeeling.

The results of two additional studies from the Partnerships for Children and Families Project's program of research also suggest that poor helping relationships in child welfare are not unusual. Maiter, Palmer, and Manji's (2003) study of families' service experiences in two southern Ontario child welfare agencies found that parents talked of negative relationships with service providers with about the same frequency as they talked about positive relationships. Harvey, Mandell, Stalker, and Frensch's (2003) workplace study of four family and children's service agencies in southern Ontario found that in a sample of 236 direct-service workers (intake, family service, and children's service workers), 36% scored in the high range on a depersonalization scale, indicating "an unfeeling and impersonal response towards recipients of one's service" (pp. 28–29).

Despite the inherent difficulties in developing constructive helping relationships in child protection services, many front-line service providers
manage to develop good relationships with families. Fine and colleagues'
(chapter 5) review of the research found that many parents and youth involved
in child welfare services encountered service providers "who were compassionate toward their failures as parents, respected them as human beings,
and reached out to support them in meeting their children's needs" (p. 210).
Furthermore, paralleling the results of research in psychotherapy, a number of studies (Drake, 1994; Maluccio, 1979; Shulman, 1978) have suggested
that good helping relationships are important to family members' satisfaction and good outcomes in child welfare. De Boer and Coady's (2003) qualitative study of exemplary helping relationships in child welfare illustrates
that, not only is it possible to develop and maintain deeply human, positive
helping relationships, even in circumstances where children are made permanent wards of the state but also that such helping relationships can have
profound, positive impacts on families.

Fine and colleagues (chapter 5) describe the qualities and actions of service providers that promote positive helping relationships. Our conviction is
that the creation of the helpful and validating actions characteristic of good
helping relationships should be a primary objective in Canadian child and
family welfare reform. Clearly there are impediments to developing positive helping relationships within the current child protection system; however, it also is evident that, even within these constraints, service providers
have some discretion about how they view and interact with families.

One front-line strategy for improving helping relationships is for service providers to empathetically consider the adverse daily living realities
faced by many children and parents, described in the introduction). This
involves striving to comprehend what it is like to live with ongoing challenges such as limited finances, bleak employment prospects, unsafe neighbourhoods, abusive relationships, social isolation and lack of social support,
addictions, and emotional and physical health problems. Such an empathetic understanding requires recognition of collective social-historical factors including inter-generational histories of poverty, physical and sexual
abuse, and addictions, as well as, particularly for Aboriginal and other minority populations, colonialism, racism, and exclusion. Furthermore, this empathetic understanding appreciates the strengths and resilience displayed by
children, parents, families, and communities who survive such histories.
Developing such an empathetic understanding can help service providers to
gain acceptance from and to work co-operatively with families.

Another front-line strategy is to acknowledge without judgment how
many clients feel about child welfare involvement. Many parents fear having their children taken away and resist the stigma of being labeled a "bad"

parent. Normalizing reactions of fear, anger, and resistence from parents and children can help service providers to respond empathically and to temper how they explain and use their legal authority.

Fine and colleagues' (chapter 5) review of child welfare clients' experiences documented how many parents and adolescents complained of feeling alienated, threatened, and/or controlled by their service involvements and of being confused due to lack of information. De Boer and Coady's (2003) study of good helping relationships in child welfare illustrates how service providers who address family member fears and anger non-defensively and empathically, give clear information about why they are involved with the family, including whether they are considering apprehending the children, and explain and use their power in a judicious manner can develop positive helping relationships with parents and children, including people who have experienced difficult relationships with other child protection service providers.

A third element in enhancing helping relationships involves softening traditional professional boundaries in favour of more humanistic, down-to-earth, and personal ways of relating. Gitterman (1988) noted the problematic tendency for some service providers to hide behind a formal professional mask. In addition, given the legal mandate of child protection, and the emotionally draining and potentially contentious nature of many encounters between service providers and families, the emotional distancing for self-protection by service providers described earlier is understandable.

Two recent studies have illustrated that parents involved with child welfare describe appreciated service providers as being more like friends and ordinary people than like "typical" professionals. Coady and Hayward (1998) found that parents and adolescents described welcome child welfare service providers as people who "seemed to really care," and "like a friend." Similarly, de Boer and Coady (2003) found that parents characterized valued child welfare service providers as "down-to-earth" and "authentic." Parents commented favourably on service providers who disclosed some personal information (for example, having children of their own, having dealt with adversity in their lives), got to know them as individuals, and shared their own feelings and emotions. Parents also liked child welfare service providers who engaged in more informal interactions with them, such as social "chit-chat" or having talks over coffee or lunch.

Notwithstanding the discovery of positive helping relationships in these studies of child protection services, the Partnerships for Children and Families Project research into alternative service-delivery infrastructures for front-line child protection services (Frensch et al., 2005) provided dramatic illustrations of how modifications to service philosophy and everyday work settings can improve helping relationships:

In this study, there was a different level of satisfaction with helping relationships [compared to earlier investigations of child protection services in 'tradition' agency settings] and all stakeholder groups across the three programs talked about the importance of establishing "good" relationships. In Guelph, almost all of the parents we spoke to described at least one good relationship with a Shelldale [community multi-service center] service provider. In Brant, two-thirds of parents shared at least one good relationship with a community-based service provider. And in Halton, almost all parents described cooperative relationships between themselves and their school-based service provider. Traits of service providers that parents appreciated included being informal, friendly, genuine, respectful, and empathetic. (p. 36)

Going the "Extra Mile" for Children, Parents, and Families

The importance of service providers doing more than was formally required in their work with families was highlighted in Fine and colleagues' (chapter 5) review of studies of parents' and adolescents' experiences in child welfare. Family members refer positively to things service providers do that are beyond agency mandates or what they would expect of most professionals. Examples include scheduling meetings outside of regular hours to accommodate parents, advocating for families with other systems (for example, school, social assistance, subsidized housing), dropping off Christmas gifts, and extending supportive work with a mother after her children have been placed permanently (de Boer & Coady, 2003).

The concept of "going the extra mile" is also closely connected to the development of empathic, supportive, and collaborative relationships with families. First, these extra efforts help to build positive relationships with families, demonstrating the commitment, concern, and humanity of the service provider. These supplementary efforts include relationship-building behaviours referred to earlier, such as getting to know individual family members, pointing out families' strengths, being sympathetic about families' struggles, and having informal meetings over coffee or lunch. Second, service providers who get to know and care about families become motivated to make these "non-mandated" efforts and do not find them onerous (de Boer & Coady, 2003). As Harvey and Stalker (chapter 7) note, a sense of engagement or involvement with one's work can be energizing and help to prevent burnout. Of course, to bring the argument full circle, to facilitate and encourage a general increase in service providers' engagement with families, the types of systems-design changes discussed earlier in this chapter would be necessary.

Implications for Research

The discussions in this book provide a conceptual structure to guide an ambitious research agenda of theoretical and practical importance. The major themes from each of the proceeding chapters inform the selection of priority child and family welfare research focuses that are grouped under the headings below. These future research focuses are relevant to the improvement of child and family welfare policy and services, as well as to allied social science knowledge development.

Missing Voices

In Canadian research, very little emphasis has been placed upon hearing from the children, parents, families, and communities involved with child protection authorities. Although much has been written about these populations, it has been almost exclusively about how others perceive their lives and appropriate interventions. Perhaps because public perceptions semi-criminalize "bad" parents, and see children as unable to make decisions about their care, information, opinions, and preferences provided by child welfare populations are often received with suspicion (Frensch & Cameron, 2003). However, the case has been made in this book that most of these families are best understood as struggling with adversity and needing assistance, and that family and community well-being are integral to protecting and enhancing the well-being of children. We also have argued for the primary importance of building less adversarial and more consensual helping relationships with children, parents, families, and communities.

Given the nature of child protection systems in Canada, what is said by parents, children, and community advocates about their lives and child protection involvements undoubtedly will be very difficult for many child protection professionals to hear (Cameron & Hoy, 2003; Frensch & Cameron, 2003). But such feedback is vital to improving helping relationships and service outcomes and essential to changing dynamics between child and family welfare organizations and the populations they involve. Ideally, this type of research could provide a foundation for productive and more equal dialogues among service professionals, family members, and community repesentatives. The list of important subjects for such a research agenda is very long; for example, parents of permanent state wards, state wards, graduates of state wardship, families with children apprehended by child protection authorities, children and adolescents in foster care, families under voluntary service agreements or court supervision orders, various ethnic, religious, and racial populations, families of children with challenging behaviours, and many other groupings.

Comparisons of Alternative Approaches

A fundamental thesis of this volume has been the need to look beyond what is familiar within the Canadian child protection paradigm for possibilities for positive innovation. In this vein, a large program of research could compare the underlying social and cultural values, service delivery processes, and outcomes of various settings reflecting the child protection, family service, and community caring paradigms described in chapter 1. Of particular merit would be research comparing family experiences and service provider experiences in different settings. We also know very little about the relative costs and benefits to children and parents involved with these different child and family welfare systems.

A related program of research would focus on comparisons of experiences and outcomes between innovations in the Canadian child and family welfare system and mainstream child protection services. For example, we need to learn more from experiments with programs such as community-based child protection services, child protection services located in specialized settings such as women's shelters and schools, co-location and partnerships of child protection services with multiple social service and community organizations, intermediary or diversionary mediation or restorative justice initiatives, and professional–community/family partnerships to protect children and support families. In such investigations we would benefit from understanding helping processes and benefits and the program developmental challenges confronted.

Improving Helping Relationships

Central observations in this volume include the non-productive divide between families and child welfare service providers and the pivotal importance of improving helping relationships in Canadian child and family welfare. Important elements of a useful program of research would focus on understanding the nature of helping relationships in child welfare, as well as extrapolating the individual and organizational factors that enhance positive collaborations. It would be productive to begin to explore various ways of balancing the front-line requirements of creating co-operative engagements and implementing the investigative and enforcement elements of child protection.

Benefits for Children, Parents, and Families

Various authors in this volume question the appropriateness of the fit between what is going on in the lives of family members and the types and levels of assistance they receive from their involvement with child protection authorities. Concerns have been raised about Canadian child protection systems' capacity to protect children and enhance the lives of families (meeting of Ministers of Social Services, 2003). Surprisingly little is known about the long-term benefits for children, parents, or families from their engagements with child protection services. It would be extremely informative to initiate prospective and retrospective longitudinal investigations of the life trajectories of various groupings of children and parents during and after their child welfare involvements. This book's discussion of residential mental health care for "difficult" children suggests the particular importance of understanding how these children and their families traverse important developmental transition points and the types of supports that would enhance the life prospects for these children.

Sustainable Employment Environments

Several papers in this volume raise serious concerns about how sustainable and productive the work environments are in many child protection organizations, particularly for front-line service providers. Rapid and unwanted turnover among employees, as well as high prevalence of service provider emotional exhaustion, alienation from clients (depersonalization), and professional image violation are important subjects for verification and explanation (chapter 7; Harvey, Stalker, Mandell, & Frensch, 2003). We need to know much more about what it is like to work in a child protection agency, along with the individual, job, and organizational elements that predict employee burnout and turnover or a more productive and sustainable tenure. It also would be very instructive to know how employment satisfaction and stability vary across various approaches to child and family welfare—for example, in purposively selected international settings and in different service delivery configurations in Canada.

First Nations

Mandell and her colleagues (chapter 3) describe several different service delivery models for child and family welfare in First Nations in Canada. They also elaborate the core elements of a First Nations ideal vision for a community-caring model and the struggles facing Aboriginal communities in negotiating a satisfactory mandate for these efforts with provincial and federal authorities. Very little has been published about experiences and outcomes for these various First Nations approaches. It would also be very instructive if the mandates and resources became available for carefully documented experiments with a range of community-caring models developed by First Nations. A caveat for this program of research is that it should be developed in a culturally appropriate manner with approval from participating First Nations, and the information generated must be used to strengthen Aboriginal communities' capacity to develop, control, and deliver suitable child and family welfare services.

System Design Experiments

Throughout this volume are suggestions for innovations to improve Canadian child and family welfare. However, many of these ideas could not be tried without some modification to the policies and procedures currently regulating Canadian child protection services. Freymond and Cameron (chapter 2) argue for the timeliness of organizational and delivery systems experiments that would require the relaxation of bureaucratic controls, the support of key authorities, competent guidance, and careful documentation (see the discussion in Cameron, Karabanow, Laurendeau, & Chamberland, 2001). Some obvious candidates for such system design experiments from the previous discussions include the creation of family-friendly placements; the development of organizational supports and procedures to increase the prevalence of mutually acceptable service agreements between families and service providers; the formal use of mediation services to reduce court applications; sharing child protection and family support mandates with a coalition of service and community organizations; and mandates involving extended family and community networks in protecting children and helping families.

Conclusion

The volume raises fundamental questions about the guiding philosophy and intervention priorities for child and family welfare in Canada. It highlights areas where new thinking is required and suggests directions in which our searches may be profitable. An underlying contention in this book is that the dominant child protection paradigm in Canada has little new left to show us. Without basic shifts in values and methods, Canadian child protection systems will not achieve better outcomes for children, families, and communities. The current emphasis in our child protection system on holding stressed parents accountable for improving their families' living circumstances is an impoverished and unkind strategy. It is our intent that this volume's constructive criticisms of the Canadian protection paradigm, and its considerations of how we might learn from other approaches to child and family welfare, will stimulate creativity and encourage initiatives toward positive reforms in Canadian child and family welfare.

References

Cameron, G., de Boer, C., Frensch, K. M., & Adams, G. (2003). *Siege and response: Families everyday realities and experiences with children's residential mental health services.* Waterloo, ON: Wilfrid Laurier University, Partnerships for Children and Families Project.

Cameron, G., & Hoy, S. (2003). *Stories of mothers and child welfare.* Waterloo, ON: Wilfrid Laurier University, Partnerships for Children and Families Project.

Cameron, G., Karabanow, J., Laurendeau, M.-C., & Chamberland, C. (2001). Program implementation and diffusion. In I. Prilleltensky, G. Nelson, & L. Peirson (Eds.), *Promoting family wellness and preventing child maltreatment: Fundamentals for thinking and action* (pp. 339–374). Toronto, ON: University of Toronto Press.

Cameron, G., O'Reilly, J., Laurendeau, M.-C., & Chamberland, C. (2001). Programming for distressed and disadvantaged adolescents. In I. Prilleltensky, G. Nelson, & L. Peirson (Eds.), *Promoting family wellness and preventing child maltreatment: Fundamentals for thinking and action* (pp. 289–338). Toronto, ON: University of Toronto Press.

Coady, N., & Hayward, K. (1998). *A study of the Reconnecting Youth Project: Documenting a collaborative inter-agency process of program development and client views of the process and outcome of service.* Faculty of Social Work, Wilfrid Laurier University.

de Boer, C., & Coady, N. (2003). *Good helping relationships in child welfare: Co-authored stories of success.* Partnerships for Children and Families Project, Faculty of Social Work, Wilfrid Laurier University. http://www.wlu.ca/pcfproject

Drake, B. (1994). Relationship competencies in child welfare services. *Social Work, 39,* 595–602.

Frensch, K., & Cameron, G. (2003). *Bridging or maintaining distance: A matched comparison of parent and service provider perceptions.* Waterloo, ON: Partnerships for Children and Families Project, Faculty of Social Work, Wilfrid Laurier University, 102pp.

Frensch, K., Cameron, G., & Hazineh, L. (2005). *The Children's Aid Society of Brant: A community-based model of child welfare service delivery.* Waterloo, ON: Partnerships for Children and Families Project, Faculty of Social Work, Wilfrid Laurier University, 85pp.

Freymond, N. (2003). *Mothers' everyday realities and child placement experiences.* Waterloo, ON: Wilfrid Laurier University, Partnerships for Children and Families Project.

Gitterman, A. (1988). Teaching students to connect theory and practice. *Social Work with Groups, 11,* 33–41.

Harvey, C., Mandell, D., Stalker, C., & Frensch, K. (2003). *A workplace study of four southern-Ontario children's aid societies.* Partnerships for Children and Families Project, Faculty of Social Work, Wilfrid Laurier University. http://www.wlu.ca/pcfproject

Hertzberg, C. (November 8 -9, 2004). Overview—Executive summary: Evidence papers. *Healthy Child BC Forum*. http://www.earlylearning.ubc.ca/pub _map.htm

Hertzman, C. (2003, October). *The early years last a lifetime: The vital importance of early childhood development and how to plan for it effectively.* Keynote address at The 15th Annual Up With Kids Celebration Dinner, Guelph, Ontario.

Innocenti Research Centre (September, 2003). League table of child maltreatment deaths in rich nations. *Innocenti Report Card, Issue 5*. Retrieved November 19, 2003, from http://www.unicef-icdc.org/publications/

Leschied, A. W., Whitehead, P. C., Hurley, D., & Chiodo, D. (2003a). Protecting children is everybody's business: Investigating the increasing demand for service at the Children's Aid Society of London and Middlesex. Retrieved November 26, 2003, from http://www.caslondon.on.ca/protectingreport .htm

Leschied, A., Whitehead, P., Hurley, D., & Chiodo, D. (2003b). Protecting children is everybody's business. *OACAS Journal, 47*(3), 10–15.

Love, C. (2006). Maori perspectives on collaboration and colonization in contemporary Aotearoa/New Zealand child and family welfare and practices. In N. Freymond and G. Cameron (Eds.), *Towards positive systems of child and family welfare: International comparisons of child protection, family service, and community caring systems* (pp. 237–268). Toronto, ON: University of Toronto Press.

Maiter, S., Palmer, S., & Manji, S. (2003). *Invisible lives: The experiences of parents receiving child protective services.* Partnerships for Children and Families Project, Faculty of Social Work, Wilfrid Laurier University. http://www.wlu.ca/pcfproject

Maluccio, A. (1979). *Learning from clients.* New York: Free Press.

Meeting of Ministers of Social Services. (2002). New directions in child welfare: Background discussion document. In *4th National Child Welfare Symposium: Community Collaboration on Differential Response. Alberta Response Model: Transforming Outcomes for Children Youth and Families.*

Nelson, G., Laurendeau, M.-C., Chamberland, C., & Peirson, L. (2001). A review and analysis of programs to promote family wellness and prevent the maltreatment of pre-school and elementary school-aged children. In I. Prilleltensky, G. Nelson, & L. Peirson (Eds.), *Promoting family wellness and preventing child maltreatment: Fundamentals for thinking and action* (pp. 221–288). Toronto, ON: University of Toronto Press.

Phipps, S. (1999). *An international comparison of policies and outcomes for young children.* Ottawa, ON: Canadian Policy Research Networks Inc., Renouf Publishing Co. Ltd., study no. F/05.

Shulman, L. (1978). A study of practice skills. *Social Work, 23,* 274–281.

Tourigny, M., Mayer, M., Wright, J., Lavergne, C., Helie, S., Trocmé, N., et al. (2002). Etude sur l'incodence et les characteristics des situations d'abus, de negligence, d'abandon et de troubles de comportement serieux signalees a la direction de la protection de la jeunesse au Quebec (EIQ). Montreal, QC: Centre de liaison sur l'intervention et la prevention psychosociale.

Trocmé, N., & Chamberland, C. (2003). Re-involving the community: The need for a differential response to rising child welfare caseloads in Canada. In N. Trocmé, D. Knoke, and C. Roy (Eds.), *Community collaboration and differential response: Canadian and international research and emerging models of practice* (pp. 32–48). Ottawa, ON: Centre of Excellence for Child Welfare c/o Child Welfare League of Canada.

|Index|

Aboriginal children, 25–26; apprehension and adoption of, 8, 9, 26, 124–26, 127–29, 200; in foster care, 127–28, 351; identity of, within community, 120; in non-Native care, 26, 117, 125, 126, 127; as over-represented in child welfare system, 116–18, 125, 151; placement decisions regarding, 205; removal of, 19, 25–26, 27, 116, 120–22, 124–25; and residential schools, 8, 120–22, 122–23, 124; sexual abuse of, 127; special place of, 118–20; suicides of, 120, 127–28, 130; teaching/nurturing of, 119–20; tragedies involving, 127. *See also* Aboriginal youth; First Nations child and family welfare

Aboriginal child welfare: and Aboriginal agencies, 126, 148–49, 190, 196, 202, 207; and Aboriginal caregivers, 200, 203; and Aboriginal self-determination, 125–26, 130, 138, 139, 140; analyses of issues in, 129–32; as assimilationist, 120–22, 122–23; and concept of "ensembled selves," 60, 348–49, 360; and cultural bias/ignorance of service providers, 128–29, 144–45; and culturally appropriate practices, 139–45, 147–51; federal–provincial wrangling over, 123–25; funding for, 135–36, 142–43; and interconnections with justice system, 132–34; models for delivery of, 135–39; in Ontario, 126, 135, 137–38; and postwar social services, as prob-

lematic, 123–25; and Spallumcheen First Nation by-law, 50–51, 125–26, 138. *See also* First Nations child and family welfare

Aboriginal child welfare delivery models, 135, 152; band by-law, 50–51, 125–26, 138; delegated, 136–37, 139, 140; pre-mandated, 137–38; as research issue, 367–68; self-government, 138, 139; tripartite, 138–39. *See also* First Nations child and family welfare

Aboriginal families: children within, 118–20; and community/collective, 24–25, 26, 36, 37–38, 43–44, 51–52, 54–55, 118–20; elders within, 25, 118, 119, 120, 139, 143, 148, 149; extended, 25, 118, 120; and parent–child connection, 60, 348–49; poverty and marginalization of, 140; realities of life for, xi, xiii–xiv, xvii, 140

Aboriginal Justice Inquiry (Manitoba), 117, 132–33, 137, 146

Aboriginal peoples, assimilation of, 151–52; and Anglo-American ideology, 26–27; and marginalization, 133–34, 152; through removal of children, 8, 9, 25–26, 120–22; in residential schools, 8, 120–22, 122–23, 124

Aboriginal peoples, and justice system, 132–34; and Aboriginal concepts of justice, 36, 134; and Aboriginal system vs. British common law, 50–51, 134, 136, 145; and differences in provincial/territorial legislation/